The

American

Voice

The American Voice

Selections from the nonfiction
of representative
American writers of fiction,
1793-1934

EDITED BY

GERALD WILLEN

*Hunter College of the
City of New York*

Weybright and Talley

NEW YORK

Contents

[v]

Preface

The richest nation ever cannot pay its diplomats adequately—so Mark Twain records it. The first of the modern democracies, and "The Freedman's Case in Equity" must be pleaded by George Washington Cable more than one hundred years after George Washington became its first president. A nation priding itself on rugged individualism irritates Theodore Dreiser into writing "The Abuse of the Individual." A much-praised system of universal education for whites enrages Upton Sinclair, goading him into *The Goose-Step, A Study of American Education.* "The United States of Lyncherdom"—Mark Twain again—has become the United States of Assassination. We Americans call one another hunkies, wops, niggers, spics, kikes, dagos, micks, krauts, polacks, whitey, chinks, nips, wasps.

Hatred, assassination, miseducation, abuse of the individual, racial oppression, public penuriousness are, apparently, the historical legacies that threaten to destroy the young-old nation, our country, in which they flourish. It is easy enough to point to our achievements and to our position as a world power as a way of ignoring the cancers that afflict us. We might, those of us who do so, ponder the uses to which those achievements and that power have been put—whether they foster Life, Liberty, and the Pursuit of Happiness, or whether they aggravate our possibly fatal ailments.

Have the disadvantages of democracy—as James Fenimore Cooper intimates—prevailed over its advantages? Do we live under the principles of plutocracy or nationalism, as defined by Edward Bellamy? Is there a class struggle of the kind noted by Jack London, or is our society classless? Is the social unrest observed in 1914 by Sinclair Lewis analogous to the social unrest of our time? And so on, into the implications of the 1838 Commencement at Williams College (Nathaniel Hawthorne), New York in the 1870s (Edith Wharton), Philadelphia at the turn of the century (Henry James), the vanishing of the frontier (Hamlin Garland and Frank Norris), the position of women in America (Charles Brockden Brown, Mark Twain, Sinclair Lewis), the racial question (Cooper, Cable, Twain, Joel Chandler Harris, Sherwood Anderson, Theodore Dreiser).

That the writers concerned with such issues were primarily writers of fiction, rather than sociologists, economists, historians, or political scientists is scarcely relevant. The very subjectivity with which they approached their fiction qualifies them—and qualifies them eminently in our time—as important spokesmen on these critical questions. For, unlike the social scientist, whose professional concerns are ostensibly objective, the fiction writer plunges into the realm of individual fantasy where, to quote Emily Dickinson, "the meanings are." Here he deals with the irrational responses, controlled or uncontrolled, of the individual to the people among whom, and the environment in which, he lives. For us in our dislocated world, an understanding of these responses is absolutely crucial. Moreover, we need the kind of understanding that is informed by moral concerns—not those that are narrowly Puritanical, but rather those involving a vision of, and a commitment to, universal human values.

Whatever else he may be, the serious writer of fiction, like all serious artists, is morally committed. This commitment, when harnessed imaginatively to the fantasies worked out in art, may very well account for the power art has over us. Art, after all, in addition to being the expression of the fantasies that enable us to cope with the world, is also responsive to them. When such fantasies are uncontrolled, we go mad. When controlled, we are able to function. When ordered by form, as in art, they are, to use Alexander Pope's phrase, "nature methodized."

When our national life becomes disordered, as seems to have happened in the twentieth century, especially in the last twenty years, we would do well to take "a backward glance" (Edith Wharton) at ourselves. The difficulty here is that we must do so through someone else's eyes. Our usual inclination is to depend on the historian for a review of our past, and then to look to sociologists, economists, and political scientists for solutions to the contemporary problems that have crystallized out of it. Yet we know full well that the historian is limited to what has happened. As Aristotle put it, the historian tells us what has happened, the poet tells us what may happen according to the laws of necessity and probability; the poet is therefore the more valuable man. And surely if we were forced to choose between Thucydides and Sophocles, we would go to Sophocles: necessity and probability say more to us than does fact, even when it is filtered through an extremely perceptive mind.

In the western world, however, since the Cartesian revolution, we have permitted ourselves to be distracted by fact. The result has been that whatever deals with values, necessity, and probability has been discounted. Religion has become an anachronism, art an entertainment. I do not mean to minimize the achievements of the last three hundred years. Certainly science and the technology that flows from it have not only opened possibilities that stagger the mind, and turned many of these possibilities into actualities, but they promise considerably more for the future. Nevertheless, even as we stand on the threshold of ever-greater achievements, we are threatened with total disintegration, if not annihilation.

The threat comes not from our achievements, but from ourselves, from individual and even collective fantasies that we seem unable to control. Distracted by the world of fact, we have permitted ourselves to become alienated and to disregard our own elemental needs. We have refused to salvage from religion those fragments that are still relevant, and we have disengaged ourselves from any serious concern with the arts.* Thus stripped of the values from which our civilization evolved, we have lost our restraints and are on the verge of a new barbarism.

The aim of this barbarism is the unchecked and indiscriminating gratification of appetite. Swift showed us in *Gulliver's Travels* how it

---

* Even in our graduate schools, and consequently at all levels of instruction, the arts are viewed and studied as a kind of historical phenomenon, rather than as subjective and completely individual forms of communication. This curious approach, as is well known by now, results from our universities' stress on research and measurable results—i.e., publication—in all fields. The end result of this emphasis may well be fatal to our civilization.

might come about, Wordsworth lamented it in "The World Is Too Much with Us," Arnold warned us against it in "Culture and Anarchy," Conrad caught it in "Heart of Darkness." Contemporary American novelists as diverse as Evan S. Connell, Jr. (*Mrs. Bridge*), Saul Bellow (*Herzog*), and Hubert Selby, Jr. (*Last Exit to Brooklyn*), among many others, deal with its effects, which they represent as an almost total dislocation of life.

In a revolutionary age such as ours the dislocation of life is not a terrible thing, provided it has purpose and carries hope. But, as our poets and novelists indicate over and over again, such is not the case.* As the quality of life continues to deteriorate under the onslaught of the new barbarism and its concomitant stress on all things economic, our fantasies become nightmares. Nowhere is the evidence more compelling than in the United States and in the fiction that documents it.

Hugh Henry Brackenridge, James Fenimore Cooper, Nathaniel Hawthorne, Herman Melville, all, as the saying goes, carry the message. From 1792 (*Modern Chivalry*) on, the American voice has expressed our individual and national agony. Brackenridge's satire, Cooper's myths, Hawthorne's anguish, Melville's quasi-allegories may well be called the American conscience worked out by means of frightening fantasy. So frightening is it that D. H. Lawrence, in his *Studies in Classic American Literature,* can say, in the process of writing about Deerslayer: "The essential American soul is hard, isolate, stoic, and a killer. It has never yet melted. . . . [Deerslayer] is the very intrinsic-most American. He is at the core of all the other flux and fluff. And when *this* man breaks from his static isolation, and makes a new move, then look out, something will be happening." †

Lawrence's prophecy, needless to say, has become an actuality. The point is, however, that we did not need Lawrence to tell us what might happen—our fiction writers were there first, and not solely in their fiction. It can scarcely be claimed that their essays, speeches,

---

* An example of our myopia in this area is the publicity accorded the work of Soviet poets and novelists who are critical of their society. We thus use their work for propaganda purposes while attacking Soviet authorities for using art in the same way. That the great majority of American poets and novelists are critical of our society seems to be irrelevant; besides, nobody much reads them, anyway.
† D. H. Lawrence, "Fenimore Cooper's Leatherstocking Novels," *Studies in Classic American Literature,* Anchor Books, New York, p. 73 (1953).

journals—their nonfiction in general—are more important than their novels and short stories. What can be claimed for their nonfiction is that it speaks directly of the social, political, and economic concerns that preoccupy some of our best imaginative minds, concerns that are bound to have affected their fiction. And though it is well enough known by scholars and specialists in American literature, it remains largely unread, even among generally literate people.

The motive, then, behind the preparation of this book is to acquaint students and other interested readers with some of this nonfiction by means of representative selections from it. However, as is the case with any anthologist, I had to be quite arbitrary in a number of ways. For example, I decided to include only works published prior to the 1930s (although I did make two arbitrary exceptions) because I felt that anything published after the 1930s would have to take the Depression into account. Had I included Depression and post-Depression pieces, the book would have lost its historical unity. Everything reprinted either deals with our nineteenth-century past or develops from it, without being specifically concerned with problems arising in the twentieth century.

Another arbitrary exclusion is that of work by such authors as Edgar Allan Poe, Herman Melville, and Stephen Crane. I omitted Poe because his nonfiction deals exclusively with literary matters, and not the social, political, and economic concerns emphasized in this book. Herman Melville is not represented because he wrote practically no nonfiction (except poetry). And Stephen Crane's nonfiction consists almost wholly of newspaper pieces, which I considered unsuitable.

The work contained in the book is arranged, for the most part, chronologically. The exceptions are Mark Twain's essays (for the sake of presenting his work as a unit); the excerpt from Edith Wharton's *Looking Backward*, which I thought should follow the selection by Henry James; and the two Sinclair Lewis essays with which the book concludes, because they round out the volume more adequately than the two excerpts from Dreiser's *Tragic America* would have.

One oddity is worth noting. So far as I can determine, Charles Brockden Brown's *Alcuin; A Dialogue* has been reprinted only once

before, in a facsimile edition limited to 250 copies and published by
Carl and Margaret Rollins (New Haven, 1935), with an Introduction
by LeRoy E. Kimball; of the first edition, only seven copies are ex-
tant. I am grateful to the Rare Book Division of the New York
Public Library for permission to reproduce its copy of the first
edition.

Because I do not believe that a compiler should tamper with the
work he anthologizes, I have not edited or footnoted any of the pieces
contained herein; neither have I changed punctuation or spelling to
conform to modern usage. My suspicion is that most readers prefer
the essays and excerpts to speak for themselves. I have also omitted
headnotes and short biographical sketches on the grounds that most
of the authors represented are well known and that curious readers
can get whatever pertinent information they require from various en-
cyclopedias or the *Dictionary of American Biography*. The very occasional prefatory notes I have supplied deal only with the publishing or
editorial history (when necessary) of the work, or, in the case of
Cooper's *Notions of the Americans*, with formal matters. My hope
for the book is that it will enable readers to understand how intensely
and persistently the American writer of fiction has been concerned
with the well-being of his compatriots and his country.

G. W.
July 6, 1968

The

American

Voice

Hugh Henry Brackenridge [1748-1816]
Oration by Citizen Brackenridge,
On the Celebration of the Anniversary of
Independence. [*Pittsburgh, July 4, 1793.*]

The celebration of the day, introduces the idea of the principle that
gave it birth: Was it the wisdom of the king of Great-Britain, who
saw the growing greatness of the province, that they were now of age
to act for themselves, and bade them be independent? No—The wisdom of the parliament of Great-Britain, that seeing the inconvenience
or impossibility of our being represented in the legislature, and sensible of the unreasonableness of being bound by laws without being
represented, saw the expediency of a separation from them, and said
to us, Be independent and become an allied power? No—Nothing of
all this. The king and parliament of Great-Britain, were of opinion,
that without representation, we were bound by their laws, and though
descendants of their isle, had no right to freedom in a great forest.

[1]

Whence then our independence? It was the offspring of the understanding and the virtue of the people of America themselves. The eloquent advised; the brave fought, and we succeeded. The day on which we assumed our rights, became a festival; and every future year shall remember it with ardent exertion.

The celebration of the day, introduces the idea of the effect of it beyond the sphere of these states. The light kindled here has been reflected to France, and a new order of things has arisen. Shall we blame the intemperance of the exertions? Was there ever enthusiasm without intemperance? and was there ever a great effect without enthusiasm? Thy principles, O! Liberty, are not violent or cruel: but in the desperation of thy efforts against tyranny, is it not always possible to keep within the limit of the vengeance, necessary to defence? Do we accuse the air, or the bastile of the mountain, when the rock is burst, and the town engulphed? The air of itself is mild, and scarcely wafts a feather from its place: But restrained and imprisoned, the yielding and placid element becomes indignant, and tears the globe before it. Do we accuse the hurricane, when the mariner is tossed with the tempest, and is an incidental sufferer in the storm? The naturalist does not. He tells you that the equilibrium of the atmosphere has been disturbed, and if man has suffered more than the demerit of his transgressions it is in a struggle of nature to restore herself.

Is it the duty of these states to assist France? That we are bound by treaty, and how far, I will not say; because it is not necessary. We are bound by a higher principle, if our assistance could avail; the great law of humanity.

We might, it is true, alledge the stipulations of a treaty, and the *guarantee of her possessions to France.* But all the world would know, and we ought to avow it, that it is the cause of republicanism which would induce our efforts. The tyrant of Great-Britain alledged the stipulations of a treaty relative to the opening of the Scheldt and waiting for no requisition on the part of Holland to observe the guarantee. But all the world knew, and he might have avowed it, that it was not the opening of the Scheldt, but the attack upon monarchy, that prompted his interposition. Shall kings combine, and shall republics not unite? We have united. The heart of America feels the cause of France; she takes a part in all her councils; approves her wisdom;

blames her excesses; she is moved, impelled, elevated and depressed; with all the changes of her good and bad fortune; she feels the same fury in her veins; she is tossed and shaken with all the variety of hopes and fears, attending her situation: Why not? Can we be indifferent? Is not our fate interlaced with hers? For, O France! if thy republic perish, where is the honor due to ours? From whom respect to our flag upon the seas? Not from France restored to a monarch, and indignant at these very feelings which are now our glory: Not from the despots that are against her: These will easily recollect that the cause of their evils took their rise here.

Can we assist France by arming in her favor? I will not say that we can. But could we, and should France say, United States, your neutrality is not sufficient; we expect the junction of your arms with mine; your heroes on the soil, and your privateers on the ocean, to distress the foes; who is there would not say, It shall be so; you shall have them; our citizens shall arm; they shall attack; our oaks shall descend from the mountains; our vessels be launched upon the stream, and the voice of our war, however weak, shall be heard with yours!

If we ourselves should judge that our arms could assist France, even though the generous republic required it not, yet who would hesitate to interfere, not only at the risk of property, but life itself? Is it illusion; or do I hear France say? My daughter America! I know the dutifulness of thy heart towards me; and that thou art disposed to shew it, by taking part in this war. But I wish thee not to provoke hostilities for my sake. If I perish, I perish; but let not a mother draw in a hapless child, to suffer with herself. Is it illusion; or do I hear America reply? I do, and it is in the language of the Moabitess Ruth, to her mother-in-law, the Jewish Naomi, "Intreat me not to leave thee, or return from following thee; for whither thou goest, I will go; and where thou lodgest, I will lodge; thy people shall be my people, and thy God my God; where thou diest, I will die, and there will I be buried. God do so to me, and more also, if aught but death shall part thee and me."

But whether we assist or not, thy cause, O! France, will be triumphant. Did the enthusiasm of a small Roman people, repel their invaders, until Rome became the protectress of nations? Did the enthusiasm of a few Greeks, repel the millions of Asia, and afterwards overrun her kingdoms? Did the enthusiasm of the Saracens, in a few years spread to Spain on the one hand, and the Indus on the other? Did the enthusiasm of a few mad Crusaders, burst upon the Saracen, and establish the kingdom of Jerusalem in the centre of his empire? And shall the enthusiasm of a brave people, more numerous than the early Roman republic, the Greeks under Alexander; the Saracens of Arabia, or the Crusaders of Europe, be subdued by all that are against them? The weight will but condense resistance, and as the materials of explosion in the ordonance acquire a spring by confinement, so in proportion to the attack of this people, will their voice be terrible, their blow irresistible.

France will be independent also, and celebrate her anniversaries; and in doing so will recollect that our independence had preceded hers and made the example.—The anniversary of the independence of America will be a great epoch of Liberty throughout the world. Proceed we then to celebrate the day; advance to the festive board; pour out liberations to sentiments of liberty, and let the loud mouthed artillery be heard on the hill!

THE END.

Charles Brockden Brown [1771-1810]
Alcuin; A Dialogue [1798]

NOTE: *The first edition consists of Parts I and II. Parts III and IV were announced for publication, but never appeared. The only evidence for the existence of Parts III and IV, according to LeRoy E. Kimball, is in William Dunlap's* Life of Charles Brockden Brown *(1815) in two volumes. But since Dunlap's* Life *is frequently inaccurate, the evidence is far from overwhelming.*

ADVERTISEMENT.

The following Dialogue was put into my hands, the last spring, by a friend who resides at a distance, with liberty to make it public. I have since been informed that he has continued the discussion of the subject, in another dialogue. The reception which the present publication shall meet will probably determine the author to withhold or print the continuation.

E. H. SMITH.

New-York, March, 1798.

PART I.

I called last evening on Mrs. Carter. I had no previous acquaintance with her. Her brother is a man of letters, who, nevertheless, finds little leisure from the engagements of a toilsome profession. He scarcely spends an evening at home, yet takes care to invite, specially and generally, to his house, every one who enjoys the reputation of learning and probity. His sister became, on the death of her husband, his house-keeper. She was always at home. The guests who came in

[5]

search of the man, finding him abroad, lingered a little as politeness enjoined, but soon found something in the features and accents of the lady, that induced them to prolong their stay, for their own sake: nay, without any well-defined expectation of meeting their inviter, they felt themselves disposed to repeat their visit. We must suppose the conversation of the lady not destitute of attractions; but an additional, and, perhaps, the strongest inducement, was the society of other visitants. The house became, at length, a sort of rendezvous of persons of different ages and conditions, but respectable for talents or virtues. A commodious apartment, excellent tea, lemonade, and ice—and wholesome fruits—were added to the pleasures of instructive society: no wonder that Mrs. Carter's *coterie* became the favourite resort of the liberal and ingenious.

These things did not necessarily imply any uncommon merit in the lady. Skill in the superintendence of a tea-table, affability and modesty, promptness to inquire, and docility to listen, were all that were absolutely requisite in the mistress of the ceremonies. Her apartment was nothing, perhaps, but a lyceum open at stated hours, and to particular persons, who enjoyed, gratis, the benefits of rational discourse, and agreeable repasts. Some one was required to serve the guests, direct the menials, and maintain, with suitable vigilance, the empire of cleanliness and order. This office might not be servile, merely because it was voluntary. The influence of an unbribed inclination might constitute the whole difference between her and a waiter at an inn, or the porter of a theatre.

—

Books are too often insipid. In reading, the senses are inert and sluggish, or they are solicited by foreign objects. To spur up the flagging attention, or check the rapidity of its flights and wildness of its excursions, are often found to be impracticable. It is only on extraordinary occasions that this faculty is at once sober and vigorous, active and obedient. The revolutions of our minds may be watched and noted, but can seldom be explained to the satisfaction of the inquisitive. All that the caprice of nature has left us, is to profit by the casual presence of that which can, by no spell, be summoned or detained.

I hate a lecturer. I find little or no benefit in listening to a man who does not occasionally call upon me for my opinion, and allow me to canvass every step in his argument. I cannot, with any satisfaction, survey a column, how costly soever its materials, and classical its ornaments, when I am convinced that its foundation is sand which the next tide will wash away. I equally dislike formal debate, where each man, however few his ideas, is subjected to the necessity of drawing them out to the length of a speech. A single proof, or question, or hint, may be all that the state of the controversy, or the reflections of the speaker, suggest: but this must be amplified and iterated, till the sense, perhaps, is lost or enfeebled, that he may not fall below the dignity of an orator. Conversation, careless, and unfettered, that is sometimes abrupt and sententious, sometimes fugitive and brilliant, and sometimes copious and declamatory, is a scene for which, without being much accustomed to it, I entertain great affection. It blends, more happily than any other method of instruction, utility and pleasure. No wonder I was desirous of knowing, long before the opportunity was afforded me, how far these valuable purposes were accomplished by the frequenters of Mrs. Carter's lyceum.

In the morning I had met the doctor at the bed-side of a sick friend, who had strength enough to introduce us to each other. At parting I received a special invitation for the evening, and a general one to be in force at all other times. At five o'clock I shut up my little school, and changed an alley in the city—dark, dirty, and narrow, as all alleys are—for the fresh air and smooth footing of the fields. I had not forgotten the doctor and his lyceum. Shall I go (said I to myself), or shall I not? No, said the pride of poverty, and the bashfulness of inexperience. I looked at my unpowdered locks, my worsted stockings, and my pewter buckles. I bethought me of my embarrassed air, and my uncouth gait. I pondered on the superciliousness of wealth and talents, the awfulness of flowing muslin, the mighty task of hitting on a right movement at entrance, and a right posture in sitting, and on the perplexing mysteries of tea-table decorum: but, though confused and panic-struck, I was not vanquished.

I had some leisure, particularly in the evening. Could it be employed more agreeably or usefully? To read, to write, to meditate; to watch a declining moon, and the varying firmament, with the emotions of poetry or piety—with the optics of Dr. Young, or of De la Lande—were delightful occupations, and all at my command. Eight hours of the twenty-four were consumed in repeating the names and

scrawling the forms of the alphabet, or in engraving on infantile
memories that twice three make six; the rest was employed in supplying an exhausted, rather than craving, stomach; in sleep, that never
knew, nor desired to know, the luxury of down, and the pomp of
tissue; in unravelling the mazes of Dr. Waring; or in amplifying the
seducing suppositions of, 'if I were a king,' or, 'if I were a lover.' Few,
indeed, are as happy as Alcuin. What is requisite to perfect my felicity, but the blessings of health, which is incompatible with periodical
head-achs, and the visits of rheumatism;—of peace, which cannot
maintain its post against the hum of a school, the discord of cart-
wheels, and the rhetoric of a notable landlady;—of competence—My
trade preserves me from starving and nakedness, but not from the
discomforts of scarcity, or the disgrace of shabbiness. Money, to give
me leisure; and exercise, to give me health; these are all my lot denies:
in all other respects, I am the happiest of mortals. The pleasures of
society, indeed, I seldom taste: that is, I have few opportunities of
actual intercourse with that part of mankind whose ideas extend beyond the occurrences of the neighbourhood, or the arrangements of
their household. Not but that, when I want company, it is always at
hand. My solitude is populous, whenever my fancy thinks proper to
people it, and with the very beings that best suit my taste. These
beings are, perhaps, on account of my slender experience, too uniform, and somewhat grotesque. Like some other dealers in fiction, I
find it easier to give new names to my visionary friends, and vary
their condition, than to introduce a genuine diversity into their characters. No one can work without materials. My stock is slender.
There are times when I feel a moment's regret that I do not enjoy the
means of enlarging it.—But this detail, it must be owned, is a little
beside the purpose. I merely intended to have repeated my conversation with Mrs. Carter, but have wandered, unawares, into a disserta-
tion on my own character. I shall now return, and mention that I cut
short my evening excursion, speeded homeward, and, after japanning
anew my shoes, brushing my hat, and equipping my body in its best
geer, proceeded to the doctor's house.

    I shall not stop to describe the company, or to dwell on those
embarrassments and awkwardnesses always incident to an unpolished
wight like me. Suffice it to say, that I was in a few minutes respect-
fully withdrawn into a corner, and fortunately a near neighbour of

the lady. To her, after much deliberation and forethought, I addressed myself thus: "Pray, Madam, are you a federalist?"

The theme of discourse was political. The edicts of Carnot, and the commentary of that profound jurist, Peter Porcupine, had furnished ample materials of discussion. This was my hint. The question, to be sure, was strange; especially addressed to a lady: but I could not, by all my study, light upon a better mode of beginning discourse. She did not immediately answer. I resumed—I see my question produces a smile, and a pause.

True (said she). A smile may well be produced by its novelty, and a pause by its difficulty.

Is it so hard to say what your creed is on this subject? Judging from the slight observations of this evening, I should imagine that to you the theme was far from being new.

She answered, that she had been often called upon to listen to discussions of this sort, but did not recollect when her opinion had been asked.

Will you favour me (said I) with your opinion, notwithstanding?

Surely (she replied) you are in jest. What! ask a woman—shallow and inexperienced as all women are known to be, especially with regard to these topics—her opinion on any political question! What in the name of decency have we to do with politics? If you inquire the price of this ribbon, or at what shop I purchased that set of china, I may answer you, though I am not sure you would be wiser for my answer. These things, you know, belong to the women's province. We are surrounded by men and politicians. You must observe that they consider themselves in an element congenial to their sex and station. The daringness of female curiosity is well known; yet it is seldom so adventurous as to attempt to penetrate into the mysteries of government.

It must be owned (said I) there is sufficient reason for this forbearance. Most men have trades; but every woman has a trade. They are universally trained to the use of the needle, and the government of a family. No wonder that they should be most willing to handle topics that are connected with their daily employment, and the arts in which they are proficient.—Merchants may be expected to dwell with most zeal on the prices of the day, and those numerous incidents, domestic and foreign, by which commerce is affected. Lawyers may quote the clauses of a law, or the articles of a treaty, without forgetting their profession, or travelling, as they phrase it, out of the record. Physicians will be most attached to livid carcases and sick beds. Women are most eloquent on a fan or a tea-cup—on the furniture of the nursery, or the qualifications of a chamber-maid. How should it be otherwise? In so doing, the merchant, the lawyer, the physician, and the matron, may all equally be said to stick to their lasts. Doubtless every one's last requires some or much of his attention. The only fault lies in sometimes allowing it wholly to engross the faculties, and often in overlooking considerations that are of the utmost importance to them, even as members of a profession.

Well (said the lady), now you talk reasonably. Your inference is, that women occupy their proper sphere, when they confine themselves to the tea-table and their work-bag: but this sphere, whatever you may think, is narrow. They are obliged to wander, at times, in search of variety. Most commonly they digress into scandal; and this has been their eternal reproach; with how much reason perhaps you can tell me.

Most unjustly, as it seems to me. Women profit by their opportunities. They are trained to a particular art. Their minds are, of course, chiefly occupied by images and associations drawn from this art. If this be blameable, it is not more so in them, than in others. It is a circumstance that universally takes place. It is by no means clear, that a change in this respect is either possible or desirable. The arts of women are far from contemptible, whether we consider the skill that is required by them, or, which is a better criterion, their usefulness in society. They are more honourable than many professions allotted to the men; those of soldier and barber for example; on one of which we may justly bestow all the contempt, and on the other all the abhorrence we have to spare. But though we may strive, we can never wholly extinguish, in women, the best principle of human nature, curiosity. We cannot shut them out from all commerce with the world. We may nearly withhold from them all knowledge of the past, because that is chiefly contained in books; and it is possible to interdict them from reading, or, to speak more accurately, withhold from them those incitements to study, which no human beings bring into the world with them, but must owe to external and favourable occurrences. But they must be, in some degree, witnesses of what is passing.

There is a limited sphere, in which they are accurate observers. They
see, and hear, somewhat of the actions and characters of those around
them. These are, of course, remembered; become the topic of reflection; and, when opportunity offers, they delight to produce and compare them. All this is perfectly natural and reasonable. I cannot, for
my life, discover any causes of censure in it.

Very well, indeed (cried the lady), I am glad to meet so zealous
an advocate. I am ready enough to adopt a plausible apology for the
peculiarities of women. And yet it is a new doctrine that would
justify triflers and slanderers. According to this system, it would be
absurd to blame those who are perpetually prying into other people's
affairs, and industriously blazoning every disadvantageous or suspicious tale.

My dear Madam, you mistake me. Artists may want skill; historians may be partial. Far be it from me to applaud the malignant or
the stupid. Ignorance and envy are no favourites of mine, whether
they have or have not a chin to be shaved: but nothing would be more
grossly absurd, than to suppose these defects to be peculiar to female
artists, or the historians of the tea-table. When these defects appear in
the most flagrant degree, they are generally capable of an easy apology. If the sexes had, in reality, separate interests, and it were not
absurd to set more value on qualifications, on account of their belonging to one of our own sex, it is the women who may justly triumph.
Together with power and property, the men have likewise asserted
their superior claim to vice and folly.

If I understand you rightly (said the lady), you are of opinion
that the sexes are essentially equal.

It appears to me (answered I), that human beings are moulded by
the circumstances in which they are placed. In this they are all alike.
The differences that flow from the sexual distinction, are as nothing in
the balance.

And yet women are often reminded that none of their sex are to
be found among the formers of States, and the instructors of mankind
—that Pythagoras, Lycurgus, and Socrates, Newton, and Locke, were
not women.

True; nor were they mountain savages, nor helots, nor shoe-
makers. You might as well expect a Laplander to write Greek spontaneously, and without instruction, as that any one should be wise or

skillful, without suitable opportunities. I humbly presume one has a
better chance of becoming an astronomer by gazing at the stars
through a telescope, than in eternally plying the needle, or snapping
the scissars. To settle a bill of fare, to lard a pig, to compose a
pudding, to carve a goose, are tasks that do not, in any remarkable
degree, tend to instil the love, or facilitate the acquisition of literature
and science. Nay, I do not form prodigious expectations even of one
who reads a novel or comedy once a month, or chants once a day to
her harpsichord the hunter's foolish invocation to Phoebus or Cyn-
thia. Women are generally superficial and ignorant, because they are
generally cooks and sempstresses. Men are the slaves of habit. It is
doubtful whether the career of the species will ever terminate in
knowledge. Certain it is, they began in ignorance. Habit has given
permanence to errors, which ignorance had previously rendered universal. They are prompt to confound things, which are really distinct;
and to persevere in a path to which they have been accustomed.
Hence it is that certain employments have been exclusively assigned to
women, and that their sex is supposed to disqualify them for any
other. Women are defective. They are seldom or never metaphysi-
cians, chemists, or lawgivers. Why? Because they are sempstresses
and cooks. This is unavoidable. Such is the unalterable constitution of
human nature. They cannot read who never saw an alphabet. They
who know no tool but the needle, cannot be skillful at the pen.

Yes (said the lady); of all forms of injustice, that is the most
egregious which makes the circumstance of sex a reason for excluding one half of mankind from all those paths which lead to usefulness
and honour.

Without doubt (returned I) there is abundance of injustice in the
sentence; yet it is possible to misapprehend, and to overrate the injury
that flows from the established order of things. If a certain part of
every community must be condemned to servile and mechanical professions, it matters not of what sex they may be. If the benefits of
leisure and science be, of necessity, the portion of a few, why should
we be anxious to which sex the preference is given? The evil lies in so
much of human capacity being thus fettered and perverted. This
allotment is sad. Perhaps it is unnecessary. Perhaps that precept of
justice is practicable, which requires that each man should take his
share of the labour, and enjoy his portion of the rest: that the tasks

now assigned to a few, might be divided among the whole; and what now degenerates into ceaseless and brutalizing toil, might, by an equitable distribution, be changed into agreeable and useful exercise. Perhaps this inequality is incurable. In either case it is to be lamented, and, as far as possible, mitigated. Now, the question of what sex either of those classes may be composed, is of no importance. Though we must admit the claims of the female sex to an equality with the other, we cannot allow them to be superior. The state of the ignorant, servile, and laborious, is entitled to compassion and relief; not because they are women, nor because they are men; but simply because they are rational.—Among savage nations the women are slaves. They till the ground, and cook the victuals. Such is the condition of half of the community—deplorable, without doubt; but it would be neither more nor less so, if the sexes were equally distributed through each class.

But, the burthen is unequal (said Mrs. Carter), since the strength of the females is less.

What matters it (returned I) whether my strength be much or little, if I am tasked to the amount of it, and no more; and no task can go beyond.

But nature (said the lady) has subjected us to peculiar infirmities and hardships. In consideration of what we suffer as mothers and nurses, I think we ought to be exempted from the same proportion of labour.

It is hard (said I) to determine what is the amount of your pains as mothers and nurses. Have not ease and luxury a tendency to increase that amount? Is not the sustenance of infant offspring in every view a privilege? Of all changes in their condition, that which should transfer to men the task of nurturing the innocence, and helplessness of infancy, would, I should imagine, be to mothers the least acceptable.

I do not complain of this province. It is not, however, exempt from danger and trouble. It makes a large demand upon our time and attention. Ought not this to be considered in the distribution of tasks and duties?

Certainly. I was afraid you would imagine, that too much regard had been paid to it; that the circle of female pursuits had been too much contracted on this account.

I, indeed (rejoined the lady), think it by far too much contracted. But I cannot give the authors of our institutions credit for any such motives. On the contrary, I think we have the highest reason to complain of our exclusion from many professions which might afford us, in common with men, the means of subsistence and independence.

How far, dear Madam, is your complaint well grounded? What is it excludes you from the various occupations in use among us? Cannot a female be a trader? I know no law or custom that forbids it. You may, at any time, draw a subsistence from wages, if your station in life, or your education has rendered you sufficiently robust. No one will deride you, or punish you, for attempting to hew wood or bring water. If we rarely see you driving a team, or beating the anvil, is it not a favourable circumstance? In every family there are various duties. Certainly the most toilsome and rugged do not fall to the lot of women. If your employment be for the most part sedentary and recluse, to be exempted from an intemperate exertion of the muscles, or to be estranged from scenes of vulgar concourse, might be deemed a privilege. The last of these advantages, however, is not yours; for do we not buy most of our meat, herbs, and fruit, of women? In the distribution of employments, the chief or only difference, perhaps, is, that those which require most strength, or more unremitted exertion of it, belong to the males: and yet, there is nothing obligatory or inviolable in this arrangement. In the country, the maid that milks, and the man that ploughs, if discontented with their present office, may make an exchange, without breach of law, or offence to decorum. If you possess stock, by which to purchase the labour of others—and stock may accumulate in your hands as well as in ours—there is no species of manufacture in which you are forbidden to employ it.

But are we not (cried the lady) excluded from the liberal professions?

Why, that may admit of question. You have free access, for example, to the accompting-house. It would be somewhat ludicrous, I own, to see you at the Exchange, or superintending the delivery of a cargo. Yet, this would attract our notice, merely because it is singular; not because it is disgraceful or criminal: but if the singularity be a sufficient objection, we know that these offices are not necessary. The profession of a merchant may be pursued with success and dignity, without being a constant visitor of the quay or the coffee-house. In the trading cities of Europe, there are bankers and merchants of your sex, to whom that consideration is attached, to which they are entitled by their skill, their integrity, or their opulence.

But what apology can you make for our exclusion from the class of physicians?

To a certain extent, the exclusion is imaginary. My grandmother was a tolerable physician. She had much personal experience; and her skill was, I assure you, in much request among her neighbours. It is true, she wisely forbore to tamper with diseases of an uncommon or complicated nature. Her experience was wholly personal. But that was accidental. She might have added, if she had chosen, the experience of others to her own.

But the law——

True, we are not accustomed to see female pleaders at the bar. I never wish to see them there. But the law, as a science, is open to their curiosity, or their benevolence. It may be even practised as a source of gain, without obliging us to frequent and public exhibitions.

Well (said the lady), let us dismiss the lawyer and the physician, and turn our eye to the pulpit. That, at least, is a sanctuary which women must not profane.

It is only (replied I) in some sects that divinity, the business of explaining to men their religious duty, is a trade. In such, custom or law, or the canons of their faith, have confined the pulpit to men: perhaps the distinction, wherever it is found, is an article of their religious creed, and, consequently, is no topic of complaint, since the propriety of this exclusion must be admitted by every member of the sect, whether male or female. But there are other sects which admit females into the class of preachers. With them, indeed, this distinction, if lucrative at all, is only indirectly so; and its profits are not greater to one sex than to the other. But there is no religious society in which women are debarred from the privileges of superior sanctity. The christian religion has done much to level the distinctions of property, and rank, and sex. Perhaps, in reviewing the history of mankind, we shall find the authority derived from a real, or pretended intercourse with heaven, pretty generally divided between them. And after all, what do these restrictions amount to? If some pursuits are monopolized by men, others are appropriated to you. If it appear that your occupations have least of toil, are most friendly to purity of manners, to delicacy of sensation, to intellectual improvement, and activity, or to public usefulness; if it should appear that your skill is always in such demand as to afford you employment when you stand in need of it; if, though few in number, they may be so generally and constantly useful, as always to furnish you subsistence; or, at least, to expose you, by their vicissitudes, to the pressure of want as rarely as it is incident to men; you cannot reasonably complain: but, in my opinion, all this is true.

Perhaps not (replied the lady): yet I must own your statement is plausible. I shall not take much pains to confute it. It is evident, that, for some reason or other, the liberal professions, those which require most vigour of mind, greatest extent of knowledge, and most commerce with books and with enlightened society, are occupied only by men. If contrary instances occur, they are rare, and must be considered as exceptions.

Admitting these facts (said I), I do not see reason for drawing mortifying inferences from them. For my part, I entertain but little respect for what are called the liberal professions, and, indeed, but little for any profession whatever. If their motive be gain, and that it is which constitutes them a profession, they seem to be, all of them, nearly on a level in point of dignity. The consideration of usefulness is of more value. He that roots out a national vice, or checks the ravages of a pestilence, is, no doubt, a respectable personage: but it is no man's trade to perform these services. How does a mercenary divine, or lawyer, or physician, differ from a dishonest chimney-sweep? The most that can be dreaded from a chimney-sweep is the spoiling of our dinner, or a little temporary alarm; but what injuries may we not dread from the abuses of law, medicine, or divinity! Honesty, you will say, is the best policy. Whatever it be, it is not the road to wealth. To the purposes of a profession, as such, it is not subservient. Degrees, and examinations, and licences, may qualify us for the trade; but benevolence needs not their aid to refine its skill, or augment its activity. Some portion of their time and their efforts must be employed by those who need, in obtaining the means of subsistence. The less tiresome, boisterous and servile that task is, which necessity enjoins; the less tendency it has to harden our hearts, to benumb our intellects, to undermine our health. The more leisure it affords us to gratify our curiosity and cultivate our moral discernment, the better. Here is a criterion for the choice of a profession, and which obliges us to consider the condition of women as preferable.

I cannot perceive it. But it matters nothing what field may be open, if our education does not qualify us to range over it. What think you of female education? Mine has been frivolous. I can make a pie, and cut out a gown. For this only I am indebted to my teachers. If I have added any thing to these valuable attainments, it is through my own efforts, and not by the assistance or encouragement of others.

And ought it not to be so? What can render men wise but their own efforts? Does curiosity derive no encouragement from the possession of the power and materials? You are taught to read and to write: quills, paper, and books are at hand. Instruments and machines are forthcoming to those who can purchase them. If you be insensible to the pleasures and benefits of knowledge, and are therefore ignorant and trifling, it is not for want of assistance and encouragement.

I shall find no difficulty (said the lady) to admit that the system is not such as to condemn all women, without exception, to stupidity. As it is, we have only to lament, that a sentence so unjust is executed on, by far, the greater number. But you forget how seldom those who are most fortunately situated, are permitted to cater for themselves. Their conduct, in this case, as in all others, is subject to the controul of others who are guided by established prejudices, and are careful to remember that we are women. They think a being of this sex is to be instructed in a manner different from those of another. Schools, and colleges, and public instructors are provided in all the abstruse sciences and learned languages; but whatever may be their advantages, are not women totally excluded from them?

It would be prudent (said I), in the first place, to ascertain the amount of those advantages, before we indulge ourselves in lamenting the loss of them. Let us consider whether a public education be not unfavourable to moral and intellectual improvement; or, at least, whether it be preferable to the domestic method;—whether most knowledge be obtained by listening to hired professors, or by reading books;—whether the abstruse sciences be best studied in a closet, or a college;—whether the ancient tongues be worth learning;—whether, since languages are of no use but as avenues to knowledge, our native tongue, especially in its present state of refinement, be not the best. Before we lament the exclusion of women from colleges, all these points must be settled: unless they shall be precluded by reflecting, that places of public education, which are colleges in all respects but the name, are, perhaps, as numerous for females as for males.

They differ (said the lady) from colleges in this, that a very different plan of instruction is followed. I know of no female school where Latin is taught, or geometry, or chemistry.

Yet, Madam, there are female geometricians, and chemists, and scholars, not a few. Were I desirous that my son or daughter should become either of these, I should not deem the assistance of a college indispensible. Suppose an anatomist should open a school to pupils of both sexes, and solicit equally their attendance; would you comply with the invitation?

No; because that pursuit has no attractions for me. But if I had a friend whose curiosity was directed to it, why should I dissuade her from it?

Perhaps (said I) you are but little acquainted with the real circumstances of such a scene. If your disdain of prejudices should prompt you to adventure one visit, I question whether you would find an inclination to repeat it.

Perhaps not (said she); but that mode of instruction in all the experimental sciences is not, perhaps, the best. A numerous company can derive little benefit from a dissection in their presence. A closer and more deliberate inspection than the circumstances of a large company will allow, seems requisite. But the assembly need not be a mixed one. Objections on the score of delicacy, though they are more specious than sound, and owe their force more to our weakness than our wisdom, would be removed by making the whole company, professor and pupils, female. But this would be obviating an imaginary evil, at the price of a real benefit. Nothing has been more injurious than the separation of the sexes. They associate in childhood without restraint; but the period quickly arrives when they are obliged to take different paths. Ideas, maxims, and pursuits, wholly opposite, engross their attention. Different systems of morality, different languages, or, at least, the same words with a different set of meanings, are adopted. All intercourse between them is fettered and embarrassed. On one side, all is reserve and artifice. On the other, adulation and affected humility. The same end must be compassed by opposite means. The man must affect a disproportionable ardour; while the woman must counterfeit indifference and aversion. Her tongue has no office, but to belie the sentiments of her heart, and the dictates of her understanding.

By marriage she loses all right to separate property. The will of her husband is the criterion of all her duties. All merit is comprised in unlimited obedience. She must not expostulate or rebel. In all contests with him, she must hope to prevail by blandishments and tears; not by appeals to justice and addresses to reason. She will be most applauded when she smiles with most perseverance on her oppressor, and when, with the undistinguishing attachment of a dog, no caprice or cruelty shall be able to estrange her affection.

Surely, Madam, this picture is exaggerated. You derive it from some other source than your own experience, or even your own observation.

No; I believe the picture to be generally exact. No doubt there are exceptions. I believe myself to be one. I think myself exempt from the grosser defects of women; but by no means free from the influence of a mistaken education. But why should you think the picture exaggerated? Man is the strongest. This is the reason why, in the earliest stage of society, the females are slaves. The tendency of rational improvement is to equalize conditions; to abolish all distinctions, but those that are founded in truth and reason; to limit the reign of brute force, and uncontroulable accidents. Women have unquestionably benefited by the progress that has hitherto taken place. If I look abroad, I may see reason to congratulate myself on being born in this age and country. Women, that are no where totally exempt from servitude, no where admitted to their true rank in society, may yet be subject to different degrees or kinds of servitude. Perhaps there is no country in the world where the yoke is lighter than here. But this persuasion, though, in one view, it may afford us consolation, ought not to blind us to our true condition, or weaken our efforts to remove the evils that still oppress us. It is manifest, that we are hardly and unjustly treated. The natives of the most distant regions do not less resemble each other, than the male and female of the same tribe, in consequence of the different discipline to which they are subject. Now, this is palpably absurd. Men and women are partakers of the same nature. They are rational beings; and, as such, the same principles of truth and equity must be applicable to both.

To this I replied, Certainly, Madam: but it is obvious to inquire to which of the sexes the distinction is most favourable. In some respects, different paths are allotted to them, but I am apt to suspect that of the woman to be strewed with fewest thorns; to be beset with fewest asperities; and to lead, if not absolutely in conformity to truth and equity, yet with fewest deviations from it. There are evils incident to your condition as women. As human beings, we all lie under considerable disadvantages; but it is of an unequal lot that you complain. The institutions of society have injuriously and capriciously distinguished you. True it is, laws, which have commonly been male births, have treated you unjustly; but it has been with that species of injustice that has given birth to nobles and kings. They have distinguished you by irrational and undeserved indulgences. They have exempted you from a thousand toils and cares. Their tenderness has secluded you from tumult and noise: your persons are sacred from profane violences; your eyes from ghastly spectacles; your ears from a thousand discords, by which ours are incessantly invaded. Yours are the peacefullest recesses of the mansion: your hours glide along in sportive chat, in harmless recreation, or voluptuous indolence; or in labour so light, as scarcely to be termed encroachments on the reign of contemplation. Your industry delights in the graceful and minute: it enlarges the empire of the senses, and improves the flexibility of the fibres. The art of the needle, by the lustre of its hues and the delicacy of its touches, is able to mimic all the forms of nature, and pourtray all the images of fancy: and the needle but prepares the hand for doing wonders on the harp; for conjuring up the 'piano' to melt, and the 'forte' to astound us.

This (cried the lady) is very partial description. It can apply only to the opulent, and but to few of them. Meanwhile, how shall we estimate the hardships of the lower class? You have only pronounced a panegyric on indolence and luxury. Eminent virtue and true happiness are not to be found in this element.

True (returned I). I have only attempted to justify the male sex from the charge of cruelty. Ease and luxury are pernicious. Kings and nobles, the rich and the idle, enjoy no genuine content. Their lot is hard enough; but still it is better than brutal ignorance and unintermitted toil; than nakedness and hunger. There must be one condition of society that approaches nearer than any other to the standard of rectitude and happiness. For this it is our duty to search; and, having found it, endeavour to reduce every other condition to this desirable mean. It is useful, meanwhile, to ascertain the relative importance of different conditions; and since deplorable evils are annexed to every state, to discover in what respects, and in what degree, one is more or less eligible than another. Half of the community are females. Let the whole community be divided into classes; and let us inquire, whether the wives, and daughters, and single women, of each class, be not placed in a more favourable situation than the husbands, sons, and single men, of the same class. Our answer will surely be in the affirmative.

There is (said the lady) but one important question relative to this subject. Are women as high in the scale of social felicity and usefulness as they may and ought to be?

To this (said I) there can be but one answer: No. At present they are only higher on that scale than the men. You will observe, Madam, I speak only of that state of society which we enjoy. If you had excluded sex from the question, I must have made the same answer. Human beings, it is to be hoped, are destined to a better condition on this stage, or some other, than is now allotted them.

PART II.

This remark was succeeded by a pause on both sides. The lady seemed more inclined to listen than talk. At length I ventured to resume the conversation.

Pray, Madam, permit me to return from this impertinent digression, and repeat my question—"Are you a federalist?"

And let me (replied she) repeat my answer—What have I, as a woman, to do with politics? Even the government of our country, which is said to be the freest in the world, passes over women as if they were not. We are excluded from all political rights without the least ceremony. Law-makers thought as little of comprehending us in their code of liberty, as if we were pigs, or sheep. That females are exceptions to their general maxims, perhaps never occurred to them. If it did, the idea was quietly discarded, without leaving behind the slightest consciousness of inconsistency or injustice. If to uphold and defend, as far as woman's little power extends, the constitution, against violence; if to prefer a scheme of union and confederacy, to war and dissention, entitle me to that name, I may justly be stiled a federalist. But if that title be incompatible with a belief that, in many particulars, this constitution is unjust and absurd, I certainly cannot pretend to it.

But how should it be otherwise? While I am conscious of being an intelligent and moral being; while I see myself denied, in so many cases, the exercise of my own discretion; incapable of separate property; subject, in all periods of my life, to the will of another, on whose bounty I am made to depend for food, raiment, and shelter: when I see myself, in my relation to society, regarded merely as a beast, or an insect; passed over, in the distribution of public duties, as absolutely nothing, by those who disdain to assign the least apology for their injustice—what though politicians say I am nothing, it is impossible I should assent to their opinion, as long as I am conscious of willing and moving. If they generously admit me into the class of existence, but affirm that I exist for no purpose but the convenience of the more dignified sex; that I am not to be entrusted with the government of myself; that to foresee, to deliberate and decide, belongs to others, while all my duties resolve themselves into this precept, "listen and obey;" it is not for me to smile at their tyranny, or receive, as my gospel, a code built upon such atrocious maxims. No, I am no federalist.

You are, at least (said I), a severe and uncommon censor. You assign most extraordinary reasons for your political heresy. You have many companions in your aversion to the government, but, I suspect, are wholly singular in your motives. There are few, even among your own sex, who reason in this manner.

Very probably; thoughtless and servile creatures! but that is not wonderful. All despotism subsists by virtue of the errors and supineness of its slaves. If their discernment was clear, their persons would be free. Brute strength has no part in the government of multitudes: they are bound in the fetters of opinion.

The maxims of constitution-makers sound well. All power is derived from the people. Liberty is every one's birthright. Since all cannot govern or deliberate individually, it is just that they should elect their representatives. That every one should possess, indirectly, and through the medium of his representatives, a voice in the public councils; and should yield to no will but that of an actual or virtual majority. Plausible and specious maxims! but fallacious. What avails it to be told by any one, that he is an advocate for liberty? we must first know what he means by the word. We shall generally find that he intends only freedom to himself, and subjection to all others. Suppose

I place myself where I can conveniently mark the proceedings at a general election: "All," says the code, "are free. Liberty is the immediate gift of the Creator to all mankind, and is unalienable. Those that are subject to the laws should possess a share in their enaction. This privilege can be exercised, consistently with the maintenance of social order, in a large society, only in the choice of deputies." A person advances with his ticket. "Pray," says the officer, "are you twenty-one years of age?"—"No."—"Then I cannot receive your vote; you are no citizen." Disconcerted and abashed, he retires. A second assumes his place. "How long," says the officer, "have you been an inhabitant of this State?"—"Nineteen months and a few days."—"None has a right to vote who has not completed two years residence." A third approaches, who is rejected because his name is not found in the catalogue of taxables. At length room is made for a fourth person. "Man," cries the magistrate, "is your skin black or white?"—"Black." —"What, a sooty slave dare to usurp the rights of freemen?" The way being now clear, I venture to approach. "I am not a minor," say I to myself. "I was born in the State, and cannot, therefore, be stigmatized as a foreigner. I pay taxes, for I have no father or husband to pay them for me. Luckily my complexion is white. Surely my vote will be received. But, no, I am a woman. Neither short residence, nor poverty, nor age, nor colour, nor sex, exempt from the jurisdiction of the laws." "True," says the magistrate; "but they deprive you from bearing any part in their formation." "So I perceive, but I cannot perceive the justice of your pretentions to equality and liberty, when those principles are thus openly and grossly violated."

If a stranger question me concerning the nature of our government, I answer, that in this happy climate all men are free: the people are the source of all authority; from them it flows, and to them, in due season, it returns. But in what (says my friend) does this unrivalled and precious freedom consist? Not (say I) in every man's governing himself, literally and individually; that is impossible. Not in the controul of an actual majority; they are by much too numerous to deliberate commodiously, or decide expeditiously. No, our liberty consists in the choice of our governors: all, as reason requires, have a part in this choice, yet not without a few exceptions; for, in the first place, all females are excepted. They, indeed, compose one half of the community; but, no matter, women cannot possibly have any rights.

Secondly, those whom the feudal law calls minors, because they could
not lift a shield, or manage a pike, are excepted. They comprehend
one half of the remainder. Thirdly, the poor. These vary in number,
but are sure to increase with the increase of luxury and opulence, and
to promote these is well known to be the aim of all wise governors.
Fourthly, those who have not been two years in the land: and, lastly,
slaves. It has been sagely decreed, that none but freemen shall enjoy
this privilege, and that all men are free but those that are slaves. When
all these are sifted out, a majority of the remainder are entitled to elect
our governor; provided, however, the candidate possess certain qualifications, which you will excuse me from enumerating. I am tired of
explaining this charming system of equality and independence. Let the
black, the young, the poor, and the stranger, support their own claims.
I am a woman. As such, I cannot celebrate the equity of that scheme
of government which classes me with dogs and swine.

In this representation (said I) it must be allowed there is some
truth; but do you sufficiently distinguish between the form and spirit
of a government? The true condition of a nation cannot be described
in a few words; nor can it be found in the volumes of their laws. We
know little or nothing when our knowledge extends no farther than
the forms of the constitution. As to any direct part they bear in the
government, the women of Turky, Russia, and America, are alike;
but, surely, their actual condition, their dignity, and freedom, are very
different. The value of any government lies in the mode in which it is
exercised. If we consent to be ruled by another, our liberty may still
remain inviolate, or be infringed only when superior wisdom directs.
Our master may govern us agreeably to our own ideas, or may restrain and enforce us only when our own views are mistaken.

No government is independent of popular opinion. By that it
must necessarily be sustained and modified. In the worst despotism
there is a sphere of discretion allotted to each man, which political
authority must not violate. How much soever is relinquished by the
people, somewhat is always reserved. The chief purpose of the wise is
to make men their own governors, to persuade them to practise the
rules of equity without legal constraint: they will try to lessen the
quantity of government, without changing or multiplying the deposi-
tories of it; to diminish the number of those cases in which authority
is required to interfere. We need not complain of the injustice of

laws, if we refrain, or do not find it needful to appeal to them: if we decide amicably our differences, or refer them to an umpire of our own choice: if we trust not to the subtilty of lawyers, and the prejudice of judges, but to our own eloquence, and a tribunal of our neighbours. It matters not what power the laws give me over the property or persons of others, if I do not chuse to avail myself of the privilege.

Then (said the lady) you think that forms of government are no subjects of contest. It matters not by whom power is possessed, or how it is transferred; whether we bestow our allegiance on a child or a lunatic; whether kings be made by the accident of birth or wealth; whether supreme power be acquired by force, or transmitted by inheritance, or conferred freely and periodically by the suffrages of all that acknowledge its validity?

Doubtless (replied I) these considerations are of some moment; but cannot you distinguish between power and the exercise of power, and see that the importance of the first is derived wholly from the consideration of the last?

But how it shall be exercised (rejoined she) depends wholly on the views and habits of him that has it. Avails it nothing whether the prince be mild or austere, malignant or benevolent? If we must delegate authority, are we not concerned to repose it with him who will use it to the best, rather than the worst purposes? True it is, we should retain as much power over our own conduct, maintain the sphere of our own discretion, as large and as inviolate as possible. But we must, as long as we associate with mankind, forego, in some particulars, our self-government, and submit to the direction of another; but nothing interests me more nearly than a wise choice of a master. The wisest member of society should, if possible, be selected for the guidance of the rest.

If an hundred persons be in want of a common dwelling, and the work cannot be planned or executed by the whole, from the want of either skill or unanimity, what is to be done? We must search out one who will do that which the circumstances of the case will not allow us to do for ourselves. Is it not obvious to inquire who among us possesses most skill, and most virtue to controul him in the use of it? Or shall we lay aside all regard to skill and integrity, and consider merely who is the tallest, or richest, or fairest among us, or admit his title that can prove that such an one was his father, or that he himself is the eldest among the children of his father? In an affair which is of common concern, shall we consign the province of deciding to a part, or yield to the superior claims of a majority? If it happen that the smaller number be distinguished by more accurate discernment, or extensive knowledge, and, consequently, he that is chosen by the wiser few, will probably be, in himself, considered more worthy than the favourite of the injudicious many; yet what is the criterion which shall enable us to distinguish the sages from the fools? And, when the selection is made, what means shall we use for expunging from the catalogue all those whom age has enfeebled, or flattery or power corrupted? If all this were effected, could we, at the same time, exclude evils from our system, by which its benefits would be overweighed? Of all modes of government, is not the sovereignty of the people, however incumbered with inconveniences, yet attended by the fewest?

It is true (answered I) that one form of government may tend more than another to generate selfishness and tyranny in him that rules, and ignorance and profligacy in the subjects. If different forms be submitted to our choice, we should elect that which deserves the preference. Suppose our countrymen would be happier if they were subdivided into a thousand little independent democratical republics, than they are under their present form, or than they would be under an hereditary despot: then it behoves us to inquire by what, if by any means, this subdivision may be effected, and, which is matter of equal moment, how it can be maintained: but these, for the most part, are airy speculations. If not absolutely hurtful, they are injurious, by being of inferior utility to others which they exclude. If women be excluded from political functions, it is sufficient that, in this exercise of these functions, their happiness is amply consulted.

Say what you will (cried the lady), I shall ever consider it as a gross abuse that we are hindered from sharing with you in the power of chusing our rulers, and of making those laws to which we equally with yourselves are subject.

We claim the power (rejoined I); this cannot be denied; but I must maintain, that as long as it is equitably exercised, no alteration is desirable. Shall the young, the poor, the stranger, and the females, be admitted, indiscriminately, to political privileges? Shall we annex no condition to a voter but that he be a thing in human shape, not lunatic, and capable of locomotion; and no qualifications to a candidate but the choice of a majority? Would any benefit result from the change? Will it augment the likelihood that the choice will fall upon the wisest? Will it endow the framers and interpreters of law with more sagacity and moderation than they at present possess?

Perhaps not (said she). I plead only for my own sex. Want of property, youth, and servile condition, may, possibly, be well-founded objections; but mere sex is a circumstance so purely physical; has so little essential influence beyond what has flowed from the caprice of civil institutions on the qualities of mind or person, that I cannot think of it without impatience. If the law should exclude from all political functions every one who had a mole on his right cheek, or whose stature did not exceed five feet six inches, who would not condemn, without scruple, so unjust an institution? yet, in truth, the injustice would be less than in the case of women. The distinction is no less futile, but the injury is far greater, since it annihilates the political existence of at least one half of the community.

But you appeared to grant (said I) that want of property and servile condition are allowable disqualifications. Now, may not marriage be said to take away both the liberty and property of women? at least, does it not bereave them of that independent judgment which it is just to demand from a voter?

Not universally the property (answered she): so far as it has the effect you mention, was there ever any absurdity more palpable, any injustice more flagrant? But you well know there are cases in which women, by marriage, do not relinquish their property. All women, however, are not wives and wards. Granting that such are disqualified, what shall we say of those who are indisputably single, affluent and independent? Against these no objection, in the slightest degree plausible, can be urged. It would be strange folly to suppose women of this class to be necessarily destitute of those qualities which the station of citizen requires. We have only to examine the pretentions of those who already occupy public stations. Most of them seem not to have attained heights inaccessible to ordinary understandings; and yet the delegation of women, however opulent and enlightened, would, probably, be a more insupportable shock to the prejudices that prevail among us, than the appointment of a youth of fifteen, or a beggar, or a stranger.

If this innovation be just (said I), the period for making it has not arrived. You, Madam, are singular. Women in general do not reason in this manner. They are contented with the post assigned them. If the rights of a citizen were extended to them, they would not employ them—stay till they desire it.

If they were wise (returned the lady), they would desire it: meanwhile, it is an act of odious injustice to withhold it. This privilege is their due. By what means have you discovered that they would not exercise it, if it were granted? You cannot imagine but that some would step forth and occupy this station, when the obstruction was removed.

I know little of women (said I); I have seldom approached them, much less have I enjoyed their intimate society; yet, as a specimen of the prejudice you spoke of, I must own I should be not a little surprized to hear of a woman proferring her services as president or senator. It would be hard to restrain a smile to see her rise in a popular assembly to discuss some mighty topic. I should gaze as at a prodigy, and listen with a doubting heart: yet I might not refuse devotion to the same woman in the character of household deity. As a mother, pressing a charming babe to her bosom; as my companion in the paths of love, or poetry, or science; as partaker with me in content, and an elegant sufficiency, her dignity would shine forth in full splendour. Here all would be decency and grace. But as a national ruler; as busied in political intrigues and cares; as intrenched in the paper mounds of a secretary; as burthened with the gravity of a judge; as bearing the standard in battle; or, even as a champion in senatorial warfare, it would be difficult to behold her without regret and disapprobation. These emotions I should not pretend to justify; but such, and so difficult to vanquish, is prejudice.

Prejudices, countenanced by an experience so specious and universal, cannot be suddenly subdued. I shall tell you, however, my genuine and deliberate opinion on the subject. I have said that the inequality of the sexes was all that could be admitted; that the superiority we deny to men can, with as little justice, be ascribed to women: but this, in the strictest sense, is not true: on the contrary, it must be allowed that women are superior.

We cannot fail to distinguish between the qualities of mind and those of person. Whatever be the relation between the thinking principle, and the limbs and organs of the body, it is manifest that they are distinct; insomuch, that when we pass judgment on the qualities of the former, the latter is not necessarily taken into view, or included in it. So, when we discourse of our exterior and sensible qualities, we are supposed to exclude from our present consideration, the endowments of the mind. This distinction is loose, but sufficiently accurate for my purpose.

Have we not abundant reason to conclude that the principle of thought is, in both sexes, the same; that it is subject to like influences; that like motives and situations produce like effects? We are not concerned to know which of the sexes has occupied the foremost place on the stage of human life. They would not be beings of the same nature in whom different causes produced like effects. It is sufficient that we can trace diversity in the effects to a corresponding diversity in the circumstances; that women are such as observation exhibits them, in consequence of those laws which belong to a rational being, and which are common to both sexes: but such, beyond all doubt, must be the result of our inquiries. In this respect, then, the sexes are equal.

But what opinion must be formed of their exterior or personal qualities? Are not the members and organs of the female body as aptly suited to their purposes as those of the male? The same, indeed, may be asserted of a mouse or a grasshopper; but are not these purposes as wise and dignified, nay, are they not precisely the same? Considering the female frame as the subject of impressions, and the organ of intelligence, it appears to deserve the preference. What shall we say of the acuteness and variety of your sensations; of the smoothness, flexibility, and compass of your voice?

Beauty is a doubtful quality. Few men will scruple to resign the superiority in this respect to women. The truth of this decision may be, perhaps, physically demonstrated; or, perhaps, all our reasonings are vitiated, by this circumstance, that the reasoner and his auditors are male. We all know in what the sexual distinction consists, and what is the final cause of this distinction. It is easier to conceive than describe that species of attraction which sex annexes to the person. It would be fallacious, perhaps, to infer female superiority, in an absolute and general sense, from the devotion which, in certain cases, we are prone to pay them; which it is impossible to feel for one of our own sex; and which is mutually felt: yet, methinks, the inference is inevitable. When I reflect on the equality of mind, and attend to the feelings which are roused in my bosom by the presence of accomplished and lovely women; by the mere graces of their exterior, even when the magic of their voice sleeps, and the eloquence of their eyes is mute;—and, for the reality of these feelings, if politeness did not forbid, I might quote the experience of the present moment—I am irresistibly induced to believe, that, of the two sexes, yours is, on the whole, superior.

It is difficult, I know, to reason dispassionately on this subject: witness the universal persuasion of mankind, that in grace, symmetry, and melody, the preference is due to women. Yet, beside that opinion is no criterion of truth but to him that harbours it, when I call upon all human kind as witnesses, it is only one half of them, the individuals of one sex, that obey my call.

It may at first appear that men have generally ascribed intellectual pre-eminence to themselves. Nothing, however, can be inferred from this. It is doubtful whether they judge rightly on the question of what is or is not intrinsically excellent. Not seldom they have placed their superiority in that which, rightly understood, should have been pregnant with ignominy and humiliation. Should women themselves be found to concur in this belief, that the other sex surpasses them in intelligence, it will avail but little. We must still remember that opinion is evidence of nothing but its own existence. This opinion, indeed, is peculiarly obnoxious. They merely repeat what they have been taught; and their teachers have been men. The prevalence of this opinion, if it does not evince the incurable defects of female capacity, may, at least, be cited to prove in how mournful a degree that capacity has been neglected or perverted. It is a branch of that prejudice which has so long darkened the world, and taught men that nobles and kings were creatures of an order superior to themselves.

Here the conversation was interrupted by one of the company, who, after listening to us for some time, thought proper at last to approach, and contribute his mite to our mutual edification. I soon after seized an opportunity of withdrawing, but not without requesting and obtaining permission to repeat my visit.

James Fenimore Cooper [1789-1851]
FROM Notions of the Americans:
Picked Up by a Traveling Bachelor [1828]

☙❧

NOTE: *The book is written in epistolary form,
and appeared in two volumes. The letter writer
is presumably an Englishman, who meets John
Cadwallader, an American, on the continent.
The two decide to travel to the United States,
Cadwallader acting as guide.*

TO SIR EDWARD WALLER, BART. &C. &C.

New-York,——

The day after we had quitted Cooperstown, we saw a collection of
people assembled in front of an inn, which was the principal edifice in
a hamlet of perhaps a dozen houses. Cadwallader told me this was the
first day of the State election, and that this spot was one of the polls, a
name which answers in some degree to the English term, "hustings."
Fortunately, the stage changed horses at the inn, and I had an opportunity of examining the incipient step in that process which literally
dictates all the national policy of this great republic.

Although each State controls its own forms, not only in the
elections, but in every thing else, a description of the usages of one
poll will be sufficiently near the truth to give a correct general idea of

them all. I now speak literally only of the State of New-York, though, generally, of the whole Union. The elections occur once a year.* They last three days. In the large towns, they are stationary, there being no inconvenience in such an arrangement where the population is dense, and the distances short. But in the country they are held on each successive day at a different place, in order to accommodate the voters. The State is divided into counties, which cover, on an average, 900 square miles each. Some are, however, larger, and some smaller. These counties are again subdivided into townships, covering, perhaps, eighty or ninety square miles. There is, also, great inequality in the size of these minor districts. These are the two great divisions of territory for all the ordinary purposes of government and police. The counties have courts of their own, and a certain sort of legislative body, which regulates many of their financial affairs. In order that the whole subject, however, may be rendered as clear as possible, we will begin at the base, and ascend to the superstructure of their government.

The most democratic assemblage known to the laws, in which legal and binding resolutions can be enacted, are the town meetings. Any number of the people may assemble when and where they please, to remonstrate, to petition, or even to plot, if they see fit; but their acts can only be recommendatory. The town meetings are held annually, and every citizen who has attained his majority can vote. A moderator (no bad name for a perfectly popular assembly) is chosen by acclamation to preside. The meeting is commonly held in some school-house, but very often in the open air. In some places, though rarely, there are town-houses. At these meetings, all the town officers are chosen. They consist of a supervisor; three assessors, who apportion all the taxes on the individuals, whether imposed by town, county, state, or United States; collectors, who collect all the taxes, except those laid by the United States government, which in time of peace, are just nothing at all; a town-clerk, who keeps certain registers; constable, poor-officers, overseers of highways, path-masters, and a few others. The names of most of these officers indicate their duties.

* There is one State where they occur twice—the little State of Rhode Island, which is still governed by the form of its ancient charter, as granted by Charles II. in 1663. As this is practically the most democratic State in the Union, it affords pretty good evidence that the experiment of a democratic government is not so new in America as some pretend.

The overseers of the highway are the men who lay out the ordinary roads of the town, and who say how much tax each individual shall contribute in work or in money; and the path-masters inspect the labour. Men of property and education frequently seek the latter employment. The voting in this popular assembly may be by ballot, but it is generally done by acclamation. There is a penalty if an individual refuse to serve, though they are sometimes excused by the citizens, if a good reason can be rendered. The courts have also a discretionary power in imposing and in laying fines. I was present during the course of this excursion at one of these town meetings. There might have been two hundred citizens assembled before the door of a large school-house. Much good-humour was blended with a sufficient despatch of business. The Americans mingle with a perfect consciousness of their influence on the government, an admirable respect for the laws and institutions of their country. I heard jokes, and one or two open nominations of men of property and character, to fill the humble offices of constable and pound-keeper; but the most perfect good sense and practical usefulness appeared to distinguish all their decisions. There was a contest for the office of supervisor, and it was decided by a close vote. The two candidates were present, and on seemingly very good terms. They were respectable looking yeomen, and he who lost told his rival that he thought the people had shown their judgment. There was no noise, no drinking, nor any excitement beyond that which one would feel in seeing an ordinary foot-race. One farmer observed, that the crows had got the taste of his corn, and unless something was done, there could be little hope for the year's crop. He therefore would propose that a reward of six cents should be paid for every dozen that should be killed, within their town, for the next six months. The resolution was opposed by a hatter, who insisted that he could take care of his hats, and that the farmers ought to take care of their corn. This logic was unsuccessful; the price was reduced a trifle, and the resolution was passed. It was then just as much a law as that which hangs a man for murder. The sum voted to meet the expense was to be apportioned with the other taxes, among the citizens, by the assessors, collected by the collector, received and paid by another officer, &c. &c. After this important act of legislation, the meeting adjourned.

The next body in the scale of the government is the board of supervisors. It is composed of the supervisors of each town in a county, who have a very similar legislative authority over the more familiar interests of the county, as is possessed by their constituents in the towns themselves. They impose taxes for all objects connected with the expenses of the county. Their authority is, however, a good deal circumscribed; enactments by the State legislature being often necessary to enforce their recommendations. When the question involves an expense heavier than common, and its effects are entirely local, the question is often referred to a final decision of the people in their town meetings. This board audits the accounts, and I believe it appoints a treasurer for the county. So far you see the process of government is exceedingly simple. The whole legislative duty is discharged in three or four days, and yet the decisions have great influence on the comfort and property of the people. The duties of the officers named, continue for one year, but the same incumbents are frequently continued for a whole life, especially the collectors, treasurers, constables, and clerks.

Each town is also subdivided into school districts, and road districts. There are overseers of the schools, who regulate all that belongs to the familiar duties of the common schools of the country, to which any body may go.

Each township is also a petty electoral district of itself, for all the ordinary purposes of the State and the United States' elections, which are held at the same time and place. The three stations taken for the convenience of the elections, as already mentioned, are selected by the inspectors of the poll, who are five or six of the town officers, named by law, and of course chosen annually by the people in their original capacity. Each county chooses its own representatives to the lower branch of the State legislature, the number being according to the amount of the population. The State is again divided into what are called senatorial districts, composed of several contiguous counties, each of which chooses a certain number of representatives, who sit in the upper body of the State legislature. Each State has a right to send to the lower House of Congress a number of representatives, in proportion to its entire population. These representatives must be chosen by the people, but the States themselves may regulate the form. Some choose them by a general ticket; that is to say, each citizen votes for the whole number; and some choose them by districts, in which case each citizen votes for the member, or members, who represent his particular district. The latter is the course adopted by New-York, and in most of the other large States, in which it is difficult for the characters of so many individuals to be intimately known to every body.

Now, complicated as this system may seem in words, it is perfectly simple in practice. It is astonishing how clearly it is understood by those who exercise it, and how difficult it is to make a foreigner get a correct idea of its details. All the elections, except those which are made at the town meetings, where other duties necessarily assemble the citizens, are held at the same time, and at the same place. Thus an American, in one of the more populous States, can exercise all his constitutional rights at an expense commonly of a ride of four or five miles at the outside, and of three hours of time.

The election on the present occasion embraced senators, (always for the State,) representatives in the assembly,* governor, lieutenant-governor, &c. The inspectors were assembled in a quiet room of the inn, with the ballot-boxes placed before them, on a table. The voters entered at their leisure, and delivered their different ballots to the officers, who, holding them up as lottery numbers are usually exhibited, called the name of the voter aloud, and then deposited the ballot in its proper box. "I challenge that vote," cried an individual, as the name of one man was thus proclaimed. It appeared that there were doubts of its legality. An inquiry was instituted, an oath proffered, explanations were made, and the challenge was withdrawn. The vote was then received. Any one who votes may challenge. Nothing could be more quiet and orderly than this meeting. A few handbills were posted around the house, proclaiming the names, and extolling the qualities of the different candidates, and I heard one or two men disputing the wisdom of certain public measures, rather in irony than in heat. The election was not, however, esteemed a warm one, and perhaps quite one third of the people did not attend the polls at all. Mr. Clinton, the governor, under whose administration the canal policy, as it is called, has been fostered, had declined a re-election, at the expiration of the official term preceding the one now in existence.

* The more popular branch of the State legislature, as it is sometimes called, though both are popular alike. The difference is principally in the term of service, and in some little exercise of power.

His place had been filled by another. In the mean time, his political adversaries, profiting by a momentary possession of a legislative majority, had ventured to assail him in a manner the people were not disposed to relish. He was removed from a seat at the "canal board," a measure which was undoubtedly intended to separate him, as far as possible, from a policy that was already conferring incalculable advantage on the State. The instant Cadwallader was told of this ill-advised and illiberal measure, he exclaimed, that the political adversaries of this gentle man had reseated him in the chair of the government. When asked for an explanation, my friend answered, that the people, though they sometimes visited political blunders with great severity, rarely tolerated persecution. The event has justified his predictions. Although a popular candidate was selected to oppose him, Mr. Clinton has triumphed in this election by an immense majority, and, in a few days, he will become governor of the State for another term of two years.*

After quitting the poll, we familiarly discussed the merits and demerits of this system of popular elections. In order to extract the opinions of my friend, several of the more obvious and ordinary objections were started, with a freedom that induced him to speak with some seriousness.

"You see a thousand dangers in universal suffrage," he said, "merely because you have been taught to think so, without ever having seen the experiment tried. The Austrian would be very apt to say, under the influence of mere speculation too, that it would be fatal to government to have any representation at all; and a vizier of the Grand Turk might find the mild exercise of the laws, which is certainly practised in Austria Proper, altogether fatal to good order. Now we know, not from the practice of fifty years only, but from the practice of two centuries, that it is very possible to have both order and prosperity under a form of government which admits of the utmost extension of the suffrage. It is a never-failing argument on these subjects, that American order is owing to the morality of a simple condition of life, and that our prosperity is incidental to our particular geographical situation. There are many good men, and, in

---

* No voter can put in two ballots, since all are compelled to place them in the hands of an inspector. In case two ballots are found rolled together, both are rejected. Thus fraud is impossible.

other respects, wise men, even among ourselves, who retain so much of the political theory which pervades the literature of our language, as to believe the same thing. For myself, I cannot see the truth of either of these positions. Our prosperity is owing to our intelligence, and our intelligence to our institutions. Every discreet man in America is deeply impressed with the importance of diffusing instruction among our people, just as many very well-meaning persons in your hemisphere honestly enough entertain a singular horror of the danger of school-books. Thus it is, our natural means of safety to do the very thing which must, of necessity, have the greatest possible influence on the happiness, civilization, and power, of a nation.

"There can be no doubt that, under a bald theory, a representation would be all the better if the most ignorant, profligate, and vagabond part of the community, were excluded from the right of voting. It is just as true, that if all the rogues and corrupt politicians, even including those who read Latin, and have well-lined pockets, could be refused the right of voting, honest men would fare all the better. But as it is very well known that the latter are not, nor cannot well be excluded from the right of suffrage any where, except in a despotism, we have come to the conclusion, that it is scarcely worth while to do so much violence to natural justice, without sufficient reason, as to disfranchise a man merely because he is poor. Though a trifling *qualification* of property may sometimes be useful, in particular conditions of society, there can be no greater fallacy than its *representation*. The most vehement declaimers in favour of the justice of the representation of property, overlook two or three very important points of the argument. A man may be a voluntary associate in a joint-stock company, and justly have a right to a participation in its management, in proportion to his pecuniary interest; but life is not a chartered institution. Men are born with all their wants and passions, their means of enjoyment, and their sources of misery, without any agency of their own, and frequently to their great discomfort. Now, though government is, beyond a doubt, a sort of compact, it would seem that those who prescribe its conditions are under a natural obligation to consult the rights of the whole. If men, when a little better than common, were any thing like perfect, we might hope to see power lodged with safety in the hands of a reasonable portion of the enlightened, without any danger of its abuse. But the experience of the world goes to prove, that there is a tendency to monopoly, wherever power is reposed in the hands of a minority. Nothing is more likely to be true, than that twenty wise men will unite in opinion in opposition to a hundred fools; but nothing is more certain than that, if placed in situations to control all the interests of their less gifted neighbours, the chance is, that fifteen or sixteen of them would pervert their philosophy to selfishness. This was at least our political creed, and we therefore admitted a vast majority of the community to a right of voting. Since the hour of the revolution, the habits, opinions, laws, and I may say principles of the Americans, are getting daily to be more democratic. We are perfectly aware, that while the votes of a few thousand scattered individuals can make no great or lasting impression on the prosperity or policy of the country, their disaffection at being excluded might give a great deal of trouble. I do not mean to say that the suffrage may not, in most countries, be extended too far. I only wish to show you that it is not here.

"The theory of representation of property says, that the man who has little shall not dispose of the money of him who has more.* Now, what say experience and common sense? It is the man who has *much* that is prodigal of the public purse. A sum that is trifling in his account, may constitute the substance of one who is poorer. Beyond all doubt, the government of the world, which is most reckless of the public money, is that in which power is the exclusive property of the very rich; and, beyond all doubt, the government of the world which, compared with its means, is infinitely the most sparing of its resources, is that in which they who enact the laws are compelled to consult the wishes of those who have the least to bestow. It is idle to say that an enlarged and liberal policy governs the measures of the one, and that the other is renowned for a narrowness which has lessened its influence and circumscribed its prosperity. I know not, nor care not, what men, who are dazzled with the glitter of things, may choose to say, but I am thoroughly convinced, from observation, that if the advice of those who were influenced by what is called a liberal policy, had been followed in our country, we should have been a poorer and, consequently, a less important and less happy people

---

* When the numbers of those who have nothing, get to be so great as to make their voices of importance, it is time to think of some serious change.

than at present. The relations between political liberality, and what is called political prodigality, are wonderfully intimate.

"We find that our government is cheaper, and even stronger, for being popular. There is no doubt that the jealousy of those who have little, often induces a false economy, and that money might frequently be saved by bidding higher for talent. We lay no claims to perfection, but we do say, that more good is attained in this manner than in any other which is practised elsewhere. We look at the aggregate of advantage, and neither our calculations nor our hopes have, as yet, been greatly deceived.

"As to the forms of our elections, you see that they are beyond example simple and orderly. After an experience of near forty years, I can say that I have never seen a blow struck, nor any other violent proceeding, at a poll. These things certainly do happen, but, in comparison with the opportunities, at remarkably long intervals. So far from the frequency of elections tending to disturb society, they produce an exactly different effect. A contest which is so soon to be repeated loses half its interest by familiarity. Vast numbers of electors are content to be lookers-on, rarely approaching a poll, except to vote on some question of peculiar concern. The struggle is generally whether A or B shall enjoy the temporary honour or the trifling emolument in dispute, the community seldom being much the better or the worse for the choice. People talk of the fluctuations which are necessarily the consequences of a popular government. They do not understand what they say. Every other enlightened nation of the earth is at this moment divided between great opposing principles; whereas here, if we expect the trifling collisions of pecuniary interests, every body is of the same mind, except as to the ordinarily immaterial question of a choice between men. We have settled all the formidable points of policy, by conceding every thing that any reasonable man can ask. The only danger which exists to the duration of our confederacy (and that is not a question of a form of government, but one of mere policy), proceeds from the little that is aristocratical in our Union. The concentrated power of a State may become, like the overgrown power of an individual, dangerous to our harmony; though we think, and with very good reason, that, on the whole, even this peculiarity adds to the durability of the Union.

"It is unnecessary to say, that so far as mere convenience goes, this method of election can be practised by a hundred millions of people, as easily as by twelve. As to corruption, comparatively speaking, it cannot exist. No man can buy a state, a county, or even a town. In a hotly contested election, it is certainly sometimes practicable to influence votes enough to turn the scale; but, unless the question involve the peculiar interests of the less fortunate class of society, it is clear both parties can bribe alike, and then the evil corrects itself. If the question be one likely to unite the interests and the prejudices of the humbler classes, nine times in ten it is both more humane and wiser that they should prevail. That sort of splendid and treacherous policy, which gives a fallacious lustre to a nation by oppressing those who have the most need of support, is manifestly as unwise as it is unjust. It violates the very principles of the compact, since governments are not formed to achieve, but to protect. After a sufficient force has been obtained to effect the first great objects of the association, the governed, and not the governors, are the true agents in every act of national prosperity. Look at America. What people, or what monarch, if you will, has done half so much as we have done, (compared to our means,) in the last half century, and precisely for the reason that the government is obliged to content itself with protection, or, at the most, with that assistance which, in the nature of things, strictly requires a concentrated action.

"It is of far less importance, according to our notions, what the executive of a nation is called, than that all classes should have a direct influence on its policy. We have no king, it is true, for the word carries with it, to our ears, an idea of expenditure; but we have a head, who, for the time being, has a very reasonable portion of power. We are not jealous of him, for we have taken good care he shall do no harm.

"Though we are glad to find that principles which we have practised, and under which we have prospered so long, are coming more in fashion in Europe, I think you must do us the justice to say, that we are not a nation much addicted to the desire of proselytising. For ourselves we have no fears, and as for other people, if they make some faint imitations of our system, and then felicitate themselves on their progress, we are well content they should have all the merit of inventors. That is a miserable rivalry, which would make a monopoly of happiness. I think, as a people, we rather admire you most when we see you advancing with moderation to your object, than when we hear of the adoption of sudden and violent means. We have ever been reformers rather than revolutionists. Our own struggle for independence was not in its aspect a revolution. We contrived to give it all the dignity of a war, from the first blow. Although our generals and soldiers might not have been so well trained as those they fought against, they were far more humane, considerate, and, in the end, successful, than their adversaries. Our own progress has been gradual. It is not long since a trifling restriction existed on the suffrage of this very State. Experience proved that it excluded quite as many discreet men as its removal would admit of vagabonds. Now it is the distinguishing feature of our policy, that we consider man a reasonable being, and that we rather court, than avoid, the struggle between ignorance and intelligence. We find that this policy rarely fails to assure the victory of the latter, while it keeps down its baneful monopolies. We extended the suffrage to include every body, and while complaint is removed, we find no difference in the representation. As yet, it is rather an improvement. Should it become an evil, however, we shall find easy and moderate means to change it, since we are certain that a majority will be sufficiently sagacious to know their own interests. You have only to convince us that it is the best government, and we will become an absolute monarchy to-morrow. It is wonderful how prone we are to adopt that which expectation induces us to think will be expedient, and to reject that which experience teaches us is bad. It must be confessed that, so far, all our experiments have been in favour of democracy. I very well know that you in Europe prophesy that our career will end in monarchy. To be candid, your prophecies excite but little feeling here, since we have taken up the opinion you don't very well understand the subject. But should it prove true, *a la bonne heure;* when we find that form of government best, depend on it, we shall not hesitate to adopt it. You are at perfect liberty, if you will, to establish a journal in favour of despotism under the windows of the Capitol. I will not promise you much patronage at first, neither do I think you will be troubled with much serious opposition. At all events, there is nothing in the law to molest the speculation. Now look behind you at the "poll" we have just left; reflect on this fact, and then draw your conclusions, of our own opinion, of the stability of our institutions. We may deceive ourselves, but you of Europe must exhibit a far more accurate knowledge of the state of our country, before we shall rely on your crude prognostics rather than on our own experience."

I could scarcely assure myself that Cadwallader was not laughing at me during a good deal of the time he was speaking, but after all, it must be confessed there is some common sense in what he said. There were three or four other passengers in the stage, men of decent and sober exterior, among whom I detected certain interchanges of queer glances, though none of them appeared to think the subject of any very engrossing interest. Provoked at their unreasonable indifference to a theme so delightful as liberty, I asked one of them "If he did not apprehend there would be an end to the republic, should General Jackson become the next President?" "I rather think not," was his deliberate, and somewhat laconic answer. "Why not? he is a soldier, and a man of ambition." My unmoved yeoman did not care to dispute either of these qualities, but he still persevered in thinking there was not much danger, since "he did not know any one in his neighbourhood who was much disposed to help a man in such an undertaking."

It is provoking to find a whole nation dwelling in this species of alarming security, for no other reason than that their vulgar and every-day practices teach them to rely on themselves, instead of trusting to the rational inferences of philanthropic theorists, who have so long been racking their ingenuity to demonstrate that a condition of society which has delusively endured for nearly two hundred years, has been in existence all that time in direct opposition to the legitimate deductions of the science of government.

TO SIR EDWARD WALLER, BART. &C. &C.

New-York, —

It is an age since I wrote to any of the club. But though my pen has been necessarily quiet, the intervening time has not been unemployed. In the interval, I have run over an immense surface in the southern and western States. It would be idle to attempt to describe all I have seen, and there would be the constant danger of leading you astray by exceptions, should I descend into detail. Still, as there is a great deal that is distinctive, I shall endeavour to convey to you some general ideas on the subject.

The first, and by far the most important feature, which distinguishes these States from their northern sisters, is slavery. Climate and productions induce some other immaterial differences. The laws, usages, institutions, and political opinions, with such exceptions as unavoidably grow out of states of society marked by such distinctions as the use or the absence of domestic slaves, are essentially the same.

There is a broad, upland region, extending through the interior of Virginia, the two Carolinas, and Georgia, where slaves are used, more as they were formerly used in New-York and in the eastern States, than as they are now used in the other sections of the States named. That is to say, the farmer is the master of three or four labourers, and works in the field at their sides, instead of being a planter, who keeps a driver, and what are called gangs. Tennessee, and Kentucky also, with some exceptions, employ the negroes in a similar manner; while on the Mississippi, the Gulf of Mexico, and along the coast of the Atlantic, as far north as the Chesapeake, slavery exists much in the same forms as it is found in the English West India islands.

The country, on the whole coast of the United States, until one gets far northward and eastward, is low and champaign. It is healthy, or not, according to the degrees of latitude, and to local situation. The uplands are invariably salubrious. There is no region on earth more beautiful, or more fertile, than large parts of Virginia, Kentucky, and Tennessee. There is also much barren, or otherwise little valuable land, in the former State, as there is in the neighbouring States of North and South Carolina.

South Carolina and Louisiana are the only two States which, at the census of 1820, contained more blacks than whites. The former had 231,812 white inhabitants, and 258,497 blacks; leaving a balance of 26,685 in favour of the latter. Of the blacks, 251,783 were slaves, being 19,971 more slaves than whites. Louisiana had, at the same time, 73,383 whites, and 79,540 blacks; of the latter, 69,064 were slaves, being rather fewer slaves than whites. All people having black blood are enumerated as blacks. Georgia is the next considerable community, which has so large a proportion of blacks. It had, in 1820, 189,566 whites, and 151,439 blacks. Virginia had 603,008 whites, and 462,042 blacks; and North Carolina, 419,200 whites, and 219,629 blacks, or nearly two whites to one black. In Kentucky there were 434,644 whites to 129,491 blacks; and in Tennessee, which is much disposed to the habits of a free State, there were 339,727 whites to 82,826 blacks; a proportion of the latter not greater than what formerly existed in New-York and New-Jersey. Most of the blacks, in all these States, are slaves.

In 1790, there were 757,208 blacks in the United States; in 1800, 1,001,729; in 1810, 1,377,810; in 1820, 1,764,836. By making premises of these facts, and taking the past rate of increase as a rule for the future, it would be found that there are now (1828) about 2,000,000 of blacks in the United States. In 1820, there were 233,400 *free* blacks in the United States. As the free blacks do not increase at the same rate as the slaves, this number cannot have accumulated in a full proportion, by natural causes. But emancipation has been busy since. New-York, alone, has liberated more than 10,000 slaves since 1820. We will therefore assume that natural increase and emancipation have kept the free blacks up to the level of the increase of the whole number. This would leave us something like 1,750,000 for the whole amount of slaves in the country, at the present moment (1828.) This result is probably not far from the truth. You will see, however, that my premises are a little faulty, because the increase of blacks between the years 1800 and 1810 was a good deal greater, in comparison with whole numbers, than between 1810 and 1820. This fact is owing to the abolition of the slave trade, which occurred between the two censuses of 1800 and of 1810, and which being known by a prospective law, induced extraordinary importations. Thus the increase between 1800 and 1810 was 376,581, whereas between 1810 and 1820 it was only 387,026, although there was so much larger a stock to increase from. Still, I think the amount of slaves cannot be much short of the number I have named. The white population, in the whole country, is now about 10,000,000. Of this number, however, at least 6,000,000, and probably a great many more, are in the free States. If we put the entire white population of the slave-holding States at 3,500,000, we shall probably give them quite as many as they possess. This would be making two whites to one slave in those States, and it is probably as near the truth as one can get at this distance of time from the census. But it has already been seen, that in many of these States the proportion of blacks is much larger than in others; South Carolina actually possessing more slaves than whites; and Tennessee having four whites to one black. There are, again, districts in these very States, in which the proportion of the whites to the blacks, and of the blacks to the whites, is even still greater.

In addition to these facts, it may be well to state that the whole white population of the country is known to have increased faster than that of the coloured, though the black population of the southern, or slave-holding States, is thought to have increased a little faster than that of the whites.

In considering the question of slavery, as now existing in the United States, the subject naturally divides itself into the past, the present, and the future. It has been often said, that a people, claiming to be the freest of the earth, ought to have brought their practice more in conformity with their professions, and to have abolished slavery at the time they declared their independence. There are many unanswerable reasons to this allegation; or reasons that will be deemed unanswerable, by that portion of mankind who regard life as it actually exists, in its practical aspects and influences. There is not now, nor has there ever been since the separation of the colonies from the mother country, any power to emancipate the slaves, except that which belongs to their masters. This reason might satisfy most practical men of the impossibility of instantly achieving so desirable an object. That sort of humanity, which regards the evils of a distant and alien people, and which, at the same time, turns a cold eye on the sufferings of those at hand, is, to say the least, as useless as it is suspicious. There is scarcely a nation in Europe, if, indeed, there be one, that has not a proportion of its population, that is quite equal to the proportion the slaves of America bear to the whites, which is not quite as low in moral debasement, the name of liberty alone excepted, and which, as a whole, endure much more of physical suffering than the negroes of America.

The condition of the American slave varies, of course, with circumstances. In some few portions of the country, he is ill dealt by. In most districts his labour is sufficiently light, his clothing is adapted to the climate, and his food is, I believe, every where abundant. The strongest evidence, after all, which can be given, that the amount of animal suffering among the American slaves is not great, (there are exceptions, of course,) is the fact that they are a light-hearted and a laughing race. I am very ready to grant that ignorance, and absence of care, are apt to produce hilarity, and that some of the most degraded and least intellectual people of the earth, are among the gayest; but I believe that it is a rule in nature, that where there is much animal suffering there is an animal exhibition of its existence.

There is still a higher, and a very numerous class of American slaves, who are far better instructed, better clothed, and better fed, and who are altogether a superior race to the lowest class of the European peasants. I mean the domestic servants, and those who labour as mechanics and artisans.

While on this branch of the subject, I shall take occasion to say, that yearly meliorations in the condition of the slaves (and of the blacks generally,) are taking place in some one part of the country or other. Several unjust and exceedingly oppressive laws, that were the fruits of colonial policy, have been repealed, or greatly qualified; and public opinion is making a steady advance to the general improvement, and, I think, to the final liberation of the race. Although these changes are not as rapid as they might be, even with a due regard to policy, and far less rapid than most good men could wish, it is a course that is more likely to be attended with less positive injury to the race of beings that true philanthropy would so gladly serve, than one as headlong and as ill-advised as mere declaimers and pretenders would dictate.

I think no candid man will deny the difficulty of making two or three millions of people, under any circumstances, strip themselves, generally of half their possessions, and, in many instances, of all. There are few nations in Europe, at this hour, in which the poorer classes would not be relieved from serious pressure, would they, who have the means, tax themselves to discharge the debts which are the causes of so much of the heavy impositions of their respective governments. Now, this would be a measure that would do good to millions, great and almost inconceivable good, and harm to none but to them that paid; whereas, a sudden, or any very violent emancipation of the slaves of America, would ruin those who did it, and scarcely do less than ruin half, or even more, of those in whose behalf the charitable act would be performed. Let me be understood. I do not mean to say that much more than is done might not be done, prudently, and with safety; nor do I mean to say that most of those who find themselves in possession of a species of property, that they have been educated to think a natural and just acquisition, think much of the matter at all; but what I would wish to express is, that they who do think calmly and sincerely on the subject, see and feel all these difficulties, and that they weaken efforts that would otherwise produce an effect more visible than the sentiment which I think is silently working its way throughout the whole of this nation.

In considering the question of American slavery, in reference to the past, it is plain that Europe has been an equal participator in all that there is of shame, or sin, in the transaction. There can be no charge more vapid and unjust, than for an European to reproach the American with the existence of slavery in his country. That the American is in the enjoyment of greater power to do natural justice than the European, is just as true, as that, in most things, he does it. That slavery is an evil of which the great majority of the Americans themselves, who have no present agency in its existence, would gladly be rid of, is manifest, since they have abolished it in so many States already; but that it is an evil not to be shaken off by sounding declarations, and fine sentiments, any man, who looks calmly into the subject, must see. But so far as a comparison between Europe and America is concerned, let us, for an instant, examine the exceedingly negative merit of the former. Is it not a fact that the policy of all America was for more than a century controlled by Europe, and was not this scourge introduced under that policy? Has that policy, in Europe, been yet abandoned? Let us take the two most prominent nations boldly to task at once; does England or France, for instance, at this moment, own a foot of land on earth, where black slaves can be profitable, and where they do not use them?* It is absurd for France, or for England, to say, we have no slaves in our respective kingdoms, properly so called, when every body knows that the one is at this moment filled with white beggars, and the other with paupers who are supported by the public purse, and both for the simple reason that they are overflowing with population. It is true, that two centuries ago, when they had more room, they did not import negroes from Guinea; but it is, also, just as true, that they sent their ships to convey them to colonies which are situated in climates where they might repay them for their trouble. It is as puerile as it is unjust, therefore, for these two countries, (most others might be included,) to pretend to any exclusive exemption from the sin or the shame of slavery.

The merit of Christendom on the subject of the wrongs of Africa, is, at the best, but equivocal. Yet, such as it is, the meed is better due to the United States than to any other nation. They were

* It is well known that a negro would be next to nothing in the Canadas, &c.

the first to abolish the trade in human flesh, though the nation, of all others, that might most have reaped that short-sighted, but alluring profit, which tempted men to the original wrong. Had not the Congress of the United States abolished this trade, there is no doubt millions of acres might have sooner been brought into lucrative cultivation, and the present generation at least would have been millions the richer. The whole body of the whites might have become a set of taskmasters to gather wealth from the labour of the blacks. No doubt true policy dictated the course they have taken, and they have but a very negative merit in pursuing it: still it should always be remembered, that what has been done, was done by those who might have profited in security by a different course, and by those, too, who had been educated in the shackles of a deeply-rooted prejudice on the subject.

In reproaching the Americans with incongruity between their practices and their professions, two or three points are very necessary to be remembered. In the first place, it is not true, as respects near 7,000,000 of the ten that comprise their population; for *they* have given freedom and (essentially) equal rights to those blacks who remain among them. The very condensation of the interests of slavery adds, however, to the difficulty of the subject, since it makes the loss fall on a comparatively reduced number. The northern men had to do one of two things; to separate their fortunes from a portion of their countrymen, to whom they were bound by the ties of fellowship, blood, common interests, and common descent, or submit to be parties to an union in which some of the other parties were slave-holders. They were, in fact, slave-holders themselves, at the time of the compact, so that it would have been absurd to be very fastidious in the matter; and there would have been but little wisdom in rejecting so much positive good, in order to assert an abstract principle, that could be attended with no single practical benefit. The southern States would have held their slaves, had the northern refused to have joined them to make one nation; and, so far as humanity is concerned, the negroes would not have been so well off, since they now feel the influence of northern policy, while war and bloodshed, and all the evils of a dangerous rivalry that would have arisen between men whom nature had made friends and brothers, are avoided. In short, this is a reproach against the northern man, that is more likely to be made by those who view the Union, and the continued harmony which pervades these vast regions, with unquiet jealousy, than by any reasoning and practical philanthropist.

As to the southern man himself, he is placed, like so many nations of other quarters of the globe, in an unfortunate predicament, that time and society, and all the multiplied interests of life, render so difficult to change. The profession of the southern man is unquestionably that of equal rights; and it is undeniable that he holds the black in slavery: but this does not involve quite so great an absurdity as one would at first imagine. The slave-holders of the present day (viewed as a body) are just as innocent of the creation of slavery, as their fellowcitizens of New-York or Connecticut; and the citizens of New-York or Connecticut are just as innocent of the creation of slavery as the citizens of London or Paris. But the citizens of the two former States have a merit in the matter, that the citizens of neither of the towns named can claim, since they have stripped themselves of property to give freedom to their blacks, while those who were parties to the original wrong have contributed nothing to the measure they so much urge. But is it not possible to assert a principle under acknowledged limitations? The black man in the southern States of this Union is not considered a citizen at all. It would not be safe to consider him a citizen, in a country of equal political rights, since he is far too ignorant, and must, for a generation at least, remain too ignorant, to exercise, with sufficient discretion, the privileges of a citizen in a free government. It would, if any thing, be more prudent for the Virginian and Carolinian to admit boys of twelve years of age to vote and to legislate, than to admit their blacks, in their present moral condition, without having any reference to the danger of a personal dissension. Equal rights do not, in any part of America, imply a broad, general, and unequivocal equality. It is the glory of the institutions of this country, that they have never run into practical excesses, in order to satisfy craving theories. By equal rights, the citizen of Connecticut, (and, I believe, no man doubts his rational and unlimited freedom,) understands that all who have reached a certain standard of qualification, shall be equal in power and that all others shall be equal in protection. He does not give political power to the pauper, nor to females, nor to minors, nor to idiots, nor yet even to his priests. All he aims at is justice; and in order to do justice, he gives political rights to all those who, he thinks, can use them without abuse. He would be culpable only, if any class existed in his community, who might, with a little care, freely enjoy these rights, did he neglect to resort to that care. He therefore excludes only those who, on great, general, and lasting principles, are disqualified from exercising political power. The situation of the Carolinian is different, but his principle is quite the same: he excludes more; for, unhappily, when he arrived at the knowledge and the practice of a liberal policy himself, he found a numerous class of human beings existing within his borders, who were not competent to its exercise. He had but a choice between a seeming inconsistency, or the entire abandonment of what he thought a great good. He chose to make all equal, who could bear equality; and in that, he has done exactly what his northern countryman has done, and no more. Should he unnecessarily neglect, however, to qualify these exceptions to enjoy a better state of being, he then becomes inconsistent.

I think these considerations must lead us to the conclusion, that most of the merits of this question lie in the fact of how much has been done and is now doing, towards effecting a change in what is admitted to be a prodigious evil. I feel confident that no discreet father, or husband, or brother, could ask a Carolinian, who was existing in a state of highly polished society, and who enjoyed all the advantages of great moral improvement, to admit, at once, a body of men who had been nurtured in the habits of slavery, with all their ignorance and animal qualities, and who are numerically superior, to a participation of equal political rights. Such a measure would induce an absolute abandonment of their country and property on the part of the whites, or it would involve a degradation, and abuses that are horrible to reflect on. Individuals may and have parted with their means of personal indulgence to give liberty to their slaves; but it is too much to expect it from communities: nor would discreet individuals do it, if it were to be a general act, since a disorganization of society would be an inevitable consequence.

The true question, and that in which the friends of humanity should feel the deepest interest, is that connected with the steps that are taken to lead to the general emancipation, which must sooner or later arrive.

At the period of the declaration of the independence of the United States, slavery existed in all the British colonies. The blacks were not numerous in the northern provinces, for, there, the white was the better labourer. Still there were slaves in every one of the thirteen original States of this Union. The proportion of slaves in some of the middle States was nearly equal to what it now is in some of the southern. Massachusetts (which in 1790 had 5,463 blacks,) put such a construction on its own bill of rights as abolished slavery. This was the first measure of the sort that was ever taken on the American continent, I presume. The example has been successively followed, at different periods, by all the northern and middle States, until slavery is either abolished in fact, or by laws that have a prospective operation, in nine out of the fourteen States that adopted the present constitution in 1789. You may form some idea of the difficulty of getting rid of such an evil as slavery, by observing the caution with which these comparatively little encumbered States have approached the subject. Perhaps twenty years are necessary to effect the object humanely, even after the policy of a community is perfectly decided.

Numberless influences have, at the same time, been at work, however, to extend the limits in which slavery might exist. Alabama and Mississippi formed parts of Georgia; Kentucky and Tennessee were within the ancient limits of Virginia; and Louisiana, and Missouri, and the Floridas, were acquired by purchase. The people of Virginia and Georgia, in ceding their territory, were not disposed to cede the right of emigration, with the privilege of carrying their wealth with them; and slavery, in consequence, became extended over the four States named. Slaves were found in the two others, and in the Floridas. In this manner the eleven present slave-holding States came into existence. In the meanwhile, the States of Ohio, Indiana, and Illinois, were organized off what was once called the north-western territory. These, added to the nine States that had abolished the policy of slavery, and by the subsequent acquisition of Maine, brought their whole number up to thirteen.

I think that the influence of free opinions, if I may so express it, is steadily on the increase. It is not the smallest evil of slavery, that it begets in the master an indifference to its existence, and that it gives birth and durability to cruel and lasting prejudices. That these prejudices must be rooted out of the majority of the citizens of the southern States themselves, ere slavery shall cease to exist, is indisputable, since no power but their own can extinguish it. But my friend assures me, that within his recollection, an immense change has taken place in this particular. Twenty years ago, even in New-York, a general and deep prejudice existed against this unfortunate class of human beings. It is rapidly disappearing. It is true, that the sort of commingling of the races, which a certain class of philanthropists are much fonder of proclaiming than they would be fond of practising, does not occur, nor is it likely very soon to occur in this country. Still there is every disposition to do the blacks justice, though there is none whatever to mingle the blood. I have heard of instances in which human beings of peculiar colour and form were esteemed in Europe as curiosities; but I fancy, if they abounded in any country, there would be found the same natural desire, in that portion of its inhabitants who believed themselves to possess the physical advantage, to retain it, as is now found here. It is odd enough, that Europe, which, for so many centuries, has been making patents of nobility obstacles to matrimony, should decry so loudly against a people who hesitate a little at intermingling colours.

But there will still be a greater objection against this mingling of the races, for at least a long time to come. With few exceptions, the blacks of America belong to an ill-educated and inferior class. When free, they are left, like other men, to look after their own interests; and most of those, who have character and talent enough to rise above the condition of menials, push their fortunes in countries where they are not daily and hourly offended by the degradation of their caste. I think this circumstance must long keep them in a station which will prevent intermarriages. You will admit, too, that matrimony is very much an affair of taste; and, although there well may be, and there are, portions of the world where white colour is not greatly admired, such is not the case here. The deep reluctance to see one's posterity exhibiting a hue different from one's own, is to be overcome, ere any extensive intercourse can occur between the blacks and the whites.

The probable future fate of the blacks of America, is a subject of deep and painful interest. I confess, however, I am not one of those who see any great danger to the whites in their increasing numbers. While they remain ignorant, their efforts must always be feeble and divided, and, as they become enlightened, they must see the utter impossibility of any continued success in a rising against a force numerically and morally so superior. Although the distances in America seem very great on the map, the inhabitants have contrived the means of bringing themselves wonderfully near to each other. The whites in the whole country increase faster than the blacks; and I think it will be found, that as emancipations multiply, the disproportion in numbers will be still greater, and always in favour of the former. It would not only be the duty of the northern men, but it would be a duty readily performed, to fly, in case of need, to the assistance of their southern neighbours. It is not easy to suppose circumstances in which the white population of the southern States, already (as a whole) two to one against the slaves, armed, intelligent, organized, and possessing the immense moral superiority of their domestic relations, should not be sufficient of themselves to protect their persons and property against a rising. The only circumstances in which the danger could be very imminent or extensive, would be in the event of a foreign war; and then their common country would be a party, and the aid of States that will shortly number of themselves twenty or thirty millions, could be commanded in their defence.

But the danger of slavery, so far as it is connected with numbers, has its own cure. No man will keep a negro after he ceases to be profitable, any more than he will keep an extra supply of other animal force. If Carolina can bear 500,000 slaves, Carolina will probably accumulate that number; but after she has reached the point where policy says she must stop, instead of resorting to laws to retain her negroes, she will have recourse to laws to get rid of them. This, to an European, and particularly to an Englishman, who knows that excessive population is the greatest burthen of his own country, may seem difficult; but in order to form a correct opinion of a question purely American, it is necessary to consider the actual state of things on this side of the Atlantic.

The already vast, and constantly increasing coasting trade of the United States, offers an easy, natural, and perfectly practicable drain, to the black population of the south. The blacks furnish, already, thousands of sailors, and quite useful sailors too, and they constitute a very important material of the supply of seamen, in considering the future commercial and nautical power of this confederation. The demand for domestics at the north, too, will, for many years, continue beyond the probability of a white supply. You will remember that experience has' shown that the free blacks have very little natural increase, and both these growing demands must therefore meet with most of their supplies from the slave-holding States. Then, again, the proximity of the West Indies, of Mexico, and of the South American States, in which a commingled population already exists, offers facilities for emigration, that Europe does not present. The slave population of the United States may reach 4 or 5,000,000, but (after a very short time) at a diminishing rate of increase,* and then I think it will be found that new means will be taken to get rid of them.

In forming these conjectures, I have not regarded the narrowing of the limits of slavery by the constant advancement of opinion. It is true, that the surface on which slavery, in fact, exists, has, on the whole, been rather enlarged than otherwise, since the existence of the confederation; but we should not lose sight of the circumstances under which this extension of the slave region has been effected.

It has spread with the diffusion of population, over districts that were originally the property of the slave-holders; and in no respect, except in mere territorial division, has there been any virtual enlargement of its political limits, unless one can thus call the enlargement of the borders of society. It is true, that when Missouri was admitted to the Union, an effort was made by the friends of the blacks (I use the term technically) to abolish slavery in that State. Had they succeeded, it would have been an inroad on the ancient limits; but their defeat ought not to be deemed an extension of the surface occupied by slaves, since slaves were there before. It was a sort of attempt to turn the flank of slavery, or to get into its rear; whereas I think it manifest that the great victory over habits and prejudices, which true policy will be sure to gain in time, is to be gained by pressing steadily on, in an open, manly, but cautious and conciliating manner, in its front. Ardent and steady a friend of universal liberty as you know me to be, I am by no means sure, that, had I been a member of that Congress, I would have given so violent an alarm to the slave-holders of the south, as to have contributed to attempt to carry that law.

* At present the slave-holder has a motive for increasing his slaves, since he can sell them in the new States; but this demand will, of course, cease as the new States get full. Louisiana has recently passed a law, prohibiting the importation of slaves; a fact which the writer thinks proves the truth of his theory. The reader will always recollect that slaves cannot be *imported* into the United States, but that they can be *transported* from one State to another, unless prohibitions are made by the States themselves. This was part of the original compact, without which the southern States would not have consented to the present constitution.

It is only necessary to witness the immense superiority that free labour possesses over slave labour, and to examine the different conditions of society in a State without slaves, and in one with, to see that a close contact must be destructive to the principles of slavery. The friends of emancipation have now a noble front, extending from the Atlantic to the Mississippi. I even think that accident has contributed to throw those communities most in advance, which are the least likely to retard the progress of emancipation. The honest and affluent, but quiet population of Pennsylvania, for instance, is much less suited to give the alarm to their neighbours of Maryland, than would be done by the more restless, ever-busy people of New-England; while their example is left to produce its undiminished effect. If I have been correctly informed, public opinion and sounder views of policy are making great progress in the latter State. The inhabitants begin to see that they would be richer and more powerful without their slaves than with them. This is the true entering wedge of argument; and juster views of moral truth will be sure to follow convictions of interest, as they have followed, and are still following, emancipation further north.

The first and surest sign of a disposition to give freedom to the slaves, is the accumulation of the free blacks, since they are not only a positive proof that emancipation exists, but they argue an indifference to slavery in the whole community. In Maryland, there were 145,429 blacks in 1810, and 147,128 in 1820. During the same time, the whites increased from 235,117 to 260,222. Emigration retarded the increase of the two races, no doubt; and yet, you see, contrary to the law of increase in most of the slave-holding States, the whites grew faster than the blacks. Now, of this number of 147,128 blacks, 39,730 were free. This is a very large proportion, and I hail it as a most auspicious omen. In point of fact, there were 4,109 fewer slaves in Maryland in 1820, than in 1810; while the whites had increased 25,105. Indeed, I heard very many enlightened and respectable men in Maryland regret that slavery existed among them at all; and the opinion is getting to be quite common, that free labour is the most profitable. Even in Virginia, the whites have increased 51,474, during the same ten years, while the blacks have increased only 38,954. It is true, the emigration renders these results a little doubtful; but the fact that there were, in 1820, 36,889 free blacks in Virginia, proves something. It is also of importance, that there exist, in so many of the slave-holding States, large bodies of their respective communities, who have very little interest in the perpetuation of the evil, except as their own personal welfare is connected with that of society. Although the latter influence is one of moment, it is also one that may influence a man both ways, since he may be as likely to believe that the interests of society call for some relief against the evil, as to think he ought to support it.

I have endeavoured to lay this important subject before you in a practical form. It has been done rapidly, and, I am quite certain, very imperfectly. It is proper to understand, there is so much of intimate detail necessary to view the state of American slavery with discretion, that it is highly probable I may have fallen into error; but I still think you will find the views I have taken of it not without some plausibility. I shall sum them up, together with the leading facts, in as few words as possible.

I think liberal sentiments towards the blacks are rapidly gaining ground in most of the southern States.* Positive, political freedom is granted, or is in the course of being granted to them, in thirteen of the twenty-four communities of the confederation. Emancipation, geographically speaking, has now reached a formidable point of resistance (on account of the numbers of the slaves,) but it is steadily advancing through the powerful agency of public opinion. When it has passed this point, its subsequent march will, I think, be easier and more rapid. Tennessee and Kentucky, the States that flank Virginia, have by no means as deep an interest in the maintenance of slavery, as the States further south; and I think it is not chimerical to hope that, by the aid of prospective laws, many are now living who may see slavery limited to the shores of the Atlantic, and to the Gulf of Mexico, with perhaps a belt for a little distance on each side of the Mississippi. In the mean time, the advance of opinion is steady and great. Unless the Christian world recedes, its final success is inevitable. I shall not incur the charge of empiricism by pretending to predict the precise period.

I do not think that slavery, under any circumstances, can entail very serious danger to the dominion of the whites in this country, for at least a century or two. Districts might be ravaged, beyond a doubt;

---

* The writer does not mean that every man becomes in some degree sensible of the evil, but that a vast number do, and of men, too, who are likely to have an effect on legislation.

but the prodigious superiority of the whites, in every thing that constitutes force, is the pledge of their power.

I am of opinion that the number of the slaves will be limited, as a
matter of course, by necessity. There is a point beyond which they
would be a burden. Nor is that point so distant as we commonly
imagine. Perhaps it has been already obtained in some of the older
States.

I think that the free black population (except in the way of
emancipation) does not increase, or, at least, not materially; and that
the proportion between the whites and the blacks is steadily growing
in favour of the former; that, in future, it will even grow faster; that
emigration, the navy, commerce, and unsettled habits, will tend to
repress the increase of the blacks, and to consume their numbers; and
that the time of the intermingling of the races to any great extent is
still remote.

Though there is much in these views to excite the regrets of a
man of pure philanthropy, it appears to me that the cause of emancipation is far from being as bad as it is generally supposed to be in
Europe. Impatience is a characteristic of zeal. But impatience, though
creditable to the feelings of the European, sometimes leads him, on this
subject, into assertions that might provoke comparisons which would
not be so honourable to his own society, perhaps, as he is apt to fancy.
Impatience, however, on the part of the American, may even do worse;
it may retard the very consummation he wishes. Mildness, candour, and
conciliation, are his weapons; and I think they will be irresistible.
Although an ardent wisher of the happy moment of general emancipation, I always turn with disgust from these cold and heartless para-
graphs which occasionally appear in the northern journals of this
country, and which, under a superficial pretension to humanity, trifle
with the safety and happiness of two of their fellow-citizens, in order
to give an affected aid to the undoubtedly righteous cause of one black
man. If this species of irritating language did good, if it did no harm by
hardening men in their opinions, it would be disagreeable; but under
the actual state of things, it is far worse than useless. The general tone
of the press, however, is sufficiently amicable; and all those who understand the difference between argumentation and judgment, have reason
to hope it may long continue so.

But physical suffering, especially in a country like this, is not the prominent grievance of slavery. It is the deep moral degradation, which no man has a right to entail on another, that forms the essence of its shame. God has planted in all our spirits secret but lasting aspirations after a state of existence higher than that which we enjoy, and no one has a right to say that such are the limits beyond which your reason, and, consequently, your mental being, shall not pass. That men, equally degraded, exist under systems that do not openly avow the principle of domestic slavery, is no excuse for the perpetuation of such a scourge, though circumstances and necessity may urge a great deal in extenuation of its present existence.

FROM *The American Democrat* [1838]

ADVANTAGES OF A DEMOCRACY.

The principal advantage of a democracy, is a general elevation in the character of the people. If few are raised to a very great height, few are depressed very low. As a consequence, the average of society is much more respectable than under any other form of government. The vulgar charge that the tendency of democracies is to levelling, meaning to drag all down to the level of the lowest, is singularly untrue, its real tendency being to elevate the depressed to a condition not unworthy of their manhood. In the absence of privileged orders, entails and distinctions, devised permanently to separate men into social castes, it is true none are great but those who become so by their acts, but, confining the remark to the upper classes of society, it would be much more true to say that democracy refuses to lend itself to unnatural and arbitrary distinctions, than to accuse it of a tendency to level those who have a just claim to be elevated. A denial of a favor, is not an invasion of a right.

Democracies are exempt from the military charges, both pecuniary and personal, that become necessary in governments in which the majority are subjects, since no force is required to repress those who, under other systems, are dangerous to the state, by their greater physical power.

As the success of democracies is mainly dependant on the intelligence of the people, the means of preserving the government are precisely those which most conduce to the happiness and social progress of man. Hence we find the state endeavoring to raise its citizens in the scale of being, the certain means of laying the broadest foundation of national prosperity. If the arts are advanced in aristocracies, through the taste of patrons, in democracies, though of slower growth, they will prosper as a consequence of general information; or as a superstructure reared on a wider and more solid foundation.

Democracies being, as nearly as possible, founded in natural justice, little violence is done to the sense of right by the institutions, and men have less occasion than usual, to resort to fallacies and false principles in cultivating the faculties. As a consequence, common sense is more encouraged, and the community is apt to entertain juster notions of all moral truths, than under systems that are necessarily sophisticated. Society is thus a gainer in the greatest element of happiness, or in the right perception of the different relations between men and things.

Democracies being established for the common interests, and the publick agents being held in constant check by the people, their general tendency is to serve the whole community, and not small portions of it, as is the case in narrow governments. It is as rational to suppose that a hungry man will first help his neighbor to bread, when master of his own acts, as to suppose that any but those who feel themselves to be truly publick servants, will first bethink themselves of the publick, when in situations of publick trust. In a government of one, that one and his parasites will be the first and best served; in a government of a few, the few; and in a government of many, the many. Thus the general tendency of democratical institutions is to equalize advantages, and to spread its blessings over the entire surface of society.

Democracies, other things being equal, are the cheapest form of government, since little money is lavished in representation, and they who have to pay the taxes, have also, directly or indirectly, a voice in imposing them.

Democracies are less liable to popular tumults than any other polities, because the people, having legal means in their power to redress wrongs, have little inducement to employ any other. The man who can right himself by a vote, will seldom resort to a musket. Grievances, moreover, are less frequent, the most corrupt representatives of a democratick constituency generally standing in awe of its censure.

As men in bodies usually defer to the right, unless acting under erroneous impressions, or excited by sudden resentments, democracies pay more respect to abstract justice, in the management of their foreign concerns, than either aristocracies or monarchies, an appeal always lying against abuses, or violations of principle, to a popular sentiment, that, in the end, seldom fails to decide in favor of truth.

In democracies, with a due allowance for the workings of personal selfishness, it is usually a motive with those in places of trust, to consult the interests of the mass, there being little doubt, that in this system, the entire community has more regard paid to its wants and wishes, than in either of the two others.

ON THE DISADVANTAGES OF DEMOCRACY.

Democracies are liable to popular impulses, which, necessarily arising from imperfect information, often work injustice from good motives. Tumults of the people are less apt to occur in democracies than under any other form of government, for, possessing the legal means of redressing themselves, there is less necessity to resort to force, but, public opinion, constituting, virtually, the power of the state, measures are more apt to be influenced by sudden mutations of sentiment, than under systems where the rulers have better opportunities and more leisure for examination. There is more feeling and less design in the movements of masses than in those of small bodies, except as design emanates from demagogues and political managers.

The efforts of the masses that are struggling to obtain their rights, in monarchies and aristocracies, however, are not to be imputed to democracy; in such cases, the people use their natural weapon, force, merely because they are denied any participation in the legal authority.

When democracies are small, these impulses frequently do great injury to the public service, but in large states they are seldom of

sufficient extent to produce results before there is time to feel the
influence of reason. It is, therefore, one of the errors of politicians to
imagine democracies more practicable in small than in large communities, an error that has probably arisen from the fact that, the ignorance of masses having hitherto put men at the mercy of the combinations of the affluent and intelligent, democracies have been permitted
to exist only in countries insignificant by their wealth and numbers.

Large democracies, on the other hand, while less exposed to the
principal evil of this form of government, than smaller, are unable to
scrutinize and understand character with the severity and intelligence
that are of so much importance in all representative governments, and
consequently the people are peculiarly exposed to become the dupes of
demagogues and political schemers, most of the crimes of democracies
arising from the faults and designs of men of this character, rather than
from the propensities of the people, who, having little temptation to do
wrong, are seldom guilty of crimes except through ignorance.

Democracies are necessarily controlled by publick opinion, and
failing of the means of obtaining power more honestly, the fraudulent
and ambitious find a motive to mislead, and even to corrupt the common sentiment, to attain their ends. This is the greatest and most
pervading danger of all large democracies, since it is sapping the foundations of society, by undermining its virtue. We see the effects of this
baneful influence, in the openness and audacity with which men avow
improper motives and improper acts, trusting to find support in a
popular feeling, for while vicious influences are perhaps more admitted
in other countries, than in America, in none are they so openly
avowed.

It may also be urged against democracies, that, nothing being more
corrupting than the management of human affairs, which are constantly demanding sacrifices of permanent principles to interests that
are as constantly fluctuating, their people are exposed to assaults on
their morals from this quarter, that the masses of other nations escape.
It is probable, however, that this evil, while it ought properly to be
enumerated as one of the disadvantages of the system, is more than
counterbalanced by the main results, even on the score of morals.

The constant appeals to public opinion in a democracy, though
excellent as a corrective of public vices, induce private hypocrisy,
causing men to conceal their own convictions when opposed to those

of the mass, the latter being seldom wholly right, or wholly wrong. A want of national manliness is a vice to be guarded against, for the man who would dare to resist a monarch, shrinks from opposing an entire community. That the latter is quite often wrong, however, is abundantly proved by the fact, that its own judgments fluctuate, as it reasons and thinks differently this year, or this month even, from what it reasoned and thought the last.

The tendency of democracies is, in all things, to mediocrity, since the tastes, knowledge and principles of the majority form the tribunal of appeal. This circumstance, while it certainly serves to elevate the average qualities of a nation, renders the introduction of a high standard difficult. Thus do we find in literature, the arts, architecture and in all acquired knowledge, a tendency in America to gravitate towards the common center in this, as in other things; lending a value and estimation to mediocrity that are not elsewhere given. It is fair to expect, however, that a foundation so broad, may in time sustain a superstructure of commensurate proportions, and that the influence of masses will in this, as in the other interests, have a generally beneficial effect. Still it should not be forgotten that, with the exception of those works, of which, as they appeal to human sympathies or the practices of men, an intelligent public is the best judge, the mass of no community is qualified to decide the most correctly on any thing, which, in its nature, is above its reach.

It is a besetting vice of democracies to substitute publick opinion for law. This is the usual form in which masses of men exhibit their tyranny. When the majority of the entire community commits this fault it is a sore grievance, but when local bodies, influenced by local interests, pretend to style themselves the publick, they are assuming powers that properly belong to the whole body of the people, and to them only under constitutional limitations. No tyranny of one, nor any tyranny of the few, is worse than this. All attempts in the publick, therefore, to do that which the publick has no right to do, should be frowned upon as the precise form in which tyranny is the most apt to be displayed in a democracy.

Democracies, depending so much on popular opinion are more liable to be influenced to their injury, through the management of foreign and hostile nations, than other governments. It is generally known that, in Europe, secret means are resorted to, to influence sentiment in this way, and we have witnessed in this country open appeals to the people, against the acts of their servants, in matters of foreign relations, made by foreign, not to say, hostile agents. Perhaps no stronger case can be cited of this weakness on the part of democracies, than is shown in this fact, for here we find men sufficiently audacious to build the hope of so far abusing opinion, as to persuade a people to act directly against their own dignity and interests.

The misleading of publick opinion in one way or another, is the parent of the principal disadvantages of a democracy, for in most instances it is first corrupting a community in order that it may be otherwise injured. Were it not for the counteracting influence of reason, which, in the end, seldom, perhaps never fails to assert its power, this defect would of itself, be sufficient to induce all discreet men to decide against this form of government. The greater the danger, the greater the necessity that all well-intentioned and right-minded citizens should be on their guard against its influence.

It would be hazardous, however, to impute all the peculiar faults of American character, to the institutions, the country existing under so many unusual influences. If the latter were overlooked, one might be induced to think frankness and sincerity of character were less encouraged by popular institutions than was formerly supposed, close observers affirming that these qualities are less frequent here, than in most other countries. When the general ease of society is remembered, there is unquestionably more deception of opinion practised than one would naturally expect, but this failing is properly to be imputed to causes that have no necessary connection with democratical institutions, though men defer to publick opinion, right or wrong, quite as submissively as they defer to princes. Although truths are not smothered altogether in democracies, they are often temporarily abandoned under this malign influence, unless there is a powerful motive to sustain them at the moment. While we see in our own democracy this manifest disposition to defer to the wrong, in matters that are not properly subject to the common sentiment, in deference to the popular will of the hour, there is a singular boldness in the use of personalities, as if men avenged themselves for the restraints of the one case by a licentiousness that is without hazard.

The base feelings of detraction and envy have more room for exhibition, and perhaps a stronger incentive in a democracy, than in other forms of government, in which the people get accustomed to personal deference by the artificial distinctions of the institutions. This is the reason that men become impatient of all superiority in a democracy, and manifest a wish to prefer those who affect a deference to the publick, rather than those who are worthy.

ON DEMAGOGUES.

A demagogue, in the strict signification of the word, is "a leader of the rabble." It is a Greek compound, that conveys this meaning. In these later times, however, the signification has been extended to suit the circumstances of the age. Thus, before the art of printing became known, or cheap publications were placed within the reach of the majority, the mass of all nations might properly enough be termed a rabble, when assembled in bodies. In nations in which attention is paid to education, this reproach is gradually becoming unjust, though a body of Americans, even, collected under what is popularly termed an "excitement," losing sight of that reason and respect for their own deliberately framed ordinances, which alone distinguish them from the masses of other people, is neither more nor less than a rabble. Men properly derive their designations from their acts, and not from their professions.

The peculiar office of a demagogue is to ⸱. lvance his own interests, by affecting a deep devotion to the interests of the people. Sometimes the object is to indulge malignancy, unprincipled and selfish men submitting but to two governing motives, that of doing good to themselves, and that of doing harm to others. The true theatre of a demagogue is a democracy, for the body of the community possessing the power, the master he pretends to serve is best able to reward his efforts. As it is all important to distinguish between those who labor in behalf of the people on the general account, and those who labor in behalf of the people on their own account, some of the rules by which each may be known shall be pointed out.

The motive of the demagogue may usually be detected in his conduct. The man who is constantly telling the people that they are unerring in judgment, and that they have all power, is a demagogue. Bodies of men being composed of individuals, can no more be raised above the commission of error, than individuals themselves, and, in many situations, they are more likely to err, from self-excitement and the division of responsibility. The power of the people is limited by the fundamental laws, or the constitution, the rights and opinions of the minority, in all but those cases in which a decision becomes indispensable, being just as sacred as the rights and opinions of the majority; else would a democracy be, indeed, what its enemies term it, the worst species of tyranny. In this instance, the people are flattered, in order to be led: as in kingdoms, the prince is blinded to his own defects, in order to extract favor from him.

The demagogue always puts the people before the constitution and the laws, in face of the obvious truth that the people have placed the constitution and the laws before themselves.

The local demagogue does not distinguish between the whole people and a part of the people, and is apt to betray his want of principles by contending for fancied, or assumed rights, in favor of a county, or a town, though the act is obviously opposed to the will of the nation. This is a test that the most often betrays the demagogue, for while loudest in proclaiming his devotion to the majority, he is, in truth, opposing the will of the entire people, in order to effect his purposes with a part.

The demagogue is usually sly, a detractor of others, a professor of humility and disinterestedness, a great stickler for equality as respects all above him, a man who acts in corners, and avoids open and manly expositions of his course, calls blackguards gentlemen, and gentlemen folks, appeals to passions and prejudices rather than to reason; and is in all respects, a man of intrigue and deception, of sly cunning and management, instead of manifesting the frank, fearless qualities of the democracy he so prodigally professes.

The man who maintains the rights of the people on pure grounds, may be distinguished from the demagogue by the reverse of all these qualities. He does not flatter the people, even while he defends them, for he knows that flattery is a corrupting and dangerous poison. Having nothing to conceal, he is frank and fearless, as are all men with the consciousness of right motives. He oftener chides than commends, for power needs reproof and can dispense with praise.

He who would be a courtier under a king, is almost certain to be a demagogue in a democracy. The elements are the same, though, brought into action under different circumstances, ordinary observers are apt to fancy them the extremes of opposite moral castes. Travellers have often remarked, that, Americans, who have made themselves conspicuous abroad for their adulation of rank and power, have become zealous advocates of popular supremacy, on returning home. Several men of this stamp are, at this moment, in conspicuous political stations in the country, having succeeded by the commonest arts of courtiers.

There is a large class of political men in this country, who, while they scarcely merit the opprobrium of being termed demagogues, are not properly exempt from the imputation of falling into some of their most dangerous vices. These are they, whose habits, and tastes, and better opinions, indeed, are all at variance with vulgar errors and vulgar practices, but, who imagine it a necessary evil in a democracy to defer to prejudices, and ignorance, and even to popular jealousies and popular injustice, that a safe direction may be given to the publick mind. Such men deceive themselves, in the first place, as to their own motives, which are rather their private advancement than the publick good, and, admitting the motives to be pure, they err greatly both in their mode of construing the system under which they live, and in the general principles of correcting evil and of producing good. As the greatest enemy of truth is falsehood, so is the most potent master of falsehood, truth. These qualities are correlatives; that which is not true, being false; and that which is not false, being true. It follows, as a pervading rule of morals, that the advancement of one is the surest means of defeating the other. All good men desire the truth, and, on all publick occasions on which it is necessary to act at all, the truth would be the most certain, efficient, and durable agency in defeating falsehoods, whether of prejudices, reports, or principles. The perception of truth is an attribute of reason, and the ground-work of all institutions that claim to be founded in justice, is this high quality. Temporary convenience, and selfish considerations, beyond a doubt, are both favored by sometimes closing the eyes to the severity of truth, but in nothing is the sublime admonition of God in his commandments, where he tells us that he "will visit the sins of the fathers unto the third and fourth generations of their children," more impressively verified, than in the inevitable punishments that await every sacrifice of truth.

Most of the political men of the day belong to this class of doubtful moralists, who, mistaking a healthful rule, which admonishes us that even truth ought not to be too offensively urged, in their desire to be moderate, lend themselves to the side of error. The ingenuity of sophisms, and the audacity of falsehoods receive great support from this mistaken alliance, since a firm union of all the intelligent of a country, in the cause of plain and obvious truths, would exterminate their correlative errors, the publick opinion which is now enlisted in the support of the latter, following to the right side, as a matter of course, in the train of combined knowledge. This is the mode in which opinions rooted in the wrong have been gradually eradicated, by the process of time, but which would yield faster, were it not for the latitude and delusion that selfishness imposes on men of this class, who flatter themselves with soothing a sore that they are actually irritating. The consequence of this mistaken forbearance, is to substitute a new set of errors, for those which it has already taken ages to get rid of.

On the subject of government and society, it is a misfortune that this country is filled with those who take the opposite extremes, the one side clinging to prejudices that were founded in the abuses of the feudal times, and the other to the exaggerations of impracticable theories. That the struggle is not fiercer, is probably owing to the overwhelming numbers of the latter class, but, as things are, truth is a sufferer.

The American *doctrinaire* is the converse of the American demagogue, and, in his way, is scarcely less injurious to the publick. He is as much a visionary on one side, as the extreme theoretical democrat is a visionary on the other. The first deals in poetry, the last in cant. The first affirms a disinterestedness and purity in education and manners, when exposed to the corruption of power, that all experience refutes; and the last an infallibility in majorities that God himself has denied. These opposing classes produce the effect of all counter-acting forces, resistance, and they provoke each other's excesses.

In the *doctrinaire,* or theorist of the old school, we see men clinging to opinions that are purely the issue of arbitrary facts, ages after the facts themselves have ceased to exist, confounding cause with effect; and, in the demagogue, or his tool, the impracticable democrat, one who permits envy, jealousy, opposition, selfishness, and the unconsciousness of his own inferiority and demerits, so far to blind his faculties, as to obscure the sense of justice, to exclude the sight of positive things, and to cause him to deny the legitimate consequences of the very laws of which he professes to be proud. This is the dupe who affirms that, "one man is as good as another."

These extremes lead to the usual inconsistencies and follies. Thus do we see men, who sigh for titles and factitious and false distinctions, so little conscious of truth, as to shrink from asserting the real distinctions of their social station, or those they actually and undeniably possess; as if nature ever intended a man for an aristocrat, who has not the manhood to maintain his just rights; and those, again, who cant of equality and general privileges, while they stubbornly refuse to permit others to enjoy in peace a single fancied indulgence or taste, unless taken in their company, although nature, education and habits have all unfitted them to participate, and their presence would be sure to defeat what they could not, in the nature of things, enjoy.

The considerate, and modest, and just-minded man, of whatever social class, will view all this differently. In asserting his own rights, he respects those of others; in indulging his own tastes, he is willing to admit there may be superior; in pursuing his own course, in his own manner, he knows his neighbor has an equal right to do the same; and, most of all, is he impressed with the great moral truths, that flatterers are inherently miscreants, that fallacies never fail to bring their punishments, and that the empire of God is reason.

ON THE PUBLICK.

There is a disposition, under popular governments, to mistake the nature and authority of the publick. Publick opinion, as a matter of course, can only refer to that portion of the community that has cognizance of the particular circumstances it affects, but in all matters of law, of rights, and of principles, as they are connected with the general relations of society, the publick means the entire constituency, and that, too, only as it is authorized to act, by the fundamental laws, or the constitution. Thus the citizen who asserts his legal rights in opposition to the wishes of a neighborhood, is not opposing the publick, but maintaining its intentions, while the particular neighborhood is arrogating to itself a power that is confided to the whole body of the state.

Tyranny can only come from the publick, in a democracy, since individuals are powerless, possessing no more rights than it pleases the community to leave in their hands. The pretence that an individual oppresses the publick, is, to the last degree, absurd, since he can do no more than exercise his rights, as they are established by law; which law is enacted, administered and interpreted by the agents of the publick.

As every man forms a portion of the publick, if honest and influenced by right principles, the citizen will be cautious how he takes sides against particular members of the community, for he is both deciding in his own case, a circumstance under which few make impartial judges, and combining with the strong to oppress the weak.

In this country, in which political authority is the possession of the body that wields opinion, influences that elsewhere counteract each other, there is a strong and dangerous disposition to defer to the publick, in opposition to truth and justice. This is a penalty that is paid for liberty, and it depends on the very natural principle of flattering power. In a monarchy, adulation is paid to the prince; in a democracy to the people, or the publick. Neither hears the truth, as often as is wholesome, and both suffer for the want of the corrective. The man who resists the tyranny of a monarch, is often sustained by the voices of those around him; but he who opposes the innovations of the publick in a democracy, not only finds himself struggling with power, but with his own neighbors. It follows that the oppression of the publick is of the worst description, and all real lovers of liberty, should take especial heed not to be accessaries to wrongs so hard to be borne. As between the publick and individuals, therefore, the true bias of a democrat, so far as there is any doubt of the real merits of the controversy, is to take sides with the latter. This is opposed to the popular notion, which is to fancy the man who maintains his rights against the popular will, an aristocrat, but it is none the less true; the popular will, in cases that affect popular pleasure, being quite as likely to be wrong, as an individual will, in cases that affect an individual interest.

It ought to be impressed on every man's mind, in letters of brass, *"That, in a democracy, the publick has no power that is not expressly conceded by the institutions, and that this power, moreover, is only to be used under the forms prescribed by the constitution. All beyond this, is oppression, when it takes the character of acts, and not unfrequently when it is confined to opinion."* Society has less need of the corrective of publick opinion, under such a system, than under a narrow government, for possessing all the power, the body of the community, by framing the positive ordinances, is not compelled to check abuses by resisting, or over-awing the laws. Great care should be had, therefore, to ascertain facts, before the citizen of a free country suffers himself to inflict the punishment of publick opinion, since it is aiding oppression in its worst form, when in error, and this too, without a sufficient object.

Another form of oppression practised by the publick, is arrogating to itself a right to inquire into, and to decide on the private acts of individuals, beyond the cognizance of the laws.

Men who have designs on the favor of the publick invite invasions on their privacy, a course that has rendered the community less scrupulous and delicate than it ought to be. All assumptions of a power to decide on conduct, that is unaccompanied by an authority to investigate facts, is adding the danger of committing rank injustice, to usurpation. The practice may make hypocrites, but it can never mend morals.

The publick, every where, is proverbially soulless. All feel when its rights, assumed or real, are invaded, but none feel its responsibilities. In republicks, the publick is, also, accused of ingratitude to its servants. This is true, few citizens of a democracy retaining the popular favor, without making a sacrifice of those principles, which conflict with popular caprices. The people, being sovereign, require the same flattery, the same humouring of their wishes, and the same sacrifices of truths, as a prince.

It is not more true, however, that the people in a democracy, are ungrateful, than that monarchs are ungrateful. The failing is common to all power, which, as a rule, is invariably as forgetful of services as it is exacting. The difference in the rewards of the servants of a prince, and the rewards of the servants of a democracy, is to be found in the greater vigilance of the first, who commonly sees the necessity of paying well. No dignities or honors conferred on a subject, moreover, can raise him to a level with his master, while a people reluctantly yield distinctions that elevate one of their own number above themselves.

In America, it is indispensable that every well wisher of true liberty should understand that acts of tyranny can only proceed from the publick. The publick, then, is to be watched, in this country, as, in other countries kings and aristocrats are to be watched.

The end of liberty is the happiness of man, and its means, that of leaving the greatest possible personal freedom of action, that comports with the general good. To supplant the exactions of the laws, therefore, by those of an unauthorized publick, is to establish restraints without the formalities and precision of legal requirements. It is putting the prejudices, provincialisms, ignorance and passions of a neighborhood in the place of statutes; or, it is establishing a power equally without general principles, and without responsibility.

Although the political liberty of this country is greater than that of nearly every other civilized nation, its personal liberty is said to be less. In other words, men are thought to be more under the control of extra-legal authority, and to defer more to those around them, in pursuing even their lawful and innocent occupations, than in almost every other country. That there is much truth in this opinion, all observant travellers agree, and it is a reproach to the moral civilization of the country that it should be so. It is not difficult to trace the causes of such a state of things, but the evil is none the less because it is satisfactorily explained. One principal reason, beyond a question, is the mistake that men are apt to make concerning the rights and powers of the publick in a popular government.

The pretence that the publick has a right to extend its jurisdiction beyond the reach of the laws, and without regard to the principles and restraints of the fundamental compact that binds society together, is, indeed, to verify the common accusation of the enemies of democracy, who affirm that, by substituting this form of government for that of a despotism, people are only replacing one tyrant by many. This saying is singularly false as respects the political action of our institutions, but society must advance farther, the country must collect more towns, a denser population, and possess a higher degree of general civilization, before it can be as confidently pronounced that it is untrue as respects the purely social.

The disgraceful desire to govern by means of mobs, which has lately become so prevalent, has arisen from misconceiving the rights of the publick. Men know that the publick, or the community, rules, and becoming impatient of any evil that presses on them, or which they fancy presses on them, they overstep all the forms of law, overlook deliberation and consultation, and set up their own local interests, and not unfrequently their passions, in the place of positive enactments and the institutions. It is scarcely predicting more than the truth will warrant, to say, that if this substitution of the caprices, motives and animosities of a portion of the publick, for the solemn ordinances of the entire legal publick, should continue, even those well affected to a popular government, will be obliged to combine with those who wish its downfall, in order to protect their persons and property, against the designs of the malevolent; for no civilized society can long exist, with an active power in its bosom that is stronger than the law.

ON PUBLICK OPINION.

Publick opinion is the lever by which all things are moved, in a democracy. It has even become so powerful in monarchies, as, virtually, to destroy despotism in all really civilized countries, holding in check the will and passions of princes.

Publick opinion, however, like all things human, can work evil in proportion to its power to do good. On the same principle that the rebound is proportioned to the blow in physics, there can be no moral agent capable of benefitting man that has not an equal power to do him harm. Publick opinion rightly directed is the highest source of national virtue, as publick opinion, which has taken a wrong direction, is the surest means of serving the devil.

In a democracy, as a matter of course, every effort is made to seize upon and create publick opinion, which is, substantially, securing power. One of the commonest arts practised, in connection with this means of effecting objects, is to simulate the existence of a general feeling in favor, or against, any particular man, or measure; so great being the deference paid to publick opinion, in a country like this, that men actually yield their own sentiments to that which they believe to be the sentiment of the majority.

In politics, however, and, indeed, in all other matters that are of sufficient magnitude to attract general attention, there are adverse sentiments, which, were it not for the absurdity of the phrase, might almost be termed two publick opinions. This is the result of party feeling, which induces men to adopt in gross, the prejudices, notions and judgments of the particular faction to which they belong, often without examination, and generally without candor. When two men of equal intelligence, of the same means of ascertaining facts, and of the same general fairness of disposition, hold the opposite extremes of opinion on the character of a particular individual, or of a particular measure, we see the extent to which a bias may be carried, and the little value that those who wish only to support the truth ought to attach even to publick opinion, in matters that will admit of doubt.

As no reparation can ever be made, in this world, to the individual who has been wronged by publick opinion, all good men are cautious how they listen to accusations that are unsupported by testimony, vulgar report being more likely to be wrong than to be right.

In matters that admit of investigation and proof, publick opinion in the end, when passion, prejudice and malice have had their day, is very apt to come to a just decision, but this is often too late to repair the wrong done to the sufferer. In matters that, by their nature, cannot be clearly established, artifice, the industry of the designing, and studied misrepresentations, permanently take the place of facts, history itself being, as a whole, but an equivocal relation of all the minor events, and a profound mystification as to motives.

Publick opinion will be acted on in this country, by its enemies, as the easiest and most effectual mode of effecting their purposes, bodies of men never being sufficiently clear-sighted to detect remote consequences. It is said to be a common practice in Europe, for the governments to incite commotions, when they wish to alarm the country on the subject of any particular opinion, as the surest and promptest method of checking its advance. The excesses of the French revolution are now attributed to the schemes of agents of this sort; the opponents of liberty finding it impossible to stem the torrent, having recourse to the opposite policy of pushing it into revolting extremes.

Excitement is a word that, as regards the publick in a country like this, ought to be expunged from its dictionary. In full possession of the power, there is every motive for deliberation and enquiry on the part of the people, and every inducement to abstain from undue agitation. "Excitement," may favor the views of selfish individuals, but it can never advance the interests of truth. All good citizens should turn a deaf ear to every proposal to aid in producing an "excitement," as it is calling into existence a uniform enemy of reason, and the most certain agent of defeating the intention of the institutions, which are based on investigation and common sense.

Whenever the government of the United States shall break up, it will probably be in consequence of a false direction having been given to publick opinion. This is the weak point of our defences, and the part to which the enemies of the system will direct all their attacks. Opinion can be so perverted as to cause the false to seem the true; the enemy, a friend, and the friend, an enemy; the best interests of the nation to appear insignificant, and trifles of moment; in a word, the right the wrong, and the wrong the right.

In a country where opinion has sway, to seize upon it, is to seize upon power. As it is a rule of humanity that the upright and well intentioned are comparatively passive, while the designing, dishonest and selfish are the most untiring in their efforts, the danger of publick opinion's getting a false direction, is four-fold, since few men think for themselves. Perhaps there is not, in all America, apart from general principles, a sentiment that is essentially just, and which is recognized as publick opinion; a sufficient proof of which is to be found in the fact that publick opinion is constantly vibrating around truth, which alone is unchangeable.

Publick opinion has got a wrong, if not a dangerous direction, already, in this country, on several essential points. It has a fearfully wrong direction on the subject of the press, which it sustains in its tyranny and invasions on private rights, violating all sanctity of feeling, rendering men indifferent to character, and, indeed, rendering character itself of little avail, besides setting up an irresponsible and unprincipled power that is stronger than the government itself. One of its consequences is a laxity of opinion on the subject of wrongs committed by the press, that amounts to a denial of justice. Another, and a still graver result, is to give an unrestrained supremacy to an engine that is quite as able, and perhaps more likely, to corrupt and destroy society than to reform it. This fearful state of things, which is better adapted than any other, to restrain good, and to prefer bold and bad men, has been brought about by the action of the press, itself, on publick opinion, and is an example of the manner in which this tremendous agent can be perverted to evil, in a popular government. It follows, that publick opinion should be watched and protected from receiving a wrong bias, as we would protect and overlook the first impressions of a child.

Publick opinion in America is exposed to another danger, growing out of the recent colonial origin of the country. There is no question that the people of this country defer in an unusual manner to foreign opinions, more particularly to those of the nation from which they are derived. The proof of this is ample, but one may constantly see quotations from English journals, in support of the pretensions of politicians, writers, artists, and all others, who are liable to the decisions of their fellow citizens for the estimation in which they are held. An opinion is seldom given in Europe, of any thing American, unless from impure motives. The country attracts too little attention in the other hemisphere, to be included in the ordinary comments of the civilized world. There are, and may be, an occasional exception, but this is the rule. As many of the interests of this country are opposed to the interests of European nations, efforts are constantly made to influence opinion here, in favor of interests there. The doctrine of free trade, as it is called, has this origin, having been got up by English writers, to prevent other states from resorting to the same expedients to foster industry, that have so well succeeded in Great Britain. The factitious condition of all things in that great empire, renders any derangement hazardous, and while America trifles with her welfare, like a vigorous youth who is careless of his health through reliance on his constitution, England watches over every material concern, with the experience, vigilance and distrust of age. Hence it is that every means is resorted to, to extol men who have become the dupes of English sophistry, and to depreciate those who resist her schemes.

We have lately seen, on the part of France, an open and a direct attempt to interfere between the people and the government, in an affair touching the character and highest interests of the country, and although the appeal injured the cause of those who urged it, by exposing their sophistry and bad faith, it proves the reliance that foreign powers have on their ability to influence publick opinion, here, even in matters touching our own dearest interests!

Another familiar and recent instance of the efforts of foreigners to influence American opinion, may be cited in connection with the late quarrel with France. It is known that the English government mediated to prevent a war. This mediation was accepted on the part of the American government, with the express reservation that France must comply with the terms of the treaty. In other words, we merely conditioned to delay acting, until the effort should be made to induce France to comply with all we asked. France saw reasons to change her policy, and to comply with our terms, before the acceptance of the

English mediation was known, and yet strong efforts have been made to persuade the American people that the accommodation was produced through English mediation, and that England was pledged to see this accommodation effected, in the character of an arbitrator. The first is untrue as to fact, and the last is opposed to all the principles of arbitration, as nothing was placed at the decision of the English government. The case is a recent proof of the vigilance that is necessary to keep publick opinion independent of foreign domination.

Opinion is the moving power of this country, and it would be extreme weakness to suppose that other nations, which are ever ready to lavish their treasure and to shed their blood, in order to effect their purposes, would neglect means so sure, easy and noiseless, as that of acting on the common mind. The danger of evil from this source will increase with the growing power of the country, or, as her policy will be likely to influence foreign interests, in a ratio proportioned to her strength and wealth.

No nation can properly boast of its independence while its opinion is under the control of foreigners, and least of all, a nation with institutions dependant on the popular will.

Nathaniel Hawthorne [1804-1864]
FROM The American Notebooks [1868]

❦

NOTE: *Hawthorne's notebooks were edited and published in several volumes by his widow (1868, 1869, 1870, 1872). In the process of editing, Mrs. Hawthorne omitted materials she thought offensive and overly personal. Editions of the notebooks prepared by Randall Stewart (1932, 1941) are more exact. The passage below was written in 1838.*

Commencement at Williams College, 1838

Wednesday, August 15th.—I went to Commencement at Williams College,—five miles distant. At the tavern were students with ribbons, pink or blue, fluttering from their buttonholes, these being the badges of rival societies. There was a considerable gathering of people, chiefly arriving in wagons or buggies, some in barouches, and very few in chaises. The most characteristic part of the scene was where the pedlers, gingerbread-sellers, etc., were collected, a few hundred yards from the meeting-house. There was a pedler there from New York State, who sold his wares by auction, and I could have stood and listened to him all day long. Sometimes he would put up a heterogeny of articles in a lot,—as a paper of pins, a lead-pencil, and a shaving-box,—and knock them all down, perhaps for ninepence. Bunches of lead-pencils, steel-pens, pound-cakes of shaving-soap, gilt finger-rings, bracelets, clasps, and other jewelry, cards of pearl buttons, or steel ("there is some steel about them, gentlemen, for my brother stole 'em, and I bore him out in it"), bundles of wooden combs, boxes of matches, suspenders, and, in short, everything,— dipping his hand down into his wares with the promise of a wonderful lot, and producing, perhaps, a bottle of opodeldoc, and joining it with a lead-pencil,—and when he had sold several things of the same kind, pretending huge surprise at finding "just one more," if the lads lingered; saying, "I could not afford to steal them for the price; for the remorse of conscience would be worth more,"—all the time keeping an eye upon those who bought, calling for the pay, making change with silver or bills, and deciding on the goodness of banks; and saying to the boys who climbed upon his cart, "Fall down, roll down, tumble down, only get down"; and uttering everything in the queer, humorous recitative in which he sold his articles. Sometimes he would pretend that a person had bid, either by word or wink, and raised a laugh thus; never losing his self-possession, nor getting out of humor. When a man asked whether a bill were good: "No! do you suppose I'd give you good money?" When he delivered an article, he exclaimed, "You're the lucky man," setting off his wares with the most extravagant eulogies. The people bought very freely, and seemed also to enjoy the fun. One little boy bought a shaving-box, perhaps meaning to speculate upon it. This character could not possibly be overdrawn; and he was really excellent, with his allusions to what was passing, intermingled, doubtless, with a good deal that was studied. He was a man between thirty and forty, with a face expressive of other ability, as well as of humor.

A good many people were the better or the worse for liquor. There was one fellow,—named Randall, I think,—a round-shouldered, bulky, ill-hung devil, with a pale, sallow skin, black beard, and a sort of grin upon his face,—a species of laugh, yet not so much mirthful as indicating a strange mental and moral twist. He was very riotous in the crowd, elbowing, thrusting, seizing hold of people; and at last a ring was formed, and a regular wrestling-match commenced between him and a farmer-looking man. Randall brandished his legs about in the most ridiculous style, but proved himself a good wrestler, and finally threw his antagonist. He got up with the same grin upon his features,—not a grin of simplicity, but intimating knowingness. When more depth or force of expression was required, he

could put on the most strangely ludicrous and ugly aspect (suiting
his gesture and attitude to it) that can be imagined. I should like to
see this fellow when he was perfectly sober.

There were a good many blacks among the crowd. I suppose
they used to emigrate across the border, while New York was a slave
State. There were enough of them to form a party, though greatly in
the minority; and, a squabble arising, some of the blacks were
knocked down, and otherwise maltreated. I saw one old negro, a
genuine specimen of the slave negro, without any of the foppery of
the race in our part of the State,—an old fellow, with a bag, I suppose of broken victuals, on his shoulder, and his pockets stuffed out
at his hips with the like provender; full of grimaces and ridiculous
antics, laughing laughably, yet without affectation; then talking with
a strange kind of pathos about the whippings he used to get while he
was a slave;—a singular creature, of mere feeling, with some glimmering of sense. Then there was another gray old negro, but of a
different stamp, politic, sage, cautious, yet with boldness enough, talking about the rights of his race, yet so as not to provoke his audi-
ence; discoursing of the advantage of living under laws, and the
wonders that might ensue, in that very assemblage, if there were no
laws; in the midst of this deep wisdom, turning off the anger of a
half-drunken fellow by a merry retort, a leap in the air, and a
negro's laugh. I was interested—there being a drunken negro ascend-
ing the meeting-house steps, and near him three or four well-dressed
and decent negro wenches—to see the look of scorn and shame and
sorrow and painful sympathy which one of them assumed at this disgrace of her color.

The people here show out their character much more strongly
than they do with us; there was not the quiet, silent, dull decency of
our public assemblages, but mirth, anger, eccentricity,—all manifesting themselves freely. There were many watermelons for sale, and
people burying their muzzles deep in the juicy flesh of them. There
were cider and beer. Many of the people had their mouths half
opened in a grin, which, more than anything else, I think, indicates a
low stage of refinement. A low-crowned hat—very low—is common.
They are respectful to gentlemen.

A bat being startled, probably, out of the meeting-house, by the
commotion around, flew blindly about in the sunshine, and alighted

on a man's sleeve. I looked at him,—a droll, winged, beast-insect, creeping up the man's arm, not over-clean, and scattering dust on the man's coat from his vampire wings. The man stared at him, and let the spectators stare for a minute, and then shook him gently off; and the poor devil took a flight across the green to the meeting-house, and then, I believe, alighted on somebody else. Probably he was put to death. Bats are very numerous in these parts.

There was a drunken man, annoying people with his senseless talk and impertinences, impelled to perform eccentricities by an evil spirit in him; and a pale little boy, with a bandaged leg, whom his father brought out of the tavern and put into a barouche. Then the boy heedfully placed shawls and cushions about his leg to support it, his face expressive of pain and care,—not transitory, but settled pain, of long and forcedly patient endurance; and this painful look, per-haps, gave his face more intelligence than it might otherwise have had, though it was naturally a sensitive face. Well-dressed ladies were in the meeting-house in silks and cambrics,—the sunburnt necks in contiguity with the delicate fabrics of the dresses showing the yeomen's daughters.

Country graduates,—rough, brown-featured, school-master-looking, half-bumpkin, half-scholarly figures, in black ill-cut broad-cloth,—their manners quite spoilt by what little of the gentleman there was in them.

The landlord of the tavern keeping his eye on a man whom he suspected of an intention to bolt.

The next day after Commencement was bleak and rainy from midnight till midnight, and a good many guests were added to our table in consequence. Among them were some of the Williamstown students, gentlemanly young fellows, with a brotherly feeling for each other, a freedom about money concerns, a half-boyish, half-manly character; and my heart warmed to them. They took their departure—two for South Adams and two across the Green Moun-tains—in the midst of the rain. There was one of the graduates with his betrothed, and his brother-in-law and wife, who stayed during the day,—the graduate the very model of a country schoolmaster in his Sunday clothes, being his Commencement suit of black broad-cloth and pumps. He is engaged as assistant teacher of the academy at Shelburne Falls. There was also the high sheriff of Berkshire, Mr. Twining, with a bundle of writs under his arm, and some of them peeping out of his pockets. Also several Trojan men and women, who had been to Commencement. Likewise a young clergyman, graduate of Brown College, and student of the Divinity School at Cambridge. He had come across the Hoosic, or Green Mountains, about eighteen miles, on foot, from Charlemont, where he is preaching, and had been to Commencement. Knowing little of men and matters, and desiring to know more, he was very free in making acquaintance with people, but could not do it handsomely. A singular smile broke out upon his face on slight provocation. He was awkward in his manners, yet it was not an ungentlemanly awkwardness, —intelligent as respects book-learning, but much deficient in worldly tact. It was pleasant to observe his consciousness of this deficiency, and how he strove to remedy it by mixing as much as possible with people, and sitting almost all day in the bar-room to study character. Sometimes he would endeavor to contribute his share to the general amusement,—as by growling comically, to provoke and mystify a dog; and by some bashful and half-apropos observations.

In the afternoon there came a fresh bevy of students onward from Williamstown; but they made only a transient visit, though it was still raining. These were a rough-hewn, heavy set of fellows, from the hills and woods in this neighborhood,—great unpolished bumpkins, who had grown up farmer-boys, and had little of the literary man, save green spectacles and black broadcloth (which all of them had not), talking with a broad accent, and laughing clown-like, while sheepishness overspread all, together with a vanity at being students. One of the party was six feet seven inches high, and all his herculean dimensions were in proportion; his features, too, were cast in a mould suitable to his stature. This giant was not ill-looking, but of a rather intelligent aspect. His motions were devoid of grace, but yet had a rough freedom, appropriate enough to such a figure. These fellows stayed awhile, talked uncouthly about college matters, and started in the great open wagon which had brought them and their luggage hither. We had a fire in the bar-room almost all day,—a great, blazing fire,—and it was pleasant to have this day of bleak November weather, and cheerful fireside talk, and wet garments smoking in the fireside heat, still in the summer-time. Thus the day wore on with a sort of heavy, lazy pleasantness; and night set in, still stormy.

In the morning it was cloudy, but did not rain, and I went with the little clergyman to Hudson's Cave. The stream which they call the North Branch, and into which Hudson's Brook empties, was much swollen, and tumbled and dashed and whitened over the rocks, and formed real cascades over the dams, and rushed fast along the side of the cliffs, which had their feet in it. Its color was deep brown, owing to the washing of the banks which the rain had poured into it. Looking back, we could see a cloud on Graylock; but on other parts of Saddle Mountain there were spots of sunshine, some of most glorious brightness, contrasting with the general gloom of the sky, and the deep shadow which lay on the earth.

We looked at the spot where the stream makes its entrance into the marble cliff, and it was (this morning, at least) the most striking view of the cave. The water dashed down in a misty cascade, through what looked like the portal of some infernal subterranean structure; and far within the portal we could see the mist and the falling water; and it looked as if, but for these obstructions of view, we might have had a deeper insight into a gloomy region.

After our return, the little minister set off for his eighteen miles' journey across the mountain; and I was occupied the rest of the forenoon with an affair of stealing,—a woman of forty or upwards being accused of stealing a needle-case and other trifles from a factory-girl at a boarding-house. She came here to take passage in a stage; but Putnam, a justice of the peace, examined her and afterwards ordered her to be searched by Laura and Eliza, the chambermaid and table-waiter. Hereupon was much fun and some sympathy. They searched, and found nothing that they sought, though she gave up a pair of pantalets, which she pretended to have taken by mistake. Afterwards, she being in the parlor, I went in; and she immediately began to talk to me, giving me an account of the affair, speaking with the bitterness of a wronged person, with a sparkling eye, yet with great fluency and self-possession. She is a yellow, thin, and battered old thing, yet rather country-lady-like in aspect and manners. I heard Eliza telling another girl about it, under my window; and she seemed to think that the poor woman's reluctance to be searched arose from the poorness of her wardrobe and of the contents of her band-box.

At parting, Eliza said to the girl, "What do you think I heard somebody say about you? That it was enough to make anybody's eyes start square out of their head to look at such red cheeks as yours." Whereupon the girl turned off the compliment with a laugh, and took her leave.

There is an old blind dog, recognizing his friends by the sense of smell. I observe the eager awkwardness with which he accomplishes the recognition, his carefulness in descending steps, and generally in his locomotion. He evidently has not forgotten that he once had the faculty of sight; for he turns his eyes with earnestness towards those who attract his attention, though the orbs are plainly sightless.

Here is an Englishman,—a thorough-going Tory and Monarchist,—upholding everything English, government, people, habits, education, manufactures, modes of living, and expressing his dislike of all Americanisms,—and this in a quiet, calm, reasonable way, as if it were quite proper to live in a country and draw his subsistence from it, and openly abuse it. He imports his clothes from England, and expatiates on the superiority of English boots, hats, cravats, etc. He is a man of unmalleable habits, and wears his dress of the same fashion as that of twenty years ago.

Joel Chandler Harris [1848-1908]
Observations From New England [1883]

NOTE: *Reprinted are the second and third of a series of three letters written for the* Atlanta Constitution.

When the first part of these desultory and rambling notes was brought to a close last week, I was on the point of entering Priscilla's bower. Let us pause, however, to consider the purport of the invasion. What is to be done? What is to be the outcome of the excursion? These are questions which I put to myself, and to which I could find no very definite answer. There was a vague desire to see the real New England so far as the reality could make itself apparent to a temporary sojourner. Curiosity was at the bottom of the whole business. I was curious to know whether the people of New England were as different from the people of the South as the gentlemanly publicists of both sections are in the habit of claiming. The question seems to be a very interesting one. If there were two distinct white races occupying the East and the South this difference as to traits could not be more strenuously pressed on the attention of the public. The books are full of it and presently, if we are not careful, the stage will teem with it. When ignorance and prejudice go into cahoots to push a theory they are a very tough pair to handle. They bristle so with eagerness and are so full of the pluck and enterprise necessary to the success of their adventures that one hesitates to challenge them. It is so comfortable to let them alone; it is so easy to permit misinformation to strut around in the highways and in the public places that a peaceably disposed person is inclined to sit in a shady place and bet with the talent, as they say at the races.

We have all, first and last, had a pretty hard time of it in attempting to blink facts and to make something important out of partisan matters. One side yells out, "Look at your poor white trash!" The other yells back, "You are a lot of mudsills!" One side sneers at the mention of chivalry and honor, and the other professes contempt for the money-getting faculty. This had been going on for thirty years when the war brought the disputants together with a crash that came near tearing the republic up by the roots. The Yankees poured billions and billions of dollars into this bloody whirlpool, and the Southerners followed suit with every dollar they had accumulated. When old Judge Sewall, a friend and contemporary of Cotton Mather, was courting a buxom Puritan widow, he mentions in his diary that he gave her a book which cost eight shillings, and adds, with startling emphasis, "Jehovah jireh!" The consoling remark sounds almost like an objurgation, but what would the pennywise old judge have said if he could have seen the sacrifice of treasures demanded by the war? The serious part of the controversy was practically settled by that event, but we still see ignorance and prejudice running around irritating the two sections with the fragments of that bloody feast. In one way and another the impression has been created that the war was fought out by two dissimilar peoples, and, so far as I know, there has been no serious effort made to correct the impression. The Tackies, who have made little or no progress since the revolution, are somehow made to represent our whole people, and the symptoms of unthrift, which are to be found in all communities and in all sections are made to stand for the whole South.

My main object, therefore, in knocking at Miss Priscilla's garden gate—apart from the pleasure of visiting a section which by its energy and its art has impressed its individuality so powerfully on the republic—was to see whether, after all, there was not something of a family resemblance, tempered by climate and other physical conditions. I had intended to fish around modestly for such symptoms as might appear to a careful observer, and to present them cautiously, as became a person treading on dangerous ground; but no sooner had I entered Priscilla's bower than the situation became comical. Here, waiting for me with smiles of welcome, were my old friend Major Joseph Jones, of Pineville, Simon Suggs, the Hon. Potiphar Peagreen, and all the rest of the characters who are identified with rural life in the South. Here, too, was Bud Stuckey, the Georgia Tacky, though what he was doing hanging barefooted around the little station of Bethel on the Vermont Central the Lord only knows. Yet there was one visible improvement; his one "gallus," instead of being fastened by a thorn was held in place by a glittering little wire dagger, which must have shone once in some fair lady's hair. Bud Stuckey's New England name, so he told me, is Webb Brown; but what is in a name? He wore here the same striped shirt and red jeans trousers he used to wear in Georgia, and he had the same pale, watery blue eyes, the same straggling sandy beard, and the same habit of fingering his weak chin and mouth. And, then, when the train-boy, with true Southern accent, called out "Northampton," why should a group of E. W. Kemble's Georgia "crackers" be standing near the station? All this is more than I can make out, unless the leagues that stretch between Vermont and Georgia are a dream and sectionalism a myth. But Vermont is not singular in this matter. Wherever I have gone in New England I have found representatives of this "poor white trash." They are perhaps not so numerous as they are in the South, for prosperity strikes deep and goes far in New England; nor so unthrifty as a general rule, for out of the unfruitfulness of the soil and the sharp, imperative demands of the climate springs the stress and necessity of industry.

And yet, here they are—the Sandhillers, the Dirteaters, the Crablanders, the Tackies—as large as life and quite as natural. Poverty is a forlorn affair at best. It is the inward resentment of its limitations and conditions that lies at the bottom of the progress and development of the race. Yet, forlornest of all is the poverty that is acquiesced in—that has become a habit. It is found here in New England, and it is not isolated and cut off into communities as in the South, but it hovers on the edge of prosperity—a somewhat somber trimming to what would otherwise be a very gay piece of holiday goods.

The wonder is, not that New England should have its Tackies and its "poor white trash," but that the restless Northern correspondents should not have found it out. Or did they think their discovery would give offense? The truth is, the most of those correspondents—always excepting, of course, those who were sent south for political purposes—had no cut-and-dried programme, but followed the large orders of perfect innocence. From the windows of the railway coaches they beheld shabbiness—the country generally having an unaccountable tendency to back against the railroad lines and expose its nakedness to view. The correspondents beheld shabbiness and its accompaniments in the shape of what seemed to be a shiftless population; and the result of this vision is the impression both at home and abroad that the South is made up of run-down establishments and a lazy and thriftless population. There has been a good deal of fretting over this, but now, since I have seen the "poor white trash" of New England, and talked with them, I feel that Providence has succeeded in preserving the unities, as it usually does. If there is any difference at all, it is in favor of the Southern poor white. He has larger opportunities, so far as the means of existence are concerned, than his New England brother. He has no such terrible climate to contend with and no such unfruitful soil to depend on. The little Southern patch will produce something if the weeds and grass are kept down. The New England patch must be waxed with hard work. I have never been able to clearly understand the real intent of the comparison that has been set up in literature and out of it between New England and the South. Neither side gives a fair view of the other. The South purchased its negroes from New England, and went into the slavery business cursing the bargaining and trading proclivities of the Yankees. Then the Yankees, seeing that slave labor had been made a success in the South began to curse the slaveholders as a pampered and luxuriant race. Right here the sectional controversy, unreasoning and ignorant on both sides, had its origin, and it has been kept up with more or less volubility ever since, chiefly for the benefit of the politicians. Meanwhile, in the beginning and for many years thereafter the Southern planters were engaged in making wives of the Yankee school-ma'ams who, driven from home by the pressure of hard conditions, sought a livelihood beneath friendlier skies. These pioneer matrons quickly discovered that the oriental luxury imputed to the slave owners was a myth taken from the book of Arabian Nights. They discovered that the duty of looking after the irresponsible blacks, was not only in the nature of unceasing drudgery, but involved the upbuilding and upholding of a patriarchal institution out of which grew new and grave responsibilities. It is true that the Yankee school-ma'ams were not numerous enough to make any impression on the native stock even if they had been of a different race, but the point I wish to make is that the old Southern planters not only found these school-ma'ams to be fair, but found them to be of the same bone and flesh as the Southern people—highstrung, quick-witted and hard-headed.

I don't know which has had the hardest time, the people of New England, with their hard climate and unfruitful soil, or the people of the South with their great negro problem. President Lincoln's proclamation emancipated the whites rather than the blacks.

I stood once watching a company of negro militiamen celebrating emancipation. A lady who had spent the best years of her life in looking after the domestic establishment of a large plantation, paused to inquire what the drumming and strumming was about. When told exclaimed, "Ah! this is a day that ought to be celebrated by the Southern women!" This remark can only be appreciated by those who know of the ceaseless demands which, in the days of slavery, were made on all who were interested in the management of the plantations. In the case of the negroes, the anxieties of those who had charge of them were sharpened by the humanity which the situation called for. It is perhaps not popular to make such a remark as this, but the sooner that the Americans realize the facts of the case, the sooner they will be proud of the great fundamental fact that American slavery differed in kind and degree from slavery anywhere else in the world. Dr. Mayo, pursuing a discussion which the *Constitution* had made the most of years ago, and using almost the same words employed by the present writer, declared that American slavery in the Southern States was, in all the essentials which made up that institution, a great university in which the savage African was brought into personal contact with Christianity and civilization. Several years ago when it was suggested that the affair known as slavery had been the means of developing a savage into a citizen, a well-known journal refused to enter into the discussion on the ground that the whole matter was above and beyond the domain of politics. To this day it remains above and beyond that domain, and there has been found no man rash enough to antagonize the views which, from a Southern standpoint, take the whole question of slavery out of partisan politics and carry it into the realm of philosophy.

It is beyond the power of partisan politics to degrade or to misrepresent an institution which, under Providence, grew into a university in which millions of savages served an apprenticeship to religion and civilization, and out of which they graduated into American citizens. We cannot perceive in these momentous results anything less powerful than the hand of the Almighty. Man was merely a blind instrument employed for the furtherance of the Lord's will. The processes of Providence we do not always recognize, but surely no one can mistake the large results that confront us.

The Negro Problem, of which we make so much at the South, is not without its New England connections. In the South it chiefly concerns the whites, and has been twisted and tangled into all sorts of political shapes; in New England, it chiefly concerns the blacks, and is a very serious matter. In the South, the whites are interested in the question whether, through political agitation, the ignorant negroes shall be permitted to take charge of affairs and touch the trigger of destruction as they did during the period of disorder and corruption which followed the war; in New England the negroes are interested in the question whether they shall be permitted to take advantage of the opportunities which their abilities open to them. Here are two very serious sections of the negro question, and we may as well make ourselves comfortable over them, for they promise to be enduring, and those who discuss them have the gift of longwindedness.

I find that the prejudice in New England against the negro is more intense and more widespread than in the South. It is more unreasoning and more unjustifiable. In the South, we are afraid of the "nigger" problem, and in a general way we recognize the fact that it is neither pleasant nor safe to have large numbers of an alien and an inferior race, armed with the power and dignity of its citizenship, and yet totally ignorant and careless of its responsibilities. We regard the situation as somewhat menacing, though in a vague way. Yet, when it comes to the individual "nigger," we are fond of him. His color and his character remind us of associations that were pleasant if not profitable; we are tolerant of his weaknesses, and always ready to help him along in the way that destiny has marked out for him.

Queerly enough, it is the race—the vague and undefinable mass— that New England is fond of, and not the individual. So far as I could see the individual "nigero" has no standing whatever in the land where philanthropy claims to have its nidus. It may be that all the attractive qualities of his character have been blotted and washed out by his residence in a cold and an uncongenial clime, but, what- ever the reason, the negro cuts a very lonely figure in New England. He is thrown absolutely on his own resources, and they seemed to me to be pitifully few. It is true I did not investigate the matter closely, but I saw no negro engaged in what might be termed a profitable business. The competition of the whites is too strenuous. In Springfield, Mass., I saw three negroes driving drays or wagons. There may be more, but these three were all I saw, and their color made them conspicuous. They held themselves proudly as if they had achieved some sort of distinction—or so it seemed. What points of superiority these three negroes have over the rest of their race in that neighborhood I do not know, but it would be interesting to dis- cover whether the positions they hold were won by superior educa- tion or by reason of native and inborn individuality.

On a Cambridge street car a very peculiar incident happened which, more than anything else, tended to open my eyes to the real status of the negroes here. There were many ladies standing, and many men were sitting—a fact which made me exceedingly uncom- fortable. Presently a negro woman got on the car. She was well dressed and pleasant looking, apparently about fifty years old. She had no sooner entered the car than a little man with side-whiskers jumped up and offered her his seat. Then, the little man, hanging to a strap, looked furtively around to see what the effect of his unusual politeness had been. He was not kept in doubt a moment. He found the white women glaring at him scornfully, and the men who had witnessed his performance jeered at him. When the little man found that what he had done was displeasing, he held his head as high as he could, and I think I shall never see on the face of mortal man a more luminous expression of self-satisfaction. The little episode was as unexpected and as comical as anything you see on the stage, and it lit up the situation as brilliantly and as suddenly as if a flash light had been turned on.

Reflecting over the matter I have come to the conclusion that there was something more sinister in the jeering than appeared on the surface. The scorn and contempt expressed in this futile and boyish way needed just one suggestion to make the situation serious. A great many people in New England to whom I described the incident had never seen anything like it, and I suppose, indeed, that it was one of those curious and inexplicable phenomena which fate or circumstance is pleased to throw in the way of the observant traveller. I remember, too, that whenever I told about it, the conversation turned into the pleasant channel of inquisitiveness. What would have happened if such an incident had occurred at the South? It was in vain I told the seekers after information that such a thing could not possibly happen at the South—that the lowest and most wretched apology for a man would not sit in a street car while there is a woman standing. This was not satisfactory. What would be the result if the Cambridge incident had occurred in the South—there being no impossible combinations in whist or in human experience? I was therefore compelled, with some of the reluctance of a Ku Klux caught in the act, to admit that if any reformer in the South, side-whiskered or smooth-faced, were to give his seat to a negro woman after having ostentatiously refused to give it to a white woman, he would probably be seized by the scruff of the neck and the slack of the trousers and bundled out of the car. This would be done not because he gave the negro woman his seat—men do this every day in Atlanta—but because he offered a deliberate insult to the public sentiment about him, and violated the race instinct, which ought to be as strong as his patriotism. I could not see that there was any approval of this programme on the part of those who insisted on having it. In their eyes they had that inward and peculiar look which no man can justify himself against.

I tried to see how far disapproval went, and I discovered this much—that there was no objection to the race instinct, or to the color line, and no particular objection to the suppositious lamming received by the imaginary man. What seemed to shock and surprise, and tumble the loose emotions about was the fact that, after everything had been forgotten and forgiven, so to speak, there should be anything like a scrapping match or a scrimmage in the progressive South. I think there is a vague idea in the minds of many good people at the North that reconstruction is only another name for regeneration, and that its practical failure is the result of hardness of heart and a perverted understanding. I tried to show, that while it might be rude to bundle a man off a street-car the very knowledge that it could and would be done on a pinch was a powerful preventive. How far success attended this effort it would be hard to say, but I think that for many years yet the average New England mind will regard what would be an incident at the North as an "outrage" at the South—and this without malice or prejudice so far as I can see, but in a sort of friendly and historic way. But I am getting away from the colored brother, and heaven forbid that I should neglect or ignore the sinctum-sanctum of modern politics.

Whatever the attitude of the reformers and philanthropists may be, the average New England man thoroughly despises the negro, and this is the more singular, since the negro is the most insignificant feature to be found here. There is no problem about him. Few in numbers, he has almost the distinction of variety. He bothers nobody, but attends to his business with an air of docility that reminds the interested observer of the days of slavery. Even his tendency to "jaw back" under provocation is suggestive. In slavery times "jawin' back" was one of the privileges of the system which was not allowed to languish for lack of use.

It is a curious fact, however, that the negroes of New England are further away from the white people than the negroes of the South. "The Negro, I am told," said an old gentleman at the Massasoit House in Springfield, "are getting along very well." The sonorous emphasis he placed on the word Negro was delicious, and yet misleading. There was such a personal flavor about it that I thought he was speaking of the old negro who was at that moment trundling a wheelbarrow across the street. The barrow contained a barrel of whitewash, that glistening emblem of civilization and advancement. "Yes," said I, replying to the old gentleman, "he is getting along tolerably well, but he might get along better. That negro yonder has a very good education, but you see what he is doing." The old gentleman regarded me almost with amazement. All interest died out of his face. "I was speaking of the Southern Negro," he remarked, and said no more. A minute later he was absorbed in the editorial page of the *Republican*.

It was clear to me that this old gentleman, prosperous and kindly, had permitted his mind to dwell on the Southern negro and his newspaper woes until he had grown somewhat sentimental on the subject. It was clear, too, that the Northern negro had no place in his regard. To say that this old gentleman's attitude toward the negroes at his door is typical would be an assumption, of course, but it would be warranted by a great deal that I saw and heard. Perhaps the old negro who was trundling the wheelbarrow across the street was not a fair type of the New England negro, yet he was very interesting. I had talked with him before I fell in and fell out with the old gentleman whose remarks I have just quoted. He was fifty-four years old, and a native of New England. His father came from Maryland and his mother from Missouri. I judged from his conversation that he had an excellent education. There was not the slightest trace of negro speech in his talk except when referring to his parents. He called them "Daddy" and "Mammy," terms which the Southern blacks have preserved from the colonial period. He had three sons and a daughter. One of his sons had gone west. The other two sons and the girl were at home. Did the boys have a trade? No! What good would it do them to have a trade? There were so many white people with trades, that colored people had mighty little chance. He didn't have any trade himself, but he could do a little of anything. He just piddled about and did odd jobs, and got along very well considering the hard times everywhere.

I have transcribed my notes made at the time instead of enlarging on them—not because this was the most interesting talk I had with a New England negro, but because the negro seemed to represent the average. Some speak with great bitterness, not of the treatment they receive, but of the lack of treatment. A youngish negro man of whom I asked some topographical information in Boston—for Boston is wildly topographical at all seasons—talked very bitterly of the lack of treatment the colored people received at the North. They were crowded out of business, out of the professions, out of the trades, and out of everything except the most menial and unprofitable employments. Yet the negro who was making these remarks was "dressed to kill," as the phrase goes. His toggery suggested prosper-

ity, and his fluency was such as is rarely heard outside the walls of a
literary institution. He told me with some degree of pride that he
was a billiard-marker for a negro hotel. This seems to be a comical
combination—dude, missionary and billiard-marker—but if this negro
could get before the Northern negroes with his tale of woe, I have
no doubt his fluency would make things interesting. But it would
accomplish nothing, except to emphasize, intensify and aggravate the
conditions which now exist. Making allowance for the sparse negro
element at the North, and for the clearer and more intimate knowledge of the negro character at the South, these conditions are precisely the same in both sections. The South, on account of outside
pressure and inside warnings, is alive to the various problems that
dance attendance on the negro question. The North, on the other
hand, is utterly indifferent to the negro at its doors, whatever vague
views it may have of the Southern negro, and this indifference grows
out of thorough contempt for the race.

It will be seen that the situation is difficult to describe. It is full
of contradictions and surprises. Where you see one man here who is
ready to make a social martyr of himself for the sake of the colored
barber, you see a thousand who know nothing and care nothing for
him except in so far as the black phantom of Southern politics may
have aroused their political susceptibilities—to touch gingerly a pep-
pery matter. What is more, they care nothing whatever for the white
martyr. Indifference is nothing, and yet it is everything. It is the wall,
unseen and impalpable, that always presents the same cold, hard surface, and I do not see how the Northern negro will ever climb over
it. As a matter of fact, he doesn't want to climb over it, and this is
thoroughly characteristic of his race. Without being at all aware of
it, or intending it, he meets indifference with indifference. He is indifferent not only to the attitude of the Northern white man, but to
the results of this indifference. I am speaking now of the real negro
who is by birth and education a native of the North.

The statement has been made that the negro is almost a rarity in
New England, and it is a statement that must be qualified. He is a
rarity in New England only when we compare the relation he bears
to the population here with the preponderating mass of negroes in
the South. There are a good many negroes here when you come to
hunt for them, but they are as completely in the background as if

they never existed. They exist and that is all. They are overlooked and ignored. When you hear the negro spoken of in a kindly way you may be sure the Southern negro is meant. When the missionary or the philanthropist goes to the telephone to speak a few words in behalf of the blacks, the South is at the other end of the wire. The eye whose vision reaches across the continent is utterly blind to facts nearer home. I do not mean to say that the condition of the negro in New England demands the calling out of the troops or the passage of a force bill, but I do mean to say that it is no better in any respect than the condition of the Southern negroes—and, in some respects, which I have already tried to indicate, it is infinitely worse. A few negroes perceive this and protest against it, but the great majority seem to be well satisfied. This being the case, we need not trouble ourselves about the matter except to call it to the attention of the political sectionalists when their buzzing becomes irritating.

George Washington Cable [1844-1925]
The Freedman's Case in Equity [1885]

I. THE NATION'S ATTITUDE

The greatest social problem before the American people today is, as it has been for a hundred years, the presence among us of the Negro.

No comparable entanglement was ever drawn round itself by any other modern nation with so serene a disregard of its ultimate issue, or with a more distinct national responsibility. The African slave was brought here by cruel force, and with everybody's consent except his own. Everywhere the practice was favored as a measure of common aggrandizement. When a few men and women protested, they were mobbed in the public interest, with the public consent. There rests, therefore, a moral responsibility on the whole nation never to lose sight of the results of African-American slavery until they cease to work mischief and injustice.

It is true these responsibilities may not fall everywhere with the same weight; but they are nowhere entirely removed. The original seed of trouble was sown with the full knowledge and consent of the nation. The nation was to blame; and so long as evils spring from it, their correction must be the nation's duty.

The late Southern slave has within two decades risen from slavery to freedom, from freedom to citizenship, passed on into political ascendency, and fallen again from that eminence. The amended Constitution holds him up in his new political rights as well as a mere constitution can. On the other hand, certain enactments of Congress, trying to reach further, have lately been made void by the highest court of the nation. And another thing has happened. The popular mind in the old free states, weary of strife at arm's length, bewildered by its complications, vexed by many a blunder, eager to turn to the cure of other evils, and even tinctured by that race feeling whose grosser excesses it would so gladly see suppressed, has retreated from its uncomfortable dictational attitude and thrown the whole matter over to the states of the South. Here it rests, no longer a main party issue, but a group of questions which are to be settled by each of these states separately in the light of simple equity and morals, and which the genius of American government is at least loath to force upon them from beyond their borders. Thus the whole question, become secondary in party contest, has yet reached a period of supreme importance.

II. OLD SOUTH AND NEW

Before slavery ever became a grave question in the nation's politics— when it seemed each state's private affair, developing unmolested—it had two different fates in two different parts of the country. In one, treated as a question of public equity, it withered away. In the other, overlooked in that aspect, it petrified and became the cornerstone of the whole social structure; and when men sought its overthrow as a national evil, it first brought war upon the land, and then grafted into the citizenship of one of the most intelligent nations in the world six millions of people from one of the most debased races on the globe.

And now this painful and wearisome question, sown in the African slave trade, reaped in our Civil War, and garnered in the national adoption of millions of an inferior race, is drawing near a second seedtime. For this is what the impatient proposal to make it a dead and buried issue really means. It means to recommit it to the silence and concealment of the covered furrow. Beyond that incubative retirement no suppressed moral question can be pushed; but all such questions, ignored in the domain of private morals, spring up and expand once more into questions of public equity; neglected as matters of public equity, they blossom into questions of national interest; and, despised in that guise, presently yield the red fruits of revolution.

This question must never again bear that fruit. There must arise, nay, there has arisen, in the South itself a desire to see established the equities of the issue; to make it no longer a question of endurance between one group of states and another, but between the moral debris of an exploded evil and the duty, necessity, and value of planting society firmly upon universal justice and equity. This, and this only, can give the matter final burial. True, it is still a question between states; but only secondarily, as something formerly participated in, or as it concerns every householder to know that what is being built against his house is built by level and plummet. It is the interest of the Southern states first, and *consequently* of the whole land, to discover clearly these equities and the errors that are being committed against them.

If we take up this task, the difficulties of the situation are plain. We have, first, a revision of Southern state laws which has forced into them the recognition of certain human rights discordant with the sentiments of those who have always called themselves the community; second, the removal of the entire political machinery by which this forcing process was effected; and, third, these revisions left to be interpreted and applied under the domination of these antagonistic sentiments. These being the three terms of the problem, one of three things must result. There will arise a system of vicious evasions eventually ruinous to public and private morals and liberty, or there will be a candid reconsideration of the sentiments hostile to these enactments, or else there will be a division, some taking one course and some the other.

This is what we should look for from our knowledge of men and history; and this is what we find. The revised laws, only where they could not be evaded, have met that reluctant or simulated acceptance of their narrowest letter which might have been expected —a virtual suffocation of those principles of human equity which the unwelcome decrees do little more than shadow forth. But in different regions this attitude has been made in very different degrees of emphasis. In some the new principles have grown, or are growing, into the popular conviction, and the opposing sentiments are correspondingly dying out. There are even some districts where they have received much practical acceptance. While, again, other limited sections lean almost wholly toward the old sentiments; an easy choice, since it is the conservative, the unyielding attitude, whose strength is in the absence of intellectual and moral debate.

Now, what are the gains, what the losses of these diverse attitudes? Surely these are urgent questions to any one in our country who believes it is always a losing business to be in the wrong. Particularly in the South, where each step in this affair is an unprecedented experience, it will be folly if each region, small or large, does not study the experiences of all the rest. And yet this, alone, would be superficial; we would still need to do more. We need to go back to the roots of things and study closely, analytically, the origin, the present foundation, the rationality, the rightness of those sentiments surviving in us which prompt an attitude qualifying in any way peculiarly the black man's liberty among us. Such a treatment will be less abundant in incident, less picturesque; but it will be more thorough.

III. THE ROOTS OF THE QUESTION

First, then, what are these sentiments? Foremost among them stands the idea that he is of necessity an alien. He was brought to our shores a naked, brutish, unclean, captive, pagan savage,* to be and remain a kind of connecting link between man and the beasts of burden. The great changes to result from his contact with a superb race of masters were not taken into account. As a social factor he was intended to be as purely zero as the brute at the other end of his plowline. The occasional mingling of his blood with that of the white man worked no change in the sentiment; one, two, four, eight multi-

---

* Sometimes he was not a mere savage but a trading, smithing, weaving, town-building, crop-raising barbarian.

plied upon or divided into zero still gave zero for the result. Generations of American nativity made no difference; his children and children's children were born in sight of our door, yet the old notion
held fast. He increased to vast numbers, but it never wavered. He
accepted our dress, language, religion, all the fundamentals of our
civilization, and became forever expatriated from his own land; still
he remained, to us, an alien. Our sentiment went blind. It did not see
that gradually, here by force and there by choice, he was fulfilling a
host of conditions that earned at least a solemn moral right to that
naturalization which no one at first had dreamed of giving him. Frequently he even bought back the freedom of which he had been
robbed, became a taxpayer, and at times an educator of his children
at his own expense; but the old idea of alienism passed laws to banish
him, his wife, and children by thousands from the state, and threw
him into loathsome jails as a common felon for returning to his
native land.*

It will be wise to remember that these were the acts of an enlightened, God-fearing people, the great mass of whom have passed
beyond all earthly accountability. They were our fathers. I am the son
and grandson of slaveholders. These were their faults; posterity will
discover ours; but these things must be frankly, fearlessly taken into
account if we are ever to understand the true interests of our peculiar
state of society.

Why, then, did this notion, that the man of color must always
remain an alien, stand so unshaken? We may readily recall how,
under ancient systems, he rose, not only to high privileges, but often
to public station and power. Singularly, with us the trouble lay in a
modern principle of liberty. The whole idea of American government rested on all men's equal, inalienable right to secure their life,
liberty, and the pursuit of happiness by governments founded in their
own consent. Hence, our Southern forefathers, shedding their blood,
or ready to shed it, for this principle, yet proposing in equal good
conscience to continue holding the American black man and mulatto
and quadroon in slavery, had to anchor that conscience, their conduct, and their laws in the conviction that the man of African tinc-
ture was, not by his master's arbitrary assertion merely, but by
nature and unalterably, an alien. If that hold should break, one single

* Notably in Louisiana in 1810 and subsequently.

wave of irresistible inference would lift our whole Southern social
fabric and dash it upon the rocks of Negro emancipation and enfranchisement. How was it made secure? Not by books, though they
were written among us from every possible point of view, but, with
the mass of our slaveowners, by the calm hypothesis of a positive,
intuitive knowledge. To them the statement was an axiom. They
abandoned the methods of moral and intellectual reasoning and fell
back upon this assumption of a God-given instinct, nobler than reason, and which it was an insult to a free man to ask him to prove on
logical grounds.

Yet it was found not enough. The slave multiplied. Slavery was a
dangerous institution. Few in the South today have any just idea how
often the slave plotted for his freedom. Our Southern ancestors were
a noble, manly people, springing from some of the most highly intelligent, aspiring, upright, and refined nations of the modern world;
from the Huguenot, the French chevalier, the Old Englander, the
New Englander. Their acts were not always right; whose are? But
for their peace of mind they had to believe them so. They therefore
spoke much of the Negro's contentment with that servile condition
for which nature had designed him. Yet there was no escaping the
knowledge that we dared not trust the slave caste with any power
that could be withheld from them. So the perpetual alien was made
also a perpetual menial, and the belief became fixed that this, too, was
nature's decree, not ours.

Thus we stood at the close of the Civil War. There were always
a few Southerners who did not justify slavery, and many who cared
nothing whether it was just or not. But what we have described was
the general sentiment of good Southern people. There was one modi-
fying sentiment. It related to the slave's spiritual interests. Thousands
of pious masters and mistresses flatly broke the shameful laws that
stood between their slaves and the Bible. Slavery was right; but religion, they held, was for the alien and menial as well as for the citizen
and master. They could be alien and citizen, menial and master, in
church as well as out; and they were.

Yet over against this lay another root of today's difficulties. This
perpetuation of the alien, menial relation tended to perpetuate the
vices that naturally cling to servility, dense ignorance, and a hopeless
separation from true liberty; and as we could not find it in our minds

to blame slavery with this perpetuation, we could only assume as a further axiom that there was, by nature, a disqualifying moral taint in every drop of Negro blood. The testimony of an Irish, German, Italian, French, or Spanish beggar in a court of justice was taken on its merits; but the colored man's was excluded by law wherever it weighed against a white man. The colored man was a prejudged culprit. The discipline of the plantation required that the difference between master and slave be never lost sight of by either. It made our master caste a solid mass, and fixed a common masterhood and subserviency between the ruling and the serving race.* Every one of us grew up in the idea that he had, by birth and race, certain broad powers of police over any and every person of color.

All at once the tempest of war snapped off at the ground every one of these arbitrary relations, without removing a single one of the sentiments in which they stood rooted. Then, to fortify the Freedman in the tenure of his new rights, he was given the ballot. Before this grim fact the notion of alienism, had it been standing alone, might have given way. The idea that slavery was right did begin to crumble almost at once. "As for slavery," said an old Creole sugar planter and former slaveowner to me, "it was damnable." The revelation came like a sudden burst of light. It is one of the South's noblest poets who has but just said:

> *I am a Southerner;*
> *I love the South; I dared for her*
> *To fight from Lookout to the sea,*
> *With her proud banner over me:*
> *But from my lips thanksgiving broke,*
> *As God in battle-thunder spoke,*
> *And that Black Idol, breeding drouth*
> *And dearth of human sympathy*
> *Throughout the sweet and sensuous South,*
> *Was, with its chains and human yoke,*
> *Blown hellward from the cannon's mouth,*
> *While Freedom cheered behind the smoke!* †

---

* The old Louisiana Black Code says, "That free people of color ought never to . . . presume to conceive themselves equal to the white; but, on the contrary, that they ought to yield to them in every occasion, and never speak or answer to them but with respect, under the penalty of imprisonment according to the nature of the offense." (Section 21, p. 164.)
† Maurice Thompson, in the *Independent*.

IV. WHAT THE WAR LEFT

With like readiness might the old alien relation have given way if we could only, while letting that pass, have held fast by the other old ideas. But they were all bound together. See our embarrassment. For more than a hundred years we had made these sentiments the absolute essentials to our self-respect. And yet if we clung to them, how could we meet the Freedman on equal terms in the political field? Even to lead would not compensate us; for the fundamental profession of American politics is that the leader is servant to his followers. It was too much. The ex-master and ex-slave—the quarterdeck and the forecastle, as it were—could not come together. But neither could the American mind tolerate a continuance of martial law. The agonies of Reconstruction followed.

The vote, after all, was a secondary point, and the robbery and bribery on one side, and whipping and killing on the other were but huge accidents of the situation. The two main questions were really these: on the Freedman's side, how to establish republican state government under the same recognition of his rights that the rest of Christendom accorded him; and on the former master's side, how to get back to the old semblance of republican state government, and—allowing that the Freedman was *de facto* a voter—still to maintain a purely arbitrary superiority of all whites over all blacks, and a purely arbitrary equality of all blacks among themselves as an alien, menial, and dangerous class.

Exceptionally here and there some one in the master caste did throw off the old and accept the new ideas, and, if he would allow it, was instantly claimed as a leader by the newly liberated thousands around him. But just as promptly the old master race branded him also an alien reprobate, and in ninety-nine cases out of a hundred, if he had not already done so, he soon began to confirm by his actions the brand on his cheek. However, we need give no history here of the dreadful episode of Reconstruction. Under an experimentative truce its issues rest today upon the pledge of the wiser leaders of the master class: Let us but remove the hireling demagogue, and we will see to it that the Freedman is accorded a practical, complete, and cordial recognition of his equality with the white man before the

law. As far as there has been any understanding at all, it is not that
the originally desired ends of Reconstruction have been abandoned,
but that the men of North and South have agreed upon a new, gentle, and peaceable method for reaching them; that, without change as
to the ends in view, compulsory Reconstruction has been set aside
and a voluntary Reconstruction is on trial.

It is the fashion to say we paused to let the "feelings engendered
by the war" pass away, and that they are passing. But let not these
truths lead us into error. The sentiments we have been analyzing, and
upon which we saw the old compulsory Reconstruction go hard
aground—these are not the "feelings engendered by the war." We
must disentangle them from the "feelings engendered by the war,"
and by Reconstruction. They are older than either. But for them
slavery would have perished of itself, and emancipation and Reconstruction been peaceful revolutions.

Indeed, as between master and slave, the "feelings engendered by
the war," are too trivial, or at least were too short-lived, to demand
our present notice. One relation and feeling the war destroyed: the
patriarchal tie and its often really tender and benevolent sentiment of
dependence and protection. When the slave became a Freedman, the
sentiment of alienism became for the first time complete. The abandonment of this relation was not one-sided; the slave, even before the
master, renounced it. Countless times, since Reconstruction began,
the master has tried, in what he believed to be everybody's interest,
to play on that old sentiment. But he found it a harp without strings.
The Freedman could not formulate, but he could see, all our old
ideas of autocracy and subserviency, of master and menial, of an
arbitrarily fixed class to guide and rule, and another to be guided and
ruled. He rejected the overture. The old master, his well-meant con-
descensions slighted, turned away estranged, and justified himself in
passively withholding that simpler protection without patronage
which any one American citizen, however exalted, owes to any other,
however humble. Could the Freedman in the bitterest of those days
have consented to throw himself upon just that one old relation, he
could have found a physical security for himself and his house
such as could not, after years of effort, be given him by constitutional amendments, Congress, United States marshals, regiments of
regulars, and ships of war. But he could not; the very nobility of the

civilization that had held him in slavery had made him too much a
man to go back to that shelter; and by his manly neglect to do so he
has proved to us who once ruled over him that, be his relative standing among the races of men what it may, he is worthy to be free.

V. FREED—NOT FREE

To be a free man is his still distant goal. Twice he has been a Freedman. In the days of compulsory Reconstruction he was freed in the
presence of his master by that master's victorious foe. In these days
of voluntary Reconstruction he is virtually freed by the consent of
his master, but the master retaining the exclusive right to define the
bounds of his freedom. Many everywhere have taken up the idea that
this state of affairs is the end to be desired and the end actually
sought in Reconstruction as handed over to the states. I do not
charge such folly to the best intelligence of any American community; but I cannot ignore my own knowledge that the average
thought of some regions rises to no better idea of the issue. The belief is all too common that the nation, having aimed at a wrong result
and missed, has left us of the Southern states to get now such other
result as we think best. I say this belief is not universal. There are
those among us who see that America has no room for a state of
society which makes its lower classes harmless by abridging their
liberties, or, as one of the favored class lately said to me, has "got 'em
so they don't give no trouble." There is a growing number who see
that the one thing we cannot afford to tolerate at large is a class of
people less than citizens; and that every interest in the land demands
that the Freedman be free to become in all things, as far as his own
personal gifts will lift and sustain him, the same sort of American
citizen he would be if, with the same intellectual and moral caliber,
he were white.

Thus we reach the ultimate question of fact. Are the Freedman's
liberties suffering any real abridgment? The answer is easy. The
letter of the laws, with a few exceptions, recognizes him as entitled to
every right of an American citizen; and to some it may seem unimportant that there is scarcely one public relation of life in the South
where he is not arbitrarily and unlawfully compelled to hold toward
the white man the attitude of an alien, a menial, and a probable

reprobate, by reason of his race and color. One of the marvels of future history will be that it was counted a small matter, by a majority of our nation, for six millions of people within it, made by its own decree a component part of it, to be subjected to a system of oppression so rank that nothing could make it seem small except the fact that they had already been ground under it for a century and a half.

Examine it. It proffers to the Freedman a certain security of life and property, and then holds the respect of the community, that dearest of earthly boons, beyond his attainment. It gives him certain guarantees against thieves and robbers, and then holds him under the unearned contumely of the mass of good men and women. It acknowledges in constitutions and statutes his title to an American's freedom and aspirations, and then in daily practice heaps upon him in every public place the most odious distinctions, without giving ear to the humblest plea concerning mental or moral character. It spurns his ambition, tramples upon his languishing self-respect, and indignantly refuses to let him either buy with money, or earn by any excellence of inner life or outward behavior, the most momentary immunity from these public indignities even for his wife and daughters. Need we cram these pages with facts in evidence, as if these were charges denied and requiring to be proven? They are simply the present avowed and defended state of affairs peeled of its exteriors.

Nothing but the habit, generations old, of enduring it could make it endurable by men not in actual slavery. Were we whites of the South to remain every way as we are, and our six million blacks to give place to any sort of whites exactly their equals, man for man, in mind, morals, and wealth, provided only that they had tasted two years of American freedom, and were this same system of tyrannies attempted upon them, there would be as bloody an uprising as this continent has ever seen. We can say this quietly. There is not a scruple's weight of present danger. These six million Freedmen are dominated by nine million whites immeasurably stronger than they, backed by the virtual consent of thirty-odd millions more. Indeed, nothing but the habit of oppression could make such oppression possible to a people of the intelligence and virtue of our Southern whites, and the invitation to practice it on millions of any other than the children of their former slaves would be spurned with a noble indignation.

Suppose, for a moment, the tables turned. Suppose the courts of our Southern states, while changing no laws requiring the impaneling of jurymen without distinction as to race, etc., should suddenly begin to draw their thousands of jurymen all black, and well-nigh every one of them counting, not only himself, but all his race, better than any white man. Assuming that their average of intelligence and morals should be not below that of jurymen as now drawn, would a white man, for all that, choose to be tried in one of those courts? Would he suspect nothing? Could one persuade him that his chances of even justice were all they should be, or all they would be were the court not evading the law in order to sustain an outrageous distinction against him because of the accidents of his birth? Yet only read white man for black man, and black man for white man, and that—I speak as an eye-witness—has been the practice for years, and is still so today; an actual emasculation, in the case of six million people both as plaintiff and defendant, of the right of trial by jury.

In this and other practices the outrage falls upon the Freedman. Does it stop there? Far from it. It is the first premise of American principles that whatever elevates the lower stratum of the people lifts all the rest, and whatever holds it down holds all down. For twenty years, therefore, the nation has been working to elevate the Freedman. It counts this one of the great necessities of the hour. It has poured out its wealth publicly and privately for this purpose. It is confidently hoped that it will soon bestow a royal gift of millions for the reduction of the illiteracy so largely shared by the blacks. Our Southern states are, and for twenty years have been, taxing themselves for the same end. The private charities alone of the other states have given twenty millions in the same good cause. Their colored seminaries, colleges, and normal schools dot our whole Southern country, and furnish our public colored schools with a large part of their teachers. All this and much more has been or is being done in order that, for the good of himself and everybody else in the land, the colored man may be elevated as quickly as possible from all the debasements of slavery and semi-slavery to the full stature and integrity of citizenship. And it is in the face of all this that the adherent of the old regime stands in the way to every public privilege and place—steamer landing, railway platform, theater, concert hall, art display, public library, public school, courthouse, church, everything —flourishing the hot branding iron of ignominious distinctions. He forbids the Freedman to go into the water until *he* is satisfied that he knows how to swim and, for fear he should learn, hangs millstones about his neck. This is what we are told is a small matter that will settle itself. Yes, like a roosting curse, until the outraged intelligence of the South lifts its indignant protest against this stupid firing into our own ranks.

VI. ITS DAILY WORKINGS

I say the outraged intelligence of the South; for there are thousands of Southern-born white men and women, in the minority in all these places—in churches, courts, schools, libraries, theaters, concert halls, and on steamers and railway carriages—who see the wrong and folly of these things, silently blush for them, and withhold their open protests only because their belief is unfortunately stronger in the futility of their counsel than in the power of a just cause. I do not justify their silence; but I affirm their sincerity and their goodly numbers. Of late years, when condemning these evils from the platform in Southern towns, I have repeatedly found that those who I had earlier been told were the men and women in whom the community placed most confidence and pride—they were the ones who, when I had spoken, came forward with warmest hand grasps and expressions of thanks, and pointedly and cordially justified my every utterance. And were they the young South? Not by half. The graybeards of the old times have always been among them, saying in effect, not by any means as converts, but as fellow discoverers, "Whereas we were blind, now we see."

Another sort among our good Southern people make a similar but feeble admission, but with the timeworn proviso that expediency makes a more imperative demand than law, justice, or logic, and demands the preservation of the old order. Somebody must be outraged, it seems; and if not the Freedman, then it must be a highly refined and enlightened race of people constantly offended and grossly discommoded, if not imposed upon, by a horde of tatterdemalions, male and female, crowding into a participation in their reserved privileges. Now look at this plea. It is simply saying in another way that though the Southern whites far outnumber the blacks, and though we hold every element of power in greater degree

than the blacks, and though the larger part of us claim to be sealed
by nature as an exclusive upper class, and though we have the courts
completely in our own hands, with the police on our right and the
prisons on our left, and though we justly claim to be an intrepid
people, and though we have a superb military experience, with ninety-
nine hundredths of all the military equipment and no scarcity of all
the accessories, yet with all these facts behind us we cannot make
and enforce that intelligent and approximately just assortment of persons in public places and conveyances on the merits of exterior
decency that is made in all other enlightened lands. On such a plea
are made a distinction and separation that not only are crude, invidious, humiliating, and tyrannous, but which do not reach their
ostensible end or come near it; and all that saves such a plea from
being a confession of driveling imbecility is its utter speciousness. It
is advanced sincerely; and yet nothing is easier to show than that
these distinctions on the line of color are really made not from any
necessity, but simply for their own sake—to preserve the old arbitrary supremacy of the master class over the menial without regard
to the decency or indecency of appearance or manners in either the
white individual or the colored.

See its everyday working. Any colored man gains unquestioned
admission into innumerable places the moment he appears as the
menial attendant of some white person, where he could not cross the
threshold in his own right as well-dressed and well-behaved master of
himself. The contrast is even greater in the case of colored women.
There could not be a system which when put into practice would
more offensively condemn itself. It does more: it actually creates the
confusion it pretends to prevent. It blunts the sensibilities of the ruling class themselves. It waives all strict demand for painstaking in
either manners or dress of either master or menial, and, for one result, makes the average Southern railway coach more uncomfortable
than the average of railway coaches elsewhere. It prompts the average Southern white passenger to find less offense in the presence of a
profane, boisterous, or unclean white person than in that of a quiet,
well-behaved colored man or woman attempting to travel on an
equal footing with him without a white master or mistress. The
holders of the old sentiments hold the opposite choice in scorn. It is
only when we go on to say that there are regions where the riotous

expulsion of a decent and peaceable colored person is preferred to his inoffensive company that it may seem necessary to bring in evidence. And yet here again it is prima-facie evidence; for the following extract was printed in the Selma (Alabama) *Times* not six months ago,* and not as a complaint, but as a boast:

"A few days since, a Negro minister, of this city, boarded the eastbound passenger train on the E. T., V. & G. Railway and took a seat in the coach occupied by white passengers. Some of the passengers complained to the conductor and brakemen, and expressed considerable dissatisfaction that they were forced to ride alongside of a Negro. The railroad officials informed the complainants that they were not authorized to force the colored passenger into the coach set apart for the Negroes, and they would lay themselves liable should they do so. The white passengers then took the matter in their own hands and ordered the ebony-hued minister to take a seat in the next coach. He positively refused to obey orders, whereupon the white men gave him a sound flogging and forced him to a seat among his own color and equals. We learned yesterday that the vanquished preacher was unable to fill his pulpit on account of the severe chastisement inflicted upon him. Now [says the delighted editor] the query that puzzles is, 'Who did the flogging?' "

And as good an answer as we can give is that likely enough they were some of the men for whom the whole South has come to a halt to let them get over the "feelings engendered by the war." Must such men, such acts, such sentiments stand alone to represent us of the South before an enlightened world? No. I say, as a citizen of an extreme Southern state, a native of Louisiana, an ex-Confederate soldier, and a lover of my home, my city, and my state, as well as of my country, that this is not the best sentiment in the South, nor the sentiment of her best intelligence; and that it would not ride up and down that beautiful land dominating and domineering were it not for its tremendous power as the *traditional* sentiment of a conservative people. But is not silent endurance criminal? I cannot but repeat my own words, spoken near the scene and about the time of this event. Speech may be silvern and silence golden; but if a lump of gold is only big enough, it can drag us to the bottom of the sea and hold us there while all the world sails over us.

* In the summer of 1884.

The laws passed in the days of compulsory Reconstruction requiring "equal accommodations," etc., for colored and white persons were Freedmen's follies. On their face they defeated their ends; for even in theory they at once reduced to half all opportunity for those more reasonable and mutually agreeable self-assortments which public assemblages and groups of passengers find it best to make in all other enlightened countries, making them on the score of conduct, dress, and price. They also led the whites to overlook what they would have seen instantly had these invidious distinctions been made against themselves: that their offense does not vanish at the guarantee against the loss of physical comforts. But we made, and are still making, a mistake beyond even this. For years many of us have carelessly taken for granted that these laws were being carried out in some shape that removed all just ground of complaint. It is common to say, "We allow the man of color to go and come at will, only let him sit apart in a place marked off for him." But marked off how? So as to mark him instantly as a menial. Not by railings and partitions merely, which, raised against any other class in the United States with the same invidious intent, would be kicked down as fast as put up, but by giving him besides, in every instance and without recourse, the most uncomfortable, uncleanest, and unsafest place; and the unsafety, uncleanness, and discomfort of most of these places are a shame to any community pretending to practice public justice. If any one can think the Freedman does not feel the indignities thus heaped upon him, let him take up any paper printed for colored men's patronage, or ask any colored man of known courageous utterance. Hear them:

"We ask not Congress, nor the Legislature, nor any other power, to remedy these evils, but we ask the people among whom we live. Those who *can* remedy them if they *will*. Those who have a high sense of honor and a deep moral feeling. Those who have one vestige of human sympathy left. . . . Those are the ones we ask to protect us in our weakness and ill-treatments. . . . As soon as the colored man is treated by the white man as a *man*, that harmony and pleasant feeling which should characterize all races which dwell together shall be the bond of peace between them."

Surely their evidence is good enough to prove their own feelings. We need not lean upon it here for anything else. I shall not bring forward a single statement of fact from them or any of their white friends who, as teachers and missionaries, share many of their humiliations, though my desk is covered with them. But I beg to make the same citation from my own experience that I made last June * in the far South. It was this: One hot night in September of last year † I was traveling by rail in the state of Alabama. At rather late bedtime there came aboard the train a young mother and her little daughter of three or four years. They were neatly and tastefully dressed in cool, fresh muslins, and as the train went on its way they sat together very still and quiet. At the next station there came aboard a most melancholy and revolting company. In filthy rags, with vile odors and the clanking of shackles and chains, nine penitentiary convicts chained to one chain, and ten more chained to another, dragged laboriously into the compartment of the car where in one corner sat this mother and child, and packed it full, and the train moved on. The keeper of the convicts told me he should take them in that car two hundred miles that night. They were going to the mines. My seat was not in that car, and I staid in it but a moment. It stank insufferably. I returned to my own place in the coach behind, where there was, and had all the time been, plenty of room. But the mother and child sat on in silence in that foul hole, the conductor having distinctly refused them admission elsewhere because they were of African blood, and not because the mother was, but because she was *not*, engaged at the moment in menial service. Had the child been white, and the mother not its natural but its hired guardian, she could have sat anywhere in the train, and no one would have ventured to object, even had she been as black as the mouth of the coalpit to which her loathsome fellow passengers were being carried in chains.

Such is the incident as I saw it. But the illustration would be incomplete here were I not allowed to add the comments I made upon it when in June last I recounted it, and to state the two opposite tempers in which my words were received. I said: "These are the facts. And yet you know and I know we belong to communities that, after years of hoping for, are at last taking comfort in the assurance of the nation's highest courts that no law can reach and stop this

* 1884.
† 1883.

shameful foul play until we choose to enact a law to that end ourselves. And now the East and North and West of our great and prosperous and happy country, and the rest of the civilized world, as far as it knows our case, are standing and waiting to see what we will write upon the white page of today's and tomorrow's history, now that we are simply on our honor and on the mettle of our far and peculiarly famed Southern instinct. How long, then, shall we stand off from such ringing moral questions as these on the flimsy plea that they have a political value, and, scrutinizing the Constitution, keep saying, 'Is it so nominated in the bond? I cannot find it; 'tis not in the bond.' "

With the temper that promptly resented these words through many newspapers of the neighboring regions there can be no propriety in wrangling. When regions so estranged from the world's thought carry their resentment no further than a little harmless invective, it is but fair to welcome it as a sign of progress. If communities nearer the great centers of thought grow impatient with *them*, how shall we resent the impatience of these remoter ones when their oldest traditions are, as it seems to them, ruthlessly assailed? There is but one right thing to do: it is to pour in upon them our reiterations of the truth without malice and without stint.

But I have a much better word to say. It is for those who, not voiced by the newspapers around them, showed both then and constantly afterward in public and private during my two days' subsequent travel and sojourn in the region, by their cordial, frequent, specific approval of my words, that a better intelligence is longing to see the evils of the old regime supplanted by a wiser and more humane public sentiment and practice. And I must repeat my conviction that if the unconscious habit of oppression were not already there, a scheme so gross, irrational, unjust, and inefficient as our present caste distinctions could not find place among a people so generally intelligent and high-minded. I ask attention to their bad influence in a direction not often noticed.

VII. THE "CONVICT LEASE SYSTEM"

In studying, about a year ago, the practice of letting out public convicts to private lessees to serve out their sentences under private management, I found that it does not belong to all our once slave states nor to all our once seceded states.* Only it is no longer in practice outside of them. Under our present condition in the South, it is beyond possibility that the individual black should behave mischievously without offensively rearousing the old sentiments of the still dominant white man. As we have seen, too, the white man virtually monopolizes the jury box. Add another fact: the Southern states have entered upon a new era of material development. Now, if with these conditions in force the public mind has been captivated by glowing pictures of the remunerative economy of the convict lease system, and by the seductive spectacle of mines and railways, turnpikes and levees that everybody wants and nobody wants to pay for, growing apace by convict labor that seems to cost nothing, we may almost assert beforehand that the popular mind will—not so maliciously as unreflectingly—yield to the tremendous temptation to hustle the misbehaving black man into the state prison under extravagant sentence and sell his labor to the highest bidder who will use him in the construction of public works. For ignorance of the awful condition of these penitentiaries is extreme and general, and the hasty half-conscious assumption naturally is that the culprit will survive this term of sentence, and its fierce discipline "teach him to behave himself."

But we need not argue from cause to effect only. Nor need I repeat one of the many painful rumors that poured in upon me the moment I began to investigate this point. The official testimony of the prisons themselves is before the world to establish the conjectures that spring from our reasoning. After the erroneous takings of the census of 1880 in South Carolina had been corrected, the population was shown to consist of about twenty blacks to every thirteen whites. One would therefore look for a preponderance of blacks on the prison lists; and inasmuch as they are a people only twenty years ago released from servile captivity, one would not be surprised to see that preponderance large. Yet, when the actual numbers confront us, our speculations are stopped with a rude shock; for what is to account for the fact that in 1881 there were committed to the state prison at Columbia, South Carolina, 406 colored persons and but 25

* See "The Convict Lease System in the Southern States," in [the *Century* for Feb. 1884].

whites? The proportion of blacks sentenced to the whole black population was one to every 1488; that of the whites to the white population was but one to every 15,644. In Georgia the white inhabitants decidedly outnumber the blacks; yet in the state penitentiary October 20, 1880, there were 115 whites and 1071 colored; or if we reject the summary of its tables and refer to the tables themselves (for the one does not agree with the other), there were but 102 whites and 1083 colored. Yet of 52 pardons granted in the two years then closing, 22 were to whites and only 30 to blacks. If this be a dark record, what shall we say of the records of lynch law? But for them there is not room here.

VIII. IN THE SCHOOLHOUSE

A far pleasanter aspect of our subject shows itself when we turn from courts and prisons to the schoolhouse. And the explanation is simple. Were our educational affairs in the hands of that not high average of the community commonly seen in jury boxes, with their transient sense of accountability and their crude notions of public interests, there would most likely be no such pleasant contrast. But with us of the South, as elsewhere, there is a fairly honest effort to keep the public-school interests in the hands of the state's most highly trained intelligence. Hence our public educational work is a compromise between the unprogressive prejudices of the general mass of the whites and the progressive intelligence of their best minds. Practically, through the great majority of our higher educational officers, we are fairly converted to the imperative necessity of elevating the colored man intellectually, and are beginning to see very plainly that the whole community is sinned against in every act or attitude of oppression, however gross or however refined.

Yet one thing must be said. I believe it is wise that all have agreed not to handicap education with the race question, but to make a complete surrender of that issue, and let it find adjustment elsewhere first and in the schools last. And yet, in simple truth and justice and in the kindest spirit, we ought to file one exception for that inevitable hour when the whole question must be met. There can be no more real justice in pursuing the Freedman's children with humiliating arbitrary distinctions and separations in the schoolhouses than in putting them upon him in other places. If, growing out of their peculiar mental structure, there are good and just reasons for their isolation, by all means let them be proved and known; but it is simply tyrannous to assume them without proof. I know that just here looms up the huge bugbear of Social Equality. Our eyes are filled with absurd visions of all Shantytown pouring its hordes of unwashed imps into the company and companionship of our own sunny-headed darlings. What utter nonsense! As if our public schools had no gauge of cleanliness, decorum, or moral character! Social Equality! What a godsend it would be if the advocates of the old Southern regime could only see that the color line points straight in the direction of social equality by tending toward the equalization of all whites on one side of the line and of all blacks on the other. We may reach the moon some day, not social equality; but the only class that really effects anything toward it are the makers and holders of arbitrary and artificial social distinctions interfering with society's natural self-distribution. Even the little children everywhere are taught, and begin to learn almost with their A B Cs, that they will find, and must be guided by, the same variations of the social scale in the public school as out of it; and it is no small mistake to put them or their parents off their guard by this cheap separation on the line of color.

IX. THE QUESTION OF INSTINCT

But some will say this is not a purely artificial distinction. We hear much about race instinct. The most of it, I fear, is pure twaddle. It may be there is such a thing. We do not know. It is not proved. And even if it were established, it would not necessarily be a proper moral guide. We subordinate instinct to society's best interests as apprehended in the light of reason. If there is such a thing, it behaves with strange malignity toward the remnants of African blood in individuals principally of our own race, and with singular indulgence to the descendants of—for example—Pocahontas. Of mere race *feeling* we all know there is no scarcity. Who is stranger to it? And as another man's motive of private preference no one has a right to forbid it or require it. But as to its being an instinct, one thing is plain: if there is such an instinct, so far from excusing the malignant indignities prac-

ticed in its name, it furnishes their final condemnation; for it stands
to reason that just in degree as it is a real thing it will take care of
itself.

It has often been seen to do so, whether it is real or imaginary. I
have seen in New Orleans a Sunday-school of white children every
Sunday afternoon take possession of its two rooms immediately upon
their being vacated by a black school of equal or somewhat larger
numbers. The teachers of the colored school are both white and
black, and among the white teachers are young ladies and gentlemen
of the highest social standing. The pupils of the two schools are alike
neatly attired, orderly, and in every respect inoffensive to each other.
I have seen the two races sitting in the same public high-school and
grammar-school rooms, reciting in the same classes, and taking recess
on the same ground at the same time, without one particle of detri-
ment that any one ever pretended to discover, although the fiercest
enemies of the system swarmed about it on every side. And when in
the light of these observations I reflect upon the enormous educational task our Southern states have before them, the inadequacy of
their own means for performing it, the hoped-for beneficence of the
general government, the sparseness with which so much of our
Southern population is distributed over the land, the thousands of
school districts where, consequently, the multiplication of schools
must involve both increase of expense and reductions of efficiency, I
must enter some demurrer to the enforcement of the tyrannous sentiments of the old regime until wise experiments have established
better reasons than I have yet heard given.

X. THE CASE SUBMITTED

What need to say more? The question is answered. Is the Freedman
a free man? No. We have considered his position in a land whence
nothing can, and no man has a shadow of right to drive him, and
where he is being multiplied as only oppression can multiply a people. We have carefully analyzed his relations to the finer and prouder
race, with which he shares the ownership and citizenship of a region
large enough for ten times the number of both. Without accepting
one word of his testimony, we have shown that the laws made for his
protection against the habits of suspicion and oppression in his late

master are being constantly set aside, not for their defects, but for such merit as they possess. We have shown that the very natural source of these oppressions is the surviving sentiments of an extinct and now universally execrated institution; sentiments which no intelligent or moral people should harbor a moment after the admission that slavery was a moral mistake. We have shown the outrageousness of these tyrannies in some of their workings, and how distinctly they antagonize every state and national interest involved in the elevation of the colored race. Is it not well to have done so? For, I say again, the question has reached a moment of special importance. The South stands on her honor before the clean equities of the issue. It is no longer whether constitutional amendments, but whether the eternal principles of justice, are violated. And the answer must—it shall—come from the South. And it shall be practical! It will not cost much. We have had a strange experience: the withholding of simple rights has cost much blood; such concessions of them as we have made have never yet cost a drop. The answer is coming. Is politics in the way? Then let it clear the track or get run over, just as it prefers. But, as I have said over and over to my brethren in the South, I take upon me to say again here, that there is a moral and intellectual intelligence there which is not going to be much longer beguiled out of its moral right of way by questions of political punctilio, but will seek that plane of universal justice and equity which it is every people's duty before God to seek, not along the line of politics—God forbid!—but across it and across it and across it as many times as it may lie across the path, until the whole people of every once slaveholding state can stand up as one man, saying, "Is the Freedman a free man?" and the whole world shall answer, "Yes."

Edward Bellamy [1850-1898]
Plutocracy or Nationalism [1889]

When Rome was the world's center, it used to be said that all roads
led to Rome; so now, when the burden upon the heart of the world
is the necessity of evolving a better society, it may be said that all
lines of thought lead to the social question. For the sake of clearness,
however, I shall this afternoon take up but a single thread of a single
line of argument, namely, the economic. I shall speak of the present
tendency to the concentration of the industrial and commercial business of the country in few and constantly fewer hands. The "Trust,"
or "Syndicate," in which this tendency finds its fullest expression, is
recognized as one of the most significant phenomena of the day. In
seeking a comparison for the bewildering effect produced by the
appearance of the Trust above the business horizon, one can only
think of the famous comets of past centuries and the terrors their
rays diffused, turning nations into flocks of sheep and perplexing
kings with fear of change. The advent of the Trust marks a crisis
more important than a hundred presidential elections rolled into one
—no less a crisis, in fact, than the beginning of the end of the com-

petitive system in industry. And the end is going to be rather near the beginning. It is in vain that the newspapers sit up nights with the patient and the legislatures feed it with tonics. It is moribund. The few economists who still seriously defend the competitive system are heroically sacrificing their reputations in the effort to mask the evacuation of a position which, as nobody knows better than our hard-headed captains of industry, has become untenable. Surely there have been few, if any, events in history on which the human race can be so unreservedly congratulated as the approaching doom of the competitive system. From the beginning, Christianity has been at odds with its fundamental principle—the principle that the only title to the means of livelihood is the strength and cunning to get and keep. Between Christianity and the competitive system a sort of *modus vivendi* has indeed been patched up, but Christianity has not thriven upon it, and the friends of Christianity are today vigorously repudiating it. As for the humane and philanthropic spirit, it has always found itself set at naught, and practically dammed up, by a system of which sordid self-seeking is so absolutely the sole idea that kindliness, humanity and generous feeling simply will not mix with it, while charity deranges the whole machine.

The final plea for any form of brutality in these days is that it tends to the survival of the fittest; and very properly this plea has been advanced in favor of the system which is the sum of all brutalities. But the retort is prompt and final. If this were indeed so, if the richest were the best, there would never have been any social question. Disparities of condition would have been willingly endured, which were recognized as corresponding to virtue or public service. But so far is this from being the case that the competitive system seems rather to tend to the survival of the unfittest. Not that the rich are worse than the poor, but that the competitive system tends to develop what is worst in the character of all, whether rich or poor. The qualities which it discourages are the noblest and most generous that men have, and the qualities which it rewards are those selfish and sordid instincts which humanity can only hope to rise above by outgrowing. But perhaps the explanation of the panic which the critical condition of the competitive system excites in some quarters lies in a belief that whatever may be said as to the immoral aspects of it, it is nevertheless so potent a machine for the production of wealth as to be indispensable. If such a belief be entertained, it is certainly the most groundless of superstitions. The problem before any system of national industry is to get the greatest result out of the natural resources of a country and the capital and labor of a people. In what way then, let us inquire, has the competitive system undertaken to solve this problem? It would seem a matter of obvious common sense that it should of course proceed upon some carefully digested and elaborated system of work to begin with. We should expect to see a close and constant oversight to secure perfect cooperation and coordination between all departments of work and all the workers. But in fact the competitive system offers nothing of the sort. Instead of a carefully digested plan of operation, there is no general plan at all; there are as many plans as there are workers, some twenty millions. There is no general oversight even of an advisory sort. Every worker not only has his own plan but is his own commander-in-chief. Not only is there no cooperation between the workers, but each is doing all he possibly can to hinder those who are working near him. Finally, not only are they not working in cooperation, but they are not even working for the same end—that is, the general wealth; but each to get the most for himself. And this he does, as frequently as not, by courses not only not contributory to the general wealth, but destructive of it.

If one of you should apply the same method of planlessness, lack of oversight and utter lack of cooperation, to your own factory or farm, your friends would have you in an asylum in twenty-four hours, and be called long suffering at that. Not a man in the country would undertake to cultivate a quarter of an acre, not a woman would undertake Spring cleaning, without more plan, more system for economy of effort, than goes to the correlated management of the industries of the United States.

If you would form a vivid conception of the economical absurdity of the competitive system in industry, consider merely the fact that its only method of improving the quality or reducing the price of goods is by overdoing their production. Cheapness, in other words, can only result under competition from duplication and waste of effort. But things which are produced with waste of effort are really dear, whatever they may be called. Therefore, goods produced under competition are made cheap only by being made dear. Such is the *reductio ad absurdum* of the system. It is in fact often true that the goods we pay the least for are in the end the most expensive to the nation owing to the wasteful competition which keeps down the price. All waste must in the end mean loss and, therefore, about once in seven years the country has to go into insolvency as the result of a system which sets three men to fighting for work which one man could do.

To speak of the moral iniquities of competition would be to enter on too large a theme for this time, and I only advert in passing to one feature of our present industrial system in which it would be hard to say whether inhumanity or economic folly predominated, and refer to the grotesque manner in which the burden of work is distributed. The industrial press-gang robs the cradle and the grave, takes the wife and mother from the fireside, and old age from the chimney-corner, while at the same time hundreds of thousands of strong men fill the land with clamors for an opportunity to work. The women and children are delivered to the task-masters, while the men can find nothing to do. There is no work for the fathers but there is plenty for the babies.

What then is the secret of this alarm over the approaching doom of a system under which nothing can be done properly without doing it twice, which can do no business without overdoing it, which can produce nothing without over-production, which in a land full of want cannot find employment for strong and eager hands, and finally which gets along at all only at a cost of a total collapse every few years, followed by a lingering convalescence?

When a bad king is mourned by his people, the conclusion must be that the heir to the throne is a worse case still. That appears to be, in fact, the explanation of the present distress over the decay of the competitive system. It is because there is fear of going from bad to worse, and that the little finger of combination will be thicker than the loins of competition; that while the latter system has chastised the people with whips, the Trust will scourge them with scorpions. Like the children of Israel in the desert, this new and strange peril causes the timid to sigh even for the iron rule of Pharaoh. Let us see if there be not also in this case a promised land, by the prospect of which faint hearts may be encouraged.

Let us first enquire whether a return to the old order of things, the free competitive system, is possible. A brief consideration of the causes which have led to the present world-wide movement for the substitution of combination in business for competition will surely convince any one that, of all revolutions, this is the least likely to go backward. It is a result of the increase in the efficiency of capital in great masses, consequent upon the inventions of the last and present generations. In former epochs the size and scope of business enterprises were subject to natural restrictions. There were limits to the amount of capital that could be used to advantage by one management. Today there are no limits, save the earth's confines, to the scope of any business undertaking; and not only no limit to the amount of capital that can be used by one concern, but an increase in the efficiency and security of the business proportionate to the amount of capital in it. The economies in management resulting from consolidation, as well as the control over the market resulting from the monopoly of a staple, are also solid business reasons for the advent of the Trust. It must not be supposed, however, that the principle of combination has been extended to those businesses only which call themselves Trusts. That would be greatly to under-estimate the movement. There are many forms of combination less close than the Trust, and comparatively few businesses are now conducted without some understanding approaching to a combination with its former competitors—a combination tending constantly to become closer.

From the time that these new conditions began to prevail, the· small businesses have been disappearing before the larger; the process has not been so rapid as people fancy whose attention has but lately been called to it. For twenty years past the great corporations have been carrying on a war of extermination against the swarm of small industrial enterprises which are the red blood corpuscles of a free competitive system and with the decay of which it dies. While the economists have been wisely debating whether we could dispense with the principle of individual initiative in business, that principle has passed away, and now belongs to history. Except in a few obscure corners of the business world, there is at present no opportunity for individual initiative in business unless backed by a large capital; and the size of the capital needed is rapidly increasing. Meanwhile, the same increase in the efficiency of capital in masses, which has destroyed the small businesses, has reduced the giants which have destroyed them to the necessity of making terms with one another. As in Bulwer Lytton's fancy of the coming race, the people of the Vril-ya had to give up war because their arms became so destructive as to threaten mutual annihilation, so the modern business world finds that the increase in the size and powers of the organizations of capital demands the suppression of competition between them, for the sake of self-preservation.

The first great group of business enterprises which adopted the principle of combining, instead of competing, made it necessary for every other group sooner or later to do the same or perish. For as the corporation is more powerful than the individual, so the syndicate overtops the corporation. The action of governments to check this logical necessity of economical evolution can produce nothing more than eddies in a current which nothing can check. Every week sees some new tract of what was once the great open sea of competition, wherein merchant adventurers used to fare forth with little capital besides their courage and come home loaded—every week now sees some new tract of this once open sea inclosed, dammed up, and turned into the private fish-pond of a syndicate.

I would also incidentally call your attention to the fact that these syndicates are largely foreign. Our new industrial lords are largely to be absentees. The British are invading the United States in these days with a success brilliantly in contrast with their former failures in that line. It is no wonder in these days, when the political basis of aristocracy is going to pieces, that foreign capitalists should rush into a market where industrial dukedoms, marquisates and baronies, richer than ever a king distributed to his favorites, are for sale. To say that from the present look of things the substantial consolidation of the various groups of industries in the country, under a few score great syndicates, is likely to be complete within fifteen years, is certainly not to venture a wholly rash statement.

So great an economic change as is involved in taking the conduct of the country's industries out of the hands of the people, and concentrating them in the management of a few great Trusts, could not, of course, be without important social reaction; and this is a reaction which is going to affect peculiarly what is called, in the hateful jargon of classes which we hope some day to do away with, the middle class. It is no longer a question merely for the poor and un-

educated what they are to do with their work; but for the educated
and well-to-do, also, where they are to find business to do and business investments to make. This difficulty cannot fail constantly to
increase, as one tract after another of the formerly free field of competition is inclosed by a new syndicate. The middle class, the business
class, is being turned into a proletarian class.

It is not difficult to forecast the ultimate issue of the concentration of industry if carried out on the lines at present indicated. Eventually, and at no very remote period, society must be divided into a
few hundred families of prodigious wealth on the one hand, a professional class dependent upon their favor but excluded from equality
with them and reduced to the state of lackeys; and underneath a vast
population of working men and women, absolutely without hope of
bettering a condition which would year by year sink them more and
more hopelessly into serfdom.

This is not a pleasant picture, but I am sure it is not an exaggerated statement of the social consequences of the syndicate system
carried out according to the plans of its managers. Are we going to
permit the American people to be rounded up, corralled and branded
as the dependents of some hundreds of great American and English
families? It is well never to despair of the Republic, but it is well to
remember that republics are saved not by a vague confidence in their
good luck, but by the clear vision and courageous action of their
citizens.

What, then, is the outcome? What way lies the Promised Land
which we may reach? For back to Egypt we cannot go. The return
to the old system of free competition and the day of small things is
not a possibility. It would involve a turning backward of the entire
stream of modern material progress.

If the nation does not wish to turn over its industries—and that
means its liberties as well—to an industrial oligarchy, there is but one
alternative; it must assume them itself. Plutocracy or Nationalism is
the choice which, within ten years, the people of the United States
will have virtually made.

Pray observe, ladies and gentlemen, that your argument is not
with me, or with those of us who call ourselves Nationalists. We are
not forcing upon you this alternative. The facts of the present state
and tendencies of national affairs are doing it. Your controversy is

with them, not with us. Convince yourself and your friends that this
talk about the invasion and appropriation of the field of general business by Trusts and Syndicates is all nonsense; satisfy yourself from a
careful study of the news of the day that there is really no tendency
toward the concentration in the hands of a comparatively few
powerful organizations of the means of the nation's livelihood, and
you can afford to disregard us entirely. Nothing is more certain than
that we cannot make a revolution with mere words, or unless the
facts are with us. Once admit, however, that the Trusts and Syndicates are facts, and that business is rapidly being concentrated in
their hands, and if you do not propose to submit to the state of
things which these admitted facts portend, you have no choice but to
be Nationalists. The burning issue of the period now upon us is to
be, is already, Nationalism against Plutocracy. In its fierce heat the
ties of old party allegiances are destined ere long to dissolve like
wax.

There have been many movements for a nobler order of society
which should embody and illustrate brotherly love, but they have
failed because the time was not right; that is to say, because the
material tendencies of the age did not work with the moral. Today
they work together. Today it matters little how weak the voice of
the preacher may be, for the current of affairs, the logic of events, is
doing his work and preaching his sermon for him. This is why there
is ground today for a higher-hearted hope that a great deliverance
for humanity is at hand than was ever before justified. When sun
and moon together pull the sea, a mighty tide is sure to come. So
today, when the spiritual and economic tendencies of the time are
for once working together; when the spirit of this age, and the divine
spirit of all ages, for once are on the same side, hope becomes reason,
and confidence is but common sense. Many, perhaps, have a vague
idea of what Nationalism is, and may wish to know in just what
ways our national assumption of the industries of the country is
going to affect the people beneficially. Briefly it may be said that the
result of this action will be to make the nation an equal industrial
partnership of its members as it already is an equal political partnership. The people will have formed themselves into a great joint
stock company for the general business of maintaining and enjoying
life. In this company every man and woman will be an equal stock-

holder, and the annual dividends will constitute their means of subsistence. While all share alike in the profits of the business, all will share according to their strength in its service, the nation undertaking to provide employment for all adapted to their gifts and guaranteeing the industrious against the idle by making industrial service obligatory. In effect the nation will then have become a universal insurance company for the purpose of assuring all its members against want, oppression, accident, or disability of whatever sort. It will be a mighty trust holding all the assets of society, moral, intellectual, and material, not only for the use of the present and passing generation, but for the benefit of the future race, looking to the ends of the world and the judgment of God. This is Nationalism.

Economically, it will be observed that the Nationalization of industry presents the logical, conclusive, and complete form of the evolution from competition toward combination which is now in progress. Every economical argument for the partial consolidation of industry already being effected, together with many new ones, tends to prove that a complete National consolidation would create a system better adapted to wealth production than any the world has seen.

It is important to state that while the economic movement toward consolidation is greatly hastening the nationalization of industries, that result will belong strictly to another line of evolution—the political. That is to say, the National idea—which is that of the union of a people to use the collective strength for the common protection and welfare,—distinctly and logically involved from the beginning the eventual nationalization of industry and the placing of the livelihood of the people under the national guarantee. If this be the true conception of a nation, then how preposterous is the notion that the mere exclusive possession, as against foreign nations, of a tract of land, in any true sense constitutes nationality. The house-lot is not a house. Such a community has merely secured a place on which to build a nation, that is all. The nation may be built or not. If it is built, it will consist in a social structure so roofed over and meetly joined together and so arranged within in all its details, as to provide in the highest possible degree for the happiness and welfare of all its people. Where are any such nations? you may well ask. And I reply that there are none, and never have been any. We consider that the

time is now arrived for building such nations, and that the first such
nation will be built in America. We call ourselves Nationalists because we have faith in this true nation that is to be, and have given
our hearts and our allegiance to it while yet it is unborn.

The fact that the use of the collective power for the common
benefit was first made in protecting the people in war, arose from the
fact that the first necessity of every community, the condition of its
further development, was protection from external foes. On the
other hand, let it be observed that the only object of this protection
from external interference was to provide the opportunity for internal development—that is, for building the social structure. It is thus
self-evident that no nation has an excuse for existing at all in which
this process of internal social evolution is not going on. The shell of
the egg is necessary to protect the vital principle within, during the
process of evolving to a complete life. That is its only use. A nation
which, having perfected its external organization, stops short there,
has failed of the object of its existence, and can be compared to nothing more savory than an addled egg.

Consider the consequences which have followed the arrest of the
development of the national idea at the point of division between the
foreign relations of the people and their internal affairs. In war, the
nation is the champion and the vindicator, against the world, of the
rights of person and property of its humblest citizen. But let peace
come, and this great archangel shrinks to the stature and functions of
a policeman. Do you protest in indignation against such an incongruity, do you demonstrate that in one week, the sufferings of citizens
from the oppressions, cruelties and maladjustments of industry exceed
in quantity and poignancy all that the nation has ever suffered from
foreign foes in its whole history? You will be told in reply that this is
all quite as it should be. It will be explained to you that the nation has
no business at all to concern itself for the welfare of its people, except
as and when that welfare may be threatened by foreigners. It has no
business to take cognizance of any trouble its people may be in, much
less to take steps to remedy it, unless it can be shown to be the result
in some way of foreign aggression. If a citizen desires the nation to
take an interest in his welfare, it is of no use at all for him to stay at
home and suffer. The nation will not regard such sufferings. It is far-
sighted and can only see the afflictions of its people when they are a

great way off. If the citizen would know how dear he is to the nation, let him go to the ends of the earth and get some foreigner to abuse him. Then indeed will he be astonished to find how devoted to his rights and his welfare his countrymen are. The very nation, which, so long as he stayed at home, did not care a pin whether he starved or lived, will incontinently, and without even stopping to find out whether he is in the right or not, enthusiastically sacrifice a hundred thousand soldiers, and double the national debt in his behalf.

May it not be well asked if mankind is, in any other respect, the victim of a theory at once so preposterous and so tragical in its consequences as that which limits the nation's guardianship of its people to their protection from foreigners? Is it any wonder that there should have arisen a sect of social reformers, under the name of Internationalists, who protest that the national organizations do but cumber the ground and block the progress of humanity? What is the use, may indeed be asked, of national distinctions, if they only fence off different sets of people to be fleeced and exploited separately? As well make the world all one pen, and save the expense of forts, fleets and armies. Nationalists, on the other hand, while admitting that the nations stand utterly condemned by their failure in the premises, yet maintain that through and by the nations, when they shall be aroused to assume and discharge their full responsibility for their people, is to come the deliverance of man.

We seek the final answer to the social question not in revolution, but in evolution; not in destruction, but in fulfillment,—the fulfillment of the hitherto stunted development of the nation according to its logical intent.

We hear much of the duty of the citizen to the country. We cannot hear too much of that, but it is time something were also said of the duty of the country to the citizen. We are taught, and taught rightly, that it is the duty of the people to die for the nation in war. Is it not time we heard something of the duty of the nation to keep the people from starving in peace? Are not these obligations properly to be regarded as reciprocal? Truly it appears to me that the account between this nation and its people shows the nation most grievously in debt to the people.

Yesterday was celebrated the sacred civic festival of our American year. As we laid the garlands upon the graves of our heroes, the memory of the day came freshly to our minds when they went forth to battle at the call of the country. We saw them turn away from wife and sweetheart, and from the dear kisses of their little ones—from the embraces of those who would die for them—to die for the country; gladly giving their heart's blood to cement her walls; eagerly proffering their tender bodies for her living barricades. How then has the country deserved, and how does she repay, this incredible devotion? this worship which the gods might envy? this tenderness which is not given to women?

Surely we may reasonably expect to find that the country cares well for such devoted citizens, and for their women and children, and that, in all ways which the collective might can support, protect and sustain them, it is employed to those ends. No doubt she sees to it that the workers who feed the world are not rewarded with oppression, but are at least guaranteed absolute security in their portion of the livelihood they create for all. To the sick, weak and infirm, and those who have no helper, we shall surely find the nation to be as the shadow of a great rock in a weary land. To the women, the nation is doubtless careful to lend of its mighty strength, that thereby they may be borne up, and not fall beneath the feet of their strong brothers; while as for the children—surely for them the nation reserves its peculiar tenderness and most vigilant watch-care. In these ways at least, as well as in a thousand others, we may confidently expect to find the nation using its strength to safeguard the people who in time of need so heroically succored it.

But no; not the least of these functions of justice, oversight, sustenance, and protection, do we find even an attempt to execute. The nation sits on high, indifferently looking on, while the people rend one another in a brutal and merciless struggle for existence, in which the weak, the old, the sick are trampled under foot. Serenely the nation looks on, while little children are driven to toil; while armies of women sell themselves for bread; while the sick and the old suffer want till the clods of the valley seem sweet to them and the earth is sodden with the tears of the widow and fatherless; while education becomes the privilege of the rich, work of the fortunate, and ignorance and poverty brood over the face of the land like a dense cloud, forbidding the light of the sun and the consolation of the stars to those who toil beneath.

Why then, since this is so, do not the people revile the country when she cries for help? How shall their passionate loyalty to a nation so ungrateful be accounted for? Were those heroes whose graves we decorated yesterday, victims of some strange madness such as has led men before in frenzy to sacrifice themselves to senseless idols? Not so. We are here come, rather, to a sacred mystery. The instinct of patriotism, like the instinct of maternity, is prophetic, and looks to the future, not the present, for its full vindication. The impulse that prompts the mother to sacrifice her life for the child, as yet not even able to understand her love, is implanted to the end that men worthy of sacrifice and capable of gratitude may later stand on the earth. So the instinct of patriotism—with difficulty to be reconciled with reason, while yet the nation so utterly fails to discharge a nation's responsibilities,—will be abundantly justified when the nation shall at last awake to them. In that day it will appear that the heroes who died that the nation might live did even better than they knew. In that day their sacrifice will be justified, and extolled in the eyes of all; their graves will blossom anew with the redoubled gratitude of men, and the spirits of the patriotic dead of all generations will see of the travail of their souls and be satisfied.

Nationalism—Principles, Purposes [1889]

No fact is better established by experience or more easily demonstrable by reason than that no republic can long exist unless a substantial equality in the wealth of citizens prevails. Wealth is power in its most concentrated, most efficient and most universally applicable form. In the presence of great disparities of wealth, social equality is at an end, industrial independence is destroyed, while mere constitutional stipulations as to the equal rights of citizens politically or before the law, become ridiculous.

One hundred years ago this Republic was founded upon a substantial equality in the condition of the people. It was not an equality established by law, but a condition resulting from a general state of poverty. For the first fifty years the increase in the wealth of the country was gradual, but within the last thirty years, owing to great mechanical and commercial inventions, it has multiplied by leaps and bounds, no longer growing from decade to decade by arithmetical, but by geometrical ratio. Instead of chiefly tending to enhance the general welfare of the people, this wealth has been mainly appropriated by a small class. At the present time the property of 100,000 men in the United States aggregates more than the total possessions of the rest of the people. Ten thousand people own nearly the whole of New York City with its 2,000,000 population. The entire bonded debt of the United States is held by 71,000 persons only, and over 60 per cent of it is in the hands of 23,000 persons. A volume of similar details might be furnished, but the situation may be summed up in one of the characteristic phrases of modern business, as follows: Mainly within thirty years 100,000 Americans have succeeded in "freezing out" their 65,000,000 co-partners as to more than half the assets of the concern, and at the rate of the last thirty years, within thirty years more will have secured the remainder.

That is the situation which has created the need for Nationalism. Those are the facts which account for the rapidity of its spread among the people.

For the sake of clearness let us distinguish the evil effects of the concentration of wealth in the hands of a few, as political, social and industrial. First as to the political effects.

The great corporations and combinations of capital dwarf our municipalities, overtop our States and are able to dictate to our National Legislature. The extent to which intimidation and bribery are employed to influence popular elections taints with the suspicion of fraud nearly all verdicts of the ballot when the majority is not large. Even in the grand appeal to the Nation the money power, by judicious concentration of corruption funds upon close States, is able to set at naught the will of the people. The titles of the Presidents of the Republic are no longer clear. What money cannot effect at the polls, by intimidation or by bribery, it does not hesitate to attempt by the corruption of individual legislators. Our municipal Council chambers are too often mere auction rooms, where public franchises are sold to the highest briber. The Legislatures of some of our greatest States are commonly said to be owned by particular corporations. The United States Senate is known as a "rich men's club," and in the lower House of Congress the schemes of capital have only to meet the sham opposition of the demagogue.

Socially, the vast disparities of wealth afford on every side inhuman contrasts of cruel want and inordinate luxury. The dazzling illustrations of pomp and power, which are the prizes of wealth, have lent to the pursuit of gain, at all times sufficiently keen, a feverish intensity and desperation never seen before in this or any other country. The moderate rewards of persistent industry seem contemptible in the midst of a universal speculative fever. In all directions the old ways of legitimate business and steady application are being abandoned for speculative projects, gambling operations and all manner of brigandage under forms of law. The spectacle presented in many instances of great riches, notoriously won by corrupt methods, has undermined the foundations of honesty. The epidemic of fraud and embezzlement, which today renders wealth so insecure, results from the general recognition that the possession of property, though it may have a legal title, is very commonly without a moral one. This is the deplorable explanation of the cynical tolerance of fraud by public opinion. Property will not, in the long run, be respected which is without some reasonable basis in industry or desert, and it is justly believed that much of the wealth of today could not stand inquiry into the means of its getting.

The consequences of the appropriation of the Nation's wealth by a few, and its further concentration by means of corporations and syndicates, have made possible a policy of monopolizing the control and profits of the industries of the country never before even imagined as among the possible perils of society. Hitherto, when oligarchies have usurped the political control of nations, they have left the conduct of business to the vulgar, but our new order of "nobility" is laying its foundations deeper by obtaining absolute mastery of the means of support of the people.

The effect of the concentration and combination of capital in the conduct of business has been directly to bring the wage-earner more completely than ever under the thumb of the employer. A chief object of combination is to control prices by restricting production—

that is to say, employment. While the competition among wage-earners for work is thus made more desperate, they are placed at the mercy of employers by the fact that in so far as employers are consolidated they no longer compete with one another.

But there could be no greater mistake than to fancy that the manual worker is peculiarly a victim of the present situation. The business men, the small tradesmen and manufacturers and the professional classes are suffering quite as much and have quite as much to dread from monopoly as has the poorest class of laborers.

As one after another the different departments of business, productive and distributive, pass under the single or syndicate control of the great capitalists, the so-called middle-class, the business men with moderate capital and plenty of wit, who used to conduct the business of the country, are crowded out of their occupation and rendered superfluous. No doubt the substitution of single for multiple control and the suppression of middle-men represents an economy. But the economy does not benefit the consumer, but goes to swell the profits of the capitalists. Meanwhile, fathers who were set up by their fathers in business find it impossible to do the like for their sons. There is now almost no opportunity left for starting in business in a moderate way; none, indeed, unless backed by large capital. What this means is, that we are rapidly approaching a time when there will be no class between the very rich, living on their capital, and a vast mass of wage and salary receivers absolutely dependent upon the former class for their livelihood. Meanwhile, as the immediate effect of the closing up of business careers to young men, the professions are being over-crowded to the starvation point. The problem before young men coming out of school or college, where to find a place in the world, was never so hard as now. Plutocracy is indeed fast leaving no place for a young man of independent and patriotic spirit, save in the party of Radical Social Reform.

The agricultural interests of the country are passing under the yoke of the money power quite as rapidly as the other forms of industry. The farmers are becoming expropriated by the operation of something like a universal mortgage system, and unless this tendency shall be checked the next generation of farmers will be a generation of tenants-at-will. The agrarian conditions of Ireland bid fair in no long time to be reproduced in portions of the West.

Such, fellow-countrymen, is the condition of political corruption, of social rottenness, of moral degeneracy, of industrial oppression, confusion and impending ruin which has resulted from the overthrow of our republican equality by the money power. If you would learn how republics perish, shut up your musty histories of Greece and Rome and look about you.

In time the money power is bound to seek protection from the rising discontent of the masses in a stronger form of government, and then the republic, long before dead, will be put out of sight. Then it will be too late to resist. Now it is not too late. The republic is being taken from us, but it is still possible to bring it back. Soon it will be too late to do so, but today there is yet time, though there is none to waste.

The Nationalists of the United States ask the cooperation of their fellow-countrymen to bring back the republic. To that end they propose a reorganization of the industrial system which shall restore the equality of the people and secure it by a perpetual guarantee.

In advocating a plan to secure equality we propose to graft no new or strange principle upon the republican idea, but the exercise of a power implied in the very idea of republicanism as ultimately necessary to its preservation. A republic is a form of government based upon and guaranteeing to all citizens a common interest in the national concern. That interest can be common only in proportion as it is substantially an equality of interest. The time has now come in America as it has come sooner or later in the history of all republics, when by the increase of wealth and by gross disparity in its distribution, this equality in its three aspects—political, social, industrial—is threatened with complete subversion. In order, under the changed conditions, to make good the original pledge of the republic to its citizens, it has become necessary to re-establish and maintain by some deliberate plan that economic equality, the basis of all other sorts of equality which, when the republic was established, existed in a substantial degree by nature. The question is not of assuming a new obligation, but whether the original ends and purposes of the republican compact shall be repudiated. We demand that the republic keep faith with the people, and propose a plan of industrial reorganization which seems to us the only possible means by which that faith can be kept. We are the true conservative party, because we are devoted to the maintenance of republican institutions against the revolution now being effected by the money power. We propose no revolution, but that the people shall resist a revolution. We oppose those who are overthrowing the republic. Let no mistake be made here. We are not revolutionists, but counter-revolutionists.

But while the guarantee of the equality of citizens is thus a measure amply justified and necessitated by merely patriotic and national considerations, without looking further for arguments, we do, in proposing this action, look both further and higher, to the ends of the earth, indeed, and the ultimate destiny of the race.

While historic, political and economic conditions require that this movement should be conducted on national lines by each people for itself, we hold the economic equality of all men a principle of universal application, having for its goal the eventual establishment of a brotherhood of humanity as wide as the world and as numerous as mankind. Those who believe that all men are brothers, and should so regard one another, must believe in the equality of men, for equals only can be brothers. Even brothers by blood do but hate each other the more bitterly for the tie when the inheritance is unequally parted between them, while strangers are presently made to feel like brothers by equality of interest and community of loss and gain. Therefore we look to the establishment of equality among men as the physical basis necessary to realize that brotherhood of humanity was regarded by the good and wise of all ages as the ideal state of society. We believe that a wonderful confluence, at the present epoch, of material and moral tendencies throughout the world, but especially in America, has made a great step in the evolution of humanity, not only possible, but necessary for the salvation of the race. We are surrounded by perils from which the only way of escape is the way upward.

The plan of industrial reorganization which Nationalism proposes is the very simple and obvious one of placing the industrial duty of citizens on the ground on which their military duty already rests. All able-bodied citizens are held bound to fight for the nation, and, on the other hand, the nation is bound to protect all citizens, whether they are able to fight or not. Why not extend this accepted principle to industry, and hold every able-bodied citizen bound to work for the nation, whether with mind or muscle, and, on the other hand, hold the nation bound to guarantee the livelihood of every citizen, whether able to work or not. As in military matters the duty to fight is

conditioned upon physical ability, while the right of protection is
conditioned only upon citizenship, so would we condition the obligation to work upon the strength to work, but the right to support
upon citizenship only.

The result would be to substitute for the present ceaseless industrial civil war, of which it would be hard to say whether it is more
brutal or more wasteful, a partnership of all the people, a great joint
stock company to carry on the business in the country for the benefit
of all equally, women with men, sick with well, strong with weak.
This plan of a national business partnership of equals we hold not
only to be demonstrably practicable, but to constitute as truly the
only scientific plan for utilizing the energy of the people in wealth
production, as it is the only basis for society consistent with justice,
with the sentiment of brotherhood, with the teachings of the founder
of Christianity, and, indeed, of the founders of all the great religions.

The realization of the proposed plan of industry requires as the
preliminary step the acquisition by the nation through its government,
national and municipal, of the present industrial machinery of the
country. It follows, therefore, that the Nationalists' programme must
begin with the progressive nationalization of the industries of the
United States. In proposing this course we are animated by no sentiment of bitterness toward individuals or classes. In antagonizing the
money power we antagonize not men but a system. We advocate no
rash or violent measures, or such as will produce derangement of
business or undue hardship to individuals. We aim to change the law
by the law, and the Constitution, if necessary, by constitutional
methods. As to the order in which industries should be nationalized,
priority should naturally be given to those the great wealth of which
renders them perilous to legislative independence, to those which deal
extortionately with the public or oppressively with employees, to
those which are highly systematized and centralized and to those
which can be readily assimilated by existing departments of government.

The following are some of the measures in the line of this policy
for which the country appears to be quite ready:

First—The nationalization of the railroads whether by constituting the United States perpetual receiver of all lines, to manage the
same for the public interest, paying over to the present security-
holders, pending the complete establishment of nationalism, such rea-

sonable dividends on a just valuation of the property as may be earned, or by some other practicable method not involving hardship to individuals.

The nationalization of the railroads is advisable for reasons apart from the Nationalist programme proper. Firstly, the railroad corporations, by the corrupt use of their vast wealth to procure and prevent legislation, are among the most formidable of the influences which are debauching our government. Secondly, the power they wield irresponsibly over the prosperity of cities, states and entire sections of the country, ought to be in the hands only of the general Government. Thirdly, the desperate rivalry of the railroads, with its incidents of reckless extension, duplication and rate wars, has long been a chief waste of the National resources and a cause of periodical business crises. Fourthly, the financial management of a large portion of the railroad system, together with its use for speculative purposes, has rendered railroad financiering the most gigantic gambling and general swindling business ever carried on in any country. Fifthly, the convenience and safety of the traveling public demand a uniform and harmonious railroad system throughout the country, nor is it likely that anything less will bring to an end the cruel slaughter of railroad employees now carried on by the corporations.

A second measure for which the people are certainly quite ready is the nationalization of the telegraphic and telephone services, and their addition to the Post Office, with which, as departments of transmission of intelligence, they should properly always have been connected.

Third—We propose that the express business of the country be assumed by the post-offices, according to the successful practices of other countries.

Fourth—We propose that the coal-mining business which at present is most rapaciously conducted as respects the public, and most oppressively as regards a great body of laborers, be nationalized, to the end that the mines may be continuously worked to their full capacity, coal furnished consumers at cost and the miners humanely dealt with. It is suggested that all mines hereafter discovered or opened shall be regarded as public property subject to just compensation for land.

Fifth—We propose that municipalities generally shall undertake lighting, heating, running of street-cars and such other municipal services as are now discharged by corporations, to the end that such services may be more cheaply and effectually rendered; that a fruitful source of political corruption be cut off and a large body of laborers be brought under humaner conditions of toil.

Pending the municipalization of all such services as have been referred to, Nationalists enter a general protest against the grant to corporations of any further franchises whether relating to transit, light, heat, water or other public services.

It is to be understood that all nationalized and municipalized businesses should be conducted at cost for use and not for profit, the amount at present paid in taxes by such businesses, being, however, charged upon them.

It is an essential feature of the method of Nationalism that as fast as industries are nationalized or municipalized, the conditions of the workers in them shall be placed upon a wholly humane basis. The hours of labor will be made reasonable, the compensation adequate, the conditions safe and healthful. Support in sickness, with pensions for disabled and superannuated workers, will be guaranteed.

The question will be asked, "How is this great force of public employees to be placed beyond the power of politicians and administrations to use for partisan purposes?" Nationalists respond by proposing a plan for organizing and maintaining all public departments of business that shall absolutely deprive parties or politicians of any direct or arbitrary power over their membership, either as to appointment, promotion or removal.

In the first place, it is understood that upon the nationalization of any business the existing force of employees and functionaries would be as a body retained. It is proposed that the service should be forthwith strictly graded and subsequently recruited exclusively by admissions to the lowest grade. All persons desiring to enter the service should be free to file applications at the proper bureau upon passing certain simple mental or physical tests, not competitive in character and adapted only to minimum grade of qualifications. Upon vacancies occurring in the force or a need of increase, the desired additions should be taken from the list of applicants on file, either in order of filed applications or, more perfectly to prevent fraud, by the drawing of the requisite number of names from a wheel containing the entire list of eligibles.

The chief of the department should be appointed at the discretion

of the political executive, whether of city, state or nation, in order
that responsibility for the general management of the business might
be brought home to an elective officer. With this exception, and
perhaps the further exceptions in some cases of the chiefs of a few
important subordinate branches of the service, all positions should be
filled by promotion in order of grades, such promotions to be determined by superiority of record and with certain requirements of
length of service. While the chief should have power of suspension,
no discharge from the service should take place save by verdict of a
tribunal expressly erected for that purpose, before which all charges
of fault or incompetence, whether by superior against subordinate, by
subordinate against superior or by the outside public against members
of the force, should be laid.

It is believed that such a plan of organization would absolutely
prevent administrative coercion of members of the public service for
partisan ends, and it is urgently recommended by Nationalists that it
be immediately applied to the Post-Office and all other business departments of the general Government, to the employees and to the
public works department of all municipalities.

The nationalization of the several great branches of public service
and productions which have been enumerated would directly affect,
greatly for the better, the condition of a million and a half of workers.

Here truly would be a bulwark against capitalism, against corporate usurpation, against industrial oppression. Here would be a mighty
nucleus for the coming industrial army. Here, too, would be a great
body of consumers whose needs would suggest and whose demands
would sustain the beginning of the coming National distributive and
productive system.

Even a single industry organized on such a basis as described and
guaranteeing to its toilers security, health, safety, dignity and justice
would be an object lesson of the advantage of Nationalism, even in its
beginnings, which would greatly hasten the general adoption of the
system. As a measure which cannot wait, seeing that at best, the
consequences of its postponement must continue to be felt long after
it is effected, we urge that such partisan support as may be needful to
enable them to attend school to the age of seventeen at least, be
provided under proper guards by the State for the children of parents
unable to maintain them without aid from their labor, and that with

this provision the employment of children should be unconditionally forbidden, and their education made rigidly compulsory, to the end that equality of educational opportunities for all be established.

Seeing that it would be manifestly inconsistent to make the education of our children compulsory while permitting the unlimited importation of adult ignorance and vice, a necessary complement to any system of education would be such regulation of foreign immigration as, without prejudice to honest intelligent poverty, should prevent the importation of persons grossly illiterate in their own language, of the defective and of criminals, merely political offenses not being considered crimes.

In reviewing the measures which have been mentioned as substantially representing, according to my belief, the present demands of Nationalists, it is observable that there is not one of them which is not demanded by considerations of humanity and public expediency quite without reference to Nationalism. A man has no need to be a Nationalist at all to advocate them. They have been freely and often favorably discussed by the press for years, and the leading political economists of this country and Europe are on record in favor of most if not all of them. As to some of the most important of these propositions, it is altogether probable that a majority of the American people, if they could be polled today would favor them. Nationalists may be, as some say, a very extravagant and fantastical set of people, but there is certainly nothing fantastical about the plan of action which they propose. There is not even anything which can be said to be greatly in advance of public opinion. This moderation is not accidental, nor yet a result of policy, but a necessary consequence of the method of Nationalism, which is essentially gradual and progressive rather than abrupt or violent, the method of evolution as opposed to that of revolution.

As to the relation of Nationalism to certain political and social issues of the day, a few words may be pertinent.

First, as to the tariff question. When the nation conducts all business for all, the common interest in every improvement will create a far stronger motive than now exists for all sorts of experiments and improvements in home industry, but owing to the public control of the production, tariffs will no longer be necessary as now to encourage private persons to undertake such new experiments. They will be tried as Government experiments are now tried, costing the country only the expense of the experimental stations, the Nation without prejudice to the experiment, continuing, if expedient, to buy in the cheapest market till its own is the cheapest.

The sectional jealousies based upon industrial rivalry, which now make States and cities enemies of each other's prosperity, and create sentiments of disunion will disappear when a National pooling of interests shall interest all equally in the prosperity of all.

As to the race issue, the industrial discipline imposed by Nationalism, while of general benefit to the white population of the South in common with that of the North, will be an ideal system for developing, guiding and elevating the recently emancipated colored race. It should be distinctly stated that the National plan will put an end to every form of sexual slavery and place feminine freedom and dignity upon an unassailable basis by making women independent of men for the means of support. We consider that by no method less radical can women's rightful equality with men be established, or, if established, maintained.

The evils of intemperance have their strongest roots in the brutalizing conditions of existing society, in the poverty of the masses, their gross ignorance, their misery and despair, in the slavish dependence of women and children upon men, and in the interest of a large class of tradesmen in the sale of intoxicants. If this be true, then the abolition of poverty, the universality of the best education, the complete enfranchisement of women, with a system of distribution which will destroy all personal motive for stimulating the sale of intoxicants, constitute surely the most promising as well as the most radical line of true temperance reform.

While the nationalizing of land in such time and by such methods as shall involve least hardships to any is a part of the National plan, and while the Nationalists meanwhile favor all practicable measures to prevent land monopoly and protect tenants and farmers, they are not persuaded that any measure applying to land alone would furnish a sufficient remedy for existing industrial and social troubles.

While sympathizing with all efforts of workers to obtain small immediate improvements in their condition, Nationalists would have them reflect that no great improvements can be gained, and if gained, can be secure, under the present industrial system, and that the only effectual and peaceable way of replacing that system by a better one is offered by Nationalism. It is also pointed out that the plan of Nationalism, by the humane and just conditions which will be secured to the employees of every industry, as it comes under the public control, offers not only the greatest ultimate results, but the speediest and surest way for immediately benefiting great bodies of workers absolutely without a risk of derangement to business.

One hundred years ago, after immemorial years of repression, the human passion for liberty, for equality, for brotherhood burst forth, convulsing Europe and establishing America. There is at hand another and far mightier outburst of the same forces, the results of which will be incomparably more profound, more far-reaching and more beneficent. Men now past middle age are likely to see in Europe the last throne fall, and in America the first complete and full-orbed republic arise, a republic at once political, industrial and social.

It is instructive for Americans to remember that there is scarcely any argument brought today against Nationalism which was not in substance brought against the experiment of political equality undertaken in this country a century ago; scarcely one which does not spring from the same low and suspicious estimate of human nature, the same distrust of the people, the same blind belief in personal and class leadership and authority; scarcely one which was not, as to principle, answered a hundred years ago by Madison, Hamilton and Jay in the 'Federalist'. And, indeed, how could it be otherwise? For what we propose is but the full development of the same republican experiment which the fathers undertook, a development now become necessary if we would preserve that experiment from ignominious failure.

In advocating equal rights for all as the only solution for the social and industrial problems of today, Nationalism follows the lines laid down by the founders of the Republic and proves itself the legitimate heir to the traditions and the spirit of 1776. Guided by those traditions, sustained by that spirit, we cannot fail.

Hamlin Garland [1860-1940]
FROM Crumbling Idols [1894]

Literary Masters

It is all a question of masters. There are masters who set free, there are masters who enslave. The best critic is he who frees, and the best criticism of the Old World has demanded of America, not imitations of the old forms, but free, faithful, characteristic work. It is the second-class critic who enslaves to the past, unable to comprehend advance.

For fifty years the best critics of England and of Europe have been calling for the native utterance of American writers. Posnett, Dowden, Taine, Véron, Freiligrath, Björnson, every critic who has perceived the forward movement of all art, has looked for a new conception, a new flavor, a new manner in American literature; and almost as constantly have the conservative and narrow critics of Boston and New York discouraged the truest, freest, utterance of the American poet and novelist. Not all have been of this hopeless type, but it remains true as a general comment. Upon the tender springing plant of American literature the frost of conservative culture has ever fallen. No wonder the young writer has turned to copying old forms, and so benumbed and sterilized his creative soul.

It really comes down to a contest, *not between the East and the West, but between sterile culture and creative work; between mere scholarship and wisdom; between conservative criticism and native original literary production.*

It is a question of books *versus* a literature of life, a struggle between adaptation to new surroundings and conformity to the ancestral type. It is only because there happen to be more conservatives in the East that the contest takes on the appearance of a war between East and West.

The East has its magnificent radicals, men who stand for free art and modern art. I do not forget the encouragement which the young writer owes to them; and yet these Eastern radicals will be the first to acknowledge the truth I write concerning the dangers of a centralization of power.

Shall our literature be a literature of the East, in mode if not in subject, or shall it be national? Is it to be only so large as the conception of New York and Boston critics, or shall it be as big and broad and democratic as the best thought of the whole nation? Is every work of art of every Western or Southern man or woman to be submitted with timid air to a jury that represents only a section of American society,—a section which is really nearer the Old World than the New,—or shall the writing be addressed to the whole nation? Is it safe to depend upon a half-dozen publishing houses, or a half-dozen magazines, for outlet? Would it not be better to have many magazines, provided, of course, the standard of excellence were high? Editors and critics are human. They are likely, at best, to be biassed by their personal likes and dislikes. It is not well that too much power be vested in any one city.

The supposition is that America finds amplest outlet in its present magazines, which are mainly in the East; but this is not true. It is a physical impossibility first; and, second, the theory is that the magazines are conducted for Eastern readers and in harmony with the traditions inherited by the East.

This is not complaint. No young writer of to-day has less cause for complaint than I. It is a statement of fact. There have arisen in the East these great magazines, hospitable in their way, but limited and inadequate to the expression of the art-life of this great nation. Their influence has been beneficent,—is yet; but there is a greater, truer, and freer expression of this people which will come only with the rise of native inland magazines.

As a matter of fact, this controversy is not sectional. It is in the East as well as in the West. All over America, in towns and cities, there are groups of readers whom our reigning monthlies do not represent. These readers have not only all the substantial acquirements of the conservatives, but possess a broader Americanism and a more intimate knowledge of American life than the aristocrat who prides himself on never having been farther west than Buffalo.

The culture represented by these radicals is not alone based upon knowledge of dead forms of art; it includes living issues of art. The number of these readers increases year by year. They stand for ideas and conditions of the future, and from them artists are rising, filled with courage and moved by convictions of their allegiance to truth. These people demand something more than smooth conventional work. They realize the tendency of young authors not to write as they really feel, but as they think the editors of the great magazines would have them write. They realize the danger which lies in putting into the hands of a few men, no matter how fine they may be, the directing power of American literature.

These cultivated and fearless radicals join Western readers in saying, "By what right do you of the conservative East assume to be final judges of American literature? What special qualifications does a residence on the extreme eastern shore of our nation give you, by which to settle all questions of a national literature?"

"The West is crude," Eastern critics are fond of saying.

"What do you mean by that? Do you mean that there are not men and women of the highest type in the West? Do you mean that we do not conform to your specific ideal of culture? Or do you mean that we have not been self-respecting enough in our own thinking? In what lies your assumed superiority over the West?"

To this the East replies: "We are the occupying claimants of the glory of the great men of this century's literature. We have also the great libraries, the museums, the great universities, which makes us the centre of critical intelligence. Granting your great railways, your stupendous enterprises, your great cities, the East still remains, and must remain, the centre of the highest literary culture in America."

The West rejoins: "That is precisely the point at issue. We deny that the East is to be the exclusive home of the broadest culture. We feel that much of this culture is barren and insincere. It has a hopeless outlook. It leads nowhere. It treads a circle, like the logic of the Koran.

"Culture is not creative power. Scholarship does not imply wisdom. We do not believe a city at our farthest East can remain the city most progressive in its art, most unbiassed in its judgment. The American city of broadest culture is henceforth to be that where the broad, free currents of American life daily ebb and flow. Such a city can know and will know all that the East knows of fundamental principles of art and literature, and will have a wider knowledge of the scope and action of American life."

The conservative of the East then says: "It will take a hundred years to make a Western city into the likeness of New York or Boston. The mellow charm of our literary atmosphere is the growth of two centuries. Our very streets are lined with suggestive walls and historical tablets. Our drawing-rooms and our clubs represent the flowering culture of ten generations."

The West quickly responds: "Keep your past. Hug your tablets to your bosom: you are welcome to all that; we are concerned with the present, and with the splendor of the future. Your culture is too largely of the moribund. Cleverness will not save you. You fail to conceive that our idea of culture is a different and, we assert, a higher form, because it refers to a culture of living forms. Besides, culture, even of the broadest, is only part of it; creative power is the crowning splendor of a nation's life. Scholarship does not necessarily imply wisdom. The study of the past does little for original genius. Libraries and universities produce few of the great leaders of American thought; all that books can give is our inheritance as well as yours."

The radical continues: "We deny that the Eastern 'art atmosphere' is necessary to the production of original works of art. We doubt the ability of New York or Boston criticism to pass final judgment upon a Western work of art, because the conditions of our life are outside the circle of its intimate knowledge. A criticism which stands for old things, we repeat, is not the criticism which is to aid the production of characteristic American art. America is not to submit itself to the past; it is to be free."

"Do you mean to say that you propose to cut loose from the past?" asks the traditionalist.

"By no means. We expect to assert our right to our day, as Russia, Norway, Germany, and others of our neighbor nations have done. The youth of all nations are in the fight. We are in the midst of one of those returning cycles of progress in art when the young man attains his majority. America has begun to attain her majority, to claim the right to a free choice in art as well as in government, to speak her own mind in her own way."

"Permit us—are you to use as a medium, Choctaw or English?" the East inquires, in strenuously polite phrase.

"That illustrates the inadequateness and the illiberality of your attitude toward us. We propose to use the speech of living men and women. We are to use actual speech as we hear it and to record its changes. We are to treat of the town and city as well as of the farm, each in its place and through the medium of characteristic speech. We propose to discard your nipping accent, your nice phrases, your balanced sentences, and your neat proprieties inherited from the eighteenth century. Our speech is to be as individual as our view of life."

The conservative replies: "Your view of life is of no interest to us. We do not see the necessity of Americans troubling to write or paint at all in future. We have books and paintings enough in the market. When we want a book, we buy a classic, and know what we are getting. When we want a painting, there are Corots and Rousseaus and Bouguereaus in the markets. Produce wheat and corn and railway-stocks yet awhile, and don't trouble yourself about literary problems. Read the classics for the improvement of your style. In the mean time, we will see that American literature is not vulgarized."

The Western radical warmly replies: "Who constituted you the guardian of American literature? What do you know of the needs or tastes of the people—"

Testily the aristocrat breaks in: "My dear sir, I care nothing for any tastes but my own. I don't like the common American in life, and I don't like him in books. Therefore—"

"There!" rejoins the radical, triumphantly. "There is a second point admitted. You have no sympathy with the American people of middle condition. You are essentially aristocratic and un-American in your position. From your library, or from the car-window, you look upon our life; that is the extent of your knowledge of our conditions, at best. For the most part you have never been west of Niagara Falls. How can you be just to this literature which springs from a life you do not know or sympathize with?

"We are forming a literature from direct contact with life, and such a literature can be estimated only by unbiassed minds and by comparison with nature and the life we live. Are you fitted to be the court of last resort upon our writing by reason of your study of English novels and your study of last-century painting? The test of a work of art is not, Does it conform to the best models? but, *Does it touch and lift and exalt men?* And we profess ability to perceive these qualities even west of the Mississippi River.

"We care little for the free-masonry of literary phrases which relates one spectacled enthusiast over dead men's books to a similar devotee of dead men's pictures. The West should aim to be wise rather than cultured. Wisdom is democratic, culture is an aristocrat. Wisdom is knowledge of principle, culture is a knowledge of forms and accepted conditions; the contention is world old, but necessary."

In the above colloquy, which may be typical in a measurable degree, I have put the Western radical over against the Eastern conservative, not because there are not conservatives in the West and radicals in the East, but because it is my sincere conviction, taking the largest view, that the interior is to be henceforth the real America. From these interior spaces of the South and West the most vivid and fearless and original utterance of the coming American democracy will come.

This is my conviction. I might adduce arguments based on the difference in races; I might speculate upon the influence of the Irish and Jews and Italians upon New York and Boston, and point out the quicker assimilation of the Teutonic races in the West, but it would only be passed over by the reader.

I confess to a certain failure to adequately portray what I mean. The things I would put in evidence are intangible. There are the mighty spaces of the West, the swarming millions of young men and women coming on in this empire of the Mississippi valley. Some imaginative Easterners caught glimpses of it at the Exposition, where the Eastern culture and accent was swallowed up and lost in the mighty flood of the middle West, unknown and inarticulate, but tremendous in its mass.

It is impossible to convey to others the immense faith in this land which intimate knowledge, gained by fifty thousand miles of travel, has built up in me. I know my West; I know its young minds. I can see their eager faces before me as I write. I know the throb of creative force everywhere thrilling the young men and women of these States, and yet I realize my inability to put it in evidence. I might mention names, writers of whose power I am assured,—they would be un-known; circumstances may crush them.

America is the most imaginative and creative of nations. Its inven-tions, its huge constructions, prove that. Only in its literature and art has it been bound by tradition. Its inventive and its original construc-tive genius arose from needs which dominated tradition. Its great railways, bridges, tunnels, transportation facilities, were perfected by minds which rose out of the common ranks of American life. The genuine American literature, in the same way, must come from the soil and the open air, and be likewise freed from tradition. Such an epoch is upon us.

Lowell felt this, in spite of his English environment. In his old age something of his early faith in America came back to him.

"No: morning and the dewy prime are born into the earth again with every child. It is our fault if drouth and dust usurp the noon. . . . Our time is not an unpoetic one. This lesson I learn from the past: that grace and goodness, the fair, the noble, and the true will never cease out of the world till the God from whom they emanate ceases out of it. . . . Lives of the great poets teach us they were the men of their generation who felt most deeply the meaning of the present."

Mark Twain [1835-1910]
Temperance and Women's Rights [1873]

The women's crusade against the rum sellers continues. It began in an Ohio village early in the new year, and has now extended itself eastwardly to the Atlantic seaboard, 600 miles, and westwardly (at a bound, without stopping by the way,) to San Francisco, about 2,500 miles. It has also scattered itself along down the Ohio and Mississippi rivers southwardly some ten or twelve hundred miles. Indeed, it promises to sweep, eventually, the whole United States, with the exception of the little cluster of commonwealths which we call New England. Puritan New England is sedate, reflective, conservative, and very hard to inflame.

The method of the crusaders is singular. They contemn the use of force in the breaking up of the whisky traffic. They only assemble before a drinking shop, or within it, and sing hymns and pray, hour after hour—and day after day, if necessary—until the publican's business is broken up and he surrenders. This is not force, at least they do not consider it so. After the surrender the crusaders march back to headquarters and proclaim the victory, and ascribe it to the powers above. They rejoice together awhile, and then go forth again in their strength and conquer another whisky shop with their prayers and hymns and their staying capacity (pardon the rudeness), and spread *that* victory upon the battle flag of the powers above. In this generous way the crusaders have parted with the credit of not less than three thousand splendid triumphs, which some carping people say they gained their own selves, without assistance from any quarter. If I am one of these, I am the humblest. If I seem to doubt that prayer is the agent that conquers these rum sellers, I do it honestly, and not in a flippant spirit. If the crusaders were to stay at home and pray for the rum seller and for his adoption of a better way of life, or if the crusaders even assembled together in a church and offered up such a prayer with a united voice, and it accomplished a victory, I would then feel that it was the praying that moved Heaven to do the miracle; for I believe that if the prayer is the agent that brings about the desired result, it cannot be necessary to pray the prayer in any particular place in order to get the ear, or move the grace, of the Deity. When the crusaders go and invest a whisky shop and fall to praying, one suspects that they are praying rather less to the Deity than *at* the rum man. So I cannot help feeling (after carefully reading the details of the rum sieges) that as much as nine tenths of the credit of each of the 3,000 victories achieved thus far belongs of right to the crusaders themselves, and it grieves me to see them give it away with such spendthrift generosity.

I will not afflict you with statistics, but I desire to say just a word or two about the character of this crusade. The crusaders are young girls and women—not the inferior sort, but the very best in the village communities. The telegraph keeps the newspapers supplied with the progress of the war, and thus the praying infection spreads from town to town, day after day, week after week. When it attacks a community it seems to seize upon almost everybody in it at once. There is a meeting in a church, speeches are made, resolutions are passed, a purse for expenses is made up, a "praying band" is appointed; if it be a large town, half a dozen praying bands, each numbering as many as a hundred women, are appointed, and the working district of each band marked out. Then comes a grand assault in force, all along the line. Every stronghold of rum is invested; first one and then another champion ranges up before the proprietor and offers up a special petition for him; he has to stand meekly there behind his bar, under the eyes of a great concourse of ladies who are better than he is and are aware of it, and hear all the secret iniquities of his business divulged to the angels above, accompanied by the sharp sting of wishes for his regeneration, which imply an amount of need for it which is in the last degree uncomfortable to him. If he holds out bravely, the crusaders hold out more bravely still—or at least more persistently; though I doubt if the grandeur of the performance would not be considerably heightened if one solitary crusader were to try praying at a hundred rum sellers in a body for a while, and see how it felt to have everybody against her instead of for her. If the man holds out the crusaders camp before his place and keep up the siege till they wear him out. In one case they besieged a rum shop two whole weeks. They built a shed before it and kept up the praying all night and all day long every day of the fortnight, and this in the bitterest winter weather, too. They conquered.

You may ask if such an investment and such interference with a man's business (in cases where he is "protected" by a license) is lawful? By no means. But the whole community being with the crusaders, the authorities have usually been overawed and afraid to execute the laws, the authorities being, in too many cases, mere little politicians, and more given to looking to chances of re-election than fearlessly discharging their duty according to the terms of their official oaths.

Would you consider the conduct of these crusaders justifiable? I do—thoroughly justifiable. They find themselves voiceless in the making of laws and the election of officers to execute them. Born with brains, born in the country, educated, having large interests at stake, they find their tongues tied and their hands fettered, while every ignorant whisky-drinking foreign-born savage in the land may hold office, help to make the laws, degrade the dignity of the former and break the latter at his own sweet will. They see their fathers, husbands, and brothers sit inanely at home and allow the scum of the country to assemble at the "primaries," name the candidates for office from their own vile ranks, and, unrebuked, elect them. They live in the midst of a country where there is no end to the laws and no beginning to the execution of them. And when the laws intended to

protect their sons from destruction by intemperance lie torpid and
without sign of life year after year, they recognize that here is a
matter which interests them personally—a matter which comes
straight home to them. And since they are allowed to lift no legal
voice against the outrageous state of things they suffer under this
regard, I think it is no wonder that their patience has broken down at
last, and they have contrived to persuade themselves that they are
justifiable in breaking the law of trespass when the laws that should
make the trespass needless are allowed by the voters to lie dead and
inoperative.

I cannot help glorying in the pluck of these women, sad as it is to
see them displaying themselves in these unwomanly ways; sad as it is
to see them carrying their grace and their purity into places which
should never know their presence; and sadder still as it is to see them
trying to save a set of men who, it seems to me, there can be no
reasonable object in saving. It does not become us to scoff at the
crusaders, remembering what it is they have borne all these years, but
it does become us to admire their heroism that boldly faces jeers,
curses, ribald language, obloquy of every kind and degree—in a word,
every manner of thing that pure-hearted, pure-minded women such as
these are naturally dread and shrink from, and remains steadfast
through it all, undismayed, patient, hopeful, giving no quarter, asking
none, determined to conquer and succeeding. It is the same old superb
spirit that animated that other devoted, magnificent, mistaken crusade
of six hundred years ago. The sons of such women as these must
surely be worth saving from the destroying power of rum.

The present crusade will doubtless do but little work against
intemperance that will be really permanent, but it will do what is as
much, or even more, to the purpose, I think. I think it will suggest to
more than one man that if women could vote they would vote on the
side of morality, even if they did vote and speak rather frantically and
furiously; and it will also suggest that when the women once made up
their minds that it was not good to leave the all-powerful "primaries"
in the hands of loafers, thieves, and pernicious little politicians, they
would not sit indolently at home as their husbands and brothers do
now, but would hoist their praying banners, take the field in force,
pray the assembled political scum back to the holes and slums where

they belong, and set up some candidates fit for decent human beings to vote for.

I dearly want the women to be raised to the political altitude of the negro, the imported savage, and the pardoned thief, and allowed to vote. It is our last chance, I think. The women will be voting before long, and then if a B. F. Butler can still continue to lord it in Congress; if the highest offices in the land can still continue to be occupied by perjurers and robbers; if another Congress (like the forty-second) consisting of 15 honest men and 296 of the other kind can once more be created, it will at last be time, I fear, to give over trying to save the country by human means, and appeal to Providence. Both the great parties have failed. I wish we might have a woman's party now, and see how that would work. I feel persuaded that in extending the suffrage to women this country could lose absolutely nothing and might gain a great deal. For thirty centuries history has been iterating and reiterating that in a moral fight woman is simply dauntless, and we all know, even with our eyes shut upon Congress and our voters, that from the day that Adam ate of the apple and told on Eve down to the present day, man, in a moral fight, has pretty uniformly shown himself to be an arrant coward.

I will mention casually that while I cannot bring myself to find fault with the women whom we call the crusaders, since I feel that they, being politically fettered, have the natural right of the oppressed to rebel, I have a very different opinion about the clergymen who have in a multitude of instances attached themselves to the movement, and by voice and act have countenanced and upheld the women in unlawfully trespassing upon whisky mills and interrupting the rum sellers' business. It seems to me that it would better become clergymen to teach their flocks to respect the laws of the land, and urge them to refrain from breaking them. But it is not a new thing for a thoroughly good and well-meaning preacher's soft heart to run away with his soft head.

꧁꧂

Diplomatic Pay and Clothes [1899]

Vienna, *January 5.*—I find in this morning's papers the statement that the government of the United States has paid to the two members of the Peace Commission entitled to receive money for their services one hundred thousand dollars each for their six weeks' work in Paris.

I hope that this is true. I will allow myself the satisfaction of considering that it *is* true, and of treating it as a thing finished and settled.

It is a precedent; and ought to be a welcome one to our country. A precedent always has a chance to be valuable (as well as the other way); and its best chance to be valuable (or the other way) is when it takes such a striking form as to fix a whole nation's attention upon it. If it come justified out of the discussion which will follow, it will find a career ready and waiting for it.

We realize that the edifice of public justice is built of precedents, from the ground upward; but we do not always realize that all the other details of our civilization are likewise built of precedents. The changes also which they undergo are due to the intrusion of new precedents, which hold their ground against opposition, and keep their place. A precedent may die at birth, or it may live—it is mainly a matter of luck. If it be imitated once, it has a chance; if twice, a better chance; if three times it is reaching a point where account must be taken of it; if four, five, or six times, it has probably come to stay—for a whole century, possibly. If a town start a new bow, or a new dance, or a new temperance project, or a new kind of hat, and can get the precedent adopted in the next town, the career of that precedent is begun; and it will be unsafe to bet as to where the end of its journey is going to be. It may not get this start at all, and may have no career; but if a crown prince introduce the precedent, it will attract vast attention, and its chances for a career are so great as to amount almost to a certainty.

For a long time we have been reaping damage from a couple of disastrous precedents. One is the precedent of shabby pay to public servants standing for the power and dignity of the Republic in foreign lands; the other is a precedent condemning them to exhibit themselves officially in clothes which are not only without grace or dignity, but are a pretty loud and pious rebuke to the vain and frivolous costumes worn by the other officials. To our day an American ambassador's official costume remains under the reproach of these defects. At a public function in a European court all foreign representatives except ours wear clothes which in some way distinguish them from the unofficial throng, and mark them as standing for their *countries*. But our representative appears in a plain black swallow-tail, which stands for neither country nor people. It has no nationality. It is found in all countries; it is as international as a night-shirt. It has no particular meaning: but our government tries to give it one; it tries to make it stand for Republican Simplicity, modesty and unpretentiousness. Tries, and without doubt fails, for it is not conceivable that this loud ostentation of simplicity deceives any one. The statue that advertises its modesty with a figleaf really brings its modesty under suspicion. Worn officially, our non-conforming swallow-tail is a declaration of ungracious independence in the matter of manners, and is uncourteous. It says to all around: "In Rome we do not choose to do as Rome does; we refuse to respect your tastes and your traditions; we make no sacrifice to any one's customs and prejudices; we yield no jot to the courtesies of life; we prefer our manners, and intrude them here."

That is not the true American spirit, and those clothes misrepresent us. When a foreigner comes among us and trespasses against our customs and our code of manners, we are offended, and justly so: but our government commands our ambassadors to wear abroad an official dress which is an offense against foreign manners and customs; and the discredit of it falls upon the nation.

We did not dress our public functionaries in undistinguished raiment before Franklin's time; and the change would not have come if he had been an obscurity. But he was such a colossal figure in the world that whatever he did of an unusual nature attracted the world's attention, and became a precedent. In the case of clothes, the next representative after him, and the next, had to imitate it. After that, the thing was custom: and custom is a petrifaction; nothing but dynamite can dislodge it for a century. We imagine that our queer official costumery was deliberately devised to symbolize our Republican Simplicity—a quality which we have never possessed, and are too old to acquire now, if we had any use for it or any leaning toward it. But it is not so; there was nothing deliberate about it: it grew naturally and heedlessly out of the precedent set by Franklin.

If it had been an intentional thing, and based upon a principle, it would not have stopped where it did; we should have applied it further. Instead of clothing our admirals and generals, for courts-martial and other public functions, in superb dress uniforms blazing with color and gold, the government would put them in swallow-tails and white cravats, and make them look like ambassadors and lackeys. If I am wrong in making Franklin the father of our curious official clothes, it is no matter—he will be able to stand it.

It is my opinion—and I make no charge for the suggestion—that, whenever we appoint an ambassador or a minister, we ought to confer upon him the temporary rank of admiral or general, and allow him to wear the corresponding uniform at public functions in foreign countries. I would recommend this for the reason that it is not consonant with the dignity of the United States of America that her representative should appear upon occasions of state in a dress which makes him glaringly conspicuous; and that is what his present undertaker-outfit does when it appears, with its dismal smudge, in the midst of the butterfly splendors of a Continental court. It is a most trying position for a shy man, a modest man, a man accustomed to being like other people. He is the most striking figure present; there is no hiding from the multitudinous eyes. It would be funny, if it were not such a cruel spectacle, to see the hunted creature in his solemn sables scuffling around in that sea of vivid color, like a mislaid Presbyterian in perdition. We are all aware that our representative's dress should not compel too much attention; for anybody but an Indian chief knows that that is a vulgarity. I am saying these things in the interest of our national pride and dignity. Our representative is the flag. He is the Republic. He is the United States of America. And when these embodiments pass by, we do not want them scoffed at; we desire that people shall be obliged to concede that they are worthily clothed, and politely.

Our government is oddly inconsistent in this matter of official dress. When its representative is a civilian who has not been a soldier, it restricts him to the black swallow-tail and white tie; but if he is a civilian who has been a soldier, it allows him to wear the uniform of his former rank as an official dress. When General Sickles was minister to Spain, he always wore, when on official duty, the dress uniform of a major-general. When General Grant visited foreign courts, he went handsomely and properly ablaze in the uniform of a full general, and was introduced by diplomatic survivals of his own Presidential Administration. The latter, by official necessity, went in the meek and lowly swallow-tail—a deliciously sarcastic contrast: the one dress representing the honest and honorable dignity of the nation; the other, the cheap hypocrisy of the Republican Simplicity tradition. In Paris our present representative can perform his official functions reputably clothed; for he was an officer in the Civil War. In London our late ambassador was similarly situated; for he also was an officer in the Civil War. But Mr. Choate must represent the Great Republic —even at official breakfast at seven in the morning—in that same old funny swallow-tail.

Our government's notions about proprieties of costume are indeed very, very odd—as suggested by that last fact. The swallow-tail is recognized the world over as not wearable in the daytime; it is a night-dress, and a night-dress only—a night-shirt is not more so. Yet, when our representative makes an official visit in the morning, he is obliged by his government to go in that night-dress. It makes the very cab-horses laugh.

The truth is, that for a while during the present century, and up to something short of forty years ago, we had a lucid interval, and dropped the Republican Simplicity sham, and dressed our foreign representatives in a handsome and becoming official costume. This was discarded by and by, and the swallow-tail substituted. I believe it is not now known which statesman brought about this change; but we all know that, stupid as he was as to diplomatic proprieties in dress, he would not have sent his daughter to a state ball in a corn-shucking costume, nor to a corn-shucking in a state ball costume, to be harshly criticized as an ill-mannered offender against the proprieties of custom in both places. And we know another thing,—*viz.* that he himself would not have wounded the tastes and feelings of a family of mourners by attending a funeral in their house in a costume which was an offense against the dignities and decorum prescribed by tradition and sanctified by custom. Yet that man was so heedless as not to reflect that *all* the social customs of civilized peoples are entitled to respectful observance, and that no man with a right spirit of courtesy in him ever has any disposition to transgress these customs.

There is still another argument for a rational diplomatic dress—a business argument. We are a trading nation; and our representative is our business agent. If he is respected, esteemed, and liked where he is stationed, he can exercise an influence which can extend our trade and forward our prosperity. A considerable number of his business activities have their field in his social relations; and clothes which do not offend against local manners and customs and prejudices are a valuable part of his equipment in this matter—would be, if Franklin had died earlier.

I have not done with gratis suggestions yet. We made a great and valuable advance when we instituted the office of ambassador. That lofty rank endows its possessor with several times as much influence, consideration, and effectiveness as the rank of minister bestows. For the sake of the country's dignity and for the sake of her advantage commercially, we should have ambassadors, not ministers, at the great courts of the world.

But not at present salaries! No; if we are to maintain present salaries, let us make no more ambassadors; and let us unmake those we have already made. The great position, without the means of respectably maintaining it—there could be no wisdom in that. A foreign representative, to be valuable to his country, must be on good terms with the officials of the capital and with the rest of the influential folk. He must mingle with this society; he cannot sit at home—it is not business, it butters no commercial parsnips. He must attend the dinners, banquets, suppers, balls, receptions, and must *return* these hospitalities. He should return as good as he gets, too, for the sake of the dignity of his country, and for the sake of Business. Have we ever had a minister or an ambassador who could do this on his salary? No—not once, from Franklin's time to ours. Other countries understand the commercial value of properly lining the pockets of their representatives; but apparently our government has not learned it. England is the most successful trader of the several trading nations;

and she takes good care of the watchmen who keep guard in her commercial towers. It has been a long time, now, since we needed to blush for our representatives abroad. It has become custom to send our fittest. We send men of distinction, cultivation, character—our ablest, our choicest, our best. Then we cripple their efficiency through the meagerness of their pay. Here is a list of salaries for English and American ministers and ambassadors:

	SALARIES	
CITY	AMERICAN	ENGLISH
Paris	$17,500	$45,000
Berlin	17,500	40,000
Vienna	12,000	40,000
Constantinople	10,000	40,000
St. Petersburg	17,500	39,000
Rome	12,000	35,000
Washington	—	32,500

Sir Julian Pauncefote, the English ambassador at Washington, has a very fine house besides—at no damage to his salary.

English ambassadors pay no house-rent; they live in palaces owned by England. Our representatives pay house-rent out of their salaries. You can judge by the above figures what kind of houses the United States of America has been used to living in abroad, and what sort of return-entertaining she has done. There is not a salary in our list which would properly house the representative receiving it, and, in addition, pay three thousand dollars toward his family's bacon and doughnuts—the strange but economical and customary fare of the American ambassador's household, except on Sundays, when petrified Boston crackers are added.

The ambassadors and ministers of foreign nations not only have generous salaries, but their governments provide them with money wherewith to pay a considerable part of their hospitality bills. I believe our government pays no hospitality bills except those incurred by the navy. Through this concession to the navy, that arm is able to do us credit in foreign parts; and certainly that is well and politic. But why the government does not think it well and politic that our diplomats should be able to do us like credit abroad is one of those myste-

rious inconsistencies which have been puzzling me ever since I
stopped trying to understand baseball and took up statesmanship as a
pastime.

To return to the matter of house-rent. Good houses, properly
furnished, in European capitals, are not to be had at small figures.
Consequently, our foreign representatives have been accustomed to
live in garrets—sometimes on the roof. Being poor men, it has been the
best they could do on the salary which the government has paid them.
How could they adequately return the hospitalities shown them? It
was impossible. It would have exhausted the salary in three months.
Still, it was their official duty to entertain the influentials after some
sort of fashion; and they did the best they could with their limited
purse. In return for champagne they furnished lemonade; in return
for game they furnished ham; in return for whale they furnished
sardines; in return for liquors they furnished condensed milk; in
return for the battalion of liveried and powdered flunkeys they furnished the hired girl; in return for the fairy wilderness of sumptuous
decorations they draped the stove with the American flag; in return
for the orchestra they furnished zither and ballads by the family; in
return for the ball—but they didn't return the ball, except in cases
where the United States lived on the roof and had room.

Is this an exaggeration? It can hardly be called that. I saw nearly
the equivalent of it once, a good many years ago. A minister was
trying to create influential friends for a project which might be worth
ten millions a year to the agriculturists of the Republic; and our
government had furnished him ham and lemonade to persuade the
opposition with. The minister did not succeed. He might not have
succeeded if his salary had been what it ought to have been—fifty or
sixty thousand dollars a year—but his chances would have been very
greatly improved. And in any case, he and his dinners and his country
would not have been joked about by the hard-hearted and pitied by
the compassionate.

Any experienced "drummer" will testify that, when you want to
do business, there is no economy in ham and lemonade. The drummer
takes his country customer to the theater, the opera, the circus; dines
him, wines him, entertains him all the day and all the night in luxuri-
ous style; and plays upon his human nature in all seductive ways. For
he knows, by old experience, that this is the best way to get a profit-

able order out of him. He has his reward. All governments except our own play the same policy, with the same end in view; and they also have their reward. But ours refuses to do business by business ways, and sticks to ham and lemonade. This is the most expensive diet known to the diplomatic service of the world.

Ours is the only country of first importance that pays its foreign representatives trifling salaries. If we were poor, we could not find great fault with these economies, perhaps—at least one could find a sort of plausible excuse for them. But we are not poor; and the excuse fails. As shown above, some of our important diplomatic representatives receive $12,000, others $17,500. These salaries are all ham and lemonade, and unworthy of the flag. When we have a rich ambassador in London or Paris, he lives as the ambassador of a country like ours ought to live, and it costs him $100,000 a year to do it. But why should we allow him to pay that out of his private pocket? There is nothing fair about it, and the Republic is no proper subject for any one's charity. In several cases our salaries of $12,000 should be $50,000; and all of the salaries of $17,500 ought to be $75,000 or $100,000, since we pay no representative's house-rent. Our State Department realizes the mistake which we are making, and would like to rectify it, but it has not the power.

When a young girl reaches eighteen she is recognized as being a woman. She adds six inches to her skirt, she unplaits her dangling braids and balls her hair on top of her head, she stops sleeping with her little sister and has a room to herself, and becomes in many ways a thundering expense. But she is in society now; and papa has to stand it. There is no avoiding it. Very well. The Great Republic lengthened her skirts last year, balled up her hair, and entered the world's society. This means that, if she would prosper and stand fair with society, she must put aside some of her dearest and darlingest young ways and superstitions, and do as society does. Of course, she can decline if she wants to; but this would be unwise. She ought to realize, now that she has "come out," that this is a right and proper time to change a part of her style. She is in Rome; and it has long been granted that when one is in Rome it is good policy to do as Rome does. To advantage Rome? No—to advantage herself.

If our government has really paid representatives of ours on the Paris Commission one hundred thousand dollars apiece for six weeks' work, I feel sure that it is the best cash investment the nation has made in many years. For it seems quite impossible that, with that precedent on the books, the government will be able to find excuses for continuing its diplomatic salaries at the present mean figure.

P. S.—Vienna, *January 10.*—I see, by this morning's telegraphic news, that I am not to be the new ambassador here, after all. This—well, I hardly know what to say. I—well, of course, I do not care anything about it; but it is at least a surprise. I have for many months been using my influence at Washington to get this diplomatic see expanded into an ambassadorship, with the idea, of course, th— But never mind. Let it go. It is of no consequence. I say it calmly; for I am calm. But at the same time— However, the subject has no interest for me, and never had. I never really intended to take the place, anyway— I made up my mind to it months and months ago, nearly a year. But now, while I am calm, I would like to say this—that so long as I shall continue to possess an American's proper pride in the honor and dignity of his country, I will not take any ambassadorship in the gift of the flag at a salary short of seventy-five thousand dollars a year. If I shall be charged with wanting to live beyond my country's means, I cannot help it. A country which cannot afford ambassadors' wages should be ashamed to have ambassadors.

Think of a seventeen-thousand-five-hundred-dollar ambassador! Particularly for *America*. Why, it is the most ludicrous spectacle, the most inconsistent and incongruous spectacle contrivable by even the most diseased imagination. It is a billionaire in a paper-collar, a king in a breechclout, an archangel in a tin halo. And, for pure sham and hypocrisy, the salary is just the match of the ambassador's official clothes—that boastful advertisement of a Republican Simplicity which manifests itself at home in Fifty-thousand-dollar salaries to insurance presidents and railway lawyers, and in domestic palaces whose fittings and furnishings often transcend in costly display and splendor and richness the fittings and furnishings of the palaces of the sceptered masters of Europe; and which has invented and exported to the Old World the palace-car, the sleeping-car, the tram-car, the electric trolley, the best bicycles, the best motor-cars, the steam-heater, the best and smartest systems of electric calls and telephonic aids to laziness and comfort, the elevator, the private bath-room (hot and cold water on tap), the palace hotel, with its multifarious conveniences, comforts, shows, and luxuries, the—oh, the list is interminable! In a word, Republican Simplicity found Europe with one shirt on her back, so to speak, as far as *real* luxuries, conveniences, and the comforts of life go, and has clothed her to the chin with the latter. We are the lavishest and showiest and most luxury-loving people on the earth; and at our masthead we fly one true and honest symbol, the gaudiest flag the world has ever seen. Oh, Republican Simplicity, there are many, many humbugs in the world, but none to which you need take off *your* hat!

The United States of Lyncherdom [1901]

I

And so Missouri has fallen, that great state! Certain of her children have joined the lynchers, and the smirch is upon the rest of us. That handful of her children have given us a character and labeled us with a name, and to the dwellers in the four quarters of the earth we are "lynchers," now, and ever shall be. For the world will not stop and think—it never does, it is not its way, its way is to generalize from a single sample. It will not say, "Those Missourians have been busy eighty years in building an honorable good name for themselves; these hundred lynchers down in the corner of the state are not real Missourians, they are renegades." No, that truth will not enter its mind; it will generalize from the one or two misleading samples and say, "The Missourians are lynchers." It has no reflection, no logic, no sense of proportion. With it, figures go for nothing; to it, figures reveal nothing, it cannot reason upon them rationally; it would say, for instance, that China is being swiftly and surely Christianized, since nine Chinese Christians are being made every day; and it would fail, with him, to notice that the fact that 33,000 pagans are *born* there every day, damages the argument. It would say, "There are a hundred lynchers there, therefore the Missourians are lynchers"; the considerable fact that there are two and a half million Missourians who are *not* lynchers would not affect their verdict.

II

Oh, Missouri!

The tragedy occurred near Pierce City, down in the southwestern corner of the state. On a Sunday afternoon a young white woman who had started alone from church was found murdered. For there are churches there; in my time religion was more general, more pervasive, in the South than it was in the North, and more virile and earnest, too, I think; I have some reason to believe that this is still the case. The young woman was found murdered. Although it was a region of churches and schools the people rose, lynched three negroes —two of them very aged ones—burned out five negro households, and drove thirty negro families into the woods.

I do not dwell upon the provocation which moved the people to these crimes, for that has nothing to do with the matter; the only question is, does the assassin *take the law into his own hands?* It is very simple, and very just. If the assassin be proved to have usurped the law's prerogative in righting his wrongs, that ends the matter; a thousand provocations are no defense. The Pierce City people had bitter provocation—indeed, as revealed by certain of the particulars, the bitterest of all provocations—but no matter, they took the law into their own hands, when by the terms of their statutes their victim would certainly hang if the law had been allowed to take its course, for there are but few negroes in that region and they are without authority and without influence in overawing juries.

Why has lynching, with various barbaric accompaniments, become a favorite regulator in cases of "the usual crime" in several parts of the country? Is it because men think a lurid and terrible punishment a more forcible object lesson and a more effective deterrent than a sober and colorless hanging done privately in a jail would be? Surely sane men do not think that. Even the average child should know better. It should know that any strange and much-talked-of event is always followed by imitations, the world being so well supplied with excitable people who only need a little stirring up to make them lose what is left of their heads and do mad things which they would not have thought of ordinarily. It should know that if a man jump off Brooklyn Bridge another will imitate him; that if a person venture down Niagara Whirlpool in a barrel another will imitate him; that if a Jack the Ripper make notoriety by slaughtering women in dark alleys he will be imitated; that if a man attempt a king's life and the newspapers carry the noise of it around the globe, regicides will crop up all around. The child should know that one much-talked-of outrage and murder committed by a negro will upset the disturbed intellects of several other negroes and produce a series of the very tragedies the community would so strenuously wish to prevent; that each of these crimes will produce another series, and year by year steadily increase the tale of these disasters instead of diminishing it; that, in a word, the lynchers are themselves the worst enemies of their women. The child should also know that by a law of our make, communities, as well as individuals, are imitators; and that a much-talked-of lynching will infallibly produce other lynchings here and there and yonder, and that in time these will breed a mania, a fashion; a fashion which will spread wide and wider, year by year, covering state after state, as with an advancing disease. Lynching has reached Colorado, it has reached California, it has reached Indiana—and now Missouri! I may live to see a negro burned in Union Square, New York, with fifty thousand people present, and not a sheriff visible, not a governor, not a constable, not a colonel, not a clergyman, not a law-and-order representative of any sort.

Increase in Lynching.—In 1900 there were eight more cases than in 1899, and probably this year there will be more than there were last year. The year is little more than half gone, and yet there are eighty-eight cases as compared with one hundred and fifteen for all of last year. The four Southern states, Alabama, Georgia, Louisiana, and Mississippi are the worst offenders. Last year there were eight cases in Alabama, sixteen in Georgia, twenty in Louisiana, and twenty in Mississippi—over one-half the total. This year to date there have been nine in Alabama, twelve in Georgia, eleven in Louisiana, and thirteen in Mississippi—again more than one-half the total number in the whole United States.—Chicago *Tribune.*

It must be that the increase comes of the inborn human instinct to imitate—that and man's commonest weakness, his aversion to being unpleasantly conspicuous, pointed at, shunned, as being on the unpopular side. Its other name is Moral Cowardice, and is the commanding feature of the make-up of 9,999 men to the 10,000. I am not offering this as a discovery; privately the dullest of us knows it to be true. History will not allow us to forget or ignore this supreme trait of our character. It persistently and sardonically reminds us that from the beginning of the world no revolt against a public infamy or oppression has ever been begun but by the one daring man in the 10,000, the rest timidly waiting, and slowly and reluctantly joining, under the influence of that man and his fellows from the other ten thousands. The abolitionists remember. Privately the public feeling was with them early, but each man was afraid to speak out until he got some hint that his neighbor was privately feeling as he privately felt himself. Then the boom followed. It always does. It will occur in New York, some day; and even in Pennsylvania.

It has been supposed—and said—that the people at a lynching enjoy the spectacle and are glad of a chance to see it. It cannot be true; all experience is against it. The people in the South are made like the people in the North—the vast majority of whom are right-hearted and compassionate, and would be cruelly pained by such a spectacle—and *would attend it,* and let on to be pleased with it, if the public approval seemed to require it. We are made like that, and we cannot help it. The other animals are not so, but we cannot help that, either. They lack the Moral Sense; we have no way of trading ours off, for a nickel or some other thing above its value. The Moral Sense teaches us what is right, and how to avoid it—when unpopular.

It is thought, as I have said, that a lynching crowd enjoys a lynching. It certainly is not true; it is impossible of belief. It is freely asserted—you have seen it in print many times of late—that the lynching impulse has been misinterpreted; that it is *not* the outcome of a spirit of revenge, but of a "mere atrocious hunger *to look upon human suffering.*" If that were so, the crowds that saw the Windsor Hotel burn down would have enjoyed the horrors that fell under their eyes. Did they? No one will think that of them, no one will make that charge. Many risked their lives to save the men and women who were in peril. Why did they do that? Because *none would disapprove.* There was no restraint; they could follow their natural impulse. Why does a crowd of the same kind of people in Texas, Colorado, Indiana, stand by, smitten to the heart and miserable, and

by ostentatious outward signs pretend to enjoy a lynching? Why does
it lift no hand or voice in protest? Only because it would be unpopular to do it, I think; each man is afraid of his neighbor's disapproval—a
thing which, to the general run of the race, is more dreaded than
wounds and death. When there is to be a lynching the people hitch up
and come miles to see it, bringing their wives and children. Really to
see it? No—they come only because they are afraid to stay at home,
lest it be noticed and offensively commented upon. We may believe
this, for we all know how *we* feel about such spectacles—also, how we
would act under the like pressure. We are not any better nor any
braver than anybody else, and we must not try to creep out of
it.

A Savonarola can quell and scatter a mob of lynchers with a mere
glance of his eye: so can a Merrill* or a Beloat.† For no mob has any
sand in the presence of a man known to be splendidly brave. Besides, a
lynching mob would *like* to be scattered, for of a certainty there are
never ten men in it who would not prefer to be somewhere else—and
would be, if they but had the courage to go. When I was a boy I saw
a brave gentleman deride and insult a mob and drive it away; and
afterward, in Nevada, I saw a noted desperado make two hundred
men sit still, with the house burning under them, until he gave them
permission to retire. A plucky man can rob a whole passenger train
by himself; and the half of a brave man can hold up a stagecoach and
strip its occupants.

Then perhaps the remedy for lynchings comes to this: station a
brave man in each affected community to encourage, support, and
bring to light the deep disapproval of lynching hidden in the secret
places of its heart—for it is there, beyond question. Then those communities will find something better to imitate—of course, being
human, they must imitate something. Where shall these brave men be
found? That is indeed a difficulty; there are not three hundred of
them in the earth. If merely *physically* brave men would do, then it
were easy; they could be furnished by the cargo. When Hobson
called for seven volunteers to go with him to what promised to be

---

* Sheriff of Carroll County, Georgia.—M.T.
† Sheriff, Princeton, Indiana. By that formidable power which lies in an
established reputation for cold pluck they faced lynching mobs and securely
held the field against them.—M.T.

certain death, four thousand men responded—the whole fleet, in fact. Because *all the world would approve.* They knew that; but if Hobson's project had been charged with the scoffs and jeers of the friends and associates, whose good opinion and approval the sailors valued, he could not have got his seven.

No, upon reflection, the scheme will not work. There are not enough morally brave men in stock. We are out of moral-courage material; we are in a condition of profound poverty. We have those two sheriffs down South who—but never mind, it is not enough to go around; they have to stay and take care of their own communities.

But if we only *could* have three or four more sheriffs of that great breed! Would it help? I think so. For we are all imitators: other brave sheriffs would follow; to be a dauntless sheriff would come to be recognized as the correct and only thing, and the dreaded disapproval would fall to the share of the other kind; courage in this office would become custom, the absence of it a dishonor, just as courage presently replaces the timidity of the new soldier; then the mobs and the lynchings would disappear, and—

However. It can never be done without some starters, and where are we to get the starters? Advertise? Very well, then, let us advertise.

In the meantime, there is another plan. Let us import American missionaries from China, and send them into the lynching field. With 1,511 of them out there converting two Chinamen apiece per annum against an uphill birth rate of 33,000 pagans per day,* it will take upward of a million years to make the conversions balance the output and bring the Christianizing of the country in sight to the naked eye; therefore, if we can offer our missionaries as rich a field at home at lighter expense and quite satisfactory in the matter of danger, why shouldn't they find it fair and right to come back and give us a trial? The Chinese are universally conceded to be excellent people, honest, honorable, industrious, trustworthy, kind-hearted, and all that—leave them alone, they are plenty good enough just as they are; and besides, almost every convert runs a risk of catching our civilization. We

* These figures are not fanciful; all of them are genuine and authentic. They are from official missionary records in China. See Doctor Morrison's book on his pedestrian journey across China; he quotes them and gives his authorities. For several years he has been the London *Times*'s representative in Peking, and was there through the siege.—M.T.

ought to be careful. We ought to think twice before we encourage a
risk like that; for, *once civilized, China can never be uncivilized again.*
We have not been thinking of that. Very well, we ought to think of it
now. Our missionaries will find that we have a field for them—and not
only for the 1,511, but for 15,011. Let them look at the following
telegram and see if they have anything in China that is more appetiz-
ing. It is from Texas:

> The negro was taken to a tree and swung in the air. Wood and
> fodder were piled beneath his body and a hot fire was made. *Then it
> was suggested that the man ought not to die too quickly, and he was
> let down to the ground while a party went to Dexter, about two miles
> distant, to procure coal oil.* This was thrown on the flames and the
> work completed.

We implore them to come back and help us in our need. Patriotism imposes this duty on them. Our country is worse off than China;
they are our countrymen, their motherland supplicates their aid in this
her hour of deep distress. They are competent; our people are not.
They are used to scoffs, sneers, revilings, danger; our people are not.
They have the martyr spirit; nothing but the martyr spirit can brave
a lynching mob, and cow it and scatter it. They can save their country, we beseech them to come home and do it. We ask them to read
that telegram again, and yet again, and picture the scene in their
minds, and soberly ponder it; then multiply it by 115, add 88; place
the 203 in a row, allowing 600 feet of space for each human torch, so
that there may be viewing room around it for 5000 Christian American men, women, and children, youths and maidens; make it night, for
grim effect; have the show in a gradually rising plain, and let the
course of the stakes be uphill; the eye can then take in the whole line
of twenty-four miles of blood-and-flesh bonfires unbroken, whereas if
it occupied level ground the ends of the line would bend down and be
hidden from view by the curvature of the earth. All being ready,
now, and the darkness opaque, the stillness impressive—for there
should be no sound but the soft moaning of the night wind and the
muffled sobbing of the sacrifices—let all the far stretch of kerosened
pyres be touched off simultaneously and the glare and the shrieks and
the agonies burst heavenward to the Throne.

There are more than a million persons present; the light from the fires flushes into vague outline against the night the spires of five thousand churches. O kind missionary, O compassionate missionary, leave China! come home and convert these Christians!

I believe that if anything can stop this epidemic of bloody insanities it is martial personalities that can face mobs without flinching; and as such personalities are developed only by familiarity with danger and by the training and seasoning which come of resisting it, the likeliest place to find them must be among the missionaries who have been under tuition in China during the past year or two. We have abundance of work for them, and for hundreds and thousands more, and the field is daily growing and spreading. Shall we find them? We can try. In 75,000,000 there must be other Merrills and Beloats; and it is the law of our make that each example shall wake up drowsing chevaliers of the same great knighthood and bring them to the front.

William Dean Howells [1837-1920]
FROM *Literature and Life* [1902]

Politics of American Authors

No thornier theme could well be suggested than I was once invited to
consider by an Englishman who wished to know how far American
politicians were scholars, and how far American authors took part in
politics. In my mind I first revolted from the inquiry, and then I cast
about, in the fascination it began to have for me, to see how I might
handle it and prick myself least. In a sort, which it would take too long
to set forth, politics are very intimate matters with us, and if one were
to deal quite frankly with the politics of a contemporary author, one
might accuse one's self of an unwarrantable personality. So, in what I
shall have to say in answer to the question asked me, I shall seek above
all things not to be quite frank.

I

My uncandor need not be so jealously guarded in speaking of authors no longer living. Not to go too far back among these, it is perfectly safe to say that when the slavery question began to divide all kinds of men among us, Lowell, Longfellow, Whittier, Curtis, Emerson, and Bryant more or less promptly and openly took sides against slavery. Holmes was very much later in doing so, but he made up for his long delay by his final strenuousness; as for Hawthorne, he was, perhaps, too essentially a spectator of life to be classed with either party, though his associations, if not his sympathies, were with the Northern men who had Southern principles until the civil war came. After the war, when our political questions ceased to be moral and emotional and became economic and sociological, literary men found their standing with greater difficulty. They remained mostly Republicans, because the Republicans were the anti-slavery party, and were still waging war against slavery in their nerves.

I should say that they also continued very largely the emotional tradition in politics, and it is doubtful if in the nature of things the politics of literary men can ever be otherwise than emotional. In fact, though the questions may no longer be so, the politics of vastly the greater number of Americans are so. Nothing else would account for the fact that during the last ten or fifteen years men have remained Republicans and remained Democrats upon no tangible issues except of office, which could practically concern only a few hundreds or thousands out of every million voters. Party fealty is praised as a virtue, and disloyalty to party is treated as a species of incivism next in wickedness to treason. If any one were to ask me why then American authors were not active in American politics, as they once were, I should feel a certain diffidence in replying that the question of other people's accession to office was, however emotional, unimportant to them as compared with literary questions. I should have the more diffidence because it might be retorted that literary men were too unpractical for politics when they did not deal with moral issues.

Such a retort would be rather mild and civil, as things go, and might even be regarded as complimentary. It is not our custom to be tender with any one who doubts if any actuality is right, or might not be bettered, especially in public affairs. We are apt to call such a one out of his name and to punish him for opinions he has never held. This may be a better reason than either given why authors do not take part in politics with us. They are a thin-skinned race, fastidious often, and always averse to hard knocks; they are rather modest, too, and distrust their fitness to lead, when they have quite a firm faith in their convictions. They hesitate to urge these in the face of practical politicians, who have a confidence in their ability to settle all affairs of State not surpassed even by that of business men in dealing with economic questions.

I think it is a pity that our authors do not go into politics at least for the sake of the material it would yield them; but really they do not. Our politics are often vulgar, but they are very picturesque; yet, so far, our fiction has shunned them even more decidedly than it has shunned our good society—which is not picturesque or apparently anything but a tiresome adaptation of the sort of drama that goes on abroad under the same name. In nearly the degree that our authors have dealt with our politics as material, they have given the practical politicians only too much reason to doubt their insight and their capacity to understand the mere machinery, the simplest motives, of political life.

II

There are exceptions, of course, and if my promise of reticence did not withhold me I might name some striking ones. Privately and unprofessionally, I think our authors take as vivid an interest in public affairs as any other class of our citizens, and I should be sorry to think that they took a less intelligent interest. Now and then, but only very rarely, one of them speaks out, and usually on the unpopular side. In this event he is spared none of the penalties with which we like to visit difference of opinion; rather they are accumulated on him.

Such things are not serious, and they are such as no serious man need shrink from, but they have a bearing upon what I am trying to explain, and in a certain measure they account for a certain attitude in our literary men. No one likes to have stones, not to say mud, thrown at him, though they are not meant to hurt him badly and may be partly thrown in joke. But it is pretty certain that if a man not in politics takes them seriously, he will have more or less mud, not to say stones, thrown at him. He might burlesque or caricature them, or misrepresent them, with safety; but if he spoke of public questions with heart and conscience, he could not do it with impunity, unless he were authorized to do so by some practical relation to them. I do not mean that then he would escape; but in this country, where there were once supposed to be no classes, people are more strictly classified than in any other. Business to the business man, law to the lawyer, medicine to the physician, politics to the politician, and letters to the literary man; that is the rule. One is not expected to transcend his function, and commonly one does not. We keep each to his last, as if there were not human interests, civic interests, which had a higher claim than the last upon our thinking and feeling. The tendency has grown upon us severally and collectively through the long persistence of our prosperity; if public affairs were going ill, private affairs were going so well that we did not mind the others; and we Americans are, I think, meridional in our improvidence. We are so essentially of to-day that we behave as if to-morrow no more concerned us than yesterday. We have taught ourselves to believe that it will all come out right in the end so long that we have come to act upon our belief; we are optimistic fatalists.

III

The turn which our politics have taken towards economics, if I may so phrase the rise of the questions of labor and capital, has not largely attracted literary men. It is doubtful whether Edward Bellamy himself, whose fancy of better conditions has become the abiding faith of vast numbers of Americans, supposed that he was entering the field of practical politics, or dreamed of influencing elections by his hopes of economic equality. But he virtually founded the Populist party, which, as the vital principle of the Democratic party, came so near electing its candidate for the Presidency some years ago; and he is to be named first among our authors who have dealt with politics on their more human side since the days of the old anti-slavery agitation. Without too great disregard of the reticence concerning the living which I promised myself, I may mention Dr. Edward Everett Hale and Colonel Thomas Wentworth Higginson as prominent authors who encouraged the Nationalist movement eventuating in Populism, though they were never Populists. It may be interesting to note that

Dr. Hale and Colonel Higginson, who later came together in their sociological sympathies, were divided by the schism of 1884, when the first remained with the Republicans and the last went off to the Democrats. More remotely, Colonel Higginson was anti-slavery almost to the point of Abolitionism, and he led a negro regiment in the war. Dr. Hale was of those who were less radically opposed to slavery before the war, but hardly so after it came. Since the war a sort of refluence of the old anti-slavery politics carried from his moorings in Southern tradition Mr. George W. Cable, who, against the white sentiment of his section, sided with the former slaves, and would, if the indignant renunciation of his fellow-Southerners could avail, have consequently ceased to be the first of Southern authors, though he would still have continued the author of at least one of the greatest American novels.

If I must burn my ships behind me in alleging these modern instances, as I seem really to be doing, I may mention Mr. R. W. Gilder, the poet, as an author who has taken part in the politics of municipal reform. Mr. Hamlin Garland has been known from the first as a zealous George man, or single-taxer. Mr. John Hay, Mr. Theodore Roosevelt, and Mr. Henry Cabot Lodge are Republican politicians, as well as recognized literary men. Mr. Joel Chandler Harris, when not writing *Uncle Remus*, writes political articles in a leading Southern journal. Mark Twain is a leading anti-imperialist.

IV

I am not sure whether I have made out a case for our authors or against them; perhaps I have not done so badly; but I have certainly not tried to be exhaustive; the exhaustion is so apt to extend from the subject to the reader, and I wish to leave him in a condition to judge for himself whether American literary men take part in American politics or not. I think they bear their share, in the quieter sort of way which we hope (it may be too fondly) is the American way. They are none of them politicians in the Latin sort. Few, if any, of our statesmen have come forward with small volumes of verse in their hands as they used to do in Spain; none of our poets or historians have been chosen Presidents of the republic as has happened to their French *confrères;* no great novelist of ours has been exiled as Victor Hugo was, or atrociously mishandled as Zola has been, though I have no doubt that if, for instance, one had once said the Spanish war wrong he would be pretty generally *conspué*. They have none of them reached the heights of political power, as several English authors have done; but they have often been ambassadors, ministers, and consuls, though they may not often have been appointed for political reasons. I fancy they discharge their duties in voting rather faithfully, though they do not often take part in caucuses or conventions.

As for the other half of the question—how far American politicians are scholars—one's first impulse would be to say that they never were so. But I have always had an heretical belief that there *were* snakes in Ireland; and it may be some such disposition to question authority that keeps me from yielding to this impulse. The law of demand and supply alone ought to have settled the question in favor of the presence of the scholar in our politics, there has been such a cry for him among us for almost a generation past. Perhaps the response has not been very direct, but I imagine that our politicians have never been quite so destitute of scholarship as they would sometimes make appear. I do not think so many of them now write a good style, or speak a good style, as the politicians of forty, or fifty, or sixty years ago; but this may be merely part of the impression of the general worsening of things, familiar after middle life to every one's experience, from the beginning of recorded time. If something not so literary is meant by scholarship, if a study of finance, of economics, of international affairs is in question, it seems to go on rather more to their own satisfaction than that of their critics. But without being always very proud of the result, and without professing to know the facts very profoundly, one may still suspect that under an outside by no means academic there is a process of thinking in our statesmen which is not so loose, not so unscientific, and not even so unscholarly as it might be supposed. It is not the effect of specific training, and yet it is the effect of training. I do not find that the matters dealt with are anywhere in the world intrusted to experts; and in this sense scholarship has not been called to the aid of our legislation or administration; but still I should not like to say that none of our politicians were scholars. That would be offensive, and it might not be true. In fact, I can think of several whom I should be tempted to call scholars if I were not just here recalled to a sense of my purpose not to deal quite frankly with this inquiry.

Frank Norris [1870-1902]
FROM *The Responsibilities of the Novelist* [1903]

᠀᠀᠀

The Frontier Gone At Last

Until the day when the first United States marine landed in China we had always imagined that out yonder somewhere in the West was the borderland where civilization disintegrated and merged into the untamed. Our skirmish-line was there, our posts that scouted and scrimmaged with the wilderness, a thousand miles in advance of the steady march of civilization.

And the Frontier has become so much an integral part of our conception of things that it will be long before we shall all understand that it is gone. We liked the Frontier; it was romance, the place of the poetry of the Great March, the firing-line where there was action and fighting, and where men held each other's lives in the crook of the forefinger. Those who had gone out came back with tremendous tales,

and those that stayed behind made up other and even more tremendous tales.

When we—we Anglo-Saxons—busked ourselves for the first stage
of the march, we began from that little historic reach of ground in the
midst of the Friesland swamps, and we set our faces Westward, feeling no doubt the push of the Slav behind us. Then the Frontier was
Britain and the sober peacefulness of land where are the ordered,
cultivated English farm-yards of to-day was the Wild West of the
Frisians of that century; and for the little children of the Frisian peat
cottages Hengist was the Apache Kid and Horsa Deadwood Dick—
freebooters, law-defiers, slayers-of-men, epic heroes, blood brothers, if
you please, of Boone and Bowie.

Then for centuries we halted and the van closed up with the
firing-line, and we filled all England and all Europe with our clamour
because for awhile we seemed to have gone as far Westward as it was
possible; and the checked energy of the race reacted upon itself, re-
bounded as it were, and back we went to the Eastward again—
crusading, girding at the Mahommedan, conquering his cities, breaking into his fortresses with mangonel, siege-engine and catapult—just
as the boy shut indoors finds his scope circumscribed and fills the
whole place with the racket of his activity.

But always, if you will recall it, we had a curious feeling that we
had not reached the ultimate West even yet, and there was still a
Frontier. Always that strange sixth sense turned our heads toward the
sunset; and all through the Middle Ages we were peeking and prying
into the Western horizon, trying to reach it, to run it down, and the
queer tales about Vineland and that storm-driven Viking's ship would
not down.

And then at last a naked savage on the shores of a little island in
what is now our West Indies, looking Eastward one morning, saw the
caravels, and on that day the Frontier was rediscovered, and promptly
a hundred thousand of the more hardy rushed to the skirmish-line and
went at the wilderness as only the Anglo-Saxon can.

And then the skirmish-line decided that it would declare itself
independent of the main army behind and form an advance column of
its own, a separate army corps; and no sooner was this done than
again the scouts went forward, went Westward, pushing the Frontier
ahead of them, scrimmaging with the wilderness, blazing the way. At

last they forced the Frontier over the Sierra Nevadas down to the edge of the Pacific. And here it would have been supposed that the Great March would have halted again as it did before the Atlantic, that here at last the Frontier ended.

But on the first of May, 1898, a gun was fired in the Bay of Manila, still farther Westward, and in response the skirmish-line crossed the Pacific, still pushing the Frontier before it. Then came a cry for help from Legation Street in Peking, and as the first boat bearing its contingent of American marines took ground on the Asian shore, the Frontier—at last after so many centuries, after so many marches, after so much fighting, so much spilled blood, so much spent treasure, dwindled down and vanished; for the Anglo-Saxon in his course of empire had circled the globe and brought the new civilization to the old civilization, and reached the starting point of history, the place from which the migrations began. So soon as the marines landed there was no longer any West, and the equation of the horizon, the problem of the centuries for the Anglo-Saxon was solved.

So, lament it though we may, the Frontier is gone, an idiosyncrasy that has been with us for thousands of years, the one peculiar picturesqueness of our life is no more. We may keep alive for many years the idea of a Wild West, but the hired cowboys and paid rough riders of Mr. William Cody are more like "the real thing" than can be found to-day in Arizona, New Mexico or Idaho. Only the imitation cowboys, the college-bred fellows who "go out on a ranch," carry the revolver or wear the concho. The Frontier has become conscious of itself, acts the part for the Eastern visitor; and this self-consciousness is a sign, surer than all others, of the decadence of a type, the passing of an epoch. The Apache Kid and Deadwood Dick have gone to join Hengist and Horsa and the heroes of the Magnusson Saga.

But observe. What happened in the Middle Ages when for awhile we could find no Western Frontier? The race impulse was irresistible. March we must, conquer we must, and checked in the Westward course of empire, we turned Eastward and expended the resistless energy that by blood was ours in conquering the Old World behind us.

To-day we are the same race, with the same impulse, the same power and, because there is no longer a Frontier to absorb our overplus of energy, because there is no longer a wilderness to conquer and because we still must march, still must conquer, we remember the old days when our ancestors before us found the outlet for their activity checked and, rebounding, turned their faces Eastward, and went down to invade the Old World. So we. No sooner have we found that our path to the Westward has ended than, reacting Eastward, we are at the Old World again, marching against it, invading it, devoting our overplus of energy to its subjugation.

But though we are the same race, with the same impulses, the same blood-instincts as the old Frisian marsh people, we are now come into a changed time and the great word of our century is no longer War, but Trade.

Or, if you choose, it is only a different word for the same race-characteristic. The desire for conquest—say what you will—was as big in the breast of the most fervid of the Crusaders as it is this very day in the most peacefully disposed of American manufacturers. Had the Lion-Hearted Richard lived to-day he would have become a "leading representative of the Amalgamated Steel Companies," and doubt not for one moment that he would have underbid his Manchester rivals in the matter of bridge-girders. Had Mr. Andrew Carnegie been alive at the time of the preachings of Peter the Hermit he would have raised a company of *gens d'armes* sooner than all of his brothers-in-arms, would have equipped his men better and more effectively, would have been first on the ground before Jerusalem, would have built the most ingenious siege-engine and have hurled the first cask of Greek-fire over the walls.

Competition and conquest are words easily interchangeable, and the whole spirit of our present commercial crusade to the Eastward betrays itself in the fact that we cannot speak of it but in terms borrowed from the glossary of the warrior. It is a commercial "invasion," a trade "war," a "threatened attack" on the part of America; business is "captured," opportunities are "seized," certain industries are "killed," certain former monopolies are "wrested away." Seven hundred years ago a certain Count Baldwin, a great leader in the attack of the Anglo-Saxon Crusaders upon the Old World, built himself a siege-engine which would help him enter the beleaguered city of Jerusalem. Jerusalem is beleaguered again to-day, and the hosts of the Anglo-Saxon commercial crusaders are knocking at the gates. And now a company named for another Baldwin—and, for all we know, a descendant of the Count—leaders of the invaders of the Old World, advance upon the city, and, to help in the assault, build an engine—only now the engine is no longer called a *mangonel*, but a locomotive.

The difference is hardly of kind and scarcely of degree. It is a mere matter of names, and the ghost of Saladin watching the present engagement might easily fancy the old days back again.

So perhaps we have not lost the Frontier, after all. A new phrase, reversing that of Berkeley's, is appropriate to the effect that "Eastward the course of commerce takes its way," and we must look for the lost battle-line not toward the sunset, but toward the East. And so rapid has been the retrograde movement that we must go far to find it, that scattered firing-line, where the little skirmishes are heralding the approach of the Great March. We must already go farther afield than England. The main body, even to the reserves, are intrenched there long since, and even continental Europe is to the rear of the skirmishers.

Along about Suez we begin to catch up with them where they are deepening the great canal, and we can assure ourselves that we are fairly abreast of the most distant line of scouts only when we come to Khiva, to Samarcand, to Bokhara and the Trans-Baikal country.

Just now one hears much of the "American commercial invasion of England." But adjust the field-glasses and look beyond Britain and search for the blaze that the scouts have left on the telegraph poles and mile-posts of Hungary, Turkey, Turkey in Asia, Persia, Baluchistan, India and Siam. You'll find the blaze distinct and the road, though rough hewn, is easy to follow. Prophecy and presumption be far from us, but it would be against all precedent that the Grand March should rest forever upon its arms and its laurels along the Thames, the Mersey and the Clyde, while its pioneers and frontiersmen are making roads for it to the Eastward.

Is it too huge a conception, too inordinate an idea to say that the American conquest of England is but an incident of the Greater Invasion, an affair of outposts preparatory to the real maneuver that shall embrace Europe, Asia, the whole of the Old World? Why not? And the blaze is ahead of us, and every now and then from far off there in the countries that are under the rising sun we catch the faint sounds of the skirmishing of our outposts. One of two things invariably happens under such circumstances as these: either the outposts fall back upon the main body or the main body moves up to the support of its outposts. One does not think that the outposts will fall back.

And so goes the great movement, Westward, then Eastward, forward and then back. The motion of the natural forces, the elemental energies, somehow appear to be thus alternative—action first, then reaction. The tides ebb and flow again, the seasons have their slow vibrations, touching extremes at periodic intervals. Not impossibly, in the larger view, is the analogy applicable to the movements of the races. First Westward with the great migrations, now Eastward with the course of commerce, moving in a colossal arc measured only by the hemispheres, as though upon the equator a giant dial hand oscillated, in gradual divisions through the centuries, now marking off the Wesward progress, now traveling proportionately to the reaction toward the East.

Races must follow their destiny blindly, but is it not possible that we can find in this great destiny of ours something a little better than mere battle and conquest, something a little more generous than mere trading and underbidding? Inevitably with constant change of environment comes the larger view, the more tolerant spirit, and every race movement, from the first step beyond the Friesland swamp to the adjustment of the first American theodolite on the Himalayan watershed, is an unconscious lesson in patriotism. Just now we cannot get beyond the self-laudatory mood, but is it not possible to hope that, as the progress develops, a new patriotism, one that shall include all peoples, may prevail? The past would indicate that this is a goal toward which we trend.

In the end let us take the larger view, ignoring the Frieslanders, the Anglo-Saxons, the Americans. Let us look at the peoples as people and observe how inevitably as they answer the great Westward impulse the true patriotism develops. If we can see that it is so with all of them we can assume that it must be so with us, and may know that mere victory in battle as we march Westward, or mere supremacy in trade as we react to the East, is not after all the great achievement of the races, but patriotism. Not our present selfish day conception of the word, but a new patriotism, whose meaning is now the secret of the coming centuries.

Consider then the beginnings of patriotism. At the very first, the seed of the future nation was the regard of family; the ties of common birth held men together, and the first feeling of patriotism was the love of family. But the family grows, develops by lateral branches, expands and becomes the clan. Patriotism is the devotion to the clan, and the clansmen will fight and die for its supremacy.

Then comes the time when the clans, tired of the roving life of herders, halt a moment and settle down in a chosen spot; the tent, becoming permanent, evolves the dwelling-house, and the encampment of the clan becomes at last a city. Patriotism now is civic pride; the clan absorbed into a multitude of clans is forgotten; men speak of themselves as Athenians, not as Greeks, as Romans, not as Italians. It is the age of cities.

The city extends its adjoining grazing fields; they include outlying towns, other cities, and finally the State comes into being. Patriotism no longer confines itself to the walls of the city, but is enlarged to encompass the entire province. Men are Hanoverians or Wurtemburgers, not Germans; Scots or Welsh, not English; are even Carolinians or Alabamans rather than Americans.

But the States are federated, pronounced boundaries fade, State makes common cause with State, and at last the nation is born. Patriotism at once is a national affair, a far larger, broader, truer sentiment than that first huddling about the hearthstone of the family. The word "brother" may be applied to men unseen and unknown, and a countryman is one of many millions.

We have reached this stage at the present, but if all signs are true, if all precedent may be followed, if all augury may be relied on and the tree grow as we see the twig is bent, the progress will not stop here.

By war to the Westward the family fought its way upward to the dignity of the nation; by reaction Eastward the nation may in patriotic effect merge with other nations, and others and still others, peacefully, the bitterness of trade competition may be lost, the business of the nations seen as a friendly *quid pro quo*, give and take arrangement, guided by a generous reciprocity. Every century the boundaries

are widening, patriotism widens with the expansion, and our countrymen are those of different race, even different nations.

Will it not go on, this epic of civilization, this destiny of the
races, until at last and at the ultimate end of all we who now arro-
gantly boast ourselves as Americans, supreme in conquest, whether of
battle-ship or of bridge-building, may realize that the true patriotism
is the brotherhood of man and know that the whole world is our
nation and simple humanity our countrymen?

Edgar Saltus [1855-1921]
FROM *The Pomps of Satin* [1904]

The Courts of Love

The 'varsities are changing their chairs. It is high time. When we
went to school we were taught everything it was easiest to forget.
Our curriculum comprised the largest possible number of subjects of
which the least possible use could be made. No doubt they were
designed for our good. Yet we are unable to conjecture what difference it would have made had they been intended for our harm. We
are unable to recall a single one of them.

Now, however, things are looking up. Oxford, for instance, is
throwing out Greek. In the States generally, instead of the mummeries
of the classics there are modern tongues and history in lieu of calculus.
That is all very well. But the change is susceptible of improvement.

Learning is not fashionable. Society has a great contempt for it. If
you do not believe us go and see. You will find it stupid to be wise all
alone. For alone you will be. The more you know the more diligently

you will be avoided. And very naturally. When your Red Badge of Culture does not put your hostess to sleep, it makes her feel ignorant. Neither proceeding is societyfied.

No, indeed. A knowledge of history, however superficial, will not bring you invitations to dinner. It is the same with languages. You may develop into a polyglot and die a bounder. The majority of us want to see our names in the papers. The ambition is quite noble, and highly American. But an acquaintance with Cicero, and even with Carnegie, won't help you to it.

It is for this reason that the change in chairs is susceptible of improvement. The better advancement and future prospects of the youth of the land demand that universities shall throw out history and languages as already they are throwing classics and calculus, and in their stead provide courses on What's What. And what is there but love and lucre?

These two little things are the motor forces of society. Beside them, barring the fashions and the charm of médisance—we say médisance because it sounds so much more cosmopolitan than tittle-tattle—nothing counts. No, nothing. Moreover, they are as potent and disintegrating as radium. Then, too, instruction regarding them is really diverting. Students who take them up will not merely learn something, they will remember it.

To be rich, for instance, seems complex. It is very simple. In an educational magazine, not long ago, Professor Carnegie, Professor Depew, and other savants indicated the process. According to Professor Carnegie you must push. Manners do not make the millionaire. Professor Depew advocated economy. A dollar in the bank is worth two on a margin. Professor Mills advised not more than eight hours' sleep. The other fellow must not catch you napping. Professor Morgan recommended investments. We believe that he has a few to unload. Now add all that up, and wealth, which looked complex, becomes easy as ping-pong.

Love is different. To love and to be loved seems simple. It is an art in itself. An art did we say? It is a philosophy, a theosophy, a pansophy in one. It is a science whereby the world, the flesh and the devil, the solar system, the universe—including what little we know of it and all that we do not—are reduced to a single being.

Sometimes to two beings. Occasionally to three. But though that

number is odd there is no luck in it. It is dangerous in addition to being inconvenient. You never have a spare moment, and are obliged to
lie like a thief. Two are less exasperating. Even with one carefully
selected being your hands are apt to be pretty full. When that being is
legally your very own you will find it advantageous to confine your
attentions to her. Anyway, it is generally admitted that it is better to
have loved your wife than never to have loved at all.

These remarks, of course, are purely ethical. Love is not that by a
long shot. Love is a vicious little chap. He is essentially selfish, and,
though little, the biggest tyrant out. A statue is not more callous. A
hyena is less cruel. Personally, we should prefer a cobra about the
house. A cobra you can elude. But not a bore—with civility at least—
and when that little chap is not sticking pins in you he rivals our best
selling novelists in the art of boring you stiff.

These observations have a false air of originality which, as is our
duty, we hasten to disclaim. They have all history for support. Out of
mythology,—and even there apart from the account which Apuleius
gave of Cupid and Pysche,—there is not a single story of happily
begun and happily ending love. No, not one. As pages turn and faces
emerge, always when they are not weeping they are yawning.

Why? Because love is not merely a philosophy. It is a poem
whose strophes age cannot construe and youth cannot scan. Because
of all subjects it is the most discussed and the least understood. Because it consists in the affection of someone else. Because affections are
like slippers, they will wear out. Because the angel who at twenty
appeals at thirty has been known to appal.

At the opera now and then you may, if you are in luck, hear
Cherubino ask the ladies who stand about to tell him what love is. The
ladies make no answer. Not because they are rude. Still less because
they are ignorant. But because Mozart did not care to have them disturb the innocence of the lad with an aria to the effect that love is the
fusion of two egotisms. Truth should be charming or else withheld.

Truth is the residuum of the sciences known as exact. Among
these sciences love, once upon a time, just escaped admittance. By way
of compensation it was codified. What is more to the point, the code
became law. Judgments in accordance therewith were rendered in
courts open and plenary.

In 1907 these courts are to be revived. They are to be revived for the pleasure, it may be, but certainly for the instruction, of visitors to an exposition which is to be then held in Milan. You may have wondered what we were driving at. There is the reason of these remarks. There, too, is a tip for St Louis. There also, perhaps, is the model of the schooling which the youth of our country lack.

We inject that "perhaps" because we are sceptical by trade. But we live in hopes. Meanwhile, Milan being remote, 1907 far away, and St Louis uncertain, a summary of the instruction may contain a few hints.

The elements of this instruction are rumoured to have originated in Broceliande, a country which, as everybody knows, lies somewhere within the confines of the Arthurian myth. By whom they were evolved is undetermined. But it has been authoritatively suspected that they were cradled in the manuals of pure courtesy with which chivalry was familiar and which society has forgot. Anyway, they once existed, and existing filtered into Provence, where a parliament of peeresses did them over into a pandect, of which the statutes survive. Here are some of them. By way of commentary we may note that licit means lawful, and illicit the reverse. There is nothing like making things clear. But oyez:

It is illicit to kiss and tell.

It is illicit to love anyone whom it would be illicit to marry.

It is illicit to love two at a time.

It is licit to be loved by two, by three, by any number.

It is illicit to be open-armed and close-fisted.

It is licit for a woman to love her husband—if she can.

It is illicit for a lover to do aught that might displease his lady.

It is licit for a lady to be less circumspect. Et cetera, and so forth.

These statutes, always candid, sometimes are profound. They disclose an understanding of the heart and its subtleties. It was over matters of this delicate nature that the Courts of Love claimed—and exercised—jurisdiction. The judges were dames of high degree. At the time, in cases of tort and even of felony, the lord of a fief possessed the right of justice, high and low. But there are crimes now which the law cannot reach. It was the same way then. There were, and are, contentions which no mere male, however enfieffed, may adjust. It was to remedy this defect that the wives of the seigneurs erected tribunals of their own. Their strength was their weakness. They were pretty, and that appealed. They were patrician, and that appeased. They took themselves seriously too, and that must have been very satisfactory. Moreover, if not always clement, occasionally they were quaint.

Here is an instance. A confidant charged by a friend with messages of love found the young person so much to his taste that he addressed her in his own behalf. Instead of being repulsed his advances were encouraged. Whereupon the injured party brought suit. The prothonotary of the court relates that the plaintiff, having humbly prayed that the fraud be submitted to the Countess of Champagne, the latter, sitting in banco with sixty dames, heard the complaint, and after due deliberation handed down the following decision:—"It is ordered that the defendants be henceforth debarred from the frequentation of honest people."

Here is another case. A knight was commanded by his lady not to say or do anything publicly in her praise. It so fell about that her name was lightly taken. The knight challenged the defamer. Thereupon the lady contended that he had forfeited all claim to her regard. Action having been brought the court decided that the defence of a lady is never illicit, and it was ordered that the knight be rehabilitated in favour and reinstated in grace. Which, the prothonotary avers, was done.

But how? There is the beautiful part of it. To the Courts of Love no sheriffs were attached. Judgments were enforced not by a constabulary but by the community. Disregard of a decision entailed not loss of liberty but loss of caste. In the case of a man there was exclusion from the field. Entrance was denied him at the tournaments. In the case of a woman the drawbridges were up. Throughout the land there was no one to receive her. As a result the delinquent was rare. So, too, was contempt of the jurists.

Such were the Courts of Love. Women then did more or less as they saw fit, and it was in order that they might do what was fittest that those tribunals were established. They had another purpose. In guiding the affections they educated them. Women were admonished to love and instructed how to. They were taught, we will assume, that they who please generally fail to please profoundly. They were further taught, we will also assume, that to please profoundly a woman should never let herself be wholly known. Even in her kisses there should be mystery. Moreover, they were taught, or ought to have been, that when to mystery there be added uncertainty, and the two be sufficiently fused, then the party of the second part is not merely profoundly pleased but confoundedly perplexed. The poor devil does not know where he is at.

For of all things mystery and perplexity disturb the imagination most. Of all factors in an enduring affection the most potent is imagination. The woman who leaves a man nothing to bother about leaves him nothing to dread. Inconstancy is the result. The brute turns to pastures new.

But the woman of whom a man is never sure has him crazy about her for the rest of his wretched career. He feels that he could cut his throat for her. When a man does not feel that way he has no feeling at all.

Maxims of this fastidious morality were, we assume without effort, handed out in the Courts of Love. But pupils, however diligent, make mistakes. Though the decisions, decretals, and mandates of the courts were highly ethical, equitable also and instructive as well, occasionally misadventures occurred. Of these one which has been disinterred from a medieval manuscript may serve as instance. It runs as follows:—

"My Lord Raymond of Roussillon was a brave baron. His wife, the Lady Marguerite, was the fairest woman in the land, the most gifted and serene. It happened that William of Cabstaing, a poor knight's son, came to the court of my lord Raymond and asked that he be received as varlet there. My Lord Raymond, seeing that he was handsome and hardy, welcomed him and told him that he might remain. William did so, and comported himself so well that my lord made him page to my lady. Now it so fell about that one day the page composed for the Lady Marguerite the song which says:

" 'Sweet are the thoughts
Which love awakes in me.'

"When Raymond of Roussillon heard that song he sent for William, led him far from the castle, cut off his head, put it in a basket, cut his heart out, and put it in the basket too. Then Raymond returned to the castle. He had the heart roasted and served at table to

his wife, and made her eat it without knowing what it was. When the
meal was over, Raymond stood up and told his wife that what she had
eaten was the heart of the Knight William, and fetched and showed
her the head, and asked her if the heart had tasted well. She understood what he said. She saw and recognised the head of the Knight
William and, answering, she replied that the heart had been so good
and appetising that never other food or other drink should take from
her mouth the savour which it had left there. Raymond ran at her
with his sword. She fled away, threw herself from a balcony, and
broke her skull.

"All this was told throughout the realm of Aragon. The King
Alphonse and all his barons and all his counts had great grief at the
death of the knight and of the lady whom Raymond had so abominably
destroyed. They made war on him, and having taken him and his
castle, and slain him there, the King Alphonse erected at Perpignan a
monument to William and to Marguerite, and all perfect lovers
prayed for their souls."

A gentleman never sees or hears anything that was not intended
for him. The lesson in pure courtesy which Raymond got from
Alphonse was well deserved. But it was insufficient. He should have
had his ghost kicked. At the same time, if episodes such as that are to
be given in the revival of the Courts of Love, we would not miss it for
a farm.

Jack London [1876-1916]

FROM *War of the Classes* [1905]

The Class Struggle

Unfortunately or otherwise, people are prone to believe in the reality
of the things they think ought to be so. This comes of the cheery
optimism which is innate with life itself; and, while it may sometimes
be deplored, it must never be censured, for, as a rule, it is productive
of more good than harm, and of about all the achievement there is in
the world. There are cases where this optimism has been disastrous, as
with the people who lived in Pompeii during its last quivering days;
or with the aristocrats of the time of Louis XVI, who confidently
expected the Deluge to overwhelm their children, or their children's
children, but never themselves. But there is small likelihood that the
case of perverse optimism here to be considered will end in such
disaster, while there is every reason to believe that the great change
now manifesting itself in society will be as peaceful and orderly in its
culmination as it is in its present development.

Out of their constitutional optimism, and because a class struggle is an abhorred and dangerous thing, the great American people are unanimous in asserting that there is no class struggle. And by "American people" is meant the recognized and authoritative mouthpieces of the American people, which are the press, the pulpit, and the university. The journalists, the preachers, and the professors are practically of one voice in declaring that there is no such thing as a class struggle now going on, much less that a class struggle will ever go on, in the United States. And this declaration they continually make in the face of a multitude of facts which impeach, not so much their sincerity, as affirm, rather, their optimism.

There are two ways of approaching the subject of the class struggle. The existence of this struggle can be shown theoretically, and it can be shown actually. For a class struggle to exist in society there must be, first, a class inequality, a superior class and an inferior class (as measured by power); and, second, the outlets must be closed whereby the strength and ferment of the inferior class have been permitted to escape.

That there are even classes in the United States is vigorously denied by many; but it is incontrovertible, when a group of individuals is formed, wherein the members are bound together by common interests which are peculiarly their interests and not the interests of individuals outside the group, that such a group is a class. The owners of capital, with their dependents, form a class of this nature in the United States; the working people form a similar class. The interest of the capitalist class, say, in the matter of income tax, is quite contrary to the interest of the laboring class; and, *vice versa*, in the matter of poll-tax.

If between these two classes there be a clear and vital conflict of interest, all the factors are present which make a class struggle; but this struggle will lie dormant if the strong and capable members of the inferior class be permitted to leave that class and join the ranks of the superior class. The capitalist class and the working class have existed side by side and for a long time in the United States; but hitherto all the strong, energetic members of the working class have been able to rise out of their class and become owners of capital. They were enabled to do this because an undeveloped country with an expanding frontier gave equality of opportunity to all. In the almost

lottery-like scramble for the ownership of vast unowned natural resources, and in the exploitation of which there was little or no competition of capital, (the capital itself rising out of the exploitation), the
capable, intelligent member of the working class found a field in
which to use his brains to his own advancement. Instead of being
discontented in direct ratio with his intelligence and ambitions, and of
radiating amongst his fellows a spirit of revolt as capable as he was
capable, he left them to their fate and carved his own way to a place
in the superior class.

But the day of expanding frontier, of a lottery-like scramble for
the ownership of natural resources, and of the upbuilding of new
industries, is past. Farthest West has been reached, and an immense
volume of surplus capital roams for investment and nips in the bud
the patient efforts of the embryo capitalist to rise through slow in-
crement from small beginnings. The gateway of opportunity after
opportunity has been closed, and closed for all time. Rockefeller has
shut the door on oil, the American Tobacco Company on tobacco,
and Carnegie on steel. After Carnegie came Morgan, who triple-
locked the door. These doors will not open again, and before them
pause thousands of ambitious young men to read the placard: No
THOROUGHFARE.

And day by day more doors are shut, while the ambitious young
men continue to be born. It is they, denied the opportunity to rise
from the working class, who preach revolt to the working class. Had
he been born fifty years later, Andrew Carnegie, the poor Scotch boy,
might have risen to be president of his union, or of a federation of
unions; but that he would never have become the builder of Home-
stead and founder of multitudinous libraries, is as certain as it is
certain that some other man would have developed the steel industry
had Andrew Carnegie never been born.

Theoretically, then, there exist in the United States all the factors
which go to make a class struggle. There are the capitalists and working classes, the interests of which conflict, while the working class is
no longer being emasculated to the extent it was in the past by having
drawn off from it its best blood and brains. Its more capable members
are no longer able to rise out of it and leave the great mass leaderless
and helpless. They remain to be its leaders.

But the optimistic mouthpieces of the great American people, who are themselves deft theoreticians, are not to be convinced by mere theoretics. So it remains to demonstrate the existence of the class struggle by a marshalling of the facts.

When nearly two millions of men, finding themselves knit together by certain interests peculiarly their own, band together in a strong organization for the aggressive pursuit of those interests, it is evident that society has within it a hostile and warring class. But when the interests which this class aggressively pursues conflict sharply and vitally with the interests of another class, class antagonism arises and a class struggle is the inevitable result. One great organization of labor alone has a membership of 1,700,000 in the United States. This is the American Federation of Labor, and outside of it are many other large organizations. All these men are banded together for the frank purpose of bettering their condition, regardless of the harm worked thereby upon all other classes. They are in open antagonism with the capitalist class, while the manifestos of their leaders state that the struggle is one which can never end until the capitalist class is exterminated.

Their leaders will largely deny this last statement, but an examination of their utterances, their actions, and the situation will forestall such denial. In the first place, the conflict between labor and capital is over the division of the joint product. Capital and labor apply themselves to raw material and make it into a finished product. The difference between the value of the raw material and the value of the finished product is the value they have added to it by their joint effort. This added value is, therefore, their joint product, and it is over the division of this joint product that the struggle between labor and capital takes place. Labor takes its share in wages; capital takes its share in profits. It is patent, if capital took in profits the whole joint product, that labor would perish. And it is equally patent, if labor took in wages the whole joint product, that capital would perish. Yet this last is the very thing labor aspires to do, and that it will never be content with anything less than the whole joint product is evidenced by the words of its leaders.

Mr. Samuel Gompers, president of the American Federation of Labor, has said: "The workers want more wages; more of the comforts of life; more leisure; more chance for self-improvement as men, as trade-unionists, as citizens. *These were the wants of yesterday; they are the wants of to-day; they will be the wants of to-morrow, and of to-morrow's morrow.* The struggle may assume new forms, but the issue is the immemorial one,—an effort of the producers to obtain an increasing measure of the wealth that flows from their production."

Mr. Henry White, secretary of the United Garment Workers of America and a member of the Industrial Committee of the National Civic Federation, speaking of the National Civic Federation soon after its inception, said: "To fall into one another's arms, to avow friendship, to express regret at the injury which has been done, would not alter the facts of the situation. Workingmen will continue to demand more pay, and the employer will naturally oppose them. The readiness and ability of the workmen to fight will, as usual, largely determine the amount of their wages or their share in the product. . . . But when it comes to dividing the proceeds, there is the rub. We can also agree that the larger the product through the employment of labor-saving methods the better, as there will be more to be divided, but again the question of the division. . . . A Conciliation Committee, having the confidence of the community, and composed of men possessing practical knowledge of industrial affairs, can therefore aid in mitigating this antagonism, in preventing avoidable conflicts, in bringing about a *truce;* I use the word 'truce' because understandings can only be temporary."

Here is a man who might have owned cattle on a thousand hills, been a lumber baron or a railroad king, had he been born a few years sooner. As it is, he remains in his class, is secretary of the United Garment Workers of America, and is so thoroughly saturated with the class struggle that he speaks of the dispute between capital and labor in terms of war,—workmen *fight* with employers; it is possible to avoid some *conflicts;* in certain cases *truces* may be, for the time being, effected.

Man being man and a great deal short of the angels, the quarrel over the division of the joint product is irreconcilable. For the last twenty years in the United States, there has been an average of over a thousand strikes per year; and year by year these strikes increase in magnitude, and the front of the labor army grows more imposing. And it is a class struggle, pure and simple. Labor as a class is fighting with capital as a class.

Workingmen will continue to demand more pay, and employers

will continue to oppose them. This is the key-note to *laissez faire*,—
everybody for himself and devil take the hindmost. It is upon this that
the rampant individualist bases his individualism. It is the let-alone
policy, the struggle for existence, which strengthens the strong, de-
stroys the weak, and makes a finer and more capable breed of men.
But the individual has passed away and the group has come, for better
or worse, and the struggle has become, not a struggle between individuals, but a struggle between groups. So the query rises: Has the
individualist never speculated upon the labor group becoming strong
enough to destroy the capitalist group, and take to itself and run for
itself the machinery of industry? And, further, has the individualist
never speculated upon this being still a triumphant expression of individualism,—of group individualism,—if the confusion of terms may be
permitted?

But the facts of the class struggle are deeper and more significant
than have so far been presented. A million or so of workmen may
organize for the pursuit of interests which engender class antagonism
and strife, and at the same time be unconscious of what is engendered.
But when a million or so of workmen show unmistakable signs of
being conscious of their class,—of being, in short, class conscious,—
then the situation grows serious. The uncompromising and terrible
hatred of the trade-unionist for a scab is the hatred of a class for a
traitor to that class,—while the hatred of a trade-unionist for the
militia is the hatred of a class for a weapon wielded by the class with
which it is fighting. No workman can be true to his class and at the
same time be a member of the militia: this is the dictum of the labor
leaders.

In the town of the writer, the good citizens, when they get up a
Fourth of July parade and invite the labor unions to participate, are
informed by the unions that they will not march in the parade if the
militia marches. Article 8 of the constitution of the Painters' and
Decorators' Union of Schenectady provides that a member must not
be a "militiaman, special police officer, or deputy marshal in the
employ of corporations or individuals during strikes, lockouts, or
other labor difficulties, and any member occupying any of the above
positions will be debarred from membership." Mr. William Potter was
a member of this union and a member of the National Guard. As a
result, because he obeyed the order of the Governor when his com-

pany was ordered out to suppress rioting, he was expelled from his union. Also his union demanded his employers, Shafer & Barry, to discharge him from their service. This they complied with, rather than face the threatened strike.

Mr. Robert L. Walker, first lieutenant of the Light Guards, a New Haven militia company, recently resigned. His reason was, that he was a member of the Car Builders' Union, and that the two organizations were antagonistic to each other. During a New Orleans street-car strike not long ago, a whole company of militia, called out to protect non-union men, resigned in a body. Mr. John Mulholland, president of the International Association of Allied Metal Mechanics, has stated that he does not want the members to join the militia. The Local Trades' Assembly of Syracuse, New York, has passed a resolution, by unanimous vote, requiring union men who are members of the National Guard to resign, under pain of expulsion, from the unions. The Amalgamated Sheet Metal Workers' Association has incorporated in its constitution an amendment excluding from membership in its organization "any person a member of the regular army, or of the State militia or naval reserve." The Illinois State Federation of Labor at a recent convention, passed without a dissenting vote a resolution declaring that membership in military organizations is a violation of labor union obligations, and requesting all union men to withdraw from the militia. The president of the Federation, Mr. Albert Young, declared that the militia was a menace not only to unions, but all workers throughout the country.

These instances may be multiplied a thousand fold. The union workmen are becoming conscious of their class, and of the struggle their class is waging with the capitalist class. To be a member of the militia is to be a traitor to the union, for the militia is a weapon wielded by the employers to crush the workers in the struggle between the warring groups.

Another interesting, and even more pregnant, phase of the class struggle is the political aspect of it as displayed by the socialists. Five men, standing together, may perform prodigies; 500 men, marching as marched the historic Five Hundred of Marseilles, may sack a palace and destroy a king; while 500,000 men, passionately preaching the propaganda of a class struggle, waging a class struggle along political lines, and backed by the moral and intellectual support of 10,000,000 more men of like convictions throughout the world, may come pretty close to realizing a class struggle in these United States of ours.

In 1900 these men cast 150,000 votes; two years later, in 1902, they cast 300,000 votes; and in 1904 they cast 450,000. They have behind them a most imposing philosophic and scientific literature; they own illustrated magazines and reviews, high in quality, dignity, and restraint; they possess countless daily and weekly papers which circulate throughout the land, and single papers which have subscribers by the hundreds of thousands; and they literally swamp the working classes in a vast sea of tracts and pamphlets. No political party in the United States, no church organization nor mission effort, has as indefatigable workers as has the socialist party. They multiply themselves, know of no effort nor sacrifice too great to make for the Cause; and "Cause," with them, is spelled out in capitals. They work for it with a religious zeal, and would die for it with a willingness similar to that of the Christian martyrs.

These men are preaching an uncompromising and deadly class struggle. In fact, they are organized upon the basis of a class struggle. "The history of society," they say, "is a history of class struggles. Patrician struggled with plebeian in early Rome; the king and the burghers, with the nobles in the Middle Ages; later on, the king and the nobles with the bourgeoisie; and to-day the struggle is on between the triumphant bourgeoisie and the rising proletariat. By 'proletariat' is meant the class of people without capital which sells its labor for a living.

"That the proletariat shall conquer," (mark the note of fatalism), "is as certain as the rising sun. *Just as the bourgeoisie of the eighteenth century wanted democracy applied to politics, so the proletariat of the twentieth century wants democracy applied to industry.* As the bourgeoisie complained against the government being run by and for the nobles, so the proletariat complains against the government and industry being run by and for the bourgeoisie; and so, following in the footsteps of its predecessor, the proletariat will possess itself of the government, apply democracy to industry, abolish wages, which are merely legalized robbery, and run the business of the country in its own interest.

"Their aim," they say, "is to organize the working class, and those in sympathy with it, into a political party, with the object of conquering the powers of government and using them for the purpose of transforming the present system of private ownership of the means of production and distribution into collective ownership by the entire people."

Briefly stated, this is the battle plan of these 450,000 men who call themselves "socialists." And, in the face of the existence of such an aggressive group of men, a class struggle cannot very well be denied by the optimistic Americans who say: "A class struggle is monstrous. Sir, there is no class struggle." The class struggle is here, and the optimistic American had better gird himself for the fray and put a stop to it, rather than sit idly declaiming that what ought not to be is not, and never will be.

But the socialists, fanatics and dreamers though they may well be, betray a foresight and insight, and a genius for organization, which put to shame the class with which they are openly at war. Failing of rapid success in waging a sheer political propaganda, and finding that they were alienating the most intelligent and most easily organized portion of the voters, the socialists lessoned from the experience and turned their energies upon the trade-union movement. To win the trade unions was well-nigh to win the war, and recent events show that they have done far more winning in this direction than have the capitalists.

Instead of antagonizing the unions, which had been their previous policy, the socialists proceeded to conciliate the unions. "Let every good socialist join the union of his trade," the edict went forth. "Bore from within and capture the trade-union movement." And this policy, only several years old, has reaped fruits far beyond their fondest expectations. To-day the great labor unions are honeycombed with socialists, "boring from within," as they picturesquely term their undermining labor. At work and at play, at business meeting and council, their insidious propaganda goes on. At the shoulder of the trade-unionist is the socialist, sympathizing with him, aiding him with head and hand, suggesting—perpetually suggesting—the necessity for political action. As the *Journal*, of Lansing, Michigan, a republican paper, has remarked: "The socialists in the labor unions are tireless workers. They are sincere, energetic, and self-sacrificing. . . . They stick to the union and work all the while, thus making a showing which, reckoned by ordinary standards, is out of all proportion to their numbers. . . . Their cause is growing among union laborers, and their long fight, intended to turn the Federation into a political organization, is likely to win."

They miss no opportunity of driving home the necessity for political action, the necessity for capturing the political machinery of society whereby they may master society. As an instance of this is the avidity with which the American socialists seized upon the famous Taft-Vale Decision in England, which was to the effect that an unincorporated union could be sued and its treasury rifled by process of law. Throughout the United States, the socialists pointed the moral in similar fashion to the way it was pointed by the *Social-Democratic Herald*, which advised the trade-unionists, in view of the decision, to stop trying to fight capital with money, which they lacked, and to begin fighting with the ballot, which was their strongest weapon.

Night and day, tireless and unrelenting, they labor at their self-imposed task of undermining society. Mr. M. G. Cunniff, who lately made an intimate study of trade-unionism, says: "All through the unions socialism filters. Almost every other man is a socialist, preaching that unionism is but a makeshift." "Malthus be damned," they told him, "for the good time was coming when every man should be able to rear his family in comfort." In one union, with two thousand members, Mr. Cunniff found every man a socialist, and from his experiences Mr. Cunniff was forced to confess, "I lived in a world that showed our industrial life a-tremble from beneath with a never-ceasing ferment."

The socialists have already captured the Western Federation of Miners, the Western Hotel and Restaurant Employees' Union, and the Patternmakers' National Association. The Western Federation of Miners, at a recent convention, declared: "The strike has failed to secure to the working classes their liberty; we therefore call upon the workers to strike as one man for their liberties at the ballot box. . . . We put ourselves on record as committed to the programme of independent political action. . . . We indorse the platform of the socialist party, and accept it as the declaration of principles of our organization. We call upon our members as individuals to commence immediately the organization of the socialist movement in their respective towns and states, and to coöperate in every way for the furtherance of the principles of socialism and of the socialist party. In states where the socialist party has not perfected its organization, we advise that every assistance be given by our members to that end. . . . We therefore call for organizers, capable and well-versed in the whole programme of the labor movement, to be sent into each state to preach the necessity of organization on the political as well as on the economic field."

The capitalist class has a glimmering consciousness of the class struggle which is shaping itself in the midst of society; but the capitalists, as a class, seem to lack the ability for organizing, for coming together, such as is possessed by the working class. No American capitalist ever aids an English capitalist in the common fight, while workmen have formed international unions, the socialists a world-wide international organization, and on all sides space and race are bridged in the effort to achieve solidarity. Resolutions of sympathy, and, fully as important, donations of money, pass back and forth across the sea to wherever labor is fighting its pitched battles.

For divers reasons the capitalist class lacks this cohesion or solidarity, chief among which is the optimism bred of past success. And, again, the capitalist class is divided; it has within itself a class struggle of no mean proportions, which tends to irritate and harass it and to confuse the situation. The small capitalist and the large capitalist are grappled with each other, struggling over what Achille Loria calls the "bi-partition of the revenues." Such a struggle, though not precisely analogous, was waged between the landlords and manufacturers of England when the one brought about the passage of the Factory Acts and the other the abolition of the Corn Laws.

Here and there, however, certain members of the capitalist class see clearly the cleavage in society along which the struggle is beginning to show itself, while the press and magazines are beginning to raise an occasional and troubled voice. Two leagues of class-conscious capitalists have been formed for the purpose of carrying on their side of the struggle. Like the socialist, they do not mince matters, but state boldly and plainly that they are fighting to subjugate the opposing class. It is the barons against the commons. One of these leagues, the National Association of Manufacturers, is stopping short of nothing in what it conceives to be a life-and-death struggle. Mr. D. M. Parry, who is the president of the league, as well as president of the National Metal Trades' Association, is leaving no stone unturned in what he

feels to be a desperate effort to organize his class. He has issued the
call to arms in terms everything but ambiguous: *"There is still time in
the United States to head off the socialistic programme, which, unrestrained, is sure to wreck our country."*

As he says, the work is for "federating employers in order that
we may meet with a united front all issues that affect us. We must
come to this sooner or later. . . . The work immediately before the
National Association of Manufacturers is, first, *keep the vicious Eight-
hour Bill off the books;* second, to *destroy the Anti-injunction Bill,*
which wrests your business from you and places it in the hands of
your employees; third, to secure the *passage of the Department of
Commerce and Industry Bill;* the latter would go through with a rush
were it not for the hectoring opposition of Organized Labor." By this
department, he further says, "business interests would have direct and
sympathetic representation at Washington."

In a later letter, issued broadcast to the capitalists outside the
League, President Parry points out the success which is already beginning to attend the efforts of the League at Washington. "We have
contributed more than any other influence to the quick passage of the
new Department of Commerce Bill. It is said that the activities of this
office are numerous and satisfactory; but of that I must not say too
much—or anything. . . . At Washington the Association is not represented too much, either directly or indirectly. Sometimes it is known
in a most powerful way that it is represented vigorously and unitedly.
Sometimes it is not known that it is represented at all."

The second class-conscious capitalist organization is called the
National Economic League. It likewise manifests the frankness of
men who do not dilly-dally with terms, but who say what they mean,
and who mean to settle down to a long, hard fight. Their letter of
invitation to prospective members opens boldly. "We beg to inform
you that the National Economic League will render its services in an
impartial educational movement *to oppose socialism and class hatred.*"
Among its class-conscious members, men who recognize that the
opening guns of the class struggle have been fired, may be instanced
the following names: Hon. Lyman J. Gage, Ex-Secretary U.S. Treasury; Hon. Thomas Jefferson Coolidge, Ex-Minister to France; Rev.
Henry C. Potter, Bishop New York Diocese; Hon. John D. Long,
Ex-Secretary U.S. Navy; Hon. Levi P. Morton, Ex-Vice President

United States; Henry Clews; John F. Dryden, President Prudential
Life Insurance Co.; John A. McCall, President New York Life Insurance Co.; J. L. Greatsinger, President Brooklyn Rapid Transit Co.;
the shipbuilding firm of William Cramp & Sons, the Southern Railway
system, and the Atchison, Topeka, & Santa Fé Railway Company.

Instances of the troubled editorial voice have not been rare during
the last several years. There were many cries from the press during
the last days of the anthracite coal strike that the mine owners, by
their stubbornness, were sowing the regrettable seeds of socialism.
The *World's Work* for December, 1902, said: "The next significant
fact is the recommendation by the Illinois State Federation of Labor
that all members of labor unions who are also members of the state
militia shall resign from the militia. This proposition has been favorably ragarded by some other labor organizations. It has done more
than any other single recent declaration or action to cause a public
distrust of such unions as favor it. *It hints of a class separation that in
turn hints of anarchy.*"

The *Outlook*, February 14, 1903, in reference to the rioting at
Waterbury, remarks, "That all this disorder should have occurred in a
city of the character and intelligence of Waterbury indicates that the
industrial war spirit is by no means confined to the immigrant or
ignorant working classes."

That President Roosevelt has smelt the smoke from the firing line
of the class struggle is evidenced by his words, "Above all we need to
remember that any kind of *class animosity in the political world* is, if
possible, even more destructive to national welfare then sectional,
race, or religious animosity." The chief thing to be noted here is
President Roosevelt's tacit recognition of class animosity in the industrial world, and his fear, which language cannot portray stronger, that
this class animosity may spread to the political world. Yet this is the
very policy which the socialists have announced in their declaration of
war against present-day society—to capture the political machinery of
society and by that machinery destroy present-day society.

The New York *Independent* for February 12, 1903, recognized
without qualification the class struggle. "It is impossible fairly to pass
upon the methods of labor unions, or to devise plans for remedying
their abuses, until it is recognized, to begin with, that unions are based
upon class antagonism and that their policies are dictated by the

necessities of social warfare. A strike is a rebellion against the owners of property. The rights of property are protected by government. And a strike, under certain provocation, may extend as far as did the general strike in Belgium a few years since, when practically the entire wage-earning population stopped work in order to force political concessions from the property-owning classes. This is an extreme case, but it brings out vividly the real nature of labor organization as a species of warfare whose object is the coercion of one class by another class."

It has been shown, theoretically and actually, that there is a class struggle in the United States. The quarrel over the division of the joint product is irreconcilable. The working class is no longer losing its strongest and most capable members. These men, denied room for their ambition in the capitalist ranks, remain to be the leaders of the workers, to spur them to discontent, to make them conscious of their class, to lead them to revolt.

This revolt, appearing spontaneously all over the industrial field in the form of demands for an increased share of the joint product, is being carefully and shrewdly shaped for a political assault upon society. The leaders, with the carelessness of fatalists, do not hesitate for an instant to publish their intentions to the world. They intend to direct the labor revolt to the capture of the political machinery of society. With the political machinery once in their hands, which will also give them the control of the police, the army, the navy, and the courts, they will confiscate with or without remuneration, all the possessions of the capitalist class which are used in the production and distribution of the necessaries and luxuries of life. By this, they mean to apply the law of eminent domain to the land, and to extend the law of eminent domain till it embraces the mines, the factories, the railroads, and the ocean carriers. In short, they intend to destroy present-day society, which they contend is run in the interest of another class, and from the materials to construct a new society, which will be run in their interest.

On the other hand, the capitalist class is beginning to grow conscious of itself and of the struggle which is being waged. It is already forming offensive and defensive leagues, while some of the most prominent figures in the nation are preparing to lead it in the attack upon socialism.

The question to be solved is not one of Malthusianism, "projected efficiency," nor ethics. It is a question of might. Whichever class is to win, will win by virtue of superior strength; for the workers are beginning to say, as they said to Mr. Cunniff, "Malthus be damned." In their own minds they find no sanction for continuing the individual struggle for the survival of the fittest. As Mr. Gompers has said, they want more, and more, and more. The ethical import of Mr. Kidd's plan of the present generation putting up with less in order that race efficiency may be projected into a remote future, has no bearing upon their actions. They refuse to be the "glad perishers" so glowingly described by Nietzsche.

It remains to be seen how promptly the capitalist class will respond to the call to arms. Upon its promptness rests its existence, for if it sits idly by, soothfully proclaiming that what ought not to be cannot be, it will find the roof beams crashing about its head. The capitalist class is in the numerical minority, and bids fair to be outvoted if it does not put a stop to the vast propaganda being waged by its enemy. It is no longer a question of whether or not there is a class struggle. The question now is, what will be the outcome of the class struggle?

The Tramp

Mr. Francis O'Neil, General Superintendent of Police, Chicago, speaking of the tramp, says: "Despite the most stringent police regulations, a great city will have a certain number of homeless vagrants to shelter through the winter." "Despite,"—mark the word, a confession of organized helplessness as against unorganized necessity. If police regulations are stringent and yet fail, then that which makes them fail, namely, the tramp, must have still more stringent reasons for succeeding. This being so, it should be of interest to inquire into these reasons, to attempt to discover why the nameless and homeless vagrant sets at naught the right arm of the corporate power of our great cities, why all that is weak and worthless is stronger than all that is strong and of value.

Mr. O'Neil is a man of wide experience on the subject of tramps. He may be called a specialist. As he says of himself: "As an old-time desk sergeant and police captain, I have had almost unlimited opportunity to study and analyze this class of floating population, which seeks the city in winter and scatters abroad through the country in the spring." He then continues: "This experience reiterated the lesson that the vast majority of these wanderers are of the class with whom a life of vagrancy is a chosen means of living without work." Not only is it to be inferred from this that there is a large class in society which lives without work, for Mr. O'Neil's testimony further shows that this class is forced to live without work.

He says: "I have been astonished at the multitude of those who have unfortunately engaged in occupations which practically force them to become loafers for at least a third of the year. And it is from this class that the tramps are largely recruited. I recall a certain winter when it seemed to me that a large portion of the inhabitants of Chicago belonged to this army of unfortunates. I was stationed at a police station not far from where an ice harvest was ready for the cutters. The ice company advertised for helpers, and the very night this call appeared in the newspapers our station was packed with homeless men, who asked shelter in order to be at hand for the morning's work. Every foot of floor space was given over to these lodgers and scores were still unaccommodated."

And again: "And it must be confessed that the man who is willing to do honest labor for food and shelter is a rare specimen in this vast army of shabby and tattered wanderers who seek the warmth of the city with the coming of the first snow." Taking into consideration the crowd of honest laborers that swamped Mr. O'Neil's station-house on the way to the ice-cutting, it is patent, if all tramps were looking for honest labor instead of a small minority, that the honest laborers would have a far harder task finding something honest to do for food and shelter. If the opinion of the honest laborers who swamped Mr. O'Neil's station-house were asked, one could rest confident that each and every man would express a preference for fewer honest laborers on the morrow when he asked the ice foreman for a job.

And, finally, Mr. O'Neil says: "The humane and generous treatment which this city has accorded the great army of homeless unfortunates has made it the victim of wholesale imposition, and this well-intended policy of kindness has resulted in making Chicago the winter Mecca of a vast and undesirable floating population." That is to say, because of her kindness, Chicago had more than her fair share of tramps; because she was humane and generous she suffered wholesale imposition. From this we must conclude that it does not do to be *humane* and *generous* to our fellow-men—when they are tramps. Mr. O'Neil is right, and that this is no sophism it is the intention of this article, among other things, to show.

In a general way we may draw the following inferences from the remarks of Mr. O'Neil: 1) The tramp is stronger than organized society and cannot be put down; (2) The tramp is "shabby," "tattered," "homeless," "unfortunate"; (3) There is a "vast" number of tramps; (4) Very few tramps are willing to do honest work; (5) Those tramps who are willing to do honest work have to hunt very hard to find it; (6) The tramp is undesirable.

To this last let the contention be appended that the tramp is only *personally* undesirable; that he is *negatively* desirable; that the function he performs in society is a negative function; and that he is the by-product of economic necessity.

It is very easy to demonstrate that there are more men than there is work for men to do. For instance, what would happen to-morrow if one hundred thousand tramps should become suddenly inspired with an overmastering desire for work? It is a fair question. "Go to work" is preached to the tramp every day of his life. The judge on the bench, the pedestrian in the street, the housewife at the kitchen door, all unite in advising him to go to work. So what would happen to-morrow if one hundred thousand tramps acted upon this advice and strenuously and indomitably sought work? Why, by the end of the week one hundred thousand workers, their places taken by the tramps, would receive their time and be "hitting the road" for a job.

Ella Wheeler Wilcox unwittingly and uncomfortably demonstrated the disparity between men and work.* She made a casual reference, in a newspaper column she conducts, to the difficulty two business men found in obtaining good employees. The first morning mail brought her seventy-five applications for the position, and at the end of two weeks over two hundred people had applied.

Still more strikingly was the same proposition recently demon-

---

* "From 43 to 52 per cent of all applicants need work rather than relief."— *Report of the Charity Organization Society of New York City.*

strated in San Francisco. A sympathetic strike called out a whole federation of trades' unions. Thousands of men, in many branches of trade, quit work,—draymen, sand teamsters, porters and packers, long-shoremen, stevedores, warehousemen, stationary engineers, sailors, marine firemen, stewards, sea-cooks, and so forth,—an interminable list. It was a strike of large proportions. Every Pacific coast shipping city was involved, and the entire coasting service, from San Diego to Puget Sound, was virtually tied up. The time was considered auspicious. The Philippines and Alaska had drained the Pacific coast of surplus labor. It was summer-time, when the agricultural demand for laborers was at its height, and when the cities were bare of their floating populations. And yet there remained a body of surplus labor sufficient to take the places of the strikers. No matter what occupation, sea-cook or stationary engineer, sand teamster or warehouseman, in every case there was an idle worker ready to do the work. And not only ready but anxious. They fought for a chance to work. Men were killed, hundreds of heads were broken, the hospitals were filled with injured men, and thousands of assaults were committed. And still surplus laborers, "scabs," came forward to replace the strikers.

The question arises: *Whence came this second army of workers to replace the first army?* One thing is certain: the trades' unions did not scab on one another. Another thing is certain: no industry on the Pacific slope was crippled in the slightest degree by its workers being drawn away to fill the places of the strikers. A third thing is certain: the agricultural workers did not flock to the cities to replace the strikers. In this last instance it is worth while to note that the agricultural laborers wailed to High Heaven when a few of the strikers went into the country to compete with them in unskilled employments. So there is no accounting for this second army of workers. It simply was. It was there all this time, a surplus labor army in the year of our Lord 1901, a year adjudged most prosperous in the annals of the United States.*

The existence of the surplus labor army being established, there

* Mr. Leiter, who owns a coal mine at the town of Zeigler, Illinois, in an interview printed in the *Chicago Record-Herald* of December 6, 1904, said: "When I go into the market to purchase labor, I propose to retain just as much freedom as does a purchaser in any other kind of a market. . . . There is no difficulty whatever in obtaining labor, *for the country is full of unemployed men*."

remains to be established the economic necessity for the surplus labor army. The simplest and most obvious need is that brought about by the fluctuation of production. If, when production is at low ebb, all men are at work, it necessarily follows that when production increases there will be no men to do the increased work. This may seem almost childish, and, if not childish, at least easily remedied. At low ebb let the men work shorter time; at high flood let them work overtime. The main objection to this is, that it is not done, and that we are considering what is, not what might be or should be.

Then there are great irregular and periodical demands for labor which must be met. Under the first head come all the big building and engineering enterprises. When a canal is to be dug or a railroad put through, requiring thousands of laborers, it would be hurtful to withdraw these laborers from the constant industries. And whether it is a canal to be dug or a cellar, whether five thousand men are required or five, it is well, in society as at present organized, that they be taken from the surplus labor army. The surplus labor army is the reserve fund of social energy, and this is one of the reasons for its existence.

Under the second head, periodical demands, come the harvests. Throughout the year, huge labor tides sweep back and forth across the United States. That which is sown and tended by few men, comes to sudden ripeness and must be gathered by many men; and it is inevitable that these many men form floating populations. In the late spring the berries must be picked, in the summer the grain garnered, in the fall the hops gathered, in the winter the ice harvested. In California a man may pick berries in Siskiyou, peaches in Santa Clara, grapes in the San Joaquin, and oranges in Los Angeles, going from job to job as the season advances, and traveling a thousand miles ere the season is done. But the great demand for agricultural labor is in the summer. In the winter, work is slack, and these floating populations eddy into the cities to eke out a precarious existence and harrow the souls of the police officers until the return of warm weather and work. If there were constant work at good wages for every man, who would harvest the crops?

But the last and most significant need for the surplus labor army remains to be stated. This surplus labor acts as a check upon all employed labor. It is the lash by which the masters hold the workers to their tasks, or drive them back to their tasks when they have revolted. It is the goad which forces the workers into the compulsory "free contracts" against which they now and again rebel. There is only one reason under the sun that strikes fail, and that is because there are always plenty of men to take the strikers' places.

The strength of the union to-day, other things remaining equal, is proportionate to the skill of the trade, or, in other words, proportionate to the pressure the surplus labor army can put upon it. If a thousand ditch-diggers strike, it is easy to replace them, wherefore the ditch-diggers have little or no organized strength. But a thousand highly skilled machinists are somewhat harder to replace, and in consequence the machinist unions are strong. The ditch-diggers are wholly at the mercy of the surplus labor army, the machinists only partly. To be invincible, a union must be a monopoly. It must control every man in its particular trade, and regulate apprentices so that the supply of skilled workmen may remain constant; this is the dream of the "Labor Trust" on the part of the captains of labor.

Once, in England, after the Great Plague, labor awoke to find there was more work for men than there were men to work. Instead of workers competing for favors from employers, employers were competing for favors from the workers. Wages went up and up, and continued to go up, until the workers demanded the full product of their toil. Now it is clear that, when labor receives its full product, capital must perish. And so the pygmy capitalists of that post-Plague day found their existence threatened by this untoward condition of affairs. To save themselves, they set a maximum wage, restrained the workers from moving about from place to place, smashed incipient organization, refused to tolerate idlers, and by most barbarous legal penalties punished those who disobeyed. After that, things went on as before.

The point of this, of course, is to demonstrate the need of the surplus labor army. Without such an army, our present capitalist society would be powerless. Labor would organize as it never organized before, and the last least worker would be gathered into the unions. The full product of toil would be demanded, and capitalist society would crumble away. Nor could capitalist society save itself as did the post-Plague capitalist society. The time is past when a handful of masters, by imprisonment and barbarous punishment, can drive the legions of the workers to their tasks. Without a surplus labor army, the courts, police, and military are impotent. In such matters the function of the courts, police, and military is to preserve order, and to fill the places of strikers with surplus labor. If there be no surplus labor to instate, there is no function to perform; for disorder arises only during the process of instatement, when the striking labor army and the surplus labor army clash together. That is to say, that which maintains the integrity of the present industrial society more potently than the courts, police, and military is the surplus labor army.

It has been shown that there are more men than there is work for men, and that the surplus labor army is an economic necessity. To show how the tramp is a by-product of this economic necessity, it is necessary to inquire into the composition of the surplus labor army. What men form it? Why are they there? What do they do?

In the first place, since the workers must compete for employment, it inevitably follows that it is the fit and efficient who find employment. The skilled worker holds his place by virtue of his skill and efficiency. Were he less skilled, or were he unreliable or erratic, he would be swiftly replaced by a stronger competitor. The skilled and steady employments are not cumbered with clowns and idiots. A man finds his place according to his ability and the needs of the system, and those without ability, or incapable of satisfying the needs of the system, have no place. Thus, the poor telegrapher may develop into an excellent wood-chopper. But if the poor telegrapher cherishes the delusion that he is a good telegrapher, and at the same time disdains all other employments, he will have no employment at all, or he will be so poor at all other employments that he will work only now and again in lieu of better men. He will be among the first let off when times are dull, and among the last taken on when times are good. Or, to the point, he will be a member of the surplus labor army.

So the conclusion is reached that the less fit and less efficient, or the unfit and inefficient, compose the surplus labor army. Here are to be found the men who have tried and failed, the men who cannot hold jobs,—the plumber apprentice who could not become a journeyman, and the plumber journeyman too clumsy and dull to retain employment; switchmen who wreck trains; clerks who cannot balance books; blacksmiths who lame horses; lawyers who cannot plead;

in short, the failures of every trade and profession, and failures, many of them, in divers trades and professions. Failure is writ large, and in their wretchedness they bear the stamp of social disapprobation. Common work, any kind of work, wherever or however they can obtain it, is their portion.

But these hereditary inefficients do not alone compose the surplus labor army. There are the skilled but unsteady and unreliable men; and the old men, once skilled, but, with dwindling powers, no longer skilled.* And there are good men, too, splendidly skilled and efficient, but thrust out of the employment of dying or disaster-smitten industries. In this connection it is not out of place to note the misfortune of the workers in the British iron trades, who are suffering because of American inroads. And, last of all, are the unskilled laborers, the hewers of wood and drawers of water, the ditch-diggers, the men of pick and shovel, the helpers, lumpers, roustabouts. If trade is slack on a seacoast of two thousand miles, or the harvests are light in a great interior valley, myriads of these laborers lie idle, or make life miserable for their fellows in kindred unskilled employments.

A constant filtration goes on in the working world, and good material is continually drawn from the surplus labor army. Strikes

---

* "Despondent and weary with vain attempts to struggle against an unsympathetic world, two old men were brought before Police Judge McHugh this afternoon to see whether some means could not be provided for their support, at least until springtime.

"George Westlake was the first one to receive the consideration of the court. Westlake is seventy-two years old. A charge of habitual drunkenness was placed against him, and he was sentenced to a term in the county jail, though it is more than probable that he was never under the influence of intoxicating liquor in his life. The act on the part of the authorities was one of kindness for him, as in the county jail he will be provided with a good place to sleep and plenty to eat.

"Joe Coat, aged sixty-nine years, will serve ninety days in the county jail for much the same reason as Westlake. He states that, if given a chance to do so, he will go out to a wood-camp and cut timber during the winter, but the police authorities realize that he could not long survive such a task."—*From the Butte (Montana) Miner, December 7th, 1904.*

" 'I end my life because I have reached the age limit, and there is no place for me in this world. Please notify my wife, No. 222 West 129th Street, New York.' Having summed up the cause of his despondency in this final message, James Hollander, fifty-six years old, shot himself through the left temple, in his room at the Stafford Hotel, to-day."—*New York Herald.*

and industrial dislocations shake up the workers, bring good men to the surface and sink men as good or not so good. The hope of the skilled striker is in that the scabs are less skilled, or less capable of becoming skilled; yet each striker attests to the efficiency that lurks beneath. After the Pullman strike, a few thousand railroad men were chagrined to find the work they had flung down taken up by men as good as themselves.

But one thing must be considered here. Under the present system, if the weakest and least fit were as strong and fit as the best, and the best were correspondingly stronger and fitter, the same condition would obtain. There would be the same army of employed labor, the same army of surplus labor. The whole thing is relative. There is no absolute standard of efficiency.

Comes now the tramp. And all conclusions may be anticipated by saying at once that he is a tramp because some one has to be a tramp. If he left the "road" and became a *very* efficient common laborer, some *ordinarily* efficient common laborer would have to take to the "road." The nooks and crannies are crowded by the surplus laborers; and when the first snow flies, and the tramps are driven into the cities, things become overcrowded and stringent police regulations are necessary.

The tramp is one of two kinds of men: he is either a discouraged worker or a discouraged criminal. Now a discouraged criminal, on investigation, proves to be a discouraged worker, or the descendant of discouraged workers; so that, in the last analysis, the tramp is a discouraged worker. Since there is not work for all, discouragement for some is unavoidable. How, then, does this process of discouragement operate?

The lower the employment in the industrial scale, the harder the conditions. The finer, the more delicate, the more skilled the trade, the higher is it lifted above the struggle. There is less pressure, less sordidness, less savagery. There are fewer glass-blowers proportionate to the needs of the glass-blowing industry than there are ditch-diggers proportionate to the needs of the ditch-digging industry. And not only this, for it requires a glass-blower to take the place of a striking glass-blower, while any kind of a striker or out-of-work can take the place of a ditch-digger. So the skilled trades are more independent, have more individuality and latitude. They may confer with

their masters, make demands, assert themselves. The unskilled laborers, on the other hand, have no voice in their affairs. The settlement
of terms is none of their business. "Free contract" is all that remains
to them. They may take what is offered, or leave it. There are plenty
more of their kind. They do not count. They are members of the
surplus labor army, and must be content with a hand-to-mouth
existence.

The reward is likewise proportioned. The strong, fit worker in a
skilled trade, where there is little labor pressure, is well compensated.
He is a king compared with his less fortunate brothers in the unskilled occupations where the labor pressure is great. The mediocre
worker not only is forced to be idle a large portion of the time, but
when employed is forced to accept a pittance. A dollar a day on
some days and nothing on other days will hardly support a man and
wife and send children to school. And not only do the masters bear
heavily upon him, and his own kind struggle for the morsel at his
mouth, but all skilled and organized labor adds to his woe. Union
men do not scab on one another, but in strikes, or when work is
slack, it is considered "fair" for them to descend and take away the
work of the common laborers. And take it away they do; for, as a
matter of fact, a well-fed, ambitious machinist or a coremaker will
transiently shovel coal better than an ill-fed, spiritless laborer.

Thus there is no encouragement for the unfit, inefficient, and
mediocre. Their very inefficiency and mediocrity make them helpless
as cattle and add to their misery. And the whole tendency for such is
downward, until, at the bottom of the social pit, they are wretched,
inarticulate beasts, living like beasts, breeding like beasts, dying like
beasts. And how do they fare, these creatures born mediocre, whose
heritage is neither brains nor brawn nor endurance? They are
sweated in the slums in an atmosphere of discouragement and despair. There is no strength in weakness, no encouragement in foul
air, vile food, and dank dens. They are there because they are so
made that they are not fit to be higher up; but filth and obscenity do
not strengthen the neck, nor does chronic emptiness of belly stiffen
the back.

For the mediocre there is no hope. Mediocrity is a sin. Poverty
is the penalty of failure,—poverty, from whose loins spring the
criminal and the tramp, both failures, both discouraged workers.

Poverty is the inferno where ignorance festers and vice corrodes, and where the physical, mental, and moral parts of nature are aborted and denied.

That the charge of rashness in splashing the picture be not incurred, let the following authoritative evidence be considered: first, the work and wages of mediocrity and inefficiency, and, second, the habitat:

The *New York Sun* on February 28, 1901, describes the opening of a factory in New York City by the American Tobacco Company. Cheroots were to be made in this factory in competition with other factories which refused to be absorbed by the trust. The trust advertised for girls. The crowd of men and boys who wanted work was so great in front of the building that the police were forced with their clubs to clear them away. The wage paid the girls was $2.50 per week, sixty cents of which went for car fare.*

Miss Nellie Mason Auten, a graduate student of the department of sociology at the University of Chicago, recently made a thorough investigation of the garment trades of Chicago. Her figures were published in the *American Journal of Sociology*, and commented upon by the *Literary Digest*. She found women working ten hours a day, six days a week, for forty cents per week (a rate of two-thirds of a cent an hour). Many women earned less than a dollar a week, and none of them worked every week. The following table will best summarize Miss Auten's investigations among a portion of the garment-workers:

INDUSTRY	AVERAGE INDIVIDUAL WEEKLY WAGES	AVERAGE NUMBER OF WEEKS EMPLOYED	AVERAGE YEARLY EARNINGS
Dressmakers	$ .90	42.	$37.00
Pants-finishers	1.31	27.58	42.41
Housewives and pants-finishers	1.58	30.21	47.49
Seamstresses	2.03	32.78	64.10
Pants-makers	2.13	30.77	75.61
Miscellaneous	2.77	29.	81.80
Tailors	6.22	31.96	211.92
General averages	$2.48	31.18	$76.74

* In the *San Francisco Examiner* of November 16, 1904, there is an account

Walter A. Wyckoff, who is as great an authority upon the worker as Josiah Flynt is on the tramp, furnishes the following Chicago experience:

"Many of the men were so weakened by the want and hardship of the winter that they were no longer in condition for effective labor. Some of the bosses who were in need of added hands were obliged to turn men away because of physical incapacity. One instance of this I shall not soon forget. It was when I overheard, early one morning at a factory gate, an interview between a would-be laborer and the boss. I knew the applicant for a Russian Jew, who had at home an old mother and a wife and two young children to support. He had had intermittent employment throughout the winter in a sweater's den,* barely enough to keep them all alive, and, after the hardships of the cold season, he was again in desperate straits for work.

"The boss had all but agreed to take him on for some sort of unskilled labor, when, struck by the cadaverous look of the man, he told him to bare his arm. Up went the sleeve of his coat and his ragged flannel shirt, exposing a naked arm with the muscles nearly gone, and the blue-white transparent skin stretched over sinews and the outline of the bones. Pitiful beyond words was his effort to give a semblance of strength to the biceps which rose faintly to the upward movement of the forearm. But the boss sent him off with an oath and a contemptuous laugh; and I watched the fellow as he turned down the street, facing the fact of his starving family with a despair at his heart which only mortal man can feel and no mortal tongue can speak."

Concerning habitat, Mr. Jacob Riis has stated that in New York

---

of the use of fire-hose to drive away three hundred men who wanted work at unloading a vessel in the harbor. So anxious were the men to get the two or three hours' job that they made a veritable mob and had to be driven off.
* "It was no uncommon thing in these sweatshops for men to sit bent over a sewing-machine continuously from eleven to fifteen hours a day in July weather, operating a sewing-machine by foot-power, and often so driven that they could not stop for lunch. The seasonal character of the work meant demoralizing toil for a few months in the year, and a not less demoralizing idleness for the remainder of the time. Consumption, the plague of the tenements and the especial plague of the garment industry, carried off many of these workers; poor nutrition and exhaustion, many more."— *From McClure's Magazine.*

City, in the block bounded by Stanton, Houston, Attorney, and Ridge streets, the size of which is 200 by 300, there is a warren of 2244 human beings.

In the block bounded by Sixty-first and Sixty-second streets, and Amsterdam and West End avenues, are over four thousand human creatures,—quite a comfortable New England village to crowd into one city block.

The Rev. Dr. Behrends, speaking of the block bounded by Canal, Hester, Eldridge, and Forsyth streets, says: "In a room 12 by 8 and 5½ feet high, it was found that nine persons slept and prepared their food. . . . In another room, located in a dark cellar, without screens or partitions, were together two men with their wives and a girl of fourteen, two single men and a boy of seventeen, two women and four boys,—nine, ten, eleven, and fifteen years old,—fourteen persons in all."

Here humanity rots. Its victims, with grim humor, call it "tenant-house rot." Or, as a legislative report puts it: "Here infantile life unfolds its bud, but perishes before its first anniversary. Here youth is ugly with loathsome disease, and the deformities which follow physical degeneration."

These are the men and women who are what they are because they were not better born, or because they happened to be unluckily born in time and space. Gauged by the needs of the system, they are weak and worthless. The hospital and the pauper's grave await them, and they offer no encouragement to the mediocre worker who has failed higher up in the industrial structure. Such a worker, conscious that he has failed, conscious from the hard fact that he cannot obtain work in the higher employments, finds several courses open to him. He may come down and be a beast in the social pit, for instance; but if he be of a certain caliber, the effect of the social pit will be to discourage him from work. In his blood a rebellion will quicken, and he will elect to become either a felon or a tramp.

If he has fought the hard fight, he is not unacquainted with the lure of the "road." When out of work and still undiscouraged, he has been forced to "hit the road" between large cities in his quest for a job. He has loafed, seen the country and green things, laughed in joy, lain on his back and listened to the birds singing overhead, unannoyed by factory whistles and bosses' harsh commands; and, most significant of all, *he has lived*. That is the point! He has not starved to death. Not only has he been care-free and happy, but he has lived! And from the knowledge that he has idled and is still alive, he achieves a new outlook on life; and the more he experiences the unenviable lot of the poor worker, the more the blandishments of the "road" take hold of him. And finally he flings his challenge in the face of society, imposes a valorous boycott on all work, and joins the far-wanderers of Hoboland, the gypsy folk of this latter day.

But the tramp does not usually come from the slums. His place of birth is ordinarily a bit above, and sometimes a very great bit above. A confessed failure, he yet refuses to accept the punishment, and swerves aside from the slum to vagabondage. The average beast in the social pit is either too much of a beast, or too much of a slave to the bourgeois ethics and ideals of his masters, to manifest this flicker of rebellion. But the social pit, out of its discouragement and viciousness, breeds criminals, men who prefer being beasts of prey to being beasts of work. And the mediocre criminal, in turn, the unfit and inefficient criminal, is discouraged by the strong arm of the law and goes over to trampdom.

These men, the discouraged worker and the discouraged criminal, voluntarily withdraw themselves from the struggle for work. Industry does not need them. There are no factories shut down through lack of labor, no projected railroads unbuilt for want of pick-and-shovel men. Women are still glad to toil for a dollar a week, and men and boys to clamor and fight for work at the factory gates. No one misses these discouraged men, and in going away they have made it somewhat easier for those that remain.

So the case stands thus: There being more men than there is work for men to do, a surplus labor army inevitably results. The surplus labor army is an economic necessity; without it, present society would fall to pieces. Into the surplus labor army are herded the mediocre, the inefficient, the unfit, and those incapable of satisfying the industrial needs of the system. The struggle for work between the members of the surplus labor army is sordid and savage, and at the bottom of the social pit the struggle is vicious and beastly. This struggle tends to discouragement, and the victims of this discouragement are the criminal and the tramp. The tramp is not an economic

necessity such as the surplus labor army, but he is the by-product of
an economic necessity.

The "road" is one of the safety-valves through which the waste
of the social organism is given off. And *being given off* constitutes
the negative function of the tramp. Society, as at present organized,
makes much waste of human life. This waste must be eliminated.
Chloroform or electrocution would be a simple, merciful solution of
this problem of elimination; but the ruling ethics, while permitting
the human waste, will not permit a humane elimination of that waste.
This paradox demonstrates the irreconcilability of theoretical ethics
and industrial need.

And so the tramp becomes self-eliminating. And not only self!
Since he is manifestly unfit for things as they are, and since kind is
prone to beget kind, it is necessary that his kind cease with him, that
his progeny shall not be, that he play the eunuch's part in this
twentieth century after Christ. And he plays it. He does not breed.
Sterility is his portion, as it is the portion of the woman on the street.
They might have been mates, but society has decreed otherwise.

And, while it is not nice that these men should die, it is ordained
that they must die, and we should not quarrel with them if they
cumber our highways and kitchen stoops with their perambulating
carcasses. This is a form of elimination we not only countenance but
compel. Therefore let us be cheerful and honest about it. Let us be as
stringent as we please with our police regulations, but for goodness'
sake let us refrain from telling the tramp to go to work. Not only is
it unkind, but it is untrue and hypocritical. We know there is no
work for him. As the scapegoat to our economic and industrial sin-
ning, or to the plan of things, if you will, we should give him credit.
Let us be just. He is so made. Society made him. He did not make
himself.

Henry James [1843-1916]
FROM *The American Scene* [1907]

Philadelphia

I

To be at all critically, or as we have been fond of calling it, analytically, minded—over and beyond an inherent love of the general many-coloured picture of things—is to be subject to the superstition that objects and places, coherently grouped, disposed for human use and addressed to it, must have a sense of their own, a mystic meaning proper to themselves to give out: to give out, that is, to the participant at once so interested and so detached as to be moved to a report of the matter. That perverse person is obliged to take it for a working theory that the essence of almost any settled aspect of anything may be extracted by the chemistry of criticism, and may give us its right name, its formula, for convenient use. From the moment the critic finds himself sighing, to save trouble in a difficult case, that the cluster of appearances can *have* no sense, from that moment he begins, and quite consciously, to go to pieces; it being the prime

business and the high honour of the painter of life always to *make* a
sense—and to make it most in proportion as the immediate aspects are
loose or confused. The last thing decently permitted him is to recognize incoherence—to recognize it, that is, as baffling; though of
course he may present and portray it, in all richness, *for* incoherence.
That, I think, was what I had been mainly occupied with in New
York; and I quitted so qualified a joy, under extreme stress of winter,
with a certain confidence that I should not have moved even a little
of the way southward without practical relief: relief which came in
fact ever so promptly, at Philadelphia, on my feeling, unmistakably,
the change of half the furniture of consciousness. This change put
on, immediately, the friendliest, the handsomest aspect—supplied my
intelligence on the spot with the clear, the salient note. I mean by
this, not that the happy definition or synthesis instantly came—came
with the perception that character and sense were there, only waiting
to be disengaged; but that the note, as I say, was already, within an
hour, the germ of these things, and that the whole flower, assuredly,
wouldn't fail to bloom. I was in fact sniffing up its fragrance after I
had looked out for three minutes from one of the windows of a particularly wide-fronted house and seen the large residential square that
lay before me shine in its native light. This light, remarkably tender,
I thought, for that of a winter afternoon, matched with none other I
had ever seen, and announced straight off fifty new circumstances—
an enormous number, in America, for any prospect to promise you
in contradistinction from any other. It was not simply that, beyond a
doubt, the outlook was more *méridional;* a still deeper impression
had begun to work, and, as I felt it more and more glimmer upon
me, I caught myself about to jump, with a single leap, to my synthesis. I of course stayed myself in the act, for there would be too
much, really, yet to come; but the perception left me, I even then
felt, in possession of half the ground on which later experience
would proceed. It was not too much to say, as I afterwards saw, that
I had in those few illumined moments put the gist of the matter into
my pocket.

Philadelphia, incontestably then, was the American city of the
large type, that didn't *bristle*—just as I was afterwards to recognize in
St. Louis the nearest approach to companionship with her in this
respect; and to recognize in Chicago, I may parenthetically add, the

most complete divergence. It was not only, moreover, at the ample, tranquil window there, that Philadelphia *didn't* "bristle" (by the record of my moment) but that she essentially couldn't and wouldn't ever; that no movement or process could be thought of, in fine, as more foreign to her genius. I do not just now go into the question of what the business of bristling, in an American city, may be estimated as consisting of; so infallibly is one aware when the thousand possible quills *are* erect, and when, haply, they are not—such a test does the restored absentee find, at least, in his pricked sensibility. A place may abound in its own sense, as the phrase is, without bristling in the least —it is liable indeed to bristle most, I think, when not too securely possessed of any settled sense to abound in. An imperfect grasp of such a luxury is not the weakness of Philadelphia—just as that admirable comprehensive flatness in her which precludes the image of the porcupine figured to me from the first, precisely, as her positive source of strength. The absence of the note of the perpetual perpendicular, the New York, the Chicago note—and I allude here to the material, the constructional exhibition of it—seemed to symbolize exactly the principle of indefinite level extension and to offer refreshingly, a challenge to horizontal, to lateral, to more or less tangential, to rotary, or, better still, to absolute centrifugal motion. If it was to befall me, during my brief but various acquaintance with the place, not to find myself more than two or three times hoisted or lowered by machinery, my prime illumination had been an absolute forecast of that immunity—a virtue of general premonition in it at which I have already glanced. I should in fact, I repeat, most truly or most artfully repaint my little picture by mixing my colours with the felt amenity of that small crisis, and by showing how this, that and the other impression to come had had, while it lasted, quite the definite prefigurement that the chapters of a book find in its table of contents. The afternoon blandness, for a fugitive from Madison Avenue in January snow, didn't mean nothing; the little marble steps and lintels and cornices and copings, all the so clear, so placed accents in the good prose text of the mildly purple houses across the Square, which seemed to wear them, as all the others did, up and down the streets, in the manner of nice white stockings, neckties, collars, cuffs, didn't mean nothing; and this was somehow an assurance that joined on to the vibration of the view produced, a few hours before, by so merely convenient a circumstance as my taking my place, at Jersey City, in the Pennsylvania train.

I had occasion, repeatedly, to find the Pennsylvania Railroad a beguiling and predisposing influence—in relation to various objectives; and indeed I quite lost myself in the singularity of this effect, which existed for me, certainly, only in that connection, touching me with a strange and most agreeable sense that the great line in question, an institution with a style and *allure* of its own, is not, even the world over, as other railroads are. It absolutely, with a little frequentation, affected me as better and higher than its office or function, and almost as supplying one with a mode of life intrinsically superior; as if it ought really to be on its way to much grander and more charming places than any that happen to mark its course—as if indeed, should one persistently keep one's seat, not getting out anywhere, it would in the end carry one to some such ideal city. One might under this extravagant spell, which always began to work for me at Twenty-third Street, and on the constantly-adorable Ferry, have fancied the train, disvulgarized of passengers, steaming away, in disinterested empty form, to some terminus too noble to be marked in *our* poor schedules. The consciousness of this devotion would have been thus like that of living, all sublimely, up in a balloon. It was not, however—I recover myself—that if I had been put off at Philadelphia I was not, for the hour, contented; finding so immediately, as I have noted, more interest to my hand than I knew at first what to do with. There was the quick light of explanation, following on everything else I have mentioned—the light in which I had only to turn round again and see where I was, and how it was, in order to feel everything "come out" under the large friendliness, the ordered charm and perfect peace of the Club, housing me with that *whole* protection the bestowal of which on occasion is the finest grace of the hospitality of American clubs. Philadelphia, manifestly, was beyond any other American city, a *society*, and was going to show as such, as a thoroughly confirmed and settled one—which fact became the key, precisely, to its extension on one plane, and to its having no pretext for bristling. Human groups that discriminate in their own favour do, one remembers, in general, bristle; but that is only when they have not been really successful, when they have not been able to discriminate enough, when they are not, like Philadelphia, settled and confirmed and content. It would clearly be impossible not to regard the place before me as possessed of this secret of serenity to a degree elsewhere—at least among ourselves—unrivalled. The basis of the advantage, the terms of the secret, would be still to make out—which was precisely the high interest; and I was afterwards to be justified of my conviction by the multiplication of my lights.

New York, in that sense, had appeared to me then not a society at all, and it was rudimentary that Chicago would be one still less; neither of them, as a human group, having been able to discriminate in its own favour with anything like such success. The proof of that would be, obviously, in one's so easily imputing to them alteration, extension, development; a change somehow unimaginable in the case of Philadelphia, which was a fixed quantity and had filled to the brim, one felt—and wasn't that really to be part of the charm?—the measure of her possibility. Boston even was thinkable as subject to mutation; had I not in fact just seemed to myself to catch her in the almost uncanny inconsequence of change? There had been for Boston the old epigram that she wasn't a place, but a state of mind; and that might remain, since we know how frequently states of mind alter. Philadelphia then wasn't a place, but a state of consanguinity, which is an absolute final condition. She had arrived at it, with nothing in the world left to bristle for, or against; whereas New York, and above all Chicago, were only, and most precariously, on the way to it, and indeed, having started too late, would probably never arrive. There were, for them, interferences and complications; they knew, and would yet know, other conditions, perhaps other beatitudes; only the beatitude I speak of—that of being, in the composed sense, a society—was lost to them forever. Philadelphia, without complications or interferences, enjoyed it in particular through having begun to invoke it in time. And now she had nothing more to invoke; she had everything; her *cadres* were all full; her imagination was at peace. This, exactly again, would be the reason of the bristling of the other places: the *cadres* of New York, Chicago, Boston, being as to a third of them empty and as to another third objectionably filled —with much consequent straining, reaching, heaving, both to attain and to eject. What makes a society was thus, more than anything else, the number of organic social relations it represents; by which logic Philadelphia would represent nothing *but* organic social relations. The degrees of consanguinity were the *cadres;* every one of them was full; it was a society in which every individual was as many times over cousin, uncle, aunt, niece, and so on through the list, as poor human nature is susceptible of being. These degrees are, when one reflects, the only really organic social relations, and when they are all there for every one the scheme of security, in a community, has been worked out. Philadelphia, in other words, would not only be a family, she would be a "happy" one, and a probable proof that the happiness comes as a matter of course if the family but be large enough. Consanguinity provides the marks and features, the type and tone and ease, the common knowledge and the common consciousness, but number would be required to make these things social. Number, accordingly, for her perfection, was what Philadelphia would have—it having been clear to me still, in my charming Club and at my illuminating window, that she couldn't *not* be perfect. She would be, of all goodly villages, the very goodliest, probably, in the world; the very largest, and flattest, and smoothest, the most rounded and complete.

II

The simplest account of such success as I was to have in putting my vision to the test will be, I think, to say that the place never for a moment belied to me that forecast of its animated intimacy. Yet it might be just here that a report of my experience would find itself hampered—this learning the lesson, from one vivid page of the picture-book to another, of how perfectly "intimate" Philadelphia is. Such an exhibition would be, prohibitively, the exhibition of private things, of private things only, and of a charmed contact with them, were it not for the great circumstance which, when what I have said has been fully said, remains to be taken into account. The state of infinite cousinship colours the scene, makes the predominant tone; but you get a light upon it that is worth all others from the moment you see it as, ever so savingly, historic. This perception moreover promptly operates; I found it stirred, as soon as I went out or began to circulate, by all immediate aspects and signs. The place "went back"; or, in other words, the social equilibrium, forestalling so that of the other cities, had begun early, had had plenty of time on its

side, and thus had its history behind it—the past that looms through
it, not at all luridly, but so squarely and substantially, to-day, and
gives it, by a mercy, an extension other than the lateral. This,
frankly, was required, it struck me, for the full comfort of one's
impression—for a certain desirable and imputable richness. The backward extension, in short, is the very making of Philadelphia; one is so
uncertain of the value one would attach to her being as she is, if she
hadn't been so by prescription and for a couple of centuries. This has
established her right and her competence; the fact is the parent, so to
speak, of her consistency and serenity; it has made the very law
under which her parts and pieces have held so closely together. To
walk her streets is to note with all promptness that William Penn
must have laid them out—no one else could possibly have done it so
ill. It was his best, though, with our larger sense for a street, it is far
from ours; we at any rate no more complain of them, nor suggest
that they might have been more liberally conceived, than we so
express ourselves about the form of the chairs in sitting through a
morning call.

I found myself liking them, then, as I moved among them, just in
proportion as they conformed, in detail, to the early pattern—the
figure, for each house, of the red-faced old gentleman whose thick
eyebrows and moustache have turned to white; and I found myself
detesting them in any instance of a new front or a new fashion.
They were narrow, with this aspect as of a double file of grizzled
veterans, or they were nothing; the narrowness had been positively
the channel or conduit of continuity of character: it made the long
pipe on which the tune of the place was played. From the moment it
was in any way corrected the special charm broke—the charm, a rare
civic possession, as of some immense old ruled and neatly-inked
chart, not less carefully than benightedly flattened out, stretching its
tough parchment under the very feet of all comings and goings. This
was an image with which, as it furthermore seemed to me, everything else consorted—above all the soothing truth that Philadelphia
was, yes, beyond cavil, solely and singly Philadelphian. There was an
interference absent, or one that I at least never met: that sharp note
of the outlandish, in the strict sense of the word, which I had already
found almost everywhere so disconcerting. I pretend here of course
neither to estimate the numbers in which the grosser aliens may

actually have settled on these bland banks of the Delaware, nor to put my finger on the principle of the shock I had felt it, and was still to feel it, in their general power to administer; for I am not now concerned so much with the impression made by one's almost everywhere meeting them, as with the impression made by one's here and there failing of it. They may have been gathered, in their hordes, in some vast quarter unknown to me and of which I was to have no glimpse; but what would this have denoted, exactly, but some virtue in the air for reducing their presence, or their effect, to naught? There precisely was the difference from New York—that they themselves had been in that place half the virtue, or the vice, of the air, and that there were few of its agitations to which they had not something to say.

The logic of the case had been visible to me, for that matter, on my very first drive from the train—from that precious "Pennsylvania" station of Philadelphia which was to strike me as making a nearer approach than elsewhere to the arts of ingratiation. There was an object or two, windowed and chimneyed, in the central sky—but nothing to speak of: I then and there, in a word, took in the admirable flatness. And if it seemed so spacious, by the same token, this was because it was neither eager, nor grasping, nor pushing. It drew its breath at its ease, clearly—never sounding the charge, the awful "Step lively!" of New York. The fury of the pavement had dropped, in fine, as I was to see it drop, later on, between Chicago and St. Louis. This affected me on the spot of symbolic, and I was to have no glimpse of anything that gainsaid the symbol. It was somehow, too, the very note of the homogeneous; though this indeed is not, oddly enough, the head under which at St. Louis my impression was to range itself. I at all events here gave myself up to the vision—that of the vast, firm chess-board, the immeasurable spread of little squares, covered *all* over by perfect Philadelphians. It was an image, in face of some of the other features of the view, dissimilar to any by which one had ever in one's life been assaulted; and this elimination of the foreign element has been what was required to make it consummate. Nothing is more notable, through the States at large, than that hazard of what one may happen, or may not happen, to see; but the only use to be made of either accident is, clearly, to let it stand and to let it serve. This intensity and ubiquity of the local tone, that of the illimitable *town*, serves so successfully for my sense of Philadelphia that I should feel as if a little masterpiece of the creative imagination had been destroyed by the least correction. And there is, further, the point to make that if I knew, all the while, that there was something more, and different, and less beatific, under and behind the happy appearance I grasped, I knew it by no glimmer of direct perception, and should never in the world have guessed it if some sound of it had not, by a discordant voice, been, all superfluously, rather tactlessly, dropped into my ear.

It was not, however, disconcerting at the time, this presentation, as in a flash, of the other side of the medal—the other side being, in a word, as was mentioned to me, one of the most lurid pages in the annals of political corruption. The place, by this revelation, was two distinct things—a Society, from far back, the society I had divined, the most genial and delightful one could think of, and then, parallel to this, and not within it, nor quite altogether above it, but beside it and beneath it, behind it and before it, enclosing it as in a frame of fire in which it still had the secret of keeping cool, a proportionate City, the most incredible that ever was, organized all for plunder and rapine, the gross satisfaction of official appetite, organized for eternal iniquity and impunity. Such were the conditions, it had been hinted to me—from the moment the medal spun round; but I even understate, I think, in speaking of the knowledge as only not disconcerting. It was better than that, for it positively added the last touch of colour to my framed and suspended picture. Here, strikingly then, was an American *case*, and presumably one of the best; one of the best, that is, for some study of the wondrous problem, admiration and amazement of the nations, who yearn over it from far off: the way in which sane Society and pestilent City, in the United States, successfully cohabit, each keeping it up with so little of fear or flutter from the other. The thing presents itself, in its prime unlikelihood, as a thorough good neighbouring of the Happy Family and the Infernal Machine—the machine so rooted as to continue to defy removal, and the family still so indifferent, while it carries on the family business of buying and selling, of chattering and dancing, to the danger of being blown up. It is all puzzled out, from afar, as a matter of the exchange, and in a large decree of the observance, from side to side, of guarantees, and the interesting thing to get at, for the

student of manners, will ever be just this mystery of the terms of the
bargain. I must add, none the less, that, though one was one's self,
inevitably and always and everywhere, that student, my attention
happened to be, or rather was obliged to be, confined to one view of
the agreement. The arrangement is, obviously, between the great
municipalities and the great populations, on the grand scale, and I
lacked opportunity to look at it all round. I had but my glimpse of
the apparently wide social acceptance of it—that is I saw but the face
of the medal most directly turned to the light of day, and could note
that nowhere so much as in Philadelphia was any carking care, in the
social mind, any uncomfortable consciousness, as of a skeleton at the
banquet of life, so gracefully veiled.

This struck me (on my looking back afterwards with more
knowledge) as admirable, as heroic, in its way, and as falling in altogether with inherent habits of sociability, gaiety, gallantry, with that
felt presence of a "temperament" with which the original Quaker
drab seems to flush—giving it, as one might say for the sake of the
figure, something of the iridescence of the breast of a well-fed dove.
The original Quaker drab is still there, and, ideally, for the picture,
up and down the uniform streets, one should see a bland, broad-
brimmed, square-toed gentleman, or a bonneted, kerchiefed, mittened
lady, on every little flight of white steps; but the very note of the
place has been the "worldly" overscoring, for most of the senses, of
the primitive monotone, the bestitching of the drab with pink and
green and silver. The mixture has been, for a social effect, admirably
successful, thanks, one seems to see, to the subtle, the charming
absence of pedantry in the Quaker purity. It flushes gracefully, that
temperate prejudice (with its predisposition to the universal *tutoie-
ment*), turning first but to the prettiest pink; so that we never quite
know where the drab has ended and the colour of the world has
begun. The "disfrocked" Catholic is too strange, the paganized Puritan too angular; it is the accommodating Friend who has most the
secret of a *modus vivendi*. And if it be asked, I may add, whether, in
this case of social Philadelphia, the genius for life, and what I have
called the gallantry of it above all, wouldn't have been better shown
by a scorn of *any* compromise to which the nefarious City could invite it, I can only reply that, as a lover, always of romantic phenomena, and an inveterate seeker for them, I should have been deprived,

by the action of that particular virtue, of the thrilled sense of a society dancing, all consciously, on the thin crust of a volcano. It is the thinness of the crust that makes, in such examples, the wild fantasy, the gay bravery, of the dance—just as I admit that a preliminary, an original extinction of the volcano would have illustrated another kind of virtue. The crust, for the social tread, would in this case have been firm, but the spectator's imagination would have responded less freely, I think, to the appeal of the scene. If I may indeed speak my whole thought for him he would so have had to drop again, to his regret, the treasure of a small analogy picked up on its very threshold.

How shall he confess at once boldly and shyly enough that the situation had at the end of a very short time begun to strike him, for all its immeasurably reduced and simplified form, as a much nearer approach to the representation of an "old order," an *ancien régime*, socially speaking, than any the field of American manners had seemed likely to regale him with? Grotesque the comparison if pushed; yet how had he encountered the similitude if it hadn't been hanging about? From the moment he adopted it, at any rate, he found it taking on touch after touch. The essence of old orders, as history lights them, is just that innocent beatitude of consanguinity, of the multiplication of the assured felicities, to which I have already alluded. From this, in Philadelphia, didn't the rest follow?—the sense, for every one, of being in the same boat with every one else, a closed circle that would find itself happy enough if only it could remain closed enough. The boat might considerably pitch, but its occupants would either float merrily together or (almost as merrily) go down together, and meanwhile the risk, the vague danger, the jokes to be made about it, the general quickened sociability and intimacy, were the very music of the excursion. There are even yet to be observed about the world fragments and ghosts of old social orders, thin survivals of final cataclysms, and it was not less positive than beguiling that the common marks by which these companies are known, and which we still distinguish through their bedimmed condition, cropped up for me in the high American light, making good my odd parallel at almost every point. Yet if these signs of a slightly congested, but still practically self-sufficing, little world were all there, they were perhaps there most, to my ear, in the fact of the little world's proper intimate idiom and accent: a dialect as much its very own, even in drawing-rooms and libraries, as the Venetian is that of Venice or the Neapolitan is that of Naples—representing the common things of association, the things easily understood and felt, and charged as no other vehicle could be with the fund of local reference. There is always the difference, of course, that at Venice and at Naples, "in society," an alternative, either that of French or of the classic, the more or less academic Italian, is offered to the uninitiated stranger, whereas in Philadelphia he is candidly, consistently, sometimes almost contagiously entertained in the free vernacular. The latter may easily become, in fact, under its wealth of idiosyncrasy and if he have the favouring turn of mind, a tempting object of linguistic study; with the bridge built for him, moreover, that, unlike the Venetian, the Neapolitan and most other local languages, it contains, itself, colloquially, a notable element of the academic and the classic. It struck me even, truly, as, with a certain hardness in it, *constituting* the society that employed it—very much as the egg is made oval by its shell; and really, if I may say all, as taking its stand a bit consciously sometimes, if not a bit defiantly, on its own proved genius. I remember the visible dismay of a gentleman, a pilgrim from afar, in a drawing-room, at the comment of a lady, a lady of one of the new generations indeed, and mistress of the tone by which I had here and there occasion to observe that such ornaments of the new generation might be known. "Listen to the creature: he speaks English!"—it was the very opposite of the indulgence or encouragement with which, in a Venetian drawing-room (I catch my analogies as I can) the sound of French or of Italian might have been greeted. The poor "creature's" dismay was so visible, clearly, for the reason that such things have only to be said with a certain confidence to create a certain confusion—the momentary consciousness of some such misdeed, from the point of view of manners, as the speaking of Russian at Warsaw. I have said that Philadelphia didn't bristle, but the heroine of my anecdote caused the so genial city to resemble, for the minute, linguistically, an unreconciled Poland.

III

But why do I talk of the new generations, or at any rate of the abyss in them that may seem here and there beyond one's shallow sounding, when, all the while, at the back of my head, hovers the image in the guise of which antiquity in Philadelphia looks most seated and most interesting? Nowhere throughout the country, I think, unless it be perchance at Mount Vernon, does our historic past so enjoy the felicity of an "important" concrete illustration. It survives there in visible form as it nowhere else survives, and one can doubtless scarce think too largely of what its mere felicity of presence, in these conditions, has done, and continues, and will continue, to do for the place at large. It may seem witless enough, at this time of day, to arrive from Pennsylvania with "news" of the old State House, and my news, I can only recognize, began but with being news for myself— in which character it quite shamelessly pretended both to freshness and to brilliancy. Why *shouldn't* it have been charming, the high roof under which the Declaration of Independence had been signed? —that was of course a question that might from the first have been asked of me, and with no better answer in wait for it than that, after all, it might just have happened, in the particular conditions, not to be; or else that, in general, one is allowed a margin, on the spot, for the direct sense of consecrated air, for that communication of its spirit which, in proportion as the spirit has been great, withholds itself, shyly and nobly, from any mere forecast. This it is exactly that, by good fortune, keeps up the sanctity of shrines and the lessons of history, to say nothing of the freshness of individual sensibility and the general continuity of things. There is positively nothing of Independence Hall, of its fine old Georgian amplitude and decency, its large serenity and symmetry of pink and drab, and its actual emphasis of detachment from the vulgar brush of things, that is *not* charming; and there is nothing, the city through, that doesn't receive a mild sidelight, that of a reflected interest, from its neighbourhood.

This element of the reflected interest, and more particularly of the reflected distinction, is for the most part, on the American scene, the missed interest—despite the ingenuities of wealth and industry and "energy" that strain so touchingly often, and even to grimace and contortion, somehow to supply it. One finds one's self, when it *has* happened to intervene, weighing its action to the last grain of gold. One even puts to one's self fantastic cases, such as the question, for instance, of what might, what might *not* have happened if poor dear reckless New York had been so distinguished or so blest—with the bad conscience she is too intelligent not to have, her power to be now and then ashamed of her "form," lodged, after all, somewhere in her interminable boots. One has of course to suppress there the prompt conviction that the blessing—that of the possession of an historical monument of the first order—would long since have been replaced by the higher advantage of a row of sky-scrapers yielding rents; yet the imagination none the less dallies with the fond vision of some respect somehow instilled, some deference somehow suggested, some revelation of the possibilities of a public *tenue* somehow effected. Fascinating in fact to speculate a little as to what a New York held in respect by something or other, some power not of the purse, might have become. It is bad, ever, for lusty youth, especially with a command of means, to grow up without knowing at least one "nice family"—if the family be not priggish; and this is the danger that the young Philadelphia, with its eyes on the superior connection I am speaking of, was enabled to escape. The charming old pink and drab heritage of the great time was to be the superior connection, playing, for the education of the place, the part of the nice family. Socially, morally, even aesthetically, the place was to be thus more or less inevitably built round it; but for which good fortune who knows if even Philadelphia too might have not been vulgar? One meets throughout the land enough instances of the opposite luck—the situation of immense and "successful" communities that have lacked, originally, anything "first-rate," as they might themselves put it, to be built round; anything better, that is, than some profitable hole in the earth, some confluence of rivers or command of lakes or railroads: and one sees how, though this deficiency may not have made itself felt at first, it has inexorably loomed larger and larger, the drawback of it growing all the while with the growth of the place. Our sense of such predicaments, for the gatherings of men, comes back, I think, and with an intensity of interest, to our sense of the way the human imagination absolutely declines everywhere to go to sleep without some apology at least for a supper. The collective consciousness, in however empty an air, gasps for a relation, as intimate as possible, to something superior, something as central as possible, from which it may more or less have proceeded and round which its life may revolve—and its dim desire is always, I think, to do it justice, that this object or presence shall have had as much as possible an heroic or romantic association. But the difficulty is that in these later times,

among such aggregations, the heroic and romantic elements, even
under the earliest rude stress, have been all too tragically obscure,
belonged to smothered, unwritten, almost unconscious private history: so that the central something, the social *point de repère*, has
had to be extemporized rather pitifully after the fact, and made to
consist of the biggest hotel or the biggest common school, the biggest
factory, the biggest newspaper office, or, for climax of desperation,
the house of the biggest billionaire. These are the values resorted to in
default of higher, for with *some* coloured rag or other the general
imagination, snatching its chance, must dress its doll.

As a real, a moral value, to the general mind, at all events, and
not as a trumped-up one, I saw the lucky legacy of the past, at Philadelphia, operate; though I admit that these are, at best, for the moon-
ing observer, matters of appreciation, mysteries of his own sensibility. Such an observer has early to perceive, and to conclude on it
once for all, that there will be little for him in the American scene
unless he be ready, anywhere, everywhere, to read "into" it as much
as he reads out. It is at its best for him when most open to that
friendly penetration, and not at its best, I judge, when practically
most closed to it. And yet how can I pretend to be able to say, under
this discrimination, what was better and what was worse in Independence Hall?—to say how far the charming facts struck me as going
of themselves, or where the imagination (perhaps on this sole patch
of ground, by exception, a meddler "not wanted anyhow") took
them up to carry them further. I am reduced doubtless to the comparative sophism of making my better sense here consist but of my
sense of the fine interior of the building. One sees them immediately
as "good," delightfully good, on architectural and scenic lines, these
large, high, wainscoted chambers, as good as any could thinkably
have been at the time; embracing what was to be done in them with
such a noble congruity (which in all the conditions they might
readily have failed of, though they were no mere tent pitched for the
purpose) that the historic imagination, reascending the centuries,
almost catches them in the act of directly suggesting the celebrated
coup. One fancies, under the high spring of the ceiling and before
the great embrasured window-sashes of the principal room, some
clever man of the period, after a long look round, taking the hint.
"*What* an admirable place for a Declaration of something! What

could one here—what *couldn't* one really declare?" And then after a
moment: "I say, why not our Independence?—capital thing always to
declare, and before any one gets in with anything tactless. You'll see
that the fortune of the place will be made." It really takes some such
frivolous fancy as that to represent with proper extravagance the
reflection irresistibly rising there and that it yet would seem pedantic
to express with solemnity: the sense, namely, of our beautiful escape
in not having had to "declare" in any way meanly, of our good fortune in having found half the occasion made to our hand.

High occasions consist of many things, and it was extraordinary
luck for our great date that not one of these, even as to surface and
appearance, should have been wanting. There might easily have been
traps laid for us by some of the inferior places, but I am convinced
(and more completely than of anything else in the whole connection) that the genius of historic decency would have kept us enslaved
rather than have seen us committed to one of those. In that light, for
the intelligent pilgrim, the Philadelphia monument becomes, under
his tread, under the touch of his hand and the echo of his voice, the
very prize, the sacred thing itself, contended for and gained; so that
its quality, in fine, is irresistible and its dignity not to be uttered. I
was so conscious, for myself, I confess, of the intensity of this perception, that I dip deep into the whole remembrance without touching bottom; by which I mean that I grope, reminiscentially, in the
full basin of the general experience of the spot without bringing up a
detail. Distinct to me only the way its character, so clear yet so
ample, everywhere hangs together and keeps itself up; distinct to me
only the large sense, in halls and spreading staircase and long-drawn
upper gallery, of one of those rare precincts of the past against
which the present has kept beating in vain. The present comes in and
stamps about and very stertorously breathes, but its sounds are as
naught the next moment; it is as if one felt there that the grand-
parent, reserved, irresponsive now, and having spoken his word, in
his finest manner, once for all, must have long ago had enough of the
exuberance of the young grandson's modernity. But of course the
great impression is that of the persistent actuality of the so auspicious room in which the Signers saw their tossing ship into port. The
lapse of time here, extraordinarily, has sprung no leak in the effect; it
remains so robust that everything lives again, the interval drops out

and we mingle in the business: the old ghosts, to our inward sensibility, still make the benches creak as they free their full coat-skirts for sitting down; still make the temperature rise, the pens scratch, the papers flutter, the dust float in the large sun-shafts; we place them as they sit, watch them as they move, hear them as they speak, pity them as they ponder, know them, in fine, from the arch of their eyebrows to the shuffle of their shoes.

I am not sure indeed that, for mere archaic insolence, the little old Hall of the Guild of Carpenters, my vision of which jostles my memory of the State House, does not carry it even with a higher hand—in spite of a bedizenment of restoration, within, which leads us to rejoice that the retouchings of the greater monument expose themselves comparatively so little. The situation of this elegant structure—of dimensions and form that scarce differ, as I recall them, from those of delicate little Holden Chapel, of the so floridly-overlaid gable, most articulate single word, in College Yard, of the small builded sense of old Harvard—comes nearer to representing an odd town-nook than any other corner of American life that I remember; American life having been organized, *ab ovo*, with an hostility to the town-nook which has left no scrap of provision for eyes needing on occasion a refuge from the general glare. The general glare seemed to me, at the end of something like a passage, in the shade of something like a court, and in the presence of something like a relic, to have mercifully intermitted, on that fine Philadelphia morning; I won't answer for the exact correspondence of the conditions with my figure of them, since the shade I speak of may have been but the shade of "tall" buildings, the vulgarest of new accidents. Yet I let my impression stand, if only as a note of the relief certain always to lurk, at any turn of the American scene, in the appearance of any individual thing within, or behind, or at the end, or in the depth, of any other individual thing. It makes for the sense of complexity, relieves the eternal impression of things all in a row and of a single thickness, an impression which the usual unprecedented length of the American alignment (always its source of pride) does by itself little to mitigate. Nothing in the array is "behind" anything else—an odd result, I admit, of the fact that so many things affirm themselves as preponderantly before. Little Carpenters' Hall *was*, delightfully, somewhere behind; so much behind, as I perhaps thus fantastically see it, that I

dare say I should not be able to find my way to it again if I were to
try. Nothing, for that matter, would induce me to revisit in fact, I
feel, the object I so fondly evoke. It might have been, for this beautiful posteriority, somewhere in the City of London.

IV

I can but continue to lose myself, for these connections, in my *whole*
sense of the intermission, as I have called it, of the glare. The mel-
lower light prevailed, somehow, *all* that fine Philadelphia morning, as
well as on two or three other occasions—and I cannot, after all, pretend I don't now see why. It was because one's experience of the
place had become immediately an intimate thing—intimate with that
intimacy that I had tasted, from the first, in the local air; so that,
inevitably, thus, there was no keeping of distinct accounts for public
and private items. An ancient church or two, of aspect as Anglican
still as you please, and taking, for another case, from the indifferent
bustle round it, quite the look of Wren's mere steepled survivals in
the backwaters of London churchyards; Franklin's grave itself, in its
own backwater of muffled undulations, close to the indifferent bustle;
Franklin's admirable portrait by Duplessis in the council-room of an
ancient, opulent Trust, a conservative Company, vague and awful to
my shy sense, that was housed after the fashion of some exclusive,
madeira-drinking old gentleman with obsequious heirs: these and
other matters, wholly thrilling at the time, float back to me as on the
current of talk and as in the flood, so to speak, of hospitality. If
Philadelphia had, in opposition to so many other matters, struck me
as coherent, there would be surely no point of one's contact at which
this might so have come home as in those mysterious chambers and
before the most interesting of the many far-scattered portraits of
Franklin—the portrait working as some sudden glimpse of the fine
old incised seal, kept in its glass cabinet, that had originally stamped
all over, for identification, the comparatively soft local wax. One
thinks of Franklin's reputation, of his authority—and however much
they may have been locally contested at the time—as marking the
material about him much as his name might have marked his under-
clothing or his pocket-books. Small surprise one had the impression of
a Society, with such a figure as that to start conversation. He seemed

to preside over it all while one lingered there, as if he had been seated, at the mahogany, relentlessly enough, near his glass of madeira; seemed to be "in" it even more freely than by the so interesting fact of his still having, in Philadelphia, in New York, in Boston, through his daughter, so numerous a posterity. The sense of life, life the most positive, most human and most miscellaneous, expressed in his aged, crumpled, canny face, where the smile wittily profits, for fineness, by the comparative collapse of the mouth, represents a suggestion which succeeding generations may well have found it all they could do to work out. It is impossible, in the place, after seeing that portrait, not to feel him still with them, with the genial generations—even though to-day, in the larger, more mixed cup, the force of his example may have suffered some dilution.

It was a savour of which, at any rate, for one's own draught, one could but make the most; and I went so far, on this occasion, as fairly to taste it there in the very quality of my company—in that of the distinguished guidance and protection I was enjoying, which could only make me ask myself in what finer modern form one would have wished to see Franklin's humanity and sagacity, his variety and ingenuity, his wealth of ideas and his tireless application of them, embodied. There was verily nothing to do, after this, but to play over the general picture that light of his assumption of the general ease of things—of things at any rate thereabouts; so that I now see each reminiscence, whatever the time or the place, happily governed and coloured by it. Times and places, in such an experience, ranged themselves, after a space, like valued objects in one of the assorted rooms of a "collection." Keep them a little, tenderly handled, wrapped up, stowed away, and they then come forth, into the room swept and garnished, susceptible of almost any pleasing arrangement. The only thing is that you shall scarce know, at a given moment, amid your abundance, which of them to take up first; there being always in them, moreover, at best, the drawback of value from mere association, that keepsake element of objects in a reliquary. Is not this, however, the drawback for exhibition of almost any item of American experience that may not pretend to deal with the mere monstrosities?—the immensities of size and space, of trade and traffic, of organisation, political, educational, economic. From the moment one's record is not, in fine, a loud statistical shout, it falls into the order of those shy things that speak, at the most (when one is one's self incapable even of the merest statistical whisper), but of the personal adventure—in other words but of one's luck and of one's sensibility. There are incidents, there are passages, that flush, in this fashion, to the backward eye, under the torch. But what solemn statement is one to make of the "importance," for example, of such a matter as the Academy soirée (as they say in London) of the Philadelphia winter, the festive commemoration of some long span of life achieved by the Pennsylvania Academy of Fine Arts? We may have been thrilled, positively, by the occasion, by the interesting encounters and discoveries, artistic and personal, to which it ministered; we may have moved from one charmed recognition to another, noting Sargents and Whistlers by the dozen, and old forgotten French friends, foreign friends in general, older and younger; noting young native upstarts, creatures of yesterday and to-morrow, who invite, with all success, a stand and a stare; but no after-sense of such vibrations, however lively, presumes to take itself as communicable.

One would regret, on the other hand, failing to sound some echo of a message everywhere in the United States so audible; that of the clamorous signs of a hungry social growth, the very pulses, making all their noise, of the engine that works night and day for a theory of civilization. There are moments at which it may well seem that, putting the sense of the spectacle even at its lowest, there is no such amusement as this anywhere supplied; the air through which everything shows is so transparent, with steps and stages and processes as distinct in it as the appearance, from a street-corner, of a crowd rushing on an alarm to a fire. The gregarious crowd "tells," in the street, and the indications I speak of tell, like chalk-marks, on the demonstrative American black-board—an impression perhaps never so much brought home to me as by a wondrous Sunday morning at the edge of a vast vacant Philadelphia street, a street not of Penn's creation and vacant of everything but an immeasurable bourgeois blankness. I had turned from that scene into a friendly house that was given over, from top to toe, to a dazzling collection of pictures, amid which I felt myself catch in the very act one of the great ingurgitations of the hungry machine, and recognize as well how perfect were all the conditions for making it a case. What could have testified less, on the face of it, than the candour of the street's insignificance?—a pair of huge parted lips protesting almost to pathos their innocence of anything to say: which was exactly, none the less, where appetite had broken out and was feeding itself to satiety. Large and liberal the hospitality, remarkably rich the store of acquisition, in the light of which the whole energy of the keen collector showed: the knowledge, the acuteness, the audacity, the incessant watch for opportunity. These abrupt and multiplied encounters, intensities, ever so various, of individual curiosity, sound the aesthetic note sometimes with unprecedented shrillness and then again with the most muffled discretion. Was the note muffled or shrill, meanwhile, as I listened to it—under a fascination I fully recognized —during an hour spent in the clustered palaestra of the University of Pennsylvania? Here the winter afternoon seemed to throw itself artfully back, across the centuries, the climates, the seasons, the very faiths and codes, into the air of old Greece and the age of gymnastic glory: artfully, I rather insist, because I scarce know what fine emphasis of modernism hung about it too. I put that question, however, only to deny myself the present luxury of answering it; so thickly do the visitor's University impressions, over the land, tend to gather, and so markedly they suggest their being reported of together. I note my palaestral hour, therefore, but because it fell through what it seemed to show me, straight into what I had conceived of the Philadelphia scheme, the happy family given up, though quite on "family" lines, to all the immediate beguilements and activities; the art in particular of cultivating, with such gaiety as might be, a brave civic blindness.

I became conscious of but one excrescence on this large smooth surface; it is true indeed that the excrescence was huge and affected me as demanding in some way to be dealt with. The Pennsylvania Penitentiary rears its ancient grimness, its grey towers and defensive moats (masses at least that uncertain memory so figures for me) in an outlying quarter which struck me as borrowing from them a vague likeness to some more or less blighted minor city of Italy or France, black Angers or dead Ferrara—yet seated on its basis of renown and wrapped in its legend of having, as the first flourishing example of the strictly cellular system, the complete sequestration of the individual prisoner, thought wonderful in its day, moved Charles Dickens to the passionate protest recorded in his *American Notes*. Of such substance was the story of these battlements; yet it was unmistakable that when one had crossed the drawbridge and passed under the portcullis the air seemed thick enough with the breath of the generations. A prison has, at the worst, the massive majesty, the sinister peace of a prison; but this huge house of sorrow affected me as, uncannily, of the City itself, the City of all the cynicisms and impunities against which my friends had, from far back, kept plating, as with the old silver of their sideboards, the armour of their social consciousness. It made the whole place, with some of its oddly antique aspects and its oddly modern freedoms, look doubly cut off from the world of light and ease. The suggestions here were vast, however; too many of them swarm, and my imagination must defend itself as it can. What I was most concerned to note was the complete turn of the wheel of fortune in respect to the measure of mere incarceration suffered, from which the worst of the rigour had visibly been drawn. Parts of the place suggested a sunny Club at a languid hour, with members vaguely lounging and chatting, with open doors and comparatively cheerful vistas, and plenty of rocking-chairs and magazines. The only thing was that, under this analogy, one found one's self speculating much on the implied requisites for membership. It was impossible not to wonder, from face to face, what these would have been, and not to ask what one would have taken them to be if the appearance of a Club had been a little more complete. I almost blush, I fear, for the crude comfort of my prompt conclusion. One would have taken them to consist, without exception, of full-blown basenesses; one couldn't, from member to member, from type to type, from one pair of eyes to another, take them for anything less. Where was the victim of circumstances, where the creature merely misled or betrayed? He fitted no type, he suffered in no face, he yearned in no history, and one felt, the more one took in his absence, that the numerous substitutes for him were good enough for each other.

The great interest was in this sight of the number and variety of ways of looking morally mean; and perhaps also in the question of how much the effect came from its being proved upon them, of how little it might have come if they had still been out in the world. Considered as criminals the moral meanness here was their explication. Considered as morally mean, therefore, would possible criminality, out in the world, have been in the same degree their sole sense? Was the fact of prison *all* the mere fact of opportunity, and the fact of freedom all the mere fact of the absence of it? One inclined to believe that—the simplification was at any rate so great for one's feeling: the cases presented became thus, consistently, cases of the vocation, and from the moment this was clear the place took on, in its way, almost the harmony of a convent. I talked for a long time with a charming reprieved murderer whom I half expected, at any moment, to see ring for coffee and cigars: he explained with all urbanity, and with perfect lucidity, the real sense of the appearance against him, but I none the less felt sure that his merit was largely in the refinement wrought in him by so many years of easy club life. He was as natural a subject for commutation as for conviction, and had had to have the latter in order to have the former—in the enjoyment, and indeed in the subtle criticism, of which, *as* simple commutation he was at his best. They were there, all those of his companions, I was able to note, unmistakably at their best. One could, as I say, sufficiently rest in it, and to do that kept, in a manner, the excrescence, as I have called it, on the general scene, within bounds. I was moreover luckily to see the general scene definitely cleared again, cleared of everything save its own social character and its practical philosophy—and at no moment with these features so brightly presented as during a few days' rage of winter round an old country-house. The house was virtually distant from town, and the conditions could but strike any visitor who stood whenever he might with his back to the fire, where the logs were piled high, as made to press on all the reserves and traditions of the general temperament; those of gallantry, hilarity, social disposability, crowned with the grace of the sporting instinct. What was it confusedly, almost romantically, like, what "old order" commemorated in fiction and anecdote? I had groped for this, as I have shown, before, but I found myself at it again. Wasn't it, for freedom of movement, for jingle of sleighbells, for breasting of the elements, for cross-country drives in the small hours, for *crânerie* of fine young men and high wintry colour of muffled nymphs, wasn't it, brogue and all, like some audible echo of close-packing, chancing Irish society of the classic time, seen and heard through a roaring blizzard? That at least, with his back to the fire, was where the restless analyst was landed.

Edith Wharton [1862-1937]
FROM A Backward Glance [1934]

❦

Little Girl

I

The depreciation of American currency at the close of the Civil War had so much reduced my father's income that, in common with many of his friends and relations, he had gone to Europe to economize, letting his town and country houses for six years to some of the profiteers of the day; but I did not learn till much later to how prosaic a cause I owed my early years in Europe. Happy misfortune, which gave me, for the rest of my life, that background of beauty and old-established order! I did not know how deeply I had felt the nobility and harmony of the great European cities till our steamer was docked at New York.

I remember once asking an old New Yorker why he never went abroad, and his answering: "Because I can't bear to cross Murray Street." It was indeed an unsavoury experience, and the shameless squalor of the purlieus of the New York docks in the 'seventies dismayed my childish eyes, stored with the glories of Rome and the architectural majesty of Paris. But it was summer; we were soon at Newport, under the friendly gables of Pencraig; and to a little girl long pent up in hotels and flats there was inexhaustible delight in the freedom of a staircase to run up and down, of lawns and trees, a meadow full of clover and daises, a pony to ride, terriers to romp with, a sheltered cove to bathe in, flower-beds spicy with "carnation, lily, rose", and a kitchen-garden crimson with strawberries and sweet as honey with Seckel pears.

The roomy and pleasant house of Pencraig was surrounded by a verandah wreathed in clematis and honey-suckle, and below it a lawn sloped to a deep daisied meadow, beyond which were a private bathing-beach and boat-landing. From the landing we used to fish for "scuppers" and "porgies", succulent little fish that were grilled or fried for high tea; and off the rocky point lay my father's and brothers' "cat-boats", the graceful wide-sailed craft that flecked the bay like sea-gulls.

Adjoining our property was Edgerston, the country home of Lewis Rutherfurd, the distinguished astronomer, notable in his day for his remarkable photographs of the moon. He and his wife were lifelong friends of my parents', and in their household, besides two grown-up daughters of singular beauty, there were two little boys, the youngest of my own age. There were also two young governesses, French and German; and as I was alone, and the German governess who had been imported for me was unsympathetic and unsatisfied, she was soon sent home, and the Rutherfurd governesses (the daughters of the house being "out," and off their hands) took me on for French, German, and whatever else, in those ancient days, composed a little girl's curriculum. This drew the two households still closer, for though I did not study with the little boys I seem to remember that I went to Edgerston for my lessons. There was certainly a continual coming and going through the private gate between the properties; but I recall a good deal more of our games than of my lessons.

Most vivid is my memory of the picturesque archery club meetings of which the grown daughters of the house, Margaret (afterward Mrs. Henry White) and her sister Louisa were among the most brilliant performers. When the club met we children were allowed to be present, and to circulate among the grown-ups (usually all three of us astride of one patient donkey); and a pretty sight the meeting was, with parents and elders seated in a semicircle on the turf behind the lovely archeresses in floating silks or muslins, with their wide leghorn hats, and heavy veils flung back only at the moment of aiming. These veils are associated with all the summer festivities of my childhood. In that simple society there was an almost pagan worship of physical beauty, and the first question asked about any youthful newcomer on the social scene was invariably: "Is she pretty?" or: "Is he handsome?"—for good looks were as much prized in young men as in maidens. For the latter no grace was rated as high as "a complexion". It is hard to picture nowadays the shell-like transparence, the luminous red-and-white, of those young cheeks untouched by paint or powder, in which the blood came and went like the lights of an aurora. Beauty was unthinkable without "a complexion", and to defend that treasure against sun and wind, and the arch-enemy sea air, veils as thick as curtains (some actually of woollen barège) were habitually worn. It must have been very uncomfortable for the wearers, who could hardly see or breathe; but even to my childish eyes the effect was dazzling when the curtain was drawn, and young beauty shone forth. My dear friend Howard Sturgis used to laugh at the "heavily veiled" heroines who lingered on so late in Victorian fiction, and were supposed to preserve their incognito until they threw back their veils; but if he had known fashionable Newport in my infancy he would have seen that the novelists' formula was based on what was once a reality.

Those archery meetings greatly heightened my infantile desire to "tell a story", and the young gods and goddesses I used to watch strolling across the Edgerston lawn were the prototypes of my first novels. The spectacle was a charming one to an imaginative child already caught in the toils of romance; no wonder I remember it better than my studies. Not that I was not eager to learn; but my long and weary illness had made my parents unduly anxious about my health, and they forbade my being taught anything that required a mental effort. Committing to memory, and preparing lessons in advance, were ruled out; it was thought that I read too much (as if a born reader could!), and that my mind must be spared all "strain". This was doubtless partly due to the solicitude of parents for a late-born child, partly to a natural reaction against the severities of their own early training. The sentimental theory that children must not be made to study anything that does not interest them was already in the air, and reinforced by the fear of "fatiguing" my brain, it made my parents turn my work into play. Being deprived of the irreplaceable grounding of Greek and Latin, I never learned to concentrate except on subjects naturally interesting to me, and developed a restless curiosity which prevented my fixing my thoughts for long even on these. Of benefits I see only one. To most of my contemporaries the enforced committing to memory of famous poems must have forever robbed some of the loveliest of their bloom; but this being forbidden me, great poetry—English, French, German and Italian— came to me fresh as the morning, with the dew on it, and has never lost that early glow.

The drawbacks were far greater than this advantage. But for the wisdom of Fräulein Bahlmann, my beloved German teacher, who saw which way my fancy turned, and fed it with all the wealth of German literature, from the Minnesingers to Heine—but for this, and the leave to range in my father's library, my mind would have starved at the age when the mental muscles are most in need of feeding.

I used to say that I had been taught only two things in my childhood: the modern languages and good manners. Now that I have lived to see both these branches of culture dispensed with, I perceive that there are worse systems of education. But in justice to my parents I ought to have named a third element in my training; a reverence for the English language as spoken according to the best usage. Usage, in my childhood, was as authoritative an element in speaking English as tradition was in social conduct. And it was because our little society still lived in the reflected light of a long-established culture that my parents, who were far from intellectual, who read little and studied not at all, nevertheless spoke their mother tongue with scrupulous perfection, and insisted that their children should do the same.

This reverence for the best tradition of spoken English—an easy idiomatic English, neither pedantic nor "literary"—was no doubt partly due to the fact that, in the old New York families of my parents' day, the children's teachers were often English. My mother and her sisters and brother had English tutors and governesses, and my own brothers were educated at home by an extremely cultivated English tutor. In my mother's family, more than one member of the generation preceding hers had been educated at Oxford or Cambridge, and one of my own brothers went to Cambridge.

Even so, however, I have never quite understood how two people so little preoccupied with letters as my father and mother had such sensitive ears for pure English. The example they set me was never forgotten; I still wince under my mother's ironic smile when I said that some visitor had stayed "quite a while", and her dry: "Where did you pick *that* up?" The wholesome derision of my grown-up brothers saved me from pomposity as my mother's smile guarded me against slovenliness; I still tingle with the sting of their ridicule when, excusing myself for having forgotten something I had been told to do, I said, with an assumption of grown-up dignity (*aetat* ten or eleven): "I didn't know that it was *imperative*."

Such elementary problems as (judging from the letters I receive from unknown readers) disturb present-day users of English in America—perplexity as to the distinction between "should" and "would", and the display of such half-educated pedantry as saying "gotten" and "you would better"—never embarrassed our speech. We spoke naturally, instinctively good English, but my parents always wanted it to be better, that is, easier, more flexible and idiomatic. This excessive respect for the language never led to priggishness, or precluded the enjoyment of racy innovations. Long words were always smiled away as pedantic, and any really expressive slang was welcomed with amusement—but used as slang, as it were between quotation marks, and not carelessly admitted into our speech. Luckily we all had a lively sense of humour, and now that my brothers were at home again the house rang with laughter. We all knew by heart "Alice in Wonderland", "The Hunting of the Snark", and whole pages of Lear's "Nonsense Book", and our sensitiveness to the quality of the English we spoke doubled our enjoyment of the incredible verbal gymnastics of those immortal works. Dear to us also, though in a lesser degree, were "Innocents Abroad", Bret Harte's parodies of novels, and, in their much later day, George Ade's "Arty", and the first volumes of that great philosopher, Mr. Dooley. I cannot remember a time when we did not, every one of us, revel in the humorous and expressive side of American slang; what my parents abhorred was not the picturesque use of new terms, if they were vivid and expressive, but the habitual slovenliness of those who picked up the slang of the year without having any idea that they were not speaking in the purest tradition. But above all abhorrent to ears piously attuned to all the inflexions and shades of meaning of our rich speech were such mean substitutes as "back of" for behind, "dirt" for earth (i.e., a "dirt road"), "any place" for anywhere, or slovenly phrases like "a great ways", soon, alas, to be followed by the still more inexcusable "a *barracks*", "a *woods*", and even "a strata", "a phenomena", which, as I grew up, a new class of the uneducated rich were rapidly introducing.

This feeling for good English was more than reverence, and nearer: it was love. My parents' ears were wounded by an unsuitable word as those of the musical are hurt by a false note. My mother, herself so little of a reader, was exaggeratedly scrupulous about the books I read; not so much the "grown-up" books as those written for children. I was never allowed to read the popular American children's books of my day because, as my mother said, the children spoke bad English *without the author's knowing it.* You could do what you liked with the language if you did it consciously, and for a given purpose—but if you went shuffling along, trailing it after you like a rag in the dust, tramping over it, as Henry James said, like the emigrant tramping over his kitchen oil-cloth—that was unpardonable, there deterioration and corruption lurked. I remember it was only with reluctance, and because "all the other children read them", that my mother consented to my reading "Little Women" and "Little Men"; and my ears, trained to the fresh racy English of "Alice in Wonderland," "The Water Babies" and "The Princess and the Goblin", were exasperated by the laxities of the great Louisa.

Perhaps our love of good English may be partly explained by the background of books which was an essential part of the old New York household. In my grand-parents' day every gentleman had what was called "a gentleman's library". In my father's day, these libraries still existed, though they were often only a background; but in our case Macaulay, Prescott, Motley, Sainte-Beuve, Augustin Thierry, Victor Hugo, the Brontës, Mrs. Gaskell, Ruskin, Coleridge, had been added to the French and English classics in their stately calf bindings. Were these latter ever read? Not often, I imagine; but they were there; they represented a standard; and perhaps some mysterious emanation disengaged itself from them, obscurely fighting for the protection of the languages they had illustrated.

A standard; the word perhaps gives me my clue. When I said, in my resentful youth, that I had been taught only languages and manners, I did not know how closely, in my parents' minds, the two were related. Bringing-up in those days was based on what was called "good breeding". One was polite, considerate of others, careful of the accepted formulas, because such were the principles of the well-bred. And probably the regard of my parents for the niceties of speech was a part of their breeding. They treated their language with the same rather ceremonious courtesy as their friends. It would have been "bad manners" to speak "bad" English, and "bad manners" were the supreme offence.

This fastidiousness of speech came chiefly from my mother's side, and my father probably acquired it under her influence. His own people, though they spoke good English, had disagreeable voices. I have noticed that wherever, in old New York families, there was a strong admixture of Dutch blood, the voices were flat, the diction was careless. My mother's stock was English, without Dutch blood, and this may account for the greater sensitiveness of all her people to the finer shades of English speech. In an article on Conrad which appeared in the *Times Literary Supplement* after his death, the author said (I quote from memory): "Conrad had worshipped the English language all his life like a lover, but he had never romped with her in the nursery"; and this it was my happy fate to do.

To the modern child my little-girl life at Pencraig would seem sadly tame and uneventful, for its chief distractions were the simple ones of swimming and riding. My mother, like most married women of her day, had long since given up exercise, my father's only active pursuits were boating and shooting, and there was no one to ride with me but the coachman—nor was our end of the island a happy place for equestrianism. I enjoyed scampering on my pony over the hard dull roads; but it was better fun to swim in our own cove, in the jolly company of brothers, cousins and young neighbours. There were always two or three "cat-boats" moored off our point, but I never shared the passion of my father and brothers for sailing. To be a passenger was too sedentary, and I felt no desire to sail the boat myself, being too wrapt in dreams to burden my mind with so exact a science. Best of all I liked our weekly walks with Mr. Rutherfurd over what we called the Rocks—the rough moorland country, at that time without roads or houses, extending from the placid blue expanse of Narragansett bay to the gray rollers of the Atlantic. Every Sunday he used to collect the children of the few friends living near us, and take them, with his own, for a tramp across this rugged country to the sea.

Yet what I recall of those rambles is not so much the comradeship of the other children, or the wise and friendly talk of our guide, as my secret sensitiveness to the landscape—something in me quite incommunicable to others, that was tremblingly and inarticulately awake to every detail of wind-warped fern and wide-eyed briar rose, yet more profoundly alive to a unifying magic beneath the diversities of the visible scene—a power with which I was in deep and solitary communion whenever I was alone with nature. It was the same tremor that had stirred in me in the spring woods of Mamaroneck, when I heard the whisper of the arbutus and the starry choir of the dogwood; and it has never since been still.

2

The old New York to which I came back as a little girl meant to me chiefly my father's library. Now for the first time I had my fill of books. Out of doors, in the mean monotonous streets, without architecture, without great churches or palaces, or any visible memorials of an historic past, what could New York offer to a child whose eyes had been filled with shapes of immortal beauty and immemorial significance? One of the most depressing impressions of my childhood is my recollection of the intolerable ugliness of New York, of its untended streets and the narrow houses so lacking in external dignity, so crammed with smug and suffocating upholstery. How could I understand that people who had seen Rome and Seville, Paris and London, could come back to live contentedly between Washington Square and the Central Park? What I could not guess was that this little low-studded rectangular New York, cursed with its universal chocolate-coloured coating of the most hideous stone ever quarried, this cramped horizontal gridiron of a town without towers, porticoes, fountains or perspectives, hide-bound in its deadly uniformity of mean ugliness, would fifty years later be as much a vanished city as Atlantis or the lowest layer of Schliemann's Troy, or that the social organization which that prosaic setting had slowly secreted would have been swept to oblivion with the rest. Nothing but the Atlantis-fate of old New York, the New York which had slowly but continuously developed from the early seventeenth century to my own childhood, makes that childhood worth recalling now.

Looking back at that little world, and remembering the "hoard of petty maxims" with which its elders preached down every sort of initiative, I have often wondered at such lassitude in the descendants of the men who first cleared a place for themselves in a new world, and then fought for the right to be masters there. What had become of the spirit of the pioneers and the revolutionaries? Perhaps the very violence of their effort had caused it to exhaust itself in the next generation, or the too great prosperity succeeding on almost unexampled hardships had produced, if not inertia, at least indifference in all matters except business or family affairs.

Even the acquiring of wealth had ceased to interest the little society into which I was born. In the case of some of its members, such as the Astors and Goelets, great fortunes, originating in a fabulous increase of New York real estate values, had been fostered by judicious investments and prudent administration; but of feverish money-making, in Wall Street or in railway, shipping or industrial enterprises, I heard nothing in my youth. Some of my father's friends may have been bankers, others have followed one of the liberal professions, usually the law; in fact almost all the young men I knew read law for a while after leaving college, though comparatively few practised it in after years. But for the most part my father's contemporaries, and those of my brothers also, were men of leisure—a term now almost as obsolete as the state it describes. It will probably seem unbelievable to present-day readers that only one of my own near relations, and not one of my husband's, was "in business". The group to which we belonged was composed of families to whom a middling prosperity had come, usually by the rapid rise in value of inherited real estate, and none of whom, apparently, aspired to be more than

moderately well-off. I never in my early life came in contact with
the gold-fever in any form, and when I hear that nowadays business
life in New York is so strenuous that men and women never meet
socially before the dinner hour, I remember the delightful week-day
luncheons of my early married years, where the men were as numerous as the women, and where one of the first rules of conversation
was the one early instilled in me by my mother: "Never talk about
money, and think about it as little as possible."

The child of the well-to-do, hedged in by nurses and governesses, seldom knows much of its parents' activities. I have only the
vaguest recollection of the way in which my father and mother spent
their days. I know that my father was a director on the principal
charitable boards of New York—the Blind Asylum and the Blooming-
dale Insane Asylum among others; and that during Lent a ladies'
"sewing class" met at our house to work with my mother for the
poor. I also recall frequent drives with my mother, when the usual
afternoon round of card-leaving was followed by a walk in the Central Park, and a hunt for violets and hepaticas in the secluded dells of
the Ramble. In the evenings my parents went occasionally to the
theatre, but never, as far as I remember, to a concert, or any kind of
musical performance, until the Opera, then only sporadic, became an
established entertainment, to which one went (as in eighteenth century Italy) chiefly if not solely for the pleasure of conversing with
one's friends. Their most frequent distraction was dining out or
dinner giving. Sometimes the dinners were stately and ceremonious
(with engraved invitations issued three weeks in advance, soups,
"thick" and "clear", and a Roman punch half way through the
menu), but more often they were intimate and sociable, though
always the occasion of much excellent food and old wine being
admirably served, and discussed with suitable gravity.

My father had inherited from his family a serious tradition of
good cooking, with a cellar of vintage clarets, and of Madeira which
had rounded the Cape. The "Jones" Madeira (my father's) and the
"Newbold" (my uncle's) enjoyed a particular celebrity even in that
day of noted cellars. The following generation, interested only in
champagne and claret, foolishly dispersed these precious stores. My
brothers sold my father's cellar soon after his death; and after my
marriage, dining in a *nouveau riche* house of which the master was

unfamiliar with old New York cousinships, I had pressed on me, as a treat not likely to have come the way of one of my modest condition, a glass of "the famous Newbold Madeira".

My mother, if left to herself, would probably not have been much interested in the pleasures of the table. My father's Dutch blood accounted for his gastronomic enthusiasm; his mother, who was a Schermerhorn, was reputed to have the best cook in New York. But to know about good cooking was a part of every young wife's equipment, and my mother's favourite cookery books (Francatelli's and Mrs. Leslie's) are thickly interleaved with sheets of yellowing note paper, on which, in a script of ethereal elegance, she records the making of "Mrs. Joshua Jones's scalloped oysters with cream", "Aunt Fanny Gallatin's fried chicken", "William Edgar's punch", and the special recipes of our two famous negro cooks, Mary Johnson and Susan Minneman. These great artists stand out, brilliantly turbaned and ear-ringed, from a Snyders-like background of game, fish and vegetables transformed into a succession of succulent repasts by their indefatigable blue-nailed hands: Mary Johnson, a gaunt towering woman of a rich bronzy black, with huge golden hoops in her ears, and crisp African crinkles under vividly patterned kerchiefs; Susan Minneman, a small smiling mulatto, more quietly attired, but as great a cook as her predecessor.

Ah, what artists they were! How simple yet sure were their methods—the mere perfection of broiling, roasting and basting—and what an unexampled wealth of material, vegetable and animal, their genius had to draw upon! Who will ever again taste anything in the whole range of gastronomy to equal their corned beef, their boiled turkeys with stewed celery and oyster sauce, their fried chickens, broiled red-heads, corn fritters, stewed tomatoes, rice griddle cakes, strawberry short-cake and vanilla ices? I am now enumerating only our daily fare, that from which even my tender years did not exclude me; but when my parents "gave a dinner", and terrapin and canvas-back ducks, or (in their season) broiled Spanish mackerel, soft-shelled crabs with a mayonnaise of celery, and peach-fed Virginia hams cooked in champagne (I am no doubt confusing all the seasons in this allegoric evocation of their riches), lima-beans in cream, corn soufflés and salads of oyster-crabs, poured in varied succulence from Mary Johnson's lifted cornucopia—ah, then, the

gourmet of that long-lost day, when cream was cream and butter
butter and coffee coffee, and meat fresh every day, and game hung
just for the proper number of hours, might lean back in his chair and
murmur "Fate cannot harm me" over his cup of Moka and his glass
of authentic Chartreuse.

I have lingered over these details because they formed a part—a
most important and honourable part—of that ancient curriculum of
house-keeping which, at least in Anglo-Saxon countries, was so soon
to be swept aside by the "monstrous regiment" of the emancipated:
young women taught by their elders to despise the kitchen and the
linen room, and to substitute the acquiring of University degrees for
the more complex art of civilized living. The movement began when
I was young, and now that I am old, and have watched it and noted
its results, I mourn more than ever the extinction of the household
arts. Cold storage, deplorable as it is, has done far less harm to the
home than the Higher Education.

And what of the guests who gathered at my father's table to
enjoy the achievements of the Dark Ladies? I remember a mild blur
of rosy and white-whiskered gentlemen, of ladies with bare sloping
shoulders rising flower-like from voluminous skirts, peeped at from
the stair-top while wraps were removed in the hall below. A great
sense of leisure emanated from their kindly faces and voices. No
motors waited to rush them on to ball or opera; balls were few and
widely spaced, the opera just beginning; and "Opera night" would
not have been chosen for one of my mother's big dinners. There
being no haste, and a prodigious amount of good food to be disposed
of, the guests sat long at table; and when my mother bowed slightly
to the lady facing her on my father's right, and flounces and trains
floated up the red velvet stair-carpet to the white-and-gold drawing-
room with tufted purple satin arm-chairs, and voluminous purple
satin curtains festooned with buttercup yellow fringe, the gentlemen
settled down again to claret and Madeira, sent duly westward, and
followed by coffee and Havana cigars.

My parents' guests ate well, and drank good wine with discernment; but a more fastidious taste had shortened the enormous repasts
and deep bumpers of colonial days, and in twenty minutes the whisk-
ered gentlemen had joined the flounced ladies on the purple settees
for another half hour of amiable chat, accompanied by the cup of tea

which always rounded off the evening. How mild and leisurely it all seems in the glare of our new century! Small parochial concerns no doubt formed the staple of the talk. Art and music and literature were rather timorously avoided (unless Trollope's last novel were touched upon, or a discreet allusion made to Mr. William Astor's audacious acquisition of a Bouguereau Venus), and the topics chiefly dwelt on were personal: the thoughtful discussion of food, wine, horses ("high steppers" were beginning to be much sought after), the laying out and planting of country-seats, the selection of "specimen" copper beeches and fern-leaved maples for lawns just beginning to be shorn smooth by the new hand-mowers, and those plans of European travel which filled so large a space in the thought of old New Yorkers. From my earliest infancy I had always seen about me people who were either just arriving from "abroad" or just embarking on a European tour. The old New Yorker was in continual contact with the land of his fathers, and it was not until I went to Boston on my marriage that I found myself in a community of wealthy and sedentary people seemingly too lacking in intellectual curiosity to have any desire to see the world.

I have always been perplexed by the incuriosity of New England with regard to the rest of the world, for New Yorkers of my day were never so happy as when they were hurrying on board the ocean liner which was to carry them to new lands. Those whose society my parents frequented did not, perhaps, profit much by the artistic and intellectual advantages of European travel, and to social opportunities they were half-resentfully indifferent. It was thought vulgar and snobbish to try to make the acquaintance, in London, Paris or Rome, of people of the class corresponding to their own. The Americans who forced their way into good society in Europe were said to be those who were shut out from it at home; and the self-respecting American on his travels frequented only the little "colonies" of his compatriots already settled in the European capitals, and only their most irreproachable members! What these artless travellers chiefly enjoyed were scenery, ruins and historic sites; places about which some sentimental legend hung, and to which Scott, Byron, Hans Andersen, Bulwer, Washington Irving or Hawthorne gently led the timid sight-seer. Public ceremonials also, ecclesiastical or royal, were much appreciated, though of the latter only distant glimpses could be caught, since it would have been snobbish to ask, through one's Legation, for reserved seats or invitations. And as for the American women who had themselves presented at the English Court—well, one had only to see with whom they associated at home!

However, ruins, snow-mountains, lakes and water-falls—especially water-falls—were endlessly enjoyable; and in the great cities there were the shops! In them, as Henry James acutely noted in "The Pension Beaurepas", the American women found inexhaustible consolation for the loneliness and inconveniences of life in foreign lands. But, lest I seem to lay undue stress on the limitations of my compatriots, it must be remembered that, even in more sophisticated societies, cultivated sight-seeing was hardly known in those days. One need only glance through the "Travels" of the early nineteenth century to see how little, before Ruskin, the average well-educated tourist of any country was prepared to observe and enjoy. The intellectual few, at the end of the eighteenth century, had been taught by Arthur Young to travel with an eye to agriculture and geology; and Goethe, in Sicily, struck Syracuse and Girgenti from his itinerary, and took the monotonous and exhausting route across the middle of the island, in order to see with his own eyes why it had been called the granary of Rome. Meanwhile the simpler majority collected scraps of marble from the Forum, pressed maidenhair fern from the temple of Vesta at Tivoli, or daisies from the grave of Shelley, and bought edelweiss gummed on card-board from the guides of Chamonix, and copies of Guido's "Aurora" and Caravaggio's "Gamesters" from the Roman picture-dealers.

At that very time a handsome blue-eyed young man with a scarred mouth was driving across the continent in his parents' travelling carriage, and looking with wondering eyes at the Giottos of the Arena Chapel and the Cimabues of Assisi; at that time a young architect, poor and unknown, was toiling through the by-ways of Castile, Galicia and Andalusia in jolting *diligences*, or over stony mule-tracks, and recording in a series of exquisite drawings the unknown wonders of Spanish architecture; and Browning was dreaming of "The Ring and the Book"—and Shelley had long since written "The

Cenci". But to the average well-to-do traveller Hawthorne's "Marble Faun", Bulwer's "Last Days of Pompeii" and Washington Irving's "Alhambra" were still the last word on Spain and Italy.

3

I have wandered far from my father's library. Though it had the leading share in my growth I have let myself be drawn from it by one scene after another of my parents' life in New York or on their travels. But the library calls me back, and I pause on its threshold, averting my eyes from the monstrous oak mantel supported on the heads of vizored knights, and looking past them at the rows of handsome bindings and familiar names. The library probably did not contain more than seven or eight hundred volumes. My father was a younger son, and my mother had a brother to whom most of the books on her side of the family went. (I remember on my uncle's shelves an unexpurgated Hogarth, splendidly bound in eighteenth century crushed Levant, with which my little cousins and I quite innocently and unharmedly beguiled ourselves.) The library to which I had access contained therefore few inherited books; I remember chiefly, in the warm shabby calf of the period, complete editions of Swift, Sterne, Defoe, the "Spectator", Shakespeare, Milton, the Percy Reliques—and Hannah More! Most of the other books must have been acquired by my father. Though few they were well-chosen, and the fact that their number was so limited probably helped to fix their contents on my memory. At any rate, long before the passing of years and a succession of deaths brought them back to me, I could at any moment visualize the books contained in those low oak bookcases. My mother, perplexed by the discovery that she had produced an omnivorous reader, and not knowing how to direct my reading, had perhaps expected the governess to do it for her. Being an indolent woman, she finally turned the difficulty by reviving a rule of her own school-room days, and decreeing that I should never read a novel without asking her permission. I was a painfully conscientious child and, conforming literally to this decree, I submitted to her every work of fiction which attracted my fancy. In order to save further trouble she almost always refused to let me read it—a fact hardly to be wondered at, since her own mother had forbidden her to read any of Scott's novels, except "Waverley", till after she was married! At all events, of the many prohibitions imposed on me—most of which, as I look back, I see little reason to regret—there is none for which I am more grateful than this, though it extended its rigours even to one of the works of Charlotte M. Yonge! By denying me the opportunity of wasting my time over ephemeral rubbish my mother threw me back on the great classics, and thereby helped to give my mind a temper which my too-easy studies could not have produced. I was forbidden to read Whyte Melville, Rhoda Broughton, "The Duchess", and all the lesser novelists of the day; but before me stretched the wide expanse of the classics, English, French and German, and into that sea of wonders I plunged at will. Nowadays a reader might see only the *lacunae* of the little library in which my mind was formed; but, small as it was, it included most of the essentials. The principal historians were Plutarch, Macaulay, Prescott, Parkman, Froude, Carlyle, Lamartine, Thiers; the diaries and letters included Evelyn, Pepys, White of Selborne, Cowper, Mme de Sévigné, Fanny Burney, Moore, the Journals of the Misses Berry; the "poetical works" (in addition to several anthologies, such as Knight's "Half Hours with the Best Authors" and Lamb's precious selections from the Elizabethan dramatists) were those of Homer (in Pope's and Lord Derby's versions), Longfellow's Dante, Milton, Herbert, Pope, Cowper, Gray, Thomson, Byron, Moore, Scott, Burns, Wordsworth, Campbell, Coleridge, Shelley (I wonder how or why?), Longfellow, Mrs. Hemans and Mrs. Browning—though not as yet the writer described in one of the anthologies of the period as "the husband of Elizabeth Barrett, and himself no mean poet". He was to come later, as a present from my sister-in-law, and to be one of the great Awakeners of my childhood.

Among the French poets were Corneille, Racine, Lafontaine and Victor Hugo, though, oddly enough, of Lamartine the poet there was not a page, nor yet of Chénier, Vigny or Musset. Among French prose classics there were, of course, Sainte-Beuve's "Lundis", bracing fare for a young mind, Sévigné the divinely loitering, Augustin Thierry and Philarète Chasles. Art history and criticism were represented by Lacroix's big volumes, so richly and exquisitely illustrated, on art, architecture and costume in the Middle Ages, by Schliemann's "Ilias" and "Troja", by Gwilt's Encyclopaedia of Archi-

tecture, by Kugler, Mrs. Jameson, P. G. Hamerton, and the Ruskin
of "Modern Painters" and the "Seven Lamps", together with a
volume of "Selections" (appropriately bound in purple cloth) of all
his purplest patches; to which my father, for my benefit, added
"Stones of Venice" and "Walks in Florence" when we returned to
Europe and the too-short days of our joint sight-seeing began.

In philosophy, I recall little but Victor Cousin and Coleridge
("The Friend" and "Aids to Reflection"); among essayists, besides
Addison, there were Lamb and Macaulay; in the way of travel, I
remember chiefly Arctic explorations. As for fiction, after the eighteenth century classics, Miss Burney and Scott of course led the list;
but, mysteriously enough, Richardson was lacking, save for an
abridged version of "Clarissa Harlowe" (and a masterly performance
that abridgement was, as I remember it). No doubt Richardson, with
Smollett and Fielding, fell to my uncle's share, and were too much
out-of-date to be thought worth replacing. Thus, except for Scott,
there was a great gap until one came to Washington Irving, that
charming hybrid on whom my parents' thoughts could dwell at ease,
because, in spite of the disturbing fact that he "wrote", he was a
gentleman, and a friend of the family. For my parents and their
group, though they held literature in great esteem, stood in nervous
dread of those who produced it. Washington Irving, Fitz-Greene
Halleck and William Dana were the only representatives of the
disquieting art who were deemed uncontaminated by it; though
Longfellow, they admitted, if a popular poet, was nevertheless a gentleman. As for Herman Melville, a cousin of the Van Rensselaers,
and qualified by birth to figure in the best society, he was doubtless
excluded from it by his deplorable Bohemianism, for I never heard
his name mentioned, or saw one of his books. Banished probably for
the same reasons were Poe, that drunken and demoralized Balti-
morean, and the brilliant wastrel Fitz James O'Brien, who was still
further debased by "writing for the newspapers". But worse still
perhaps in my parents' eyes was the case of such unhappy persons as
Joseph Drake, author of "The Culprit Fay", balanced between "fame
and infamy" as not quite of the best society, and writing not quite the
best poetry. I cannot hope to render the tone in which my mother
pronounced the names of such unfortunates, or, on the other hand,
that of Mrs. Beecher Stowe, who was so "common" yet so successful.

On the whole, my mother doubtless thought, it would be simpler if people one might be exposed to meeting would refrain from meddling with literature.

Considering the stacks of novels which she, my aunts and my grandmother annually devoured, their attitude seems singularly ungrateful; but it was probably prompted by the sort of diffidence which, thank heaven, no psycho-analyst had yet arisen to call a "complex". In the eyes of our provincial society authorship was still regarded as something between a black art and a form of manual labour. My father and mother and their friends were only one generation away from Sir Walter Scott, who thought it necessary to drape his literary identity in countless clumsy subterfuges, and almost contemporary with the Brontës, who shrank in agony from being suspected of successful novel-writing. But I am sure the chief element in their reluctance to encounter the literary was an awe-struck dread of the intellectual effort that might be required of them. They were genuinely modest and shy in the presence of any one who wrote or painted. To sing was still a drawing-room accomplishment, and I had two warbling cousins who had studied with the great opera singers; but authors and painters lived in a world unknown and incalculable. In addition to its mental atmosphere, its political and moral ideas might be contaminating, and there was a Kilmeny-touch about those who adventured into it and came back.

Meanwhile, though living authors were so remote, the dead were my most living companions. I was a healthy little girl who loved riding, swimming and romping; yet no children of my own age, and none even among the nearest of my grown-ups, were as close to me as the great voices that spoke to me from books. Whenever I try to recall my childhood it is in my father's library that it comes to life. I am squatting again on the thick Turkey rug, pulling open one after another the glass doors of the low bookcases, and dragging out book after book in a secret ecstasy of communion. I say "secret", for I cannot remember ever speaking to any one of these enraptured sessions. The child knows instinctively when it will be understood, and from the first I kept my adventures with books to myself. But perhaps it was not only the "misunderstood" element, so common in meditative infancy, that kept me from talking of my discoveries. There was in me a secret retreat where I wished no one to intrude,

or at least no one whom I had yet encountered. Words and ca-
dences haunted it like song-birds in a magic wood, and I wanted to
be able to steal away and listen when they called. When I was about
fifteen or sixteen I tried to write an essay on English verse rhythms. I
never got beyond the opening paragraph, but that came straight out
of my secret wood. It ran: "No one who cannot feel the enchant-
ment of 'Yet once more, O ye laurels, and once more', without
knowing even the next line, or having any idea whatever the context
of the poem, has begun to understand the beauty of English poetry."
For the moment that was enough of ecstasy; but I wanted to be
always free to steal away to it.

It was obvious that a little girl with such cravings, and to whom
the Old Testament, the Apocalypse and the Elizabethan dramatists
were open, could not long pine for Whyte Melville or even Rhoda
Broughton. Ah, the long music-drunken hours on that library floor,
with Isaiah and the Song of Solomon and the Book of Esther, and
"Modern Painters", and Augustin Thierry's Merovingians, and
Knight's "Half Hours", and that rich mine of music, Dana's "Household Book of Poetry"! Presently kind friends began to endow me
with a little library of my own, and I was reading "Faust" and
"Wilhelm Meister", "Philip Van Arteveld", "Men and Women" and
"Dramatis Personæ" in the intervals between "The Broken Heart"
and "The Duchess of Malfy", "Phèdre" and "Andromaque". And
there was one supreme day when, my mother having despairingly
asked our old literary adviser, Mr. North at Scribner's, "what she
could give the child for her birthday", I woke to find beside my bed
Buxton Forman's great editions of Keats and Shelly! Then the gates
of the realms of gold swung wide, and from that day to this I don't
believe I was ever again, in my inmost self, wholly lonely or
unhappy.

By the time I was seventeen, though I had not read every book
in my father's library, I had looked into them all. Those I devoured
first were the poets and the few literary critics, foremost of course
Sainte-Beuve. Ruskin fed me with visions of the Italy for which
I had never ceased to pine, and Freeman's delightful "Subject and
Neighbour Lands of Venice", Mrs. Jameson's amiable volumes, and
Kugler's "Handbook of Italian Painting", gave a firmer outline to
these visions. But the books which made the strongest impression on

me—doubtless because they reached a part of my mind that no one
had thought of arousing—were two shabby volumes unearthed
among my brother's college text-books: an abridgement of Sir William
Hamilton's "History of Philosophy" and a totally forgotten
work called "Coppée's Elements of Logic". This first introduction to
the technique of thinking developed the bony structure about which
my vague gelatinous musings could cling and take shape; and Darwin
and Pascal, Hamilton and Coppée ranked foremost among my
Awakeners.

In a day when youthful innocence was rated so high my mother
may be thought to have chosen a singular way of preserving mine
when she deprived me of the Victorian novel but made me free of
the Old Testament and the Elizabethans. Her plan was certainly not
premeditated; but had it been, she could not have shown more insight.
Those great pages, those high themes, purged my imagination; and I
cannot recall ever trying to puzzle out allusions which in tamer
garb might have roused my curiosity. Once, at the house of a little
girl friend, rummaging with her through a neglected collection of
books which her parents had acquired with the property, and never
since looked at, we came upon a small volume which seemed to burst
into fiery bloom in our hands.

> Forth, ballad, and take roses in both arms,
>   Even till the top rose touch thee in the throat
> Where the least thornprick harms;
>   And girdled in thy golden singing-coat,
> Come thou before my lady and say this:
>   Borgia, thy gold hair's colour burns in me,
> Thy mouth makes beat my blood in feverish rhymes;
>   Therefore so many as these roses be,
>   Kiss me so many times.

But this, like all the rest, merely enriched the complex music of
my strange inner world. I do not mean to defend the sheltered education
against the system which expounds physiological mysteries in
the nursery; I am not sure which is best. But I am sure that great
literature does not excite premature curiosities in normally constituted
children; and I can give a comic proof of the fact, for though
"The White Devil", "Faust" and "Poems and Ballads" were among
my early story-books, all I knew about adultery (against which we

were warned every week in church) was that those who "committed" it were penalized by having to pay higher fares in travelling: a conclusion arrived at by my once seeing on a ferry-boat the sign: "Adults 50 cents; children 25 cents"!

This ferment of reading revived my story-telling fever; but now I wanted to write and not to improvise. My first attempt (at the age of eleven) was a novel, which began: " 'Oh, how do you do, Mrs. Brown?' said Mrs. Tompkins. 'If only I had known you were going to call I should have tidied up the drawing-room'." Timorously I submitted this to my mother, and never shall I forget the sudden drop of my creative frenzy when she returned it with the icy comment: "Drawing-rooms are always tidy."

This was so crushing to a would-be novelist of manners that it shook me rudely out of my dream of writing fiction, and I took to poetry instead. It was not thought necessary to feed my literary ambitions with foolscap, and for lack of paper I was driven to begging for the wrappings of the parcels delivered at the house. After a while these were regarded as belonging to me, and I always kept a stack in my room. It never occurred to me to fold and cut the big brown sheets, and I used to spread them on the floor and travel over them on my hands and knees, building up long parallel columns of blank verse headed: "Scene: A Venetian palace", or "Dramatis Personæ" (which I never knew how to pronounce).

My dear governess, seeing my perplexity over the structure of English verse, gave me a work called "Quackenbos's Rhetoric", which warned one not to speak of the oyster as a "succulent bivalve", and pointed out that even Shakespeare nodded when he made Hamlet "take arms against a sea of troubles". Mr. Quackenbos disposed of the delicate problems of English metric by squeezing them firmly into the classic categories, so that Milton was supposed to have written in "iambic pentameters", and all superfluous syllables were got rid of (as in the eighteenth century) by elisions and apostrophes. Always respectful of the rules of the game, I tried to cabin my Muse within these bounds, and once when, in a moment of unheard-of audacity, I sent a poem to a newspaper (I think "The World"), I wrote to the editor apologizing for the fact that my metre was "irregular", but adding firmly that, though I was only a little girl, I wished this irregularity to be respected, as it was "intentional". The editor published the poem, and wrote back politely that he had no objection to irregular metres himself; and thereafter I breathed more freely. My poetic experiments, however, were destined to meet with the same discouragement as my fiction. Having vainly attempted a tragedy in five acts I turned my mind to short lyrics, which I poured out with a lamentable facility. My brother showed some of these to one of his friends, an amiable and cultivated Bostonian named Allen Thorndike Rice, who afterward became the owner and editor of the "North American Review". Allen Rice very kindly sent the poems to the aged Longfellow, to whom his mother's family were related; and on the bard's recommendation some of my babblings appeared in the "Atlantic Monthly". Happily this experiment was not repeated; and any undue pride I might have felt in it was speedily dashed by my young patron's remarking to me one day: "You know, writing lyrics won't lead you anywhere. What you want to do is to write an epic. All the great poets have written epics. Homer . . . Milton . . . Byron. Why don't you try your hand at something like 'Don Juan'?" This was a hard saying to a dreamy girl of fifteen, and I shrank back into my secret retreat, convinced that I was unfitted to be either a poet or a novelist. I did, indeed, attempt another novel, and carried this one to its close; but it was destined for the private enjoyment of a girl friend, and was never exposed to the garish light of print. It exists to this day, beautifully written out in a thick copy-book, with a title page inscribed "Fast and Loose", and an epigraph from Owen Meredith's "Lucile":

> Let Woman beware
> How she plays fast and loose with human despair,
> And the storm in Man's heart.

Title and epigraph were terrifyingly exemplified in the tale, but it closed on a note of mournful resignation, with the words: "And every year when April comes the violets bloom again on Georgie's grave."

After this I withdrew to secret communion with the Muse. I continued to cover vast expanses of wrapping paper with prose and verse, but the dream of a literary career, momentarily shadowed forth by one miraculous adventure, soon faded into unreality. How could I ever have supposed I could be an author? I had never even seen one in the flesh!

Upton Sinclair [1878-1968]
FROM *The Goose-Step, A Study of*
American Education [1923]

The Social Traitors

The failure of colleges to impart culture is a standard topic of our
time, so I shall not dwell upon it. The theme of this book is something
of far greater importance—the success of colleges in imparting a spirit
of bigotry, intolerance and suspicion toward ideas. Says a teacher in a
Pennsylvania college, who asks me not to use his name: "Our students
are climbers, strangers to idealism, or at best mere dabblers at it." Or
consider the testimony of Hendrik Willem Van Loon, who taught at
Cornell, and later at Antioch, which is trying a novel experiment in
combining education and everyday work. Van Loon declares that he
found in the students of both colleges a profound and deeply rooted
hostility toward originality, a personal resentment toward anyone
who interfered with their standardized notions. They are taught from

textbooks, and they follow the book, and refuse to think about anything that is not in the book.

To the same effect testifies Robert Herrick, after thirty years experience at the University of Chicago. Our colleges follow the English monastic tradition, says Professor Herrick; they pretend to watch over the morals of their students, but with the crowds now thronging in, the task is impossible, and the pretense is dishonest. No large university would today dare attempt any real control, nor would the parents support it; because fathers who send their sons to college with large allowances and high-powered cars know perfectly well that these young men go on "bats," and that they take girls out into the country in their cars.

What discipline they get, according to Herrick, they get from one another in their fraternities and clubs. They are uncritical, naive and barbarous, with herd feelings instead of ideas. The first requirement is that everyone shall be alike, a part of a mob. They teach the newcomer the rules; he must wear a freshman cap, and if he has opinions of his own they tell him he is too "tonguey," and proceed to knock the nonsense out of him. The faculty know of this, and think it is fine; they mix with the men, and join the fraternities, and help in the production of subservience and conformity. I quoted the above remarks to a professor in another university, and he threw up his hands. "My God!" he cried. "I am stupefied! My students accept everything that I say as gospel. If only I might once discover a crank in my classes!" And he quoted the phrase of William James, once of Harvard: "Our undisciplinables are our proudest product."

I have before me a letter from a professor in one of the "little toad-stools," Parsons College, Fairfield, Iowa. The Student Council passed a rule, which was later approved by the faculty, that all freshmen were to wear green caps. A hundred and fifty freshmen meekly submitted; but there was one "conscientious objector." My informant writes:

The upper classmen got together and announced that unless every freshman got a cap by noon of a certain day he would be subjected to the gauntlet of the paddling machine. I wish I could have gotten a picture of that mob of upper classmen on the campus of a "Christian" college, each provided with a club, as they lined up and forced Ball through the line of clubs, each taking as hearty a swat as possible—a fine specimen of the type of civilization we can expect from the

leaders we are training in the Christian colleges today! What a new
social order it will be! Through it all, the president has practically
approved the whole procedure, from the chapel platform. Ball still
refuses, in spite of a boycott by the student body, even his own fellow
freshmen; and I understand a paper is to be read in chapel next week
denouncing him, and calling for a boycott unless he submits. This is
supposed to be the daily Christian religious service—the hour of
devotion for the students!

Yet another professor compared his students to the crackers
which are packed in tin boxes by the wholesale bakeries; all cut from
certain patterns, and stamped with certain standard designs. We have
sheltered them from realities, and kept them ignorant of the problems
they are to confront. We have taught them a few formulas of morality, utterly unpractical and impossible to apply—as we prove by not
applying them ourselves. From their social life the students learn what
the real world is—a place of class distinctions based upon property;
they learn the American religion—what William James calls "the worship of the bitch-goddess Success." They throw themselves into the
social struggle with ferocious determination to get ahead; and when
they go out into the world, they carry that spirit into the commercial
struggle.

In every profession they find, of course, that the way to get ahead
is to serve the powers that rule, and to betray the general welfare. I
could take you through the professions which are taught in our universities, one after another, and show you how the prevailing ethical
standards constitute treason to the human race. I could show you in
academic teaching how these same standards are justified, in phrases
only partly veiled. Take, Harvard, for example, and the Massachusetts
Institute of Technology, admitted to have the highest standards of any
engineering school in America; we saw the professors in these institutions selling themselves to predatory corporations, and laying down
high-sounding "principles," whose sole effect and purpose is to enable
the Wholesale Pickpockets' Association to plunder the public. I have a
letter from a high official of the United States Bureau of Education,
who tells me more about these engineering traitors. He says:

I recall one man, for example, who was called in by a water
company for expert service in connection with the purity of the
water, which was being questioned by the people. He contended with
me that it was "his business" if he could find remunerative employ-

ment of that sort, and that he was under no obligation to give the public the benefit of his expert knowledge concerning the impurity of the water supply. But what aroused my ire more than anything else was the fact that he preached that kind of thing to his technical students as the standard of "loyalty" they should pursue toward the companies where they might be employed after graduation. This man was a real scientist. He was so thoroughly interested in his subject that he was willing to take considerable personal risks in conducting experiments, but he was sadly lacking in that social and religious conception which makes us realize our mutual obligations and duties.

Or take the work of inventors; they have a man at one of our greatest universities who is a famous inventor, and he makes great scientific discoveries, and then he goes to the big corporations and sells them—what? The right to use his invention and spread it throughout the world for the benefit of mankind? No; he sells them the right to suppress the invention, and deprive mankind of the use of it for a generation or two! You see, a new invention may mean the scrapping of a great deal of existing machinery; if it falls into the hands of some independent concern, it may cost the big monopolists enormous losses. So they pay for the right to suppress it, and a great inventor is turned by the social system into a kind of scientific black-mailer.

Or take the lawyers; surely I do not need to prove to you how the lawyers are betraying mankind. A professor at the University of Chicago told me of attending a class reunion, where a group of high-up corporation lawyers got drunk and began gossiping about the tricks they had played in their profession, and, as the professor said, it made him physically ill. I also have heard these high-up lawyers talking; the late James B. Dill, who was paid a million dollars to organize the Steel Trust, spent many an evening in his home telling me the game as he had seen it, and it began with bribery of judges, juries and legislators, and ended with wire-tapping and burglary. The late Francis Lynde Stetson, one of the highest paid corporation lawyers in New York, went down to Trenton on the train with Judge Dill to beat some railroad rate law, and he opened his suit-case playfully, showing that he had fifty thousand dollars in new bank-notes. "That's a fine kind of work for a pillar of the church like you," said Dill, and the other answered, with a grin: "How do I know but that I may have to pay for my lunch?"

Or if you cannot believe Judge Dill, believe Judge Lindsey, who told me about a young man who came to Denver from the Harvard Law School, full of the fine phrases of altruism with which his teachers had filled him, and when he learned what he had to do to practice corporation law in Denver, he broke down in Lindsey's office, and buried his head in his arms and cried like a baby. Afterwards, so Lindsey writes me, "he capitulated and joined the gang."

Or maybe it is medicine the young man has studied. He has heard about the nobleness of the healing art, but he has to keep an automobile, and his wife wants to get into society, and competition is keen. There is one way a physician can make a thousand dollars by a few minutes' work, and any physician who is in touch with the leisure class has women on their knees to him every week, begging him to take their money. Dr. William J. Robinson estimates that there are a million abortions performed in the United States every year, so you see that our medical schools have not steeled all their graduates against this temptation. Now we have another one added—every physician in the United States is made by law a dispenser of joviality, the seneschal of the castle, the keeper of the keys to the wine-cellar!

Or maybe the graduate becomes a newspaper reporter. One of the oldest Wall Street reporters in New York talked to me last spring, telling me a little of the way things are going there. The newspaper reporters also are keepers of the keys of the wine-cellar; they have police passes, and some of them are running a bootlegging industry between New York and Canada! Others have gone into high finance on a large scale—because, of course, a financial reporter comes on information which is worth thousands, and sometimes tens of thousands. "Nowadays," said my friend, "when a Wall Street reporter gets a tip and rushes to the telephone, you don't hear him call his city editor; you hear him call his broker." I was told of one newspaper man who had the fortune to be called in when Mr. Charles Sabin of the Guaranty Trust Company gave out some news of the German overtures for peace, and this enterprising young man cleared fifty thousand dollars from the information.

Or perhaps the young man becomes a college professor; if so, he hides his convictions and makes himself a tight little snob and reactionary, to win the favor of the college machine. He hides the truth from his students, or he "shades" it, which is the same thing, and takes his pitiful little bribe in the dignity of a full professorship. He turns out class after class of young men, as ignorant of life and as helpless against temptation as he himself was once. So reaction rules in our country, and men who plead for social justice are slandered and maligned, and turned into criminals in the public eye; all the agencies of law and justice become mobs, and the Ku Klux Klan meets every night in lonely places, and lights its fiery cross and prepares for the wholesale slaughter of the future of mankind.

Just now the rich are having it all their own way; they can do the killing and the bludgeoning and the jailing—and it never occurs to them to think what an example they are setting to the workers, and what it will mean when the tables are turned, and the disinherited of the earth have their way for a while! It ought to be the chief function of educators to point out things like this to the public; but that would be "meddling in politics," and we have seen that politics in colleges is a privilege reserved to presidents and trustees. There are going to be ferocious attacks made upon this book, and this seems as convenient a place as any in which to explain what they mean. Faculty members will rush forward to defend their institutions; in some cases, no doubt, there will be resolutions of protest, with many signatures. They will have some ammunition; for, of course no one can write a book of this size, full of such masses of facts, and not make a few slips of detail. These will be taken up and magnified into gigantic blunders, and denunciation of them spread broadcast in the capitalist press. When you read these things, bear one circumstance in mind: that any young professor who wants to become a dean in a hurry, who has a vision of himself selected as president in the course of a few years, will know that he can find no more certain way to win favor with his overlords than to find something wrong with this book, and then tell about it gallantly!

The Academic Rabbits

There are, of course, a large number of individual professors in institutions of higher learning who take their stand for what they believe to be the truth, and risk their jobs and chances of promotion. I have mentioned the existence of eight "renommir professoren." At Wellesley is Vida Scudder, who "gets by" because she is a devout Episcopalian; also Professor Ellen Hayes, who "gets by" because she is old, and because she teaches astronomy. These reasons are not my guesses, but were the statements of the president of the college, when she was asked at a women's club in Denver why she kept a notorious Socialist and labor agitator on her faculty.

Professor Hayes got this reputation by running for office on the Socialist party ticket; I visited her on my trip, and heard some funny stories. Here is one of the sweetest and most lovable old ladies you ever met, who is not mealy-mouthed about her belief in the right and destiny of the workers to control the world's industry for their own benefit. She deliberately lives in a working-class neighborhood—with rather comical results. Her neighbors are in awe of her, because she is a college professor, and a little afraid of her, because of her bad reputation; the one way she might get to know them, through the church, is not available, because Professor Hayes is a scientist.

On the other side of the continent is Guido Marx of Stanford, who shamelessly avows his sympathy with the co-operative move-ment, and likewise with faculty control of universities. Professor Marx, it is amusing to notice, teaches mechanical engineering, a sub-ject almost as safe as the stars. If there is a single professor in the United States who teaches political economy and admits himself a Socialist, that professor is a needle which I have been unable to find in our academic hay-stack.

Of course there are many radicals who conceal their views, and judiciously try to open the minds of their students without putting any label upon themselves. I have told in "The Profits of Religion" about Jowett at Oxford, who got by with the Apostles' Creed when-ever he had to recite it in public, by inserting the words "used to" between the words "I believe," saying the inserted words under his breath, thus: "I *used to* believe in the Father, the Son, and the Holy Ghost." I encountered several college professors who have equally ingenious devices for salving their consciences in their unhappy situa-tion. I might terrify the plutocratic world by stating that I know two presidents of small colleges in the United States, who in their own homes and among their trusted friends are real "reds." One of them, a young man recently appointed, was asked by his assembled trustees: "What are your views on property questions?" He answered, with an easy smile: "I fear I am far too conservative for a man of thirty-seven"—and he got by with that! The other one is head of a woman's college, and was asked by her trustees: "Are you a Socialist?" She said to me: "I could answer no with a perfectly good conscience, for I had just made up my mind that I am a convert to the Soviet form of political and industrial organization!"

Of course, it is perfectly possible to teach modern ideas without the labels, and to open the minds of your students by seeing that they hear both sides of every case. If you avoid the extremely crucial questions, such as the I. W. W. and Russia, you can get by with this in the majority of institutions, especially if you eschew outside activities and never get into the newspapers. Many professors are doing this, others have tried and slipped up, and have sacrificed promotion and security. Many professors are rovers in the academic world, staying in one place for two or three years, and when they are not able to stand it any more, moving on. There is an infinite variety of degrees and shadings in such cases; conditions differ with institutions, and with subjects taught, and with individual teachers. Some "get away" with what others dare not attempt. Some spoil their chances by bad manners or bad judgment; and, of course, many others are accused of doing this. You will seldom find a fight over a question of academic freedom where there are not other factors present or alleged, personal weaknesses or eccentricities. It is always easy to find defects in the characters and temperaments of persons whose ideas are offensive to us.

Likewise, of course, it is easy to find excuses for seeking the safest way, and holding on to our jobs. The psychoanalysts have a useful word for mental processes of this sort—they are "rationalizations"; and the masters of our educational system have provided an elaborate set of "rationalizations" for college professors who wish to avoid the painful duty of being heroes. They will be loyal to the institution and to their colleagues. They will be scholars and not propagandists. They will be judicious, instead of being "emotionally unbalanced, like Scott Nearing." They will argue that their specialty is one of unusual importance, and they are privileged beings, set apart to work at that. Or they will plead that social evolution takes a long time, and that every man's first duty is to look out for his wife and children. These, too, are phrases which I heard over and over again, and they reveal the psychology of the academic rabbits. You will perhaps be interested to meet one of these rabbits, so here is part of a letter written by a professor in a large college in New York City:

I do not believe that there is a single group of "special privilege." The human race is made up of people who are looking after their own interests first—some with energy and ability, some with weakness and folly, but not with less singleness of purpose. All such groups, in so far as they have ability enough, want to control education and all other group activities in their interest. This is perfectly natural. . . . Of course the big book corporations work for the promotion of their friends just as you and I do. If they put bad people into the schools and colleges it is the fault of the employing agencies.

Before I conclude this chapter I ought to mention one hopeful incident which happened at Lafayette College, a religious institution located at Easton, Pennsylvania. The president of this institution, MacCracken, is a product of the University of Jabbergrab; he was professor of politics there for twelve years, and has five honorary degrees. He has as the grand duke of his trustees the president of the Hazleton National Bank and the Hazleton Iron Works; and as first assistant he has Mr. Fred Morgan Kirby, president of the Woolworth stores, also of a bank and a railroad; a high-up interlocking director in railroads, lumber, insurance, gas and electricity. Mr. Kirby decided that he did not like modern ideas, so he gave a hundred thousand dollars to Lafayette, to furnish a salary of seven thousand a year for the teaching of "civil rights"; very carefully laying down his defini-tion—"those absolute rights of persons, such as . . . . the right to acquire and enjoy property as regulated and protected by law." Also he declared his purpose:

That the fallacies of Socialism and kindred theories and practices which tend to hamper and discourage and throttle individual effort, and individual energy, may be exposed and avoided . . . . . with a firm belief that the protection of the civil rights of individuals has contributed greatly to the advancement of the nation and that the encroachments, and threatened encroachments on these rights will imperil the country, and destroy the prosperity and happiness of our people, I, Fred Morgan Kirby, give to Lafayette College, etc.

These are high-sounding legal phrases, and we shall understand the situation better if we put them into plain business English, as follows:

I, Fred Morgan Kirby, having become owner of a chain of hun-dreds of stores throughout the United States, and wishing to have my descendants own these stores forever, seek to provide that the wage-slaves who work in these stores shall never organize, but shall come to be hired as individuals under the competitive-wage system. To this end I wish to hire a man to teach in a college that any proposition to have the Woolworth stores owned by the public, or democratically run by the people who work in the stores, will imperil the country and destroy the prosperity and happiness of America.

Mr. Kirby thought that seven thousand a year ought to buy a real high-up professor of political science, and his college president invited a young professor of a leading university, who asks me to omit his name in telling the story. This professor boldly asked for an opportunity to discuss the question with Mr. Kirby himself, so they sat down to luncheon, the grand duke and his university president and this young supposed-to-be rabbit. The supposed-to-be rabbit suggested that it might not be quite fair to lay down to a man of science exactly what he should teach forever after; which surprised Mr. Kirby, and rather hurt his feelings. He said that when he hired a salesman, he told him what to say and how to say it. Mr. Kirby is a nice, amiable old business gentleman, and he asked, plaintively: "Why can't I employ a college professor to sell my opinions?" The professor, who is a lawyer, said that he should be very glad to become Mr. Kirby's attorney if invited. He would give up teaching work and advocate Mr. Kirby's ideas—only the fee which Mr. Kirby offered was insufficient for a lawyer, and he would regard that merely as a retaining fee. Then the professor turned to President MacCracken, asking him if he did not think that possibly the terms of the bequest might have a tendency to control the opinions of the professor who accepted the chair. President MacCracken answered naively that he had never thought of that. Such a dear, innocent college president—he had given an honorary degree to A. Mitchell Palmer only a year before this!

The deal with this professor did not go through, and—here is the significant part of the story—President MacCracken asked one university after another to recommend a man for that chair, and not one would do it; not one economist of standing could be found who would accept seven thousand dollars a year to become the salesman of Mr. Kirby's ideas! In the end they had to take an obscure lawyer from Washington, whom no one had ever heard of before, or has ever heard of since. That is encouraging—except for the poor students at Lafayette, who are innocently swallowing Mr. Kirby's poison!

Sherwood Anderson [1876-1941]
The South [1926]

The white race is one great family, the black another. In the far east,
the yellow men. Families of brown men, scattered over the Pacific—
living on islands.

The American Pacific Coast grew alarmed at the way yellow men
pushed in and managed to squeeze them out.

Suppose you have, living in the family, in the house with you, a
man or woman who wins your affection. There is a reason why you
cannot sit with such a one at table, marry, make love with such a
one.

Something strange—a strange kind of relationship between men
and women—men and men—women and women.

Something tender—often brutal, often fine—making white men
something they would not otherwise be—making black, brown, high-
brown, velvet-brown men and women something they would not
otherwise be.

I have had in mind, for some time now, trying to write several articles about sections of the country in which I have lived. No one will take what I say too seriously. It does not matter. Writing may clarify some of my own thoughts and feelings.

I am living in a valley between mountains cutting the north off from the south and can roll down either way. One roll into West Virginia, another into North Carolina. Of these particular places I shall say nothing. There has been in me always something calling from the north, a voice calling from the south. In regard to the negro I am Southern. I have no illusions about making him my brother.

I have just come from the far south, have been living there for two or three years. The heat and mosquitoes drove me out. Some of these days I shall drift back down there.

Southern nights, soft voices, New Orleans, Mobile, the Mississippi, live oaks, ships, forests—negroes—always the negroes—setting the tempo of life.

Here I find myself sitting at my desk, trying to write of the south—wanting to do it.

Liking negroes—wanting them about—not wanting them too close. In me the southern contradiction so puzzling to the north.

To a man like myself—that is to say to the artist type of man living in America—there is something tremendously provocative in the American south, in all the life of the south. The south is to me not just a place—it is an idea—a background.

Laughter perhaps—leisure—a kind of warm joy in living.

Born in the middle west—a youth spent as a wanderer and factory hand—after years of struggle, trying to be a successful man of affairs in industrial northern cities—I went south for the first time when I was well into middle life.

Something had drawn me south—something I had felt since boyhood. It may have been the reading of Huckleberry Finn—or the talk of my father.

He was a man southern bred and proud of it.

All southern men, men whose people came from the south, tell you about it at once. The notion of a southern aristocracy persists. Whether or not it is justified is another matter. I have always had difficulty deciding just what an aristocrat is.

Innumerable Americans have had the experience of a first southern trip—by train. . . .

The little miserable towns, the badly kept plantations, lean hogs in the streets of towns, lean white men, shabbiness.

Niggers.

Shiftlessness.

I got it all that first time south and landed at last in the old city of Mobile. This was in the month of February. I went to a hotel.

I did not intend to stay there. I had saved a little money and wanted to live cheaply, while I wrote a novel. We high-brow writers have to live low.

It rained—a soft patter of rain in the streets. I put my bags in my room, ate hastily and went out into the night—my first southern night.

For how many hours did I wander, sometimes in lighted streets where white men lived, sometimes in little dark negro streets? At once I felt—how shall I explain? There was something friendly—in dark figures passing in dark streets, in buildings. Something friendly seemed to come up out of the warm earth under my feet.

In northern industrial towns at night, as you wander thus through streets of small houses, there is always something tense and harsh in voices coming out of houses. Something nervous—irritable—in people.

Life is too difficult. Everything moves too fast.

The tenseness was in my own voice, that first night in the south. I had gone south hoping to get it out.

Softness in voices, laughter, an easy careless swing to bodies of men and women. I walked in a soft cloud of words, not clearly caught, feeling warmth in sounds, in people.

There was a negro ballad I had once heard Carl Sandburg sing, a ballad about the boll weevil.

> *"I like this place,*
> *This'll be my home."*

I went murmuring the song—not being a bold singer—have been murmuring it to myself these last four or five years—while I lingered in the south.

Being northern, I yet never went south without a feeling of gladness, never have turned back northward without some feeling of inner fear—of sadness.

I got the nigger craze. All northern men of the artist type who go south get it.

Well, for those of us who tell tales, sing songs, work in colors, in stone, the negroes have something—something physical—rhythm—something we want to get into ourselves—our work.

I had not gone the length of wanting the negro to replace the white. I hadn't even gone with Abe Lincoln who said "Just because I want to see justice done the black is no sign I want to sleep with him." I wasn't thinking of justice.

Being in the south, what I most wanted was a decent sort of relationship with white southern men. In Mobile, New Orleans, Baton Rouge—other towns of the south—there is always a difficulty for the northern man to overcome.

It concerns the blacks.

You are in the south and would like to know—because you are a writer, interested in the life about you—something about the relationships of black, brown, yellow and white.

The negro race in the south is so apparently getting lighter. How does that happen? What's going on? White blood constantly creeping in from somewhere.

Northern travelers can't do it all.

Many of the negro women seen in the streets, in cities, on country roads, on river boats, about houses where you go to dine—splendid creatures.

People always whispering things. "Such and such a white man has a touch of the tar pot." It doesn't come in through white southern women. You know that.

I went walking with southern men, eating, drinking, talking with southern men.

Men are what the civilization in which they live makes them.

Be careful now.

A good deal of fear, everywhere in the south, of cheap, snap northern judgments. One of these fellows hot on justice goes south. He sees the negroes doing all the work with their hands—sees them wearing ragged clothes, eating in fence corners like dogs, gets indignant.

He can tell you all about everything in ten days.

I did not want to do it like that. The negro problem is the vast overshadowing problem of the south. No man questions that.

Try down there to associate with the negro; sit with him, eat with him, talk with him.

You would learn nothing. A white man of the right sort will tell you everything better—more clearly. You would get nothing but the contempt of both whites and blacks. Chances are you would deserve it, too.

Some days I sat for hours on the docks—watching negroes work. That wasn't for the negroes' sake. It was for my own sake. The negro had something I wanted. All sensible white men want it. There is a kind of closeness to nature, trees, rivers, the earth, more primitive men have, that men less primitive are all seeking. We want to have the cake and eat it. I know I do.

I remember a morning. I went before daylight to conceal myself in a lumber pile, lay hidden all day, negroes at work all about me.

Later many talks with southern white men. They began to open up a little—saw I hadn't come down there to tell them anything. Some grew immediately angry, flared up. Others got my point of view—seemed to like it.

Suppose strangers always coming into your house to tell you where to hang your pictures, how to place your chairs, how to treat others in your house.

In what bed to sleep. The south has had to stand a lot from the north—God knows.

Yes, it happens—boys in the country—in the cities—brown girls. How are you going to help that?

To say it does not happen—constantly—is foolish. If it did not happen there would be no problem, and there is a problem. If the negro were just an animal. He isn't. Often he is a tremendously attractive man—or alas, woman.

If you think you, being northern, a Puritan perhaps, would run your house better, be more truly what you call "moral," you're a fool.

I remember a brown man laughing. He was sweeping out my room in a house in the country. "White man and brown woman get the fun in this country. White woman and brown man get left."

Well, I have stressed the problem. I like to accept life as it comes up to me. Nothing in the life of the south shocks me. I would take my

chances with southern white men and women. Given the same problem I could not handle it better.

It seems to me that what the south needs most now is the artist—
not visiting artists—its own—but there is a difficulty.

The south needs southern expression of all phases of southern
life in song, prose, painting, music. To get that it needs acceptance of
itself, more frankness.

It needs to begin to escape the nonsense about spotless white
womanhood, insisting too much upon a kind of purity that is humanly
impossible. It needs most of all to wipe out fear of ugly puritanical
northern judgments.

The south has got to cleanse itself of the fear of facing itself.

Not an easy job.

The southern problem—that of a race living so intimately with
the white race—not living with it at all—fear of race mixture—is the
hardest problem any section of the country has to face.

Having lived in the south I believe southern white men handle it
as well as northern men ever could—perhaps better.

Chicago, talking of southern violence.

If you go on the theory that exact justice is a human possibility
everything is wrong. I do not subscribe to any such theory.

I have a notion that injustice has a place of its own in the scheme
of life.

As for the negro, I am sure he is better off in the south than in
the north. There, at least, injustice is often tempered by real affection.

The land belongs to the blacks. White men own legally the railroads, the land, the boats on the rivers, the rivers, forests, swamps, but
they are nigger boats, nigger rivers, nigger swamps, forests, railroads.

It can't be otherwise.

Any intelligent southern white would agree—laughing—"what of
it?"

The negro does the work, the dust of the fields and the water of
the rivers and swamps runs through his fingers. No white man anywhere has ever done what the negro has done with the railroad.

Songs of railroads, dreams of railroads—voyages from town to
town—a chicken for frying tucked under the arm.

> *"Have you got your ticket bought*
> *O, Lord!*
> *Have you got your ticket bought?"*

Railroading into a nigger heaven.

The land is really the negro's land because he works it, sings of it, loves it.

What of it?

The white man isn't going to let him take it away.

The white man of the south getting at his problem the best he can, perhaps. Having to put up with violent fools in his own race, having to be father to innumerable black children.

The blacks remain children.

In the country—in the south—in many households in cities, the conditions of slavery days not much changed.

A relationship between the races not frankly faced, but faced more than the north suspects.

All sorts of subtle angles—loyalty, tenderness, attempts at justice that do not show on the surface.

The negro unbelievably cunning—"cute" is the word.

Getting for himself in the south—so much the whites do not get and that does not appear on the surface.

The south—the white south getting bolder. Southern white life will yet express itself—really—in song, prose, painting, music.

The negro contributing—doing too much of the contributing now. A second-rate negro poet or artist always getting twice the credit of an equally able white man. That's northern sentimentality.

It is a difficult, delicate job to see the southern white man's angle and see it whole, but the northern man will have to do it if he wants to draw nearer the south.

To go black—think all the hope of future cultural development in the south is in the southern black, because he sings, dances, produces jazz—is hopelessness.

The puzzle remains—two races that when they meet to produce blood mixture must meet in secret, in shame.

The southern problem is the most difficult problem in America. The attitude of the north has never helped much.

I spent a few days at a southern plantation. There were several thousand acres—a village of blacks.

The seasons were long, land cheap.

Two white women owned and ran the place.

We came in the late afternoon and dined in a great room of the old house.

The management of such a house would drive a northern white woman crazy in a week.

The two southern women were handling it easily—naturally.

Delicious food—in vast abundance—dogs, cats, niggers—men, women and children.

Life squirming and writhing everywhere underfoot—nigger life, insect life, animal life.

The niggers worked the land on shares. The arrangement would be called "peonage" by a northern reformer.

Sure, all the niggers in debt to the two women, always in debt.

What grows on the place belongs to every one on the place. The niggers eat, sleep, sing, make love, work some.

As we dined one of the women told me of hogs, chickens, eggs, turkeys always being carried off secretly to be consumed in some cabin.

She had to know her blacks.

If a man stole a hog, needing it—having children to feed, having been ill—having been a good nigger when times were better—she said nothing, laughed and let it go.

She had to know what nigger stole the hog and why.

She managed to let him know she knew without too many words. There's a way.

Cunning, creeping life all about the two women. They did not dare be afraid.

I stayed four days and went back on "settlement" day.

That is the great day when the negro squares up for his year's work.

Not much chance for the whites to cheat. If they do they lose their niggers.

The negro won't go away physically.

Cheat him and he'll live on you all through the next year, doing no work.

He knows how.

Negroes aren't fools either. Trick niggers among them—but a trick negro is like the trick white workman of the north.

The two women had to know their people.

Niggers on such southern plantations are taken out sometimes and whipped.

I saw a southern white woman whip a negro man for trying to hit another negro man with an axe.

It was about a negro girl they both wanted.

The white woman knew what was coming. She was watching. She stepped in just in time to prevent a murder. Such things are not uncommon in the south.

The two women I visited knew every negro man, every negro woman and child on their place as a northern woman might know the children of her own body.

Plenty of southern white men of the same sort—on other plantations about.

The two white women were doing the job because their white men were all dead. Southern white families—the old ones are dying out. That may be one reason why so many negroes come north.

Just why the old white families are passing is another story. It may be simply the old south's passing, a new south being born. In southern cities the negro labor doesn't sing any more. The south may have to industrialize, like the east, mid-America, the far west, southern city newspapers all say so.

And the dying out of the old families may be due to something else.

The thing not talked about except among intimates—never publicly—in the south.

A gradual loss of personal dignity in white men, due to a condition—thrust into relationships too complex and difficult for the generality of men to handle.

At the plantation I visited, the plantation run by two childless women, the last of their particular family, the problem was touched upon during our visit.

After dining one evening we sat on a wide gallery. There was talk of the old days. Always talk of old days in the south.

Then later a troop of black and brown women came up to the house to sing.

The old work songs, ballads about the life of the negroes on the plantation, were taboo.

An idea had got abroad among the blacks that it was wicked to sing of work, of play. Only songs of a Baptist or Methodist God permitted.

A few wicked niggers, however. They stepped forward and sang of a wreck on the railroad that crossed the edge of the plantation some three miles from the house, of the year when the flu came and so many negroes died.

I have seldom heard the miseries of flu so aptly described.

The wicked negroes having a grand time—singing the ungodly songs—the good ones standing aside and enjoying the wickedness of the wicked.

Puritanism taking hold of the negroes, too.

The two southern white women half heroic figures in my imagination.

I got a slant on them the next day.

We drove to a small town, a southern market town and the half white negroes were all about.

A girl with straight hair and blue eyes—the hair golden brown.

A young negro man with Jewish features, plainly marked.

Traces of white blood everywhere—in blacks—making the blacks not blacks but browns.

I dared to suggest to the women—tentatively of course—well, I asked the question. . . .

Very few of the negroes of that section had ever been twenty miles from home. Few enough northern visitors came that way.

Young white men growing up—getting married—making a new white man's south as a new east, far west and mid-America is always being made.

The woman looked at me with a hard light in her eyes.

"It is true," she said. "It happens. I don't like it."

"One thing I know. You are a northern man and can't judge in such matter, but I am southern through and through." She smiled at me, deciding not to be angry.

"What you suggest happens but southern white men never have anything to do with the matter."

It was the south—all I know of the south. If you of the north lived there do you think you would do the job better?

Southern civilization began with a problem—a war was fought—the problem remains.

It cannot be solved now—in any way I know.

It can be faced.

Facing it may be the one thing needed for the flowering of a truly southern art, a truly southern contribution to an American civilization.

Theodore Dreiser [1871-1945]
FROM *Tragic America* [1931]

THE CONSTITUTION AS A SCRAP OF PAPER

Facts alone may portray the liberality or non-liberality toward all of such a document as our American Constitution, and from this liberality or its opposite shines forth the degree of its worth.

The further to comprehend the forces which conditioned the drafting of the American Constitution, and give weight to its setting in the thought and life of that day, one must return at least a little way in modern history. In seventeenth century Europe, as we all know, the great wars of religion were fought. And by the time the American Constitution was being drawn, religion, on the European continent at least, was still occupying quite the foremost place in the minds, motives and actions of its governments and peoples. Catholicism, entrenched in the South, and Protestantism in the North, wrangled to such a degree that liberty, although Montesquieu, Turgot, Voltaire, Rousseau and Lessing had written or were then writing of toleration and humaneness, was but dawning. This dominance of religion and its abuses, so trenchantly and bitterly assailed by Voltaire, existed in a day when kings, as we know, ruled by the direct will of God. And this assertion, due to the mental humbleness of those who can be led by dogmatic religion was too noble, as well as too sacred, to be questioned. Yet but a little while after all this was laughable to us here in America, as we also know. But now when we see how corporation despotism, bolstered by propaganda, can triumph, it does not seem so laughable. Dishonest and entrenched wealth is becoming sacred here; and those who question its rights and powers are not so different to the "possessed" and the "heretics" of a former day.

The first modern political revolt, as we all know, occurred in England (1640). Charles I was beheaded, and for treason. But not treason against God—the divine appointer of kings on the continent—but rather against the people of England, who, according to the very advanced thought of the radicals of that day and country, ruled by the wish and favor of the people of that country, and none other. They had come to believe, apparently, that the Lord checks up on kings. Their great thinker of the time, John Locke, expounded these conceptions of theirs so clearly that subsequently they, among other things, became strong, motivating factors in the production of the daring and noble, and yet inevitable, French Revolution. But despite this radical defiance and the subsequent superiority of Parliamentary power over the monarch, still the House of Lords remained—a forceful voice of the aristocracy,—while the commoners were either appointed by magnates or chosen from the electorate of less than one-tenth of the men of England. The idea of extending the franchise to the mass of the people of that day was not yet thought of. And of course the aristocrats of Spain, France and the German countries, as well as the nobility of Russia and Poland, considered themselves infinitely more lofty than the masses.

During the seventeenth century, however, those radical churchmen, the Calvinists, electrified Europe by stating that all men in the church were equal in the sight of God. Naturally, this did not "get much of a hand" from the nobility, and most particularly when it was hinted at or broached as a political doctrine. Only Cromwell, with his army, asserting that all men, equal in the state, should be the source of governmental authority, came near to establishing such democracy as could then be established which was little enough. But he and his

army also passed. They were quenched like a light, and their ideas
vanished or became a dusty and neglected philosophy. Yet in 1748,
Montesquieu wrote that men are born equal (a figment of the mind);
and Voltaire believed that men should possess equal rights before the
law (which is not so true as that they should have equal consideration); and Rousseau would sacrifice even liberty to gain utter equality.

Although these warm radical breezes blew on and fluttered all
that they touched, the nobility of that time, making light of them, was
wholly preoccupied by such supposedly critical matters as the growth
of Russia, the Austrian policies of the time, and the plunder of Poland.
Yet by a certain few, the radical movement was looked upon as
perhaps a natural but not a momentous matter. No one dreamed of a
complete transference of power from kings and courts to the people.
Yet with no more background ideologically than this, the English
colonies in America a little later declared their independence and
asserted that "all men are created free and equal."

It was not until eleven years later, during which time these same
ideas, and these alone were propounded, that the United States Constitution was written. The imminent French Revolution, which was to
make Kant, the dignified professor and philosopher, weep for joy, had
not even occurred. No other democracy existed. Americans in 1787
blazed out a unanimously willed democracy—a Russian Communism
of that day.

But now to contrast the Constitution with what had gone before
in this country. Pre-independence times here saw charter, proprietary
and royal government. Massachusetts, Rhode Island, Pennsylvania and
Delaware were overlorded by proprietors; New Hampshire, New
York, New Jersey, Virginia and Georgia were directly subject to the
English Crown. Under the new and wonderfully progressive (and by
that I mean better balanced) Constitution, representatives of the people, elected by them, were to raise all revenues, regulate commerce
with foreign nations and between States, and declare war. In lieu of
the prevailing religious intolerance abroad, with its strife and death,
and motivated by what idiotic superstitions and brought to bear by
what former regulations, the first Constitutional amendment, adopted
in 1791, guaranteed freedom of religious belief and the practice there-
of. Instead of a distant and infallible British government impossible of
approach by the people—an example of which was the English Gov-

ernor Berkeley of Virginia, who said: "Thank God there are no free
schools nor printing presses here"—there was granted the constitutional right to criticize by speech or through the press, and to freely
assemble and petition the government to mitigate any abuse. In short,
freedom after the severely repressive laws of the earlier day! And if
their severity be doubted, recall that in New England colonial life,
twelve offenses were punished by death, and in Virginia, seventeen!

Yet all of the class differences conditioning the British nobility
and the British proletariat existed in Colonial America. Only the gen-
tility here in America were permitted to use the prefix "Mr." or
"Mrs." Others above the rank of servant were honored by being
addressed as "goodman" and "goodwife." Catalogues of Yale and Harvard were arranged according to the rank of the student's families.
One whose estate did not amount to £200 or more, could not wear
gold or silver lace. And it was the aristocrat and the aristocrat alone,
who could wear calf-skin shoes, flowered silk, or gay-colored embroi-
dered velvet suits with wide ruffles of gold or silver lace, or have a
cane-head and snuff-box of gold or silver. The farmer and laborer
must venture to no better than a homespun shirt, neat's leather (cow-
hide) shoes, enhanced on Sundays by buckles, and leather breeches,
greased and blacked for occasions. Yet in spite of this actual practice
of British class difference, the Constitution verbally lessened the
whole business of class distinctions by prohibiting titles.

People now laud our American Constitution as a great document
that has kept up with the times. Yet what does that mean? That the
Constitution has given free sway to a corporate oligarchy which its
framers never contemplated, or to a capitalistic unionism so dominant
of the people as to exercise an undue power against them and frustrate
their every guarantee? Of course, 2,000,000 Colonists who didn't as yet
have a single daily newspaper, whose largest city was Philadelphia
(William Penn's "fair greene country town"), of 25,000 inhabitants,
and who were so excited about a stagecoach line established in 1766
and making the unprecedented time of two days between New York
and Philadelphia, that they called the stages "flying machines," could
not foretell the capitalism which now motivates and dominates the
American life. The American government to-day is not so much
government in the sense of managing for the many as it is in licensing
for and to the few—the corporate interests, no less—and with the

privilege of getting all they can for their private purposes. The strongest and final hold of capitalism to-day in the Constitution is its guarantee of private property. And in framing this clause, the Constitution-makers, thinking of real estate and personal property in terms of that day, never dreamed or imagined, let alone contemplated, the vast industrialism that later was to come and hold as personal property, not only unimaginably large amounts of stocks and bonds in holding companies, trusts and corporations, but the same in their entirety and in perpetuity. Most of the great fortunes of to-day which carry with them crucial power are personalty of this nature. And only a little while ago, the late George F. Baker, Chairman of the First National Bank of New York, died leaving hundreds of millions of dollars worth of this personal property in the form of tens of thousands of railroad, bank, etc., shares and bonds.

But now, with this change in the times, our financiers and corporation and bank-heads finding such dominance and control to their liking, have not only fought and in the main prohibited all natural and needed additions to this freedom, but have tightened and limited that naturally acquired by the Constitution nearly one hundred and fifty years ago. They have not welcomed and have not intended, if by such ways as they could devise they could frustrate it—a government of and by the people.

During the long one hundred and fifty years which have passed since the Constitution was drafted, our industrialists, and this almost unanimously (read Gustavus Myers' "History of Great American Fortunes"), have used every means in their power—money, government and the influence of connection—to filch one liberty and another from the layman. Of course, I take account of the fact that many petty regulations of olden days which mattered not to industry have disappeared. They are as nothing. Also, I pay due homage to the fact that the Constitution was drawn up by wealthy landowners, who did not intend all powers to be conferred upon the even then somewhat distrusted masses. In the large trend of affairs, however, my contention as to the primary liberality of that document is sound.

If this is doubted, an examination of the liberties of the individual citizen of to-day as contrasted with those the Constitution intended and those the corporations, who now control the Government which is supposed to abide by and enforce that Constitution, are willing to grant him, will, I think, command support for me and as only facts can.

Firstly, any scientific or cultural learning which will loosen customs or free the mind of industrial shackles, is suppressed. Free speech, free press? Our radio, public schools, colleges, pulpits? One needs only to scan the current American scene to know what already has happened as well as is now happening. If you will recall, in the chapter on Our Banks and Corporations as Government, I outlined the propaganda program in regard to private versus public ownership, and how schools and colleges, as well as newspapers and their editorial sanctums were invaded and suborned or betrayed. And to-day, if you investigate any factory, college, radio concern, newspaper office, moving picture company, library, or any other source of public information, its distribution or clarification for the masses, you will find out how quickly money—the present oligarchic program for the elevation of the few and the domination and suppression of the many—has invaded all these fields, and is saying what and how and where and why anything shall be said, and ruling always in its own interests. And that directly in the face of the line and letter of our American Constitution which guarantees the freedom or use of these to all.

But let us see now if this is not so. Students at a Brooklyn college were forbade to hear Norman Thomas, socialist leader, speak. Then at the University of Pittsburgh only recently, the Student Liberal Club of that School, prohibited from holding a meeting on the campus, assembled off the college grounds to listen to Professor Harry Elmer Barnes, of Smith College, speak on the Mooney-Billings case. For this, and this alone, one Fred Woltman, who taught philosophy, and two students were dismissed from the University. In other words, a nationally and legally acknowledged injustice to labor closed to comment in an American college. But at whose orders or wish? And next, in March, 1929, a sex questionnaire, distributed among students by psychologists and sociologists at the University of Missouri, resulted in the suspension of Professor Max F. Meyer, for many years a member of the faculty, and the dismissal of two other men. Yet the questionnaire in question had already been deemed entirely proper by scientific students of the subject at other schools as well as by the American Association of University Professors. Then why the suppression? The answer, as I took it from the mouths of some of the faculty itself, was this. The faculty itself is subject to a board of trustees. The trustees, in themselves not too highly informed, and highly conventional, publicly speaking, individuals of the moneyed and professional classes of the State, and looking to the State as well as individuals of wealth for endowments and funds, were determined not only to please these, but to see to it that their university conformed in every way, morally and otherwise, to the local as well as (as they assumed) generally current and therefore conventional notions of what a university should or should not teach and do in America. And hence the ban, which has fallen in well enough with the general feelings of our corporations, commercial and religious, which is that the less education, apart from things technical and financial (by no means political or sociologic) the better!

I sum the matter of dictation by all to the professor as to what he is to teach, in this way. A writer writes as he sees fit, a lawyer interprets the law and an educator should educate, unhampered.

But one of the most daring and subtle of all the attempts *so far* to undermine the right of free speech and, by the natural and obvious extension of the same, the right to a free press (defeated in the Supreme Court of the United States on June 1, 1931, and that after a two-year fight), began in Minneapolis in 1927, and came to be known as the Minnesota Gag Law Case. This concerned a weekly newspaper in Minneapolis: *The Saturday Press*, in which, in late September, 1927, there was printed an attack on not only one Barnett, a gangster operating gambling and vice houses in Minneapolis, but also on one Brunskill, the Chief of Police of that city, for accepting graft. Also, one Davis, of the Law Enforcement League, and Leach, the Mayor, were included. Because H. A. Guilford, who, with J. M. Near, ran the *Saturday Press*, was shot, though not killed by gangsters when the first issue of this exposure came out, I have a suspicion that most of the charges were true. At any rate, among the statutes of the State of Minneapolis at this time was one which declared that any newspaper repeatedly publishing "scandalous, malicious and defamatory" matter, could be declared a nuisance and on that ground, suppressed. Exactly how that statute came to be there (although the why of it is obvious) is yet to be explained. Nevertheless, by virtue of the authority of that, the local individuals so attacked, and through their lawyers and the police, clamped this suppression power down on this publication and ended it. Then the usual thing—the gangsters tried to force these editors to their side by offering them a share of the gambling and illicit profits. The paper, however, to be thoroughly wiped out. And for three years, or until it was, by a vote of 5 to 4 only (note the 5 to 4) voided by our Supreme Court, it ran the gamut of the State courts. And the gag law was sustained by them. And nearly so, as you see, by the Supreme Court of the United States. And that in the face of the plain mandate of the Constitution itself which says that the rights of a free press are not to be abridged.

But consider the implication of all this; the fact that a sovereign State in America should pass such a law and, next, that its Supreme Court should uphold it. And that three years had to elapse before any final decision of any kind could be reached! For under that power, assuming it had been sustained (and consider the vote 5 to 4), the government, if it chose, could have stopped any publication on any such trumped up charges, and this in the face of the question as to whether or not there existed evidence that the statements circulated were libelous or true! Or if this law had been held Constitutional, like legislation in other states would have been able also to muzzle the press.

In short, it doomed the individual, regardless of his rightness or wrongness, not only as to editorial expression of his ideas, but subjected him to financial loss as well. And this was upheld in the Courts of the State of Minnesota and enforced there until three years later, until, via funds furnished, I believe, by the American Newspaper Publishers' Association, and others, it was set aside by the Supreme Court. But even so, there were those who, editorially and in court, argued that because England has practically the same thing, it would be equitable here. But in England, total suppression, as was so decidedly effected in Minnesota, is not possible. Besides, England does not have a constitutional guarantee of freedom of the press, whereas we do. Yet this sinister attempt to dictate to and actually control the American press got as far as I have indicated.

But let me turn to a related phase: that of the power of our Government to deny at any time the use of the mails to any individual, firm or publication. This on the strength of the laws which relate to obscenity and sedition. But in practice, to-day, how does it work? You can imagine! Is there anything political or anti-corporation or anti-social as a religionist or a trust sees it? If so, and quickly, the mails are closed, and perhaps proceedings of a different character started: examinations, prosecutions, etc., on the part of the Department of Justice. No need to mention anything Communistic. Although there is nothing in the Constitution which should prevent a widespread study and discussion of that new economic theory, attempt to do that through the mails! It has not been long since several publications dealing with the new Eastern economic theory have been suppressed, and with scarcely a protest from any but the Communists. And yet labor, antagonistic to the corporations, fares no better, or very little. I cite two cases. First the booklet: "Smash the Gastonia Frame-up!"—a sharp comment on the Gastonia, N. C., labor war, which was held improper for the mails because it reflected on the State of North Carolina! And next, a second booklet, "Justice, California Style," was decreed by the New York Court of Appeals in March, 1930, as fit for the mails because the law does not contemplate libel against a State. To me, since libel is a tort, a private, civil, uncontractual wrong to an individual, the latter is the better case. But all this is just the gravy; here is the roast! Even in peace time, the Postmaster General may exclude *future* issues of a newspaper which has published nonmailable material. Our United States Supreme Court has so decided. But is the Postmaster General a sorcerer or a wizard, that he can know beforehand what is to be printed in the future issues of a newspaper, or is it merely a way for him to save himself time and trouble?

Although arbitrary suppression by the Government is an outrage, that of a *corporation* to evade the Constitutional guarantee of free speech is infinitely worse. Yet now comes radio censorship, the worst because no legal action may be taken. The corporations who want to sell radios to the tomfoolery-seekers and half-baked people who would not dare to know anything, will sign all kinds of contracts for "Madame Distingué" to tell how sub-debs with black hair and green eyes, brown hair and blue eyes, yellow hair and brown eyes, should dress, or with "Amos and Andy" for years of service, but let more serious matters be suggested, how different! Last year, for instance, in December, the National Broadcasting Company refused to broadcast speeches of the National Birth Control Congress in New York on the ground that they were evil—although the Church of England does not now appear to think so. And again, in Pittsburgh, KQV canceled, for

the alleged reason of "conflicting programs" a talk by Patrick Fagan
in which he berated the "coal and iron police."

Now turn to the Negro situation for a moment, and his place and
rights under the Constitution. As I see his problem, it is like this:
Though the Constitution freed him and gave him (and now to-day his
wife and daughter) the right to vote, this right in ten States to-day,
flagrantly and directly in opposition to the law, is interfered with.
More, our high courts in thirty States now hold that the State laws of
those States prohibiting intermarriage of whites and blacks, and in
seventeen States segregating the Negroes in schools and public conveyances, do not conflict with the Constitutional amendments that
freed them and gave them the right to vote. Yet directly under the
judge's eyes, does it not say in the Constitution that *the enumeration
of certain rights does not disparage others retained by the people?* It
would seem to me that constitutionally, at least, the Negroes have the
right to marry whom they please and to ride in all conveyances.
Why? Because by the Constitution and by gaining citizenship, all of
their privileges are protected. This 14th Amendment, though, by
which a State may now pass these crotchety or credulous acts if only
they "protect" all equally by them, is a hoax, because all of the
Negroes aren't all of the people.

More, the Negro, fast being absorbed by industry, is to-day, under
our individualistic and capitalistic approach, being put to the meanest
labor and suffering abuse involving a loss of Constitutional privileges.
For it is the Negro and the Negro alone to-day who must sweat all
night in the gas-filled, nauseating and hence enervating checker-chamber
of a steel mill, or crawl into underground sewers or repair red-hot fur-
naces. Much work of other kinds does not go to him. And in the steel
mill at Sparrow's Point, Maryland, common Negro labor is paid but
25 or 30 cents a day for 12 hours work. Again, at the Allegheny Steel
Company, near Pittsburgh, Pennsylvania, Negroes labor fourteen
hours a day. Yet one word of protest on their part, and all of their
Constitutional privileges in this matter are blotted out, as I will show
in my chapter on labor. Our Negroes, likewise, are the first to be laid
off. What happens then? They have to go back to the country. Yet
back in the country again, these same Negroes as tenant farmers
become practically the slaves of landlords, who assume actually—not
theoretically—the power of slave owners, and before whom, because

of local coöperation, these Negroes are helpless. (You will meet up with them again in the chapter on The Abuse of the Individual.) Though the crops raised on this tenant-farmer basis are supposed to be shared fifty-fifty between the landlord and tenant, the landlord who sells the crop and receives the money, keeps all he can. If a Negro protests, the landlord can, and does, have him arrested on the ground that the ignorant and unknowing Negro still owes him money, and sentenced. Or perhaps he is lynched, or just shot down in cold blood—a conclusion which is locally if not legally, passed upon as justifiable homicide. And when in 1919, Negro tenant farmers of eastern Arkansas organized to obtain a fair price for their cotton, they held a meeting, which they had a right to do under the Constitution. But upon so doing, the henchmen of local landowners fired upon the gathering and the landowners had the local militia come and kill scores of these Negroes. In cases of this nature, the local government of Arkansas then forced evidence adverse to the Negroes for use at their trial by torturing Negro witnesses on an electric chair which shocked them until they said such things as there and then transcribed could later be used against them.

But not only is the individual, black or white, misused and suppressed in this way in America, but our Government officials once they are not just duly, but, rather, swindlingly elected, and that in the face of the intentions of the individual when voting, and once inducted in office, and vested with some power, then they proceed not only to interpret the law for themselves or according to the wishes of some corporation, but they themselves proceed to grant to others authority which was never delegated to them by the Constitution or the people. And mostly this arbitrary and unconstitutional power in office is exercised to help corporations as against the public at large. Thus, the legal authorities of any given State, or the United States Government itself, via its charter or franchise-granting powers, will allow a corporation to set up a town or city within a State and give it authority to make and enforce rules and regulations for the inhabitants of said town or city which are no part of any law of the State, the while and at the same time, the same corporation thus governing a city is allowed to refuse to the State, via the franchise granted it, the right to make the corporation obey it not only in police, but other matters. In other words, elected or appointed officials, without any constitutional authority for what they do, set corporations above the State and the government itself in order that the corporation, for such favors as it may be willing to do them, can the more closely and drastically regulate those who work for it. Also, it is in such illegal and purely corporation created towns that the corporation may say what newspapers shall or shall not be read, what store or stores dealt with, what rents paid, social or mental actions indulged in, and the like. And if you doubt this, you need only recall Cœur d'Alene in Idaho, Carnegie in Pennsylvania, and Gary and other towns in Indiana and elsewhere.

In fact, in any matter relating to the American corporation to-day—its assumed rights, privileges, its power to tax, destroy, suborn, suppress, even enslave (as in the case of the chain and camp gangs in the South and elsewhere) or to imprison and otherwise abuse the individual who in any way protests or seeks to annul or frustrate its arbitrary abuses as in the case of Tom Mooney,—the Constitution and its various guarantees as to all this is as nothing. The courts, where the corporations and their interests are concerned, are no longer willing to hear the individual, let alone aid him. Concerning this case, may I quote a capitalist who said: "Practically all I know is that he has a pretty clear record of being a bad actor and is a party who would probably start this same thing all over again if he were out of jail." I could cite cases, not by the dozen but the hundreds, I am sure, but just to prove roughly that I am not talking without the machine guns of fact at my elbow, I will list these (and please read them):

1. Lochner *v.* New York, 1904. This case came to the United States Supreme Court because a Utica bakery contested the constitutionality of the New York State law *limiting* the employment of help in bakeries to ten hours a day. Our highest court held the statute *unconstitutional* on the ground that it denied "equal protection of the laws to all." In other words, it denied sufficient protection to the corporation, although incidentally it was denying *all* protection to labor. Not only that, but the majority opinion of the court proceeded to call the law a "meddlesome interference" with liberty, property and *the right to contract* (the individual's right to contract to work 14 hours a day or more if by poverty he was forced so to do, is what is meant here) guaranteed by the 14th Amendment! But what about the liberty and property and right to contract of the laborer? It is stingingly minimized.

In this case, the court would not in any way limit the right to contract, because, although the law protected the laborer from abuse, it inconvenienced the employer. I believe this is a sound statement, because the same United States Supreme Court had not hesitated to limit contracts before.

Thus, in many instances, the Government has not hesitated to limit the people's right to contract. For one example, when a municipal or state government grants a franchise, it limits the people's right to contract in this way: You and I have a right to buy a house from this company or the other, and theoretically, you and I have the right to contract with this, that, or the other gas company for gas. But when a franchise is granted, one company has a monopoly on gas. Thus, if any one wants gas, he must take it from this company or go without. The people's right to contract for gas is limited to this one company.

2. Hammer *v.* Dagenhart, 1918. Our National Child Labor Law prohibited the interstate transportation of goods made by children. Child labor was thus regulated because Congress, under its constitutional privilege as well as duty in regard to interstate commerce, the regulation of the same, so ordered. Many consider that law as protecting health, etc. Questions similar to this protection of health, however, deal with police power, and police power is held by the States according to the Constitution.

Yet this National Child Labor Law was declared unconstitutional by a 5-4 Supreme Court decision, on the ground that the subject matter of this law—that is, regulating the ages at which children can work—is really a police power. But many preëminent justices agree with me that this law definitely concerned the regulation of interstate commerce. Yet the court cast aside this right of Congress as if it was nothing. The very same court, though, had previously held that the right of Congress to regulate interstate commerce was more important and came before the right of the States to exercise police power. So there you have it. Now a thing is wrong and now it is right—but all according, apparently, to who is seeking to know. In this case, obviously, it was much to the advantage of capital to have this law declared unconstitutional. Then it could hire hundreds of thousands of children for practically nothing. And in declaring this law unconstitutional, the court even went against its own principles and past deci-

sion; because previously, it had held interstate commerce more important than police powers. Because of this and because the decision
obviously favored capital in preference to labor, it is most clear that
this decision was made to favor capital rather than to protect police
power. And in going against its principles, the court cast aside as
nothing, the constitutional privilege of Congress to regulate interstate
commerce.

3. Adair *v.* United States, 1907. One section of the Federal Erd-
man Act (resulting from the great railroad strike of 1894) to promote
arbitration between labor and capital, prohibited discrimination
against employees who belonged to unions. This section of the law
was declared unconstitutional by the Supreme Court in this case on
the grounds that it denied liberty to the individual to contract—of
course, actual liberty for the boss to hire, fire and keep whom he
pleased. (A court decision on the subject of labor *v.* capital has never
been made for labor on the grounds of his liberty, etc.) Personally,
though, I see no liberty with the power to discriminate lawfully. Yet
the court was "hipped" on this idea. It said: "No government can
legally justify such legislation in a free land." Actually, what this
court decision legalizes is this: the bosses are free by law to unite into
corporations, powerful enough to fight all labor, and so united, do
oppose all labor, but labor is not free to unite, because this decision
gives the bosses power to discriminate against unionized labor. The
liberty of contract in this instance was held to be the liberty of the
employers to enforce their demands—not liberty of both parties to
agree, a supposedly necessary mutuality if any contract is to be held as
good law.

When it comes to the individual, who is not protected by a union
or some organization of some kind, there is still another story to tell.
Thus, in many of the Southern States, like Florida and Alabama,
where laws exist saying that a man who owes his employer money
cannot leave his job until the debt is made up, individuals are forced
to sign notes and other evidences of debt, until in some cases men are
kept working all their lives at the most inadequate wages.

More, in this same area, men arrested on petty charges are victims
of a virtual press gang system which runs counter to the very
essence of the American Constitution. The old custom of the press
gang master—getting an affable sailor drunk in order to shanghai him,

and then forcing him to slave as a sailor without pay—had at least more of preliminary affability about it than which now operates against the unemployed man, in the South or West. For alleged vagrancy, the mere necessity of passing from one region to another in search of work the unemployed man of this hour is seized, jailed and then hired out as part of a prison or chain gang to work under a private contractor who makes the money. All of which is described in "Abuse to the Individual."

The chief ill of most of these abuses all over the United States is that usually they fall to individuals impotent because they are single-handed and uninformed. In this complex society of ours, with its government now almost wholly privately controlled, I have traced them either to our dominant corporations and their allied interests, or to the influence of their example now so widely known of all. For naturally, in a country where private powers able to coerce the government, and strong enough, as are our corporations, to resist regulation exist, this abuse of the individual is sure to arise. For who is he to ask of any one anything, or to complain when he considers himself abused? Was this not so long ago the land of slavery, par excellence? And has not the general and brutal attitude of our corporations and financiers since encouraged this wholesale abuse of the individual? And since that desire for slaves on the part of some in the South appears never to have died we have what we have, now. For our corporations do seek, via wealth, for themselves and poverty for all others, to enslave. And this they still seek, mainly by making reform in any and all of its phases anywhere in America a failure—and always in the teeth of the Constitution and with the aid and consent of the higher courts.

But how do corporations and our Government in aiding them (and when it is caught in so doing) get out of their jam? I will show you. There is an antiquated Constitutional privilege which says that an individual does not have to testify or answer questions which even *tend* to incriminate him. (Recall how the common man is forced by 3rd degree violence to testify.) In other words, because a man has committed a crime, he doesn't need to tell anything about it. Thus, when the proper Government officials set out to investigate something, they cannot force those who know the most about it to disclose anything, and hence they cannot obtain enough evidence even to take the case to court. Thus, in the matter of the investigation of the disgusting New York milk graft, as well as the investigation—by public prosecutors after public exposure, of course—of graft in connection with the State census of the building and equipping of public school buildings, hospitals, sewers, etc., these same were either blocked in part or thwarted entirely by this legal hocus pocus in regard to your testimony tending to incriminate or degrade you. The State officials could not answer, because, etc. Again, it was illustrated in connection with those New York judges and various prominent New York City officials who, having stolen this or that, or winked at the same for what there was in it for them, were freed because of this Constitutional privilege to sit back and while still holding their jobs, mockingly evade these investigators and their questions. Yet these same Government officials, since they had openly and publicly accepted a public trust by taking a position of trust, were certainly answerable to to the people for everything except private matters. And in so far as any public matters were concerned, these officials should not have been permitted to use this so-called immunity privilege. Accepting a government office, as I see it, at least, should carry with it in law a pledge not to take advantage of this Constitutional right. And although some lawyers say that this would be unconstitutional (forcing a man to give up his Constitutional rights) I say, and I am supported by distinguished legal opinion, that this would not be forcing him because no man is compelled to take office unless he wants to.

But be that as it may, the entire business is not only shameful but outrageously and brazenly dishonest. All of the rest of the everyday living methods of the common American citizen is not based on any such immunity idea. If a lay individual does something to be accounted for, most members of society ask him: "What about it?" "How do you explain this?" And it is natural and just that he should answer for his deeds, whether he incriminates himself or not.

The other legal hoax preventing Government investigations comes from a hazy law, used hundreds of years ago in the trials by combat and torment. And its proper place, to-day, is not among national or legal principles but among those of our corporations. And this legal hoax reads that no person "shall be twice put in jeopardy of his life for the same offense." But those who want to oppose Government investigation use this to keep what witnesses tell the Grand Jury from being admitted as evidence against them in any trial which may follow. But this is dishonest—a mere subterfuge—for even according to this legal jargon, a man isn't actually "in jeopardy" until he is actually put to trial. And when he is before a Grand Jury most certainly he is not on trial. None the less, this obviously dishonest loophole is now used in this way to free crooks who might be punished. And worse, not one American out of a thousand who would not permit, let alone sanction, this knows anything about it. It is too new a piece of legal legerdemain. Yet how often does a judge, veiled in the mystery of learning, rule out such evidence! And how many Government officials thus fix things for corporations!

Indeed, our corporations aided by "influenced" government, not only unscrupulously get out of predicaments by the misuse of these Constitutional rights, but in any labor issue and in order that they themselves may win at the workingman's expense, do flatly renounce them, thus doubly penalizing the little man for his littleness. Indeed, these denials of these privileges to labor come about through heartless wrong to the workers in the first instance. They are, at such times as the corporations choose, and regardless of past profits earned by the corporation at mainly their expense, forced to accept a 10 per cent, or 15 per cent or even 25 per cent wage cut in pay that permits as it is, for the worker, only the barest needs; or, for instance, as at the American Woolen Company in Lawence, Massachusetts, a single worker who used to operate two combs must speed his body unduly so as to run nine combs. These conditions the wage-earner cannot meet, but against these outrages he is not supposed to do a thing. As proof, I offer the data for 1930 arrests: at strikes, 1,037; at unemployment demonstrations, 1,598; at open and shop-gate meetings, 644; for distributing leaflets, 962; miscellaneous, 1,598; a total of 5,935! And this in a country where strikes are lawful and where freedom of assembly, of the press, and presentation of grievances to the Government, are Constitutional sacraments!

But to show by facts that corporations are arbitrarily helped by the courts in labor disputes, I wish to cite that injunctions have been, and are still being, issued forbidding union leaders to ask laborers to join workers' organizations or ordering labor leaders to call no strikes, and worse, to pay for no necessities of life for the striking workman, and so aiding in breaking any strike. And not only that, but the courts

have even issued injunctions to prevent legal proceedings in behalf of
workers! But then, you may ask, are the courts in this country to be
denied the underdog? Can he not be protected as to his guaranteed
rights? The answer is no, he cannot! Meetings and parades in the
present depressing state of unemployment are arbitrarily prevented,
despite the freedom of assembly guaranteed by the Constitution.
Again, the circulation of newspapers and pamphlets is forbidden, as
though a free press were no longer a valuable or valued thing and one
especially needed and craved by the workers, if not by the corporations. Any of our American judges to-day can, or at least does, decide
to and then does issue these injunctions on affidavit that life or property require protection; or that peace requires to be maintained; also
that the Sherman Anti-Trust Act (meant only for conspirators restraining trade by monopoly and not for labor) is being interfered
with. In other words, our American Constitution is now a scrap of
paper to the rich and powerful, but by no means such to the poor. For
this is the day of the corporation judge and the corporation land. Our
judges now not only establish what social regulations they see fit,
under the argument of protection to property which would probably
never be damaged (and so do in violation of the United States Constitution) but simultaneously they exercise partisan favor. For the
workers in America are not even given a hearing before the judge,
who previous to his decision and issuance of such preliminary and
restraining order as are asked for by corporations and which usually
hold for a long time before any hearings whatsoever, is supposed to
be interested to know what they, the workers, have to say. But is he?
Not he! And the little man takes his loss and goes his way. More, a
reform injunction measure cannot even now be gotten through Congress. And if it could, our all powerful corporations, legally so well
armed, would evade its purpose by some divergent and underground
channel of the law. A capitalistic failure? Certainly. And what is to be
done about it? That is yet to be seen.

Not only that, though, but our corporations and our Government
likewise use any—even the most despicable—legal loopholes to smash
any but an extremely reactionary political analysis, and this in violation of the fundamental rights relating to thought, assembly, address,
publication, distribution, written into the Constitution. Thus, the National Espionage Act, passed during the World War for purposes of

that war only and to suppress sedition supposedly, is now being in-
voked again, and for the first time in ten years. But for what? Thus
far, to keep from the mails the following Communist newspaper publications: *Revolutionary Age, Young Worker, Young Pioneer, Vida
Obrera* and *Labor Sports Monthly*. And this on the ground that
violence was advocated in them. But there is one point connected with
this legal interpretation of this advocacy of violence that I want to
make very clear. Always in America, as well as in its mother country,
England,—that even more conservative country from whence came
the Common Law upon which America's entire legal structure is
built—advocacy of a violence which is not a clear and present threat
does *not* constitute sedition. Yet the most graphic proof that the
present Government is waging a campaign against all political interpretation which is not reactionary—in other words, against Communists—is that even during the War, sedition under the Espionage Act
had to be advocacy of a clear and immediate violence. Yet in none of
the recent Communist publications has there been any specific incite-
ment to violence. None the less in their case, certainly freedom of the
press had disappeared like frost on a warmed pane. And this when for
generations, the assassination of British kings—but not a specific king,
like the present King George—could be advocated. Yet all that the
Communist literature in this country is guilty of is the use of such
words as "fight," "militant," "revolution" and "war," which in Web-
ster's Dictionary, as well as in common use, have meanings like "a
fight or war of any kind" and "revolution signifying a complete
change." And these listed not only as *prior* meanings, but naturally
connoting such in the mind of the reader.

But what mention is made, if any, of the advocacy by conservatives of violence against such enormous groups as Communists, labor
leaders, strikers, and Negroes? Lynchings, turning machine guns on
strikers, etc. No law is passed to prohibit that! Scarcely any attempt
to minimize it, even. But to return to sedition—sedition being discontent with the government. As official interpretation—arbitrary or legal
—runs now in America, the people, who are supposed merely to
entrust or delegate their power to their elected officials, have now no
longer the right to express discontent over phases of current statecraft
or action. They are to take these interpretations and acts of their
elected officials, whatsoever their nature, as legal, just and in the

interest of all, or suffer the consequences. Yet sedition with no definite act committed, only words "tending to treason" (a vagueness which makes for poor law, and already is at variance with any reputable law relating to crimes) has become a criminal offense, subject to extremely long imprisonment. But unless interpreted in the traditional, definite way, i.e., as words containing a clear and immediate threat to the Government of the United States, our sedition law is nothing more than an illegal and arbitrary denial to a specific group, and at the behest of their enemies, of an inherent Constitutional right and, as such, subject to all the abuses that usually accompany such an arbitrary denial. And that is exactly what is occurring in America today.

Not only that, but our various State sedition laws meet with an even more hazy interpretation than does the Federal Espionage Act. In Woodlawn, Pennsylvania, for instance, where stands the Jones & Laughlin Steel Works, holding relations with 2,528 families of the 2,928 in the town, and paying its laborers but 40 to 50 cents an hour on the 12-hour system, three Communists who not only disavowed even belief in the overthrow of the Government, let alone a desire to bring it about, and who had never attempted in any way so to do, were sentenced to five years in the Allegheny County Workhouse because they had in their possession some Communistic literature—not guns and ammunition—and had tried to organize a Communistic group which had almost no followers. They had not attempted or argued military revolt or siege, but were alleged to have made certain utterances.

Laws similar to this Pennsylvania Sedition Act have been passed, since 1917, in 33 states. Get that! Then conceive of a statute like California's Criminal Syndicalism law—but no worse than the others—being used against the workers in this land where all men are by no means free or equal in or out of the sight of the law—and used to jail them for years. Thus, six men, together with others, were charged under this statute on three counts: first, membership in the Communist Party (political views, a crime, would you!); second, advocacy of violence by speech and printed matter; and third, conspiracy to advocate these matters—this last in substance the same as the first count and hence an unjust addition to the duration of the sentence. The State's evidence against them consisted of Communist literature found in their possession, plus statements alleged to have been made that mass picketing and violence, such as carrying "pop" bottles (not revolvers) and the tearing up of cantaloupe vines as well as railroad trains and bridges, would be resorted to in case of a strike. Yet all of these statements relative to the advocacy of violence, etc., were testified to only by stool-pigeons (spy detectives in the union) who admitted at the trial that they had urged the workers to fight with "pop" bottles and who when asked by the defense, "Did you or did you not say to . . . that you had to provoke these Communists and that you were fixing the testimony to get a conviction?" hesitated until under furious objections by the prosecution, they answered "No." And although this embodies every important phase of their trial, none the less these six men are now serving sentences of from three to forty-two years—an undue variation in length of time or servitude which can keep these men locked up for a lifetime! And yet actually for no other reason than being Communists and having Communist literature in their possession.

Yet in America—or according to its Constitution at least—that is no crime, but rather an individual and guaranteed right. That it is now being so severely punished by an especial American exile system introduced into this land of ours is due to the growth and self-entrenchment and now would-be self-perpetuating money power, which for daring, cruelty and downright Neronic despotism is not to be rivaled anywhere. But now wanting to forfend itself against the rise of a rival and more equitable economic system in the East, it is prepared to indulge in such tactics as we have seen;—to battle and drive men who are no longer satisfied with its methods;—in short, to make a memory of the American equality idea and of America's Constitution a scrap of paper, which by now it really is.

THE ABUSE OF THE INDIVIDUAL

Corporations, the deviously won reward of skyscraper-crowned dignitaries, having catapulted their way (honestly or dishonestly) through meshes of law, public opinion, morals, theories—obviously by reason of some constructive intent on Nature's part as manifested through man—have finally reached that state of centralized power and security in America in which any attempt at opposition, correction, or even criticism, on the part of the small fry is likely to be met with drastic counter-attacks intended in quite every instance to terrify or punish, and so forestall any attempt at the same thing in the future. To realize the truth of this, one need only contemplate the fierce executive, judicial, financial, as well as social, attacks on this or that opponent of the present centralization of all powers in the hands of a few. To-day in America the individual is practically helpless; that is, any individual lower in rank than the top level.

In short, the individual in America suffers from cruelty and abuse, as well as senseless regulation: the kind of abuse and cruelty that is not only ruthless but brainless, and that, except for abnormal money greed on the part of a few, need not exist. Thus, corporation greed in connection with railroads, street cars, busses—in fact, any form of transportation or exchange—has worked untold hardship on the little person, causing him to be pushed and kicked about, browbeaten by officials and their hirelings, ignored and even laughed at by petty officials in every field. One need only consider the street car, bus, or subway—the conscienceless overcrowding; the cars with too few seats, insufficient light and air, dirty seats, floors and windows; and all because by ignoring and failing to supply even the commonest decencies of public transport, a few extra dollars can be made by an inner ring of owners already stuffed to repletion with money!

Yet no help from any official source to which the public might turn! Instead, should any complaint be made, insults from officials, petty magistrates, the police, and the hirelings, and even thugs, of money-mad corporations, until ten-, fifteen-, and even thirty-five- and forty-dollar-a-week clerk or worker in any field is ready to admit that he is a mere nothing, a beggar or dog or less, in the eyes of those who, by bribery and chicane and direct robbery in every conceivable form, have been able to take from him his right to decent service or consideration. His corporations have not only seized his privileges as a citizen, but have taxed him to death into the bargain.

One illustration of this was the abolition, not so many years ago in many cities, of the transfer system from any direct to any cross-town car line, and vice versa. This meant double and treble fares for the traveling world which originally had been assured that in return for a free franchise to the corporation, it would be protected. But no!

More millions for more money-mad dubs, and to be extracted from the many, regardless of their poverty or downright inability to pay! And in addition, in many other fields, a steady and dishonest increase in rates for light, heat, water, telephone and other public service, the while the number of those compelled to use these utilities grew and grew. And yet, and withal, the corporations, fattening by this numerical increase, still bawling about confiscatory taxes and rates not high enough to permit them (the poor corporations!) to earn seven per cent on their invariably falsely-represented investments. And so, according to them, no money for replacement of the wear and tear on their supposedly, very much injured property. And the same therefore, and on this pretext, left in all too many cases in the shabbiest condition; no decent service to the public. Go into the men's room or the ladies' room of a New York City elevated station to-day even, and see for yourself!

And what American has not only suffered from, but commented on, the really infuriating imposition of the American Pullman car, with its stuffy, narrow, and quite public berth, for the use of which he has persistently been charged not only exorbitant but preposterous prices: much more to ride, say, from New York to Pittsburgh than he would have to pay for a room in any of the best hotels of his great cities? And in addition to his regular and already exorbitant fare. And, since our corporations tax as they please, on the "take it or leave it" basis.

And similarly, the control by corporations of prices regardless of merit or (in so far as foodstuffs are concerned) seasonal supply. In New York or Chicago or other big cities, lemons, for instance, remaining at three for ten cents, whether they be plentiful or whether the extra ones have to be allowed to rot in cars or dumped in any harbor or slough in order that this price may be maintained. And this applying to other fruits and vegetables as well. At this writing there are vast piles of farm produce rotting along the railroad tracks which stretch out into the meadows between Jersey City and Newark— carload after carload dumped because otherwise the exorbitant asking price could not be obtained from the wholesaler in New York. And this destruction of food, and in the face of millions of unemployed and thousands of bread lines, not only done openly, but widely publicized. Witness the items in all the newspapers some months ago, announcing a sham battle in California with "surplus" eggs as missiles. Thousands of crates of eggs so destroyed, and in order to keep up prices, the while children all over America were suffering from malnutrition and their parents not only unable to buy eggs for them but themselves suffering from hunger or actually dying of starvation! Is life really mad? Are all men scoundrels or fools?

It is the same with bread. Ten cents a loaf the while hundreds of millions of bushels of wheat lie stored and unsalable! Not only that, but in the Northwest last winter, wheat used as fuel, and at the instigation of capitalists terming such measures "stabilization." Yet millions of men on the streets, with scarcely as much as ten cents wherewith to buy a loaf of bread! And though cattle-hides fall to almost nothing in price—a dead loss to the cattle-raiser, if not the packer—still, shoes remaining at from eight to fourteen dollars a pair! And let the unemployed, or he who has had his salary cut in half, do the best he can!

Worse, this destruction of necessities is not only condoned but now actually recommended and demanded by the Government itself. Have we not heard the vacuous and inane Farm Board telling the cotton-growers of the South that they must plow under one-third of their cotton crops so that the price of cotton may be increased? True, cotton has suffered great declines in price, and when it became evident that this year's crop would be large, the price collapsed below the cost of production, but should that mean the destruction of something that thousands of penniless individuals have need for? Yet as to this plowing under, the rich land-owners passing along the full burden of the decline in price to the "croppers," as demonstrated at Camp Hill, Alabama, where they cut off the food supplies of Negro "croppers" in order to force them to abandon their share of the crops before the cotton-picking season came around. And later shooting them for the least offense—for stealing a loaf of bread or a purse, because otherwise—and there being now nearly one hundred thousand penniless and hungry—they might turn brave and savage and take from their grafting overlords or their alleged Government something wherewith to maintain their lives. But the individual farmer, as is natural, refusing to destroy any of his own cotton, no matter how much he might approve of having the other fellow destroy his. Needless to say, and as

you can see, the Farm Board's fantastic and impractical recommendation arousing only wide opposition.

But can a more insane economic system be imagined? Because
there is too much food, people must starve! Because there is too much
cotton, people must continue to wear rags! Or say, rather, and more
truly, that because grasping corporations find themselves unable—their
indecently low wage scales having practically nullified buying power
as far as the mass is concerned—to command the exorbitant prices
they insist on, they have nothing more to offer in the way of a
solution to this economic mess than the destruction of these crops for
which there is so much dire need and the starvation of those who
grew them. And yet, as you can see, they have safely counted, and can
continue so to do, on a fawning government to support whatever they
recommend. Yet if these suggestions were not really criminal, they
would appear insanely naïve.

In fact, it is true that in the United States to-day the capitalists
having the factories and land necessary for producing them have a
stranglehold on the necessities of life, for they make the price pools
and agreements for keeping prices high. This enables our bankers and
speculators, in order to keep up the prices of everything, to dump
food on the ground to rot, to destroy crops and property in many
forms, the while the jobless go hungry. Yet in the Soviet Union,
where the workers collectively, through their government, are the
owners (really there is no such thing as private property in Russia)
every effort is made to increase production in order to improve the
conditions of life for the masses. Every surplus of goods is welcomed,
not as a menace to the prices of the few but as a means of further
raising the standard of living of the whole population.

Not only this, but in the chapters entitled "The Position of
Labor" and "The Growth of Police Power" I have cited crime after
crime against the petty individual who under this great corporation-
controlled government has neither voice nor recourse of any kind.
For, as I have just shown, not only the courts, but the police, the
press, the church, the pictures and the radio, all, all have gone over to
the side that has the most money and that can fight them the hardest,
or, assuming them to be sufficiently subservient, do the most for them.
A little brief authority, a trashy badge or uniform, or the insignia of

any small office, and behold a tyrant who sees nothing but effrontery in the least desire or pleasure of any one not possessed of authority or property or power. Is it the driver of an automobile? Then it is the pleasure as well as the purpose of the largest as well as the smallest officials connected in any least way with the regulation of traffic (its assumed furtherance, not hindrance) to irritate, browbeat, delay, threaten, and all too often arrest (and for purposes of graft, fine or tax) individuals who are seeking no more than a reasonable and just use of the public roads. And since our American railroads have been seeking to drive the individual bus-owners off the roads in order to gobble up the right to operate buses for themselves, it is no common occurrence to have the petty individual operator annoyed, delayed, and most inordinately fined, until at last, through downright weariness as well as robbery, he is compelled to dispose of his right and allow the corporation to function in his stead. And this by the aid of the local police, the county sheriff, the town marshal, and who not else, in quite every part of America. It is a commonplace, just as the driving out of the individual oil operator by the Standard Oil Company, or the individual coal operator by the combined mining and railway trust, was a commonplace of half a century ago.

In fact, I am now convinced that this is one country that, ever since it was conceived of as a possibility, has been steadily and deceit-fully, as well as fraudulently, shunted along the path of individual and later corporate control, as opposed to its written and widely-promul-gated determination to make of itself a liberal and helpful democracy in which the individual was to fare more pleasantly and comfortably than ever he had before in all the world! For here more than any-where else in the world, I do believe, the petty individual has seen himself more thoroughly coerced, robbed and frustrated, and that always in favor of the cunning individual of capitalistic leanings and with a will to power. For where other than here has been developed those superorganisms: the trust and holding company (even the *Holding Company of Holding Companies*) which, because of its ramifi-cations and strength, is now so completely in a position to obfuscate law, equity and the rules of government as to have become govern-ment, *de facto* if not *de jure*. And since these organizations have chosen to work evil as well as good, to abrogate individual as well as government rights, and to cause to be robbed, restrained, defamed,

and even slain, any and all of those who have ventured to disagree
with or oppose them, they have made of the original plan of our
government a complete failure.

The record is too great and savage to be even more than hinted at
here, but one thing is sure: the illegal, bandit actions of American
financial men in general, and from the beginning—their corporations,
trusts and holding companies, their suborned or threatened courts,
lawyers, police, politicians and officials generally—have so weakened
the faith of the little American in his government that now one of his
outstanding dreams is to obtain, by some hook or crook, an office or
uniform or robe for himself, and thus vested in authority, proceed to
tax or graft upon or otherwise ill-use as thoroughly as the corporations all those not sufficiently clever to obtain a like office.

In other words, the American scene in this sense is actually fantastic. Judges obtain their seats by bribery or corporation favor (for
services rendered, of course) and then proceed to pass upon the
bribery of others. Representatives of the people, supposedly beholden
to the voters for their positions, once they are elected do the bidding
only of the corporations or bosses and in turn lecture the people on
their duties to the Government and, if you please, its most favored
corporations: the railroads, steel trust, power trust, and what not. And
the little individual, helpless and in the main fearsome because of what
may be done to him as an individual, makes the best of it, since, as he
well knows, neither the courts, the police, nor any other officials, are
for him unless he chances to have the means wherewith to buy aid.
Thus, the little person when arrested for any offense, however small,
all too often finds himself unnecessarily detained in jail while the
judge is busy dining or calling or protracting his absence by any other
sort of foolishness. And though the worker may lose several hours or
days from his job, does that make any difference? A workingman, a
single individual, carries little weight in this régime where wealth and
office rule.

Likewise, in some States (Florida, Alabama, Georgia, Texas) men
arrested to-day on the pettiest of charges—vagrancy, for one, and
because they cannot find work—are at once victims of a virtual Government press gang system. That age-old shippers' custom of employing a press gang, getting a stupid but affable stranger drunk and then
hauling him aboard ship and forcing him to slave without pay, was no

more iniquitous than the present-day American system of seizing an
unemployed man for vagrancy or any other charge and then jailing
him and hiring him out as part of a prison gang to work for a private
contractor who makes money by paying the officials something and
the seized laborer nothing, or nearly nothing—his alleged food and
lodging! In fact, until July 1, 1928, when it was prohibited by a State
law, Alabama convicts were leased to private contractors and coal
mine owners. And under this pagan system, a certain Warden Davis
of the State was prosecuted by the State for ordering Convict Robert
Knox, who refused to work in the mines, dipped in boiling water,
which burned him to death. But how rich the favorites at the State
Capitol because of this slavery! Yet despite prohibitive measures in
Alabama to-day against contracting out prison labor, flogging the
individual with a snakeskin-whip remains as lawful as ever!

Not only that, but the attitude of the Southern white to the
Negro as well as that of the Southern landowner to his tenant, the
"cropper" with whom presently I will deal, and also that of the
average American corporation toward its employees, is of a similar
pattern and all equally cruel and evil. In our South, for instance, petty
offenders are picked up among the whites and colored to keep the
county chain gangs full. In North Carolina, which permits a convict,
guilty of only a minor offense, to labor for years, in a chain gang, fixes
no limit to other cruelties that may be inflicted on him. Indeed, persons fighting this practice in some counties have found evidence that
when the gang is short of men, a much greater number are not only
arrested but convicted. And although Alabama, after a bloody career,
no longer leases prisoners to private contractors, Idaho, Delaware and
South Carolina do. And again, in many States, although convicts in the
State prison may not be leased, those in the county jail, mostly guilty
of only minor offenses, are so leased, and unrestrainedly, to private
contractors who enslave and abuse them as they will. And this is also
true of Nebraska, Arkansas and other States—the new American
slavery, it might be called, for in thirteen States prisoners are contracted for by private citizens or companies having any kind of grimy
work to do: mining, coke-burning, etc., and used to the limit of their
strength, and as for pay, for almost nothing, or nothing.

In Virginia, North and South Carolina, the number of men in the
chain gangs is frequently twice the number confined in the State

prisons. And although experts have declared that this system of manual labor is actually a money-loser (much less efficient than machinery), these counties would apparently rather knock people around, humiliate them publicly in chains, and so totally demoralize them, than appropriate funds for a prison or devise some system whereby economically they might be made self-sustaining and so be considered worthy of at least human treatment. And in at least one case, a city, not a county—and that the notoriously anti-labor city of Greensboro, North Carolina—maintains its own chain gang.

The actual treatment which these poor fellows receive in the chain gangs is an outrage. A cage on wheels, like those for wild animals in a circus, not only transports them along the country roads but furnishes them with their only home. At night, after working from daylight until dark, eighteen of these men, still chained together, are forced to sleep in bunks measuring only eight by eighteen feet. If a man is more than a foot wide, he has to lie on his side, apparently. Drinking water and slop pails are crowded in with them, and men suffering from venereal diseases are in no way segregated. In only one county that I have heard of are diseased convicts placed in separate gangs. Some States, however, have laws enforcing isolation. In winter, the shanties erected for these chain gangs are dirty and poorly ventilated. They are set in the midst of their own sewerage, which, according to the North Carolina Board of Health, contaminates the water. Other reports show these camps alive with vermin. A convict's life here is spent constantly chained, with either single or double shackles riveted on the ankle by a blacksmith and occasionally with spikes a foot long. And these must be worn even while sleeping. But for what great offense, if any? Owing some one five or even three dollars or stealing from some one as little as a chicken!

And more, according to North Carolina laws, a second violation of such petty rules as "no smoking during working hours" calls for a flogging. Yet how inhuman to inflict such cruelty for so petty an offense! But according to the code of North Carolina, this is quite right, for it permits all the flogging which the county physician and the superintendent of a chain gang may agree that a convict can stand! In short, so little significance is placed upon the cruelty of a chain gang superintendent that mainly he is his own guide and law, and more, time after time one such, discharged for inhumane conduct in one county, has immediately been employed by another and for the same work! And though escape itself is only a misdemeanor, a man imprisoned for only a misdemeanor can be shot dead by his superintendent for attempting escape!

Although in my chapter on "Crime and Why" I cover prison conditions in America generally, here I would like to remark that the report of the Tennessee Penal Institutions Committee of March 17, 1931, has just come to my attention, and I feel it necessary to circularize the data contained therein. Although all prisons are not like this, the very fact that such exist at all is shocking. Brushy Mountain Prison was built as a temporary structure thirty-five years ago for 300 or 400 prisoners. To-day, unremodeled, it houses in a four-story building, constructed entirely of wood, 976 prisoners. Wood, as well as the old wiring, makes for a serious fire hazard. Worse, however, is the matter of health. Over 400 men sleep on the fourth floor on beds standing as close together as possible. During the recent investigation, 138 suffering with flu and pneumonia, both highly contagious, slept among the other men. The death rate is sixteen times as high as at Nashville Prison. Sodomy is practiced promiscuously, mostly by inveterate criminals upon the young. (Seventy per cent are from 18 to 30 years old.) More dreadful, if possible, is the fact that the sixty per cent having venereal disease are not only not segregated but also indulge promiscuously in sodomy.

But now let us turn to another phase, that of peonage. For although these cases have been kept secret by the Government over periods, it is known that in 1903, a Federal Grand Jury sitting at Montgomery, Alabama, made 100 indictments for forced labor or peonage as it is called. And in 1907, according to a report of the Department of Justice, 83 complaints against this forced labor were pending. Again, on April 22, 1921, Governor Hugh M. Dorsey of Georgia stated that in February, 1921, a Negro, who had run away after being arrested and brought back twice for indebtedness, was offered for sale by the planter who had illegally enslaved him, and for $55! This same Governor Dorsey told of another case: a Negro who had run away because his peonage-practicing planter employer had threatened him and then hit him in the face. This Negro had been working for this planter for $12 or $15 a month and board. Just before he ran away, the planter gave him $3 for a pair of shoes. On the

strength of this $3 debt, the Negro was arrested, charged with swin-
dling, and threatened with the chain gang if he did not return to the
planter.

Again, Governor Dorsey revealed that a Negro who had made a
contract with a planter to work for $25 a month and board during
1920, but had been paid nothing for months, finally asked the planter
for an accounting. The employer admitted that he owed the Negro
$65, but paid him only $10, whereupon the Negro ran away. He was
arrested and brought back by force.

In the pamphlet from which all this is taken, the Governor cites
the case of a Fulton County, Georgia, planter who having taken ten
Negroes out of the county chain gang worked them all day at the
point of a gun and then at night locked them in. And when two of
them ran away, they were forcibly brought back and then whipped,
but in such a brutal manner that one, begging to be killed, was shot by
the planter and his body sunk in a pond on the plantation. According
to this same Governor, one Negro claims to have seen a runaway
Negro shot by a Negro supervisor at the command of a white.

The last case I will cite from Governor Dorsey's résumé concerns a Georgia planter indicted for killing eleven Negroes. On April
8, 1921, he was convicted in a single case and sent to prison for life.
Yet in spite of this conviction and considerable publicity in connection with all of this data, the system still survives, for the present
somewhat secretly. And to this day in the South many Negroes truly
believe that their planter may and will shoot them if they tell or
complain. Yet in times of crisis, and due to newspaper reporters, in the
section, the status of at least some of these tenants, workers or slaves
occasionally becomes clear to the outside world. Thus, in connection
with the Red Cross flood relief in the South in 1927, it became known
that it, our Red Cross of blessed station, contracted with planters to
deliver Negroes from the relief station to the plantation again by
force, if necessary, when the charity work was over. So much for our
Red Cross, its noble services!

But because neither the Negroes nor the poor whites dare talk
much, most of these really dreadful cases never get publicity. Yet
while some of the States permit men to be brought back for debt,
others do prohibit planters from crossing the State lines to force men
back, a fact which should be written down to their credit. On the

whole, though, this Southern force and violence has its roots, I am sure, in the pre-Civil-War slavery tradition of the South; in other words, the assumed fitness of the Negro and the criminal for slavery, and for slavery only. Yet why? The Negro who works is law-abiding, and if not thrifty is at least economically independent and cheerful, a good and useful citizen. Can it be that due to his somewhat erotic nature, he is offensive to the Northern Puritan (in law, not fact), or is it merely that he is black? In part, its roots may lie in the world-old notion that freedom for the individual is something bestowed by the strong upon the weak, that might makes right, and that the strong may (not necessarily "must") direct the weak and helpless everywhere, and to the advantage of the strong. For the strong, being strong, are right, and the weak, being weak, are wrong or worthless— a doctrine to which all of the money powers of our modern world will most readily subscribe and, in reality, practice. If this and other chapters do not show this, then most certainly my statements are without meaning and of no authority.

Of the practice of peonage in the South, however, Professor S. H. Hobbs, of the Department of Rural Social Economics of the University of North Carolina in June, 1930, told the Southern Economic Conference in Atlanta that "more than half of all the farms in the South are to-day operated by tenants . . . the lowest type of tenure existing in the civilized world to-day, the cropper system, which is just one step removed from serfdom . . . and nearly two-thirds of the tenants in the South are whites!"

The laws in some States (Florida and Alabama) state that a worker owing money to an employer may not leave his employ until that money is paid. Yet the payment of it, however small, is no easy matter. For the planters or bosses sell the crop and divide the proceeds, equitably or not, over the heads of the ignorant tenants. Also they, and they only, keep all books and charge such exaggerated prices for rent, food, supplies, etc., that the share cropper or employee of whatsoever walk never succeeds in getting out of debt from one year to the next. In Georgia also, the code of law which makes running away from an employer when money is owed *prima facie* evidence of intent to defraud, practically secures the worker as a slave, and over very considerable periods of time. For the ignorant tenant or worker, in contracting with his planter employer, is usually made to sign away all sorts of privileges, because not being able to read or write much, he does not understand.

A typical contract is the following cited by the "American Statistical Quarterly Publications XIII," pp. 82–3:

"Said tenant further agrees that if he violates the contract or neglects or abandons or fails (or in the owner's judgment violates this contract or fails) to properly cultivate the land . . . or if he should become physically incapacitated . . . or die, or fails to gather . . . crops . . . or fails to pay rents or advances made by the owner, when due, then in that event this contract may become void and canceled at the owner's option, and all indebtedness of the tenant for advances or rent shall at once become due and payable to the owner . . . in which case the owner is hereby authorized to transfer, sell or dispose of all property thereon . . . the tenant has any interest in. It shall not be necessary to give any notice of any failure or violation of this contract . . . the execution of this lease being sufficient notice of defalcation on the part of the tenant, and shall be so construed between the parties hereto, any law, usage, or custom to the contrary notwithstanding."

In other words, this contract puts simply and completely the law into the hands of the planter—such law as he chooses to make and exercise. For it is not binding! There are property laws in the South which have grown up and protect people's interests, but these, of course, are thrown overboard. No delay or any inconvenience of legal resort, as you see! And besides, the tenants never have any money wherewith to investigate or contest such contracts. They are too wholly benighted and enslaved, and by the State! The local politicians and petty executives of all levels in this region will usually be found to be friends of either the planter employer or the system, and at best or worst, extremely unused to taking care of the legal problems of either Negroes or poor whites, and prejudiced against them into the bargain. But why? One must look to the world-old reverence for wealth as opposed to the world-old contempt for poverty. It is something which an entirely different concept of social equity, if such is humanly possible, will have to replace, or there is no hope for social decency in man's relationship to man anywhere in society, any more than there is in wild nature outside society.

To go on with this particular situation in the South, however, a tremendous and extortionate rate of interest is also forced upon these simple and powerless individuals by opulent planters and their merchants. The North Carolina College of Agriculture, in connection with twenty-seven farms in Pitt County in that State in 1928, said that charges for credit by merchants there ranged to nineteen per cent for cash advances and to seventy-two per cent for supplies in advance! And Secretary of Agriculture A. M. Hyde, in his 1930 report, stated that over the entire South, charges by merchants for credit averaged twenty-five per cent, and for fertilizer thirty-five per cent.

But to further substantiate these charges that peonage as well as such abuses as the above exist in the South to-day, I offer the following. These are recent cases—so recent in fact that most of them have not come to trial, at the time when this book goes to press. Fred Burk, a share-cropper of Etowah, Arkansas, was, on March 21, 1931, shot by Pat Cook, a planter. Reason: some complaint in regard to inequity on the part of the cropper. Burk's condition was critical. I mention this case because such quarrels as these are reported by scores in the Southern newspapers of to-day. They exist in such numbers as to be proof, it seems to me, of undue domination by planters.

Again, on January 31, 1931, Ordis Waller, of Bossier Parish, Louisiana, was under bail on a charge of violating the Federal Peonage Act by holding by force four Negro tenants. One Henry McLemore, a well-known planter of Conshatta, Louisiana, was charged, in January, 1931, with unlawfully holding five Negro laborers and share-croppers for alleged indebtedness. McLemore, who asserted their indebtedness to range between $125 and $700, went about constantly armed and it is alleged that he would threaten Negroes if they dared leave him.

Still again, James Piggott, of Bogalusa, Louisiana, sentenced to eighteen months in the Federal Prison at Atlanta for peonage, said that he had merely treated his Negroes as everybody else in the South did. Yet on December 28, 1929, Piggott was charged with holding three Negro families totaling thirteen persons on his plantation for a year and a half without pay! It was also charged that they were beaten by him with trace chains and forced to eat inferior food. Not only was every attempt at escape repulsed, but Piggott admitted going into Mississippi and by force, not process of law, bringing his workers back!

But the proof varies. Thus, Russell Owen's New York *Times* report of January 31, 1931, states that no Arkansas sharecropper may move from one plantation to another unless the second planter employing him assumes his debts (if any) to the first planter—a system indicating peonage over a wide area.

Next, on January 28, 1931, the National Association for the Advancement of Colored People wrote to United States District Attorney Mitchell, saying: "Reliable reports reaching us from the drought areas of Arkansas and Louisiana indicate that conditions of peonage are widespread there." And investigation shows that forced labor of this nature is most prevalent in the Red River basin, the inland region of Arkansas and Louisiana and the Delta region. And yet again, Mr. Walter Wilson,* social research worker, sent 118 letters to Southern ministers, professors, Government officials, etc., inquiring as to this matter. I am permitted to quote typical replies.

A well-known lawyer of Houston, Texas, writing in February, 1931, said that peonage was illegal in Texas but because of force illegally applied, was still practiced. He said: "It has a firm hold and terrorizes the tenant."

Mr. Covington Hall, of the *Industrial Democrat* of Leesville, Louisiana, on February 23, 1931, wrote: "The 'sharecropper' and tenant serfdom is confined mainly to the cotton plantations. In the sugar district, the condition of labor is that of out-and-out peonage, and it is the same in the lumber industry."

A professor in an Alabama college wrote, on March 17, 1931: "The peonage system of tenantry does exist to a certain extent."

And Deputy Commissioner of Labor Robert B. Grogg, at Austin, Texas, wrote, on February 27, 1931: "Peonage, or the system of tenantry through a credit system that actually binds tenant-croppers to the land, actually exists in this State, but the system is so plausibly organized that neither the State nor Federal authorities have ever been able to isolate a case of peonage and institute prosecution. The system is not, of course, recognized by law."

Yet leaving for the time being this depressing illustration of the wholly inhuman and unsocial and, of course, illegal attitude of the small American employer toward the individual beneath him in the economic if not the social scale, we can turn again to our major corporations and their viewpoint, which is by no means dissimilar to that of these lesser fry. A corporation like the New York Telephone

* *Forced Labor in the United States,* by Walter Wilson. (International Publishers.)

Company can become so partial, as well as so indifferent, in their business transactions as between patron and patron as to cause one—the little man without influence—to suffer heavily the while another—less weak—is better taken care of. Thus, in so far as any speedy installations are concerned, the red flag or check meaning "rush" is required. But who is to supply or command that? Some one with influence? Certainly! Otherwise, no courteous, let alone rapid, installation! One individual or thousands waiting while a few obtain immediate service. Again, on most railroads in America to-day, how frequently the local, if not the through, train is without portable ground steps! And yet heavy people who cannot possibly step up two feet without help, and so in danger of a fall! And how many conductors, without a proper sense of their responsibility (due, of course, to the inefficiency of their employers), neglect their work and the public!

But when these same corporations started out, nearly a hundred years ago, how different! Then their securities could scarcely be sold, for financing then was difficult. And hence during their brief period of struggle, and even later when profits were rolling up, all kinds of inducements were offered to the people to persuade them to ride. Round trip and excursion rate concessions! And inducements, because of fare privileges held out, for people to move to the suburbs of all cities along their lines. But now that hundreds of thousands have settled in these suburban towns, acquired property and become interested in the social communities in which they reside, the railroads, instead of dealing with them if not gratefully at least equitably, have long since pushed up the commutation rates until at this time they constitute not only a huge but conscienceless and cruel tax, many of our ogre roads asking and getting three and four times the original rates. Yet yelling "confiscation" when any tax is leveled on them! And indifferent to the question of schools for the children or a job for the head of the family, so often dependent, because of our modern suburban life, upon reasonable fares! Indeed, how great and kind our corporations now that they are so strong!

For always higher and higher rates are desired, and when these higher rate pleas are entered the railroad attorneys present the facts in so misleading a manner. Being shrewd and wise in the ways to power, these railways and their attorneys find it easy to scheme and cheat. Thus, the New York Central recently demanding a forty per cent

increase in suburban fares out of New York City, stepped forward
with the argument that although their commuters comprised sixty-five
percent of their passenger traffic, they paid only eight per cent of the
total fares. But how sly and faked! Do you not really sense injustice to
the New York commuter, who from the beginning has not only seen
his public property stolen by bribery by the New York Central—
literally billions in property and privileges—and all fair tax rates into
the bargain fought to a standstill—but himself in the matter of fares
taxed to the point of exhaustion? For of what value is a record of the
number of passengers without giving the distance traveled? And how
could a commuter riding 18 miles honestly be contrasted as to fare
with a passenger traveling 1,800 miles? Yet what about the thousands
of miles of track along and through other enormous cities? For considering the enormity of the New York Central's mileage, the length
of its various lines, and the great distance traveled by its through
passengers, eight per cent of the total fares of the whole system and as
the contribution of the passengers who use only about 50 miles of
trackage seems O.K. to me.

In this matter of robbing the people, though, our American corporations seem always to me to be trying the one to outdo the other—
never in the honest old game of competition, where each one sought
to get business by cutting prices on the other, but rather by always
raising prices to meet those charged by supposed competitors, who
happen to be charging more, not less. And with little Government
interference at any time! It evidently does not want to interfere because it does not do so. Thus, right now the New York Central is
pointing out that while the New York, New Haven & Hartford
Railroad's commutation rate to Mt. Vernon is $10.01 monthly, theirs
is only $7.15. Therefore, theirs should be $10.01! Not the New
Haven's to $7.15! For that would be lowering rates, and that is practi-
cally unheard of in America! Next, all our corporations must sell
tickets, or what you will, at prices forced by the strongest or shrewd-
est company, and these prices always the highest. In other words,
never lower a fare; raise it, or at worst, keep it where it is! Otherwise,
confiscation, the undermining of business, the lowering of the American flag, Communism, and what not else!

In my own city, New York, the New York Edison (an electric
company), and as I recall, no better and no worse than any of the

corporations the land over, has only this spring of 1931 forced most abusive rates upon its powerless patrons. Forgetful of the social value of a rational balance, even to a corporation, it is perpetrating extortion. It asserts, however, that its plan lowers charges. But what really is meant is that by a curtain of shuffling and rearrangement, it hopes to hoodwink the public the while it is bringing profits to itself. Lower rates but higher bills! The "now you see it, now you don't" system! For what they really do is to cut the price of electric current from 7 to 5 cents a kilowatt hour, the while they proceed to charge 60 cents a month for meter service, a charge never before made and one that really increases the bills of fifty-seven per cent of their customers and those—the poor people. Thus, while the lady of Park Avenue, whose bill was formerly $36.20 for 517 kilowatt hours, saves, under the new apportionment, $10.15 monthly, another woman living in a tenement house, or hundreds of thousands in one-room apartments, and who previously paid only 65 cents for 9 kilowatt hours, now pays $1.05 monthly. Save money for the rich out of pennies of the poor. The eagle standard.

Yet has there been any public outcry as to this, or any defense of the weak by anybody? That voice of the public, the press, has it said anything? Or our so-called political "representatives of the people," have they spoken? In America, I am sorry to report, they are the rubber stamps only that O.K. every corporation proposition; the individuals who "yes, yes" every individual of power. It is America, and that is how the individual is dealt with here.

But how bold, and even insolent, to assess the individual for meters or anything but the electricity which he actually uses! In the beginning, when they were anxious for people to use their electricity, the corporations were glad enough to supply the meters. But not now! And not only that, but they were willing and glad to sell direct to the consumer, whereas after a little while, finding electricity so popular, they must needs devise or at least take up with a third party—likely a subsidiary concern: the sub-metering electricity broker who, like the ticket speculator of the theater world, proceeds to show them how, by dealing through him, they can make even more money. For behold you, he will contract for some hundreds of thousands of kilowatt hours, flat or by the year, paying in advance for the current so taken, then sub-metering the same to apartment houses, office buildings and the like, and locally servicing their tenants, but at rates which yield him a handsome profit and at the same time save the main company the trouble of meter reading, collecting and the like. And at the same time giving the corporation much free money to juggle with. But as for the customer, well, as for the customer in these better apartments and office buildings, he pays, and pays well, more than he would to the company direct. A mere bagatelle, as you see, but also one more illustration of the gross and still growing greed of the wealth of America. It can never get too much and it can never give too little.

But what an undesirable precedent is this meter charge! So unethical! And opening the door to other robberies of the same nature. For next—and why not?—a fixed rate for the wires leading to the house, or the posts or tubes that carry the wires, or a salary for the meter readers! There is no difference in principle. And although just two other cities, Atlanta and San Francisco, have meter charges so far, the former receives for current only 2 cents a kilowatt hour and the latter 1½ cents. Compare these with 5 cents for every single unit of the New York Edison Company's 40 light hours! Yet Mr. Sloan, an Edison president, states that this is the only way that the New York Edison can give New York City a lower rate.

And this following upon America's hope of thirty years ago that with invention and mechanization supplying most of the necessities would come lower living charges, and so more leisure and time for this and that! Instead the rich throw away what the poor man produces and only to keep the rich still more rich. But the individual of to-day as much as ever harnessed to the task of making a living in order that those who rob him may sport! And that in an age when all cooking should be carried on by cheap electricity! More, the New York Edison is controlled by the Consolidated Gas Company. So not only one, but two, and even a score of companies must fatten on a single need of the individual.

In addition, this same New York Edison proposes to assess commercial patrons a demand charge of $1.00 a month. They are possessed with ideas! Corporation witchcraft! Why, building owners alone would pay the company about ten million dollars for installing these demand charge meters!

But now let me add one more illustration of this corporation abuse of the little fellow, and then I will turn to another matter. Our great American telephone company, which is very rich and very powerful now, taxes the individual all that it can; that is, extortionately, and from coast to coast. For practically, the courts and politicians and officeholders aiding it, it fixes its own assessment of the people through the various utilities commissions which now exist in most States and which, by reason of laws arranged by the corporations, have now the power to examine into and fix rates, for the corporations, not the people, depend on that! And in connection with these, this dear American Tel. & Tel. of ours is always "correcting inconsistencies." But these "corrections," as you learn when you come to examine them, are always in the direction of higher rates for the great bulk of the business, with occasional—and not often even there— lowering of them on some minor portion. The method of doing this is termed, by our Mr. Gifford, present President of the Company, "correction of inconsistencies." This *"correction of inconsistencies"* business has already given rise to such clever money-squeezing devices as "person to person calls" and a three-minute limit for one class of calls before an additional payment is demanded and a five-minute rate for another class. Thus, the New York Telephone Company—the greatest of all the great divisions of this great company—is now seeking to increase the rates for calling between 24 and 40 miles and to decrease those over 72 miles. But consider, if you will, the number of calls in the former group, around New York City alone, say, and with interchange of business between scores of large and prosperous suburbs and other places, and then the number of calls over the longer distance! Now which would have the larger number of calls? Can you guess? How smart you are! So even a five per cent reduction on a high charge for a call of over 72 miles is scarcely the equivalent or proper counterbalance to an increase of from 5 to 10 cents on each of these millions of necessary short calls. For short wires are so busy as compared with long ones. Just the same, this kind-hearted and very large company proposes a cut after 8.30 P.M., when business hours are over! Low charges on the dearth of business; high charges for the mass of it! But, oh, these efficiency experts! How they do earn their money from the company, and how they must sit up late devising these things! Snares, did I hear you say? Or robberies? Yet the telephone company's "line" is no different from that of the railroads and utilities. They all figure on the "up and up."

Telephone from New York to Jersey City or Forest Hills or South Orange, and note the result! For even brief talks, the operators interrupt and annoy you, always pleading for more and more money for the vulture company. And courtesy! They do not know the meaning of the word! Rather, vulgarity and even raw brutal force is their way where protest occurs. Thus, when I found that a friend whom I was trying to reach on a long distance call was out, the operator furnished me with a long report on his whereabouts, of which same, however, I was previously thoroughly cognizant. After thinking to myself that here at last was detailed and careful service, it suddenly came to me that this might really be no more than another corporation trick to get money out of me. And true enough, in reply to my inquiry as to whether I was to be charged for this report, the operator gave me the rate: a third of the total price!

"But why didn't you ask me if I cared for a report on the call, and what I would like you to inquire about the gentleman?" I asked.

"But it's our regulation," she replied.

"But I didn't want it and didn't ask for it."

"But we always do that," she insisted, trying to smooth matters over. One of the present-day American business robberies or "wrinkles," as we call them!

Concerning rate robbery charges, however, I have evidence of what seems to be a misrepresentation on the part of the New York Company. For although the New York Telephone Company stated that the increase to contract business subscribers would be from ten to fifteen per cent only, one Samuel Zirn, of Brooklyn, says that in his Brooklyn office the contract charge prior to January 1, 1931, was $8.06; that on February 1st the bill read $9.38; on June 1st, $9.70, and on July 1st, $10.70. A thirty-three per cent increase for the same service.

And although a man compelled to leave town for a period of time should most certainly be allowed to save something on his telephone bills, especially since he uses no service, the up-and-coming telephone company to-day will not so permit. What, no money for a month or two! Hence, though I leave my studio for two months, and order the service cut off to save money, upon returning and getting it connected, I find myself charged practically as much for this reconnection as I would have been for two months of service!

Yet has the individual any recourse? You know he has not! But is there not the law, and are there not the courts! Yes, there is and are! Try them—at your expense! So the crook who has boodled his franchise through a complaisant council or legislature drives you as though you were enslaved, as, in fact, you really are.

Indeed, for a long time now, as I have shown, our corporations have been free to combine against the individual. And not only that, but even to-day, now, the heads of our great industries as well as those of lesser factories are themselves advocating repeal of the antitrust laws, because, as they see it, these laws have brought on this major depression of 1928–31. But can you imagine a greater burlesque of the logic of economics in toto? No wonder voters—poor, misinformed creatures!—don't know what our Government is all about! Those who would repeal these laws argue the usual claptrap that these Sherman and Clayton Anti-Trust laws are the things which have principally induced overproduction which has in turn brought depression. And yet, without these laws, most certain it is that greater and greater mergers, with their illegal but still enforced power of taxing the people, would have combined and so taxed the people, even more.

And yet in addition to all this even, the usual American corporation "blah" concerning courage and the duty of the American people to fight through, have patience, etc. Yet at heart their attitude toward all their patrons and fellow-citizens in general and throughout all of their monopolistic activities is that of the first and original Vanderbilt (the Commodore of blessed trust memory!): "The public be damned!"

Sinclair Lewis [1885-1951]
Is America a Paradise for Women? [1929]

When our ancestress Eve still dwelt in Eden she complained a good deal to Father Adam, and to all of the animals that would listen, about the dullness of the scene and the society. She wanted to live some place else. She was certain that all the men in all the Some Place Elses were gallanter toward women, and with lips apart she listened to the first gigolo who flattered her. But that gigolo was a Serpent and not a sound domestic adviser, no matter how well he danced in the moonlight, no matter how glistening his scales.

When she took his advice and was pushed into the Great World Outside which she had desired, she found that all the time, without knowing it, she had been in Paradise.

Eve's voluble belief that Eden was not Paradise did not keep it from being Paradise. And perhaps the fable is not entirely untrue for today.

I decidedly do not maintain that these United States compose or ever will compose, an absolute Paradise for women—or men, or children, or any other breed of animals. But neither is any other country, and I do maintain that for the woman with imagination and eagerness this country presents problems and opportunities, presents a conceivable future, which are more stimulating than the beautiful peace of any other land.

I do not maintain that Mr. George F. Babbitt is any more uplifting as a husband than he is as a luncheon-club orator; I do not maintain that he makes love more exquisitely than the pretty Don Juans and Casanovas you see playing on the sands at the Lido. But I do maintain that Mrs. George F., if she has the stuff in her, has the chance here, and the invitation, to take part in creating a dramatic new world of industry, education, family life, and that her husband, poor clump, leaves her more free than any woman on earth to tickle her egotism with the flattery of the Don Juans betweenwhiles.

It would be the flattest sort of chauvinism to say that we have here all the European security of tradition, sweetness of easy gaiety, beauty of old marble—as yet. What we may have five hundred years from now no one knows save "the amateur ethnologists who have patented this Nordic supremacy myth," but now we are still awkward and self-conscious with newness, and we boast only that we may not quaver.

We can show nothing like an English drawing-room at tea-time, a French café looking on chestnuts in Spring bloom, a German mountain-top with the knapsacked hikers singing, or the slopes of Capri in Autumn sunshine as seen from the walls of Tiberias. No, we have nothing here save the spectacle of the very center of the world's greatest revolution—a revolution that makes the Bolshevik upheaval seem like a mere national election and the French Revolution like a street fight!

We need not read history for our drama—we are in history, right now! The world is changing (for good or bad) from an ill-connected series of individualist businesses to a commonwealth of gigantic industries in which each individual has no more freedom than a private (or even a general) in an army in wartime.

Whether or not this loss of freedom is compensated for by an increased sense of importance in belonging to an organization mighty and significant, whether one would prefer to be the lone trapper or the smartly uniformed corporal with his companions-in-arms, is not the question, for we have already been drafted, and, like it or not, we are in that war—the most exciting and dangerous war in history.

And women, hitherto the weeping stay-at-homes or the wailing refugees in war, have as much place in this one as any man. The woman teacher, controlling the education of a hundred men children; the woman wife, no longer regarding her man's business as a mystery but as a plain job which she can understand as well as he; the woman uplifter or politician or salesman of real estate or publisher or author —she has exactly the place in this universal army that her brains and energy and ambition demand.

She is less secure than the lady of the manor, controlling her spinning maids and the grubbers in the walled garden, four hundred dead years ago—but, then, she no longer has to remain back home in the manor!

If Eve now finds Eden dull the world allows her to go out and make her own Paradise—and the women in America who have opened the barber-shops to women and closed the barrooms to men have done that remaking of Paradise to an extent which is slightly dismaying to low, ordinary men like myself—to such an extent that I wonder whether the question here debated should not be, "Is America a Paradise for Any One *Except* Women?"

I doubt whether any of the reasons usually given so patly and fatly by most reporters of America as a female Paradise are really important. It is true that women here have more "domestic conveniences" than anywhere else in the world—more electric flat-irons and toasters and refrigerators and dish-washing machines, more gas-stoves and vacuum cleaners and oil-furnaces and garbage-incinerators. But then! For the women who are mistresses the servants are so much more expensive that the ruling class can have but a quarter as many of them as elsewhere in the world.

And for the women who are servants (it must distinctly be remembered, though discussions of women rather frequently forget it, that the wives of doctors and lawyers and authors and sales-managers do not compose the entire feminine world)—for the women servants, their apparently high wages and their laboratory-like kitchens do not always make up for the fact that most Americans do not have the reverence for good cooking nor the respect for smart servants which is to be found in Europe.

And it is true that our women have more leisure than in Europe. Think of the canned goods which permit them to prepare dinner in five minutes! "Think of the increasing number of women in service-flats whose chief daily task is to struggle out of bed and find the remains of yesterday's box of candy!" Yet this constantly offered reason why our women should be happy often means precisely nothing. It's not the heat—it's the humidity; it's not the leisure—it's what one may do with the leisure.

A man in solitary confinement in prison has complete leisure, yet I am told that he rarely gets any great ecstasy out of it. I am certain that a woman who has to work in the fields all day, but who works with her men-folk, who sings with them, who laughs as she eats her bread and cheese under the hedge, who feels strong, and resolute, and significant, is considerably happier than a woman in a workless apartment who, afternoon upon drab afternoon, has nothing to do save play bridge, go window-shopping, look at a movie.

The third reason usually given for the paradisiality of America for women—that their husbands are so generous, so complaisant, so obedient—seems to me equally bunk, because most human beings would rather be united to spouses whom they must struggle to please, but whom they respect, than to weaklings whom they can twist around their fingers, but whom they despise. Whether they are conscious of it or not, most women would rather be married to a Napoleon than to a Mr. Pickwick—and it is precisely the amiable, vague, foolishly generous virtues of a Pickwick that have been exhibited as admirable in American husbands.

I seem to be arguing against my own thesis, that America is the women's Paradise. I am not. I am trying to dispose, or suggest ways of disposing, of foolish reasons for a wise thesis, because more debates are lost by the sentimental reasoning of the advocates than by the savagery of the opponents.

No, I do not present America as desirable for women because it gives them an easy life, but precisely because it gives them a hard life—a keen, belligerent, striving, exciting life of camp and embattled field; because it gives them a part in this revolution which (whether we like it or hate it) is changing all our world from the lilac-hedged cottages of Main Street to the overpowering, the intimidating yet magnificent bastions of Park Avenue; from the chattering court following a toy monarch in glass coaches to the hard, swift procession of industrial lords in 120 h.p. cars.

Women not only can take full part in this revolution—they are taking it, and such women, though they may long to return to the lilacs and roses and peace of Main Street, are certainly not returning. If they can not utterly enjoy being warriors, they can never now enjoy anything less valiant.

Consider a woman like Miss Frances Perkins, recently appointed State Commissioner of Labor in New York—a position of considerable significance in a State where at least eight million people are classed as laborers or the families of laborers—a position considerably weightier than that of the King of Norway or Sweden or the President of the Irish Free State.

Miss Perkins has, with zest, climbed through all the grades from that of an unknown social worker struggling for fire-escapes on factories, through years as Her Honor the Judge in the Workmen's Compensation Court, to her present power. And she has managed to do it without any of that celebrated "loss of femininity," for in private life Miss Perkins is a Mrs., an extremely good wife and mother, and the most entertaining of friends.

Consider Miss Mabel Willebrandt. Whether one admire her as an enforcer of prohibition or detest her as an evangelical politician and self-advertiser, one must admit that more than any one else in the country she has won the right to be Attorney-General of the United States. Then consider a woman who was completely opposed to Miss Willebrandt in the late lamented campaign—Mrs. Henry Moskowitz, Al Smith's prime adviser and chief coach. If he had won, the credit would have belonged to her as much as to his own vivid self. And with them, view Miss Elisabeth Marbury, who is, both as politician and as producer of plays, quite the equal of any man rival.

And turning to what is sometimes known with amiable pleasantry as "the art of writing," regard women like Edith Wharton, Willa Cather, Ruth Suckow, Mary Austin, Anne Parrish, Gertrude Atherton, Dorothy Canfield, Mary Roberts Rinehart, Kathleen Norris, Alice Duer Miller, Josephine Herbst, Evelyn Scott, Katherine Mayo—at least as important as any equal number of males.

I could go on with women congressmen, researchers, actresses, heads of social settlements, editors, or women in business—developing narrow white tearooms into millionaire candy companies. I could suggest that Aimee Semple McPherson is, admire her or detest her, the most renowned figure in organized religion in America today, better known than Billy Sunday, S. Parkes Cadman, or Harry Emerson Fosdick, and more adored by her following. And the greatest religious leader of the decade before her was another woman—Mary Baker Eddy!

But these celebrated ladies I bring in only as a hint that, increasingly, the greatest careers in this country are open to women. But that fact, applying only to a few women of extraordinary vigor, or charm, or intelligence, or instinct for publicity, is less important than the fact that everywhere in America women have, if they care to seize it, a power and significance at least equal to that of the men about them.

It is most seen in the schools.

Actually, two distinguished English observers, Mr. Bertrand Russell and Mr. H. G. Wells, complain that the chief trouble with America is that women have too much control of our education and, thus, training our future citizens in the way they shall think or fear to think, have control of all our social life; that through the preponderance of women teachers in our schools all America is becoming feminized.

They politely hint that though the Typical American Businessman, with his heavy shoulders, his large spectacles, his clenched cigar, his growling about poker and golf and fishing and the stock-market, seems to the eye particularly masculine, at heart, in his fear of offending the conventions, in his obedience to public prejudice, in his negative attitude that goodness consists not in doing fine things but in failing to do dangerous things, he is tied to the apron-strings of the women teachers of his boyhood; that he has become effeminized, without having the virtues of being frankly feminine.

Whether or not Mr. Wells and Mr. Russell are anything save ingenious, it is certain that in all our schools save a few private retreats for the rather wealthy, it is women who do nine-tenths of the direct teaching. The school principals, with their fussiness about ventilation and assignments in Cæsar, may be men, but it is women who day after day give, equally to boys and to girls, their concepts of courage, learning, decency, good manners, along with the less significant instruction in the details of algebra and the exports of Sumatra.

And when the boys and girls go home, it is mother—not father, as in England or Germany—who chiefly instructs them in the ethics of sex and cleanliness. And to make it all complete, on the Sabbath day it is women who, in Sunday-school, teach them the eternal mysteries.

Women to whom Paradise is escape from responsibility, amorous flattery, and emulating the lilies of the field, will find all this rather grubby and irritating. But to women for whom Paradise is creation of life and thought, living life, this opportunity of having more power than was ever seized by any bandit dictator will be more satisfying than any condition of life that women in any other age, in any land, have ever known.

It is not alone the professional teachers, the home-determining mothers, and the religious instructors among American women who have power and the zest of activity. Everywhere in Europe, or in China or Timbuktu, for that matter, it is males who determine what books and operas and painters shall be popular, what social movements—eugenics or tenement reform or revised taxation—shall be considered momently important.

But in America these decisions are to an inconceivable extent made by our women's clubs. A curious situation, which will puzzle future historians, almost to frenzy. For ninety per cent of our male politicians, however billowing their frock coats, however *basso profundo* their voices on the radio, however noble their hawklike or Roman noses as depicted in the rotogravure sections, in private life use such brains as they may have only on the chess-like problems of political advancement.

Their utterances on the things regarding which they are supposed to be experts and representatives of the pee-pul, their opinions on prohibition, foreign affairs, pacifism, agricultural relief, and what not, are determined for them by the women's clubs back home.

It is the women, in these clubs, in their courses of study, their reading, their prejudices or lack of prejudices, who form the only really large and half-way co-ordinated "body of public opinion" in these hustling but uncontemplative States.

And when all the male editors have produced their magazines, male publishers have issued their books, male authors have composed their arguments (on, for example, such a subject as "Is America the Women's Paradise?"), when the male playwrights and producers have set forth their wares, and male critics have given judgment on novels, after this it is the women, the one sex in the country that really reads and meditates and talks to others about its reading and the fruits of its meditation, that decides what book or play, what magazine or article, shall be sufficiently approved—or vigorously enough disapproved!—to be allowed to live and have its being.

What brought prohibition to America? The Anti-Saloon League, the lauded evangelists? Not by a long shot! They do themselves too much honor!

It was the women of America, working for these past hundred and fifty years, diffidently beginning in the days when in frontier cabins they heard their men-folk yowling over fifty-cent-a-gallon corn liquor, rising at last to the women's temperance societies in all the evangelical churches, and the grim and powerful W.C.T.U.; it was the women at home, coaching their sons in the evils of alcohol and raising Cain if their husbands came home with a breath.

The women of America wanted prohibition, and got it. If they ever want any other incredibly revolutionary experiment—communism or universal church union, polygamy or vegetarianism, pacifism or cannibalism—they will get that, too, and all the walrus-voiced politicians and ingenious pamphleteers will be but megaphones for their small, invincible voices.

In fact, men have accomplished but one thing in America—they have, by some magic which one would suppose to be beyond their powers, kept women from knowing how lucky a human being is to be born a woman in these United States, to be born one of the ruling sex and not one of that pompous, waddling, slightly ridiculous, and pathetic race of belated children known as men!

But there are women, and many women, and extraordinarily intelligent and pleasant and notable women, who answer that this is all very well, and even perhaps partly true, but as for them, they do not desire this power, this influence. They want the things symbolized by the traditional beauty of Europe—husbands who are also charming lovers, children who are not automata to be filled up with feminized education, backgrounds suggesting two thousand years of building and passion and aspiration—who desire, in fact, to be not statesmen in step-ins, but to be *women!*

Well, if they desire gallantry, it is at least as much up to them as it is up to men to create among our hitherto somewhat stiff and

embarrassed people, with our subconscious theory that the good Lord
somehow made an error in creating human bodies, the suave yet
passionate atmosphere which raises Europeans above the level of
shamefaced flirtation.

And I believe that it is precisely the reckless flapper, who is so
much condemned by the long-noses for her wicked "necking," who is,
in an experimental way, beginning to create that atmosphere; I believe
that as the New York of the '70's, the plush-horse New York of the
Jim Fisks and the Boss Tweeds, has turned into a metropolis which in
elegance compares with any European capital whatever, so a generation from now American social life, the easy and unembarrassed association of men and women, will have the richness known in Europe
today.

And meanwhile, if our imprisoned Eves want Europe—why, they
can have it!

Among all the nations of earth, only in America, Britain, Germany, and Scandinavia are the women allowed to go off traveling
alone, at their own sweet wills, without having an infernal row kicked
up by their husbands, fathers, brothers, and cousins even unto the
seventh connection. And none of the three other lands gives to their
women such liberty as does America. The English squire can, without
hysterics, see his women go off to the Continent alone, but he expects
them to stick to safe, canonical places—the nice quiet hotel at Vevey,
or Cousin Ethelbert's at Hyères, or that really sweet pension at San
Remo where you *never* meet any Americans or Italians or curious
people like that.

But the American woman who feels that she must have European
spice to her Yankee corn bread may go as she pleases, if her husband
or father has money enough—or almost money enough—and he hears
with equanimity, probably with too much equanimity, that she has
stayed at a doubtful hotel in Paris, that she has gone to the Coliseum
by moonlight with a count of the most dubious countishness.

If an Italian, an Austrian, a Frenchman, a Spaniard, heard of such
capers, his wife would jolly well be told to stay there in the Coliseum
with her count, in rain and sleet as well as affable moonlight. But our
American yearner, when she tires of gigolos and galleries, can come
home at will, and at will resume her position as Lady Mussolini of the
local study club.

I do not mean to say that any large percentage of American

husbands have the money to permit their wives to indulge in such escapism. But they all have the willingness. And it is astounding how much American women in families of no great wealth do travel. The wife of the average small-town doctor or lawyer, with an income of thirty-five hundred dollars a year, expects to go across at least once. The wife of a man of corresponding income in Europe would be lucky if she were allowed to visit Aunt Marie a hundred miles away. In her family the money would be saved—for what? For her son, that he might show the smartness which in Europe belongs not to women but to the lordly male!

In no other land, in no other age, have women expected to have their cakes and eat them. The joke is that they actually get away with it!

For every native American woman who sighs that she is a martyr to live here, there is a foreign-born American woman who gloats that she is lucky to have come.

We have a young Czech maid, six years in America, who saved enough money so that last Summer she was able to go back to Bohemia to see her father and mother. She had a notion of remaining, but she returned in two months, and thus Mary explains it:

"Gee, I'm never going back to that country again. Say, gee, it was fierce. My Old Man makes my Old Woman do whatever he wants her to. She can't do nothing without he lets her. There was a fellow there wanted to marry me. He's well off, too, that fellow. But when I looks at my Old Woman, 'Nix,' I says, 'not on your life; I'm going back to America, where a woman gets what money she earns and don't get it took off her by her Old Man like they do back in the Old Country. Not on your life,' I says; 'even a cook is her own boss in America,' I says.

"And say, my Old Man, he don't need money none; he's got a mill, he's fixed good, but he keeps ahinting and ahinting about the money I'd saved and how a man ought to get what his daughter's made, and I says, 'Here's a thousand bucks,' I says, and say, he *took* it! And he didn't need it! Say! Do you know what the trouble with them Europeans is? They don't think about nothing but money!"

I had intended, with Rockefeller-like philanthropy, to present Mary's opinion to the next European who writes or lectures about Das Dollar Land and Uncle Shylock. But I donate it, instead, to all the

Eves who find Eden insufficiently like Paradise to suit them, and who are unwilling to do anything whatever to make it so.

꒰꒱

Relation of the Novel to the Present Social Unrest: The Passing of Capitalism [1914]

Extraordinarily confused is the question of what we are going to do with this world to make it a comfortable place of dwelling for all of us. You find quite amiable people who look forward with genuine satisfaction to the coming of a revolution which shall change everything. You find quite courageous souls who are perfectly satisfied with the manner in which things in general improve from year to year. But almost all of the people who do think are agreed that things are not as they should be; that education is either absurd or weightily inefficient; that under the present economic system—technically called "capitalism"—products do not get distributed as they should. Only—what is to be done?

Such is the condition of most earnest after-dinner talk—and such, precisely, is the condition of fiction, in the cases where individual dramas are seen against a background of general change.

Aside from *Tono-Bungay* of Mr. Wells, *The Iron Heel* of Mr. London, *The Jungle* of Mr. Sinclair, *The Chasm* of Mr. George Cram Cook, and a very few other novels, there are none that say out boldly, "Capitalism must pass, indeed already is passing, into collective ownership." But it is truly astonishing to find the number of slaps, tiny or resounding, at the vast monster of poverty which occur in even the lightest of modern novels, though often these are accompanied by a rather wistful bewilderment on the part of the slapper. No longer is there a Meredith to whom a mild feminism is thrillingly "advanced";

no longer does one take very seriously the belief of Hardy that his wretchedly beset characters are victims of inexplicable blind forces. The pure individualism of Wharton and James and Howells is out of the trend. It is Wells, Dreiser, Herrick, Walpole, to whom one turns for a complete criticism of life today—and in them one finds back of all the individual's actions a lowering background of People—people with clenched fists, people saying a great many impolite things, people highly discomforting the cultured and the nice by raucously demanding that they have some share in the purple and fine linen.

That Mr. H. G. Wells should be named first will be no surprise to a large number of connoisseurs of fiction. The somewhat perilous title of "*the greatest living novelist*" belongs as much to him as to any man living. And Mr. Wells terrifically sees this human spectacle in the group.

Tono-Bungay reveals to the reader to whom his own little tuppenny-ha'p'ny shop is still the center of the universe a world that is composed entirely of just such short-sighted shopkeepers. His young man comes up to the Titanic London timidly believing that this great network must needs be governed by some supreme intelligence. How otherwise can there be a London County Council and innumerable homes? And he finds that the whole enormous city is simply a hodge-podge of clumsy inefficiency, with every man sharing that youthful faith that there is some central mind which takes care of everything—and consequently blithely leaving the care of Things in General to that beautifully omniscient (and quite as beautifully non-existent) Central Mind.

Tono-Bungay looks upon High Finance, upon Large Production and Keenly Competitive Industry and the Initiative of the Entrepreneur as nothing more or less than chance and inefficiency and intolerable cruelty to those upon whose chests Chance sets the lucky. Without ranting, without saying very much about Socialism, Wells goes the whole journey and convicts Capitalism of puerile cruelty to most people, leaving in the reader's mind a strong feeling that men are about done with leaving the conduct of things in general to little men in woollen undergarments who have made a fortune by the manufacture of injurious patent medicines. He leaves a strong desire to see men get together and act like men; try seriously (at least with some part of the seriousness which an office manager puts into the selection of rubber erasers) to find out what is the matter with the economic system, and remedy it.

Behind all the charming faults and painfully fatal little virtues of *Mr. Polly*, also, Mr. Wells shows Things in General being misconducted or not conducted: The foolish haberdashery where Mr. Polly accumulated poverty and indigestion is frankly the symbol of all the State's activities. The barren shops which figure now as laundries, now as stationery shops, now as chemists' establishments, are pitiful makeshifts for a modern system of distribution, Mr. Wells assures us.

And when an author begins to attack the Modern System of Distribution he is head over heels in the strange heresy of Socialism, even though his diabolic intentions are veiled. If it were not now quite as lacking in smartness to quote Omar as it is to quote Tennyson, one might remark that Mr. Wells desires to "grasp this sorry scheme of things *entire.*" He should have sermons preached against him, for certainly his plan would stop nowhere short of taking every single man of us from our ruts—whether we be editors or oil magnates or floor-scrubbers—and turn us into part of a smoothly and consciously co-ordinated State. Which would doubtless be good for oil and editing and floor-scrubbing, but smack of Socialism and enmity to Capitalism.

Finally, in *The World Set Free*, that truly panoramic. book, Mr. Wells shows the world doing just this thing; consciously co-ordinating the activities of the States; and Capitalism, the private control of manufacture and distribution, disappears with the Theory of Armaments, and all the rest of the good old belief that the best way to keep peace is to encourage large armies to fight.

Nor is *The World Set Free* any Utopian Romance; any echo of *Looking Backward*, or *News from Nowhere*. It is founded on real life as it is, at the time of this writing, being so desperately played out in Europe. There is one thing to be said for Capitalism. Under it, an H. G. Wells can be produced.

Tono-Bungay, as an intimate study of what finance means to the financier is, however, but a brief Christmas booklet compared with the work of our own Theodore Dreiser. The very fact that this admirable novelist sees in business an adventure, a romance, quite comparable to all the crusading and hand-kissing of hackneyed fiction, is an indication that men are no longer regarding business as "shop-keeping—unfit for a gentleman" but a very big emprise worthy of admiration or bitter attack.

To Frank Cowperwood, whose experiences so continue through Mr. Dreiser's *The Financier* and *The Titan* that these books are really one, there was adventure in collecting pictures and beautiful rooms and houses, greater adventure in collecting amorous experiences, but greatest experience in collecting varieties of financial power. He experimented with stocks in Philadelphia and, pioneering in Chicago in the days before it was a commanding metropolis, cornered gas, then traction. But never did he genuinely realize that his suave skill in controlling great industries meant life and death to a very large number of men. He paid his employees well enough—but only to avoid strikes; and that tribute he easily got back from "the people" by his professional skill in bribing legislators. He never considered them as a body of followers to whom he was in any wise responsible. Indeed, it is to be doubted if Mr. Dreiser much realizes such a situation, himself. He very deeply, very dramatically, sees Frank Cowperwood as a man fighting and loving and winning and losing. But he very shallowly sees him as a part of a system. Nevertheless he cannot help so seeing him, to some extent. It stands upon page 519 of *The Titan:*

But against [Cowperwood's supporters] were the preachers—poor wind-blown sticks of unreason who saw only what the current palaver seemed to indicate. Again there were the anarchists, socialists, single-taxers and public-ownership advocates. There were the very poor who saw in Cowperwood's wealth and in the fabulous stories of his New York home and of his art-collection a heartless exploitation of their needs. At this time the feeling was spreading broadcast in America that great political and economic changes were at hand—that the tyranny of iron masters at the top was to give way to a richer, freer, happier life for the rank and file. A national eight-hour-day law was being advocated, and the public ownership of public franchises. And here now was a great street-railway corporation, serving a population of a million and a half, occupying streets which the people themselves created by their presence, taking toll from all these humble citizens to the amount of sixteen or eighteen million dollars in the year and giving in return, so the papers said, no universal transfers (as a matter of fact, there were in operation three hundred and sixty-two separate transfer points) and no adequate tax on the immense sums earned.

The working-man who read this by gas or lamplight in the kitchen or parlor of his shabby flat or cottage . . . felt himself to be de-frauded of a portion of his rightful inheritance.

It is to be suspected that, throughout this long passage, Mr. Dreiser is speaking out his own mind only in the parenthesis which defends the generosity of the almost philanthropic company in grant-ing transfers. It is probable that he genuinely admires Frank Cowper-wood, quite as much for his rather perilous faults—such as a confusing carelessness with his neighbor's wife—as for his virtues of courage and good taste. But this same growing tendency on the part of the people to demand something for themselves is precisely that tendency which they who approve it call the "beginning of the downfall of capitalism" and which the comfortably propertied call "the growing unrest and ingratitude of the masses." The type of person who writes to a news-paper that he hopes no student-waiter will lose the caste mark of the collegian gentleman by taking a tip would deplore this tendency. But there it is, if the biggest, vitalest current fiction truly mirrors the hour, and you may do what you like—only do not overlook it.

It is quite essential for the capitalist to read *Tono-Bungay* and behold how blithely Mr. Wells conceives the great financier as a clumsy player of ping-pong. It is quite essential for the Socialist to read *The Financier* and *The Titan* and see how romantic a figure is the pirate of finance to Mr. Dreiser. And it is quite essential for the reader too unimportant to have either label to read both and discover that fiction is no longer like the home life of our dear Queen.

Next to Mr. Dreiser, Mr. Robert Herrick has most interestingly pictured finance—though in the picture of industry-in-general doubt-less Mr. Frank Norris surpassed them both. In his very latest book, *Clark's Field*, Mr. Herrick fascinatingly traces the rake's progress which is society's reward to a family for the social virtue of holding a field which they could not sell. That field, once an inferior pasture near to Boston (which city Mr. Herrick remarkably disguises by calling it "B———"), becomes a nest of tenements, worth thousands a front foot. The accruing money enables a very inferior type of young heiress to buy a parasite husband, spoils her life, and her husband's, and every one's whom it touches, and never brings happi-ness to one of the bedraggled workers who toss at night in the airless tenement rooms over the old "Clark's field." After a close-knit chronicle of the gradual awakening of the heiress to the fact that she had neither right to, nor joy in, the money from the field, Mr. Herrick does not suggest any very deep-reaching solution of that oldest of questions regarding sociology, "But what can we do?" He would have her erect a market, give the tenement-dwellers something of a chance. But nothing more.

Despite this failure to suggest a wider solution (which is probably quite intentional on Mr. Herrick's part; he has long dwelt in Chicago, and such solutions as single-tax and Socialism are not, we may safely conclude, unknown to that city) he does place the problem strikingly before the reader. And not for the first time.

Already, in *A Life for a Life* he had burningly declared that the ingenious capitalists, with their cleverness at forming companies and their stupidity at being human beings, had no conceivable right to their mines, their banks, their railroads, and no real skill in their conduct. He—the efficient university instructor—had mocked bitterly the complacent university president who lets his right hand know precisely what his left is doing in order that both hands may be busily gathering in funds from rich philanthropists. He—the well-received—had in *A Life for a Life* presented wealthy society as stupid and inexcusable. Again, there is no real solution presented; no propaganda urged; but a terribly earnest picture of capitalism as a thing that should, must, will pass.

And in *The Memoirs of an American Citizen* Mr. Herrick finds a pork-packer, a would-be sincere and honest financier, blind to the rest of the world and its needs; giving up all human interests for ambition. Very cleverly, he tells the story in the first person, but wherever he gives the pork-packer's own version of his philosophy of finance, the sharp watcher may spy Mr. Herrick's mocking smile behind the pork-packer's broad shoulder.

Into *The Memoirs of an American Citizen*, as also into his *One Woman's Life* enters a remembrance of the Haymarket Riot. That incident seems to haunt every writer who mentions Chicago. It appears in *The Bomb*, by Mr. Frank Harris, of course; in Mr. Dreiser's *The Titan;* and a low echo of its explosion is heard in half a dozen other books. It was an expression of this movement which threatens the passing of capitalism—whether or no it shall effect that passing.

These novels of Chicago seem nearly all of them to be tinged with a thoughtfulness about real life. Take, for example, that very excellent recent novel, *The Precipice,* by Miss Elia W. Peattie. Take *The Pit;* which brings one to Frank Norris.

Unlike Mr. Herrick, Mr. Norris did, apparently, have a definite solution of the social confusion. As expressed at the end of *The Octopus,* his solution is that we must take all the apparent injustice of the world as necessary friction of progress. Now that is, of course, a quite tenable view. It is comforting to the capitalist. But in general *The Octopus* is not at all comforting to the capitalist. It makes us believe that injustice is everywhere prevalent and not at all to be tolerated as necessary friction. It shows men battling for fields properly theirs. It makes us rage at the power given dirty little agents of the bigger powers. Broad and visualizable as is its picture of the great San Joaquin Valley, it is broader in its picture of the human men and women who are crushed in order that the San Joaquin may have a railway.

Probably Frank Norris was not essentially what is called a "radical." Probably he could find capitalism the system that its fortunate adherents claim it to be—the only sensible means of getting things really done. But nevertheless he takes one into the hearts of crushed men so successfully that one stops to think what the meaning of capitalism is—a process equally recommended as favorable and fatal to capitalism.

Gone is Frank Norris; McTeague has staggered to his death; the tentacles of the Octopus are still; but today, in the year of Tagore and the siege of Liège, young men are still discovering *The Octopus,* and, reading it, asking themselves the why and how of Society-in-General. And if enough young men do that we shall have something—it may be a new capitalism, it may be an autocracy, it may be a complete anarchism, but it will be a condition of society in which such men as they of the San Joaquin shall not reap thistles.

Gone, perhaps, is Mr. Upton Sinclair, too, for today one hears of him not as a novelist but as an experimenter in diet, and as a revolutionist who is either a complete traitor or a quiet hero, depending on your economic theories. But Mr. Sinclair did one novel which first gave an almost painfully brilliant picture of life in brogans, and unhesitatingly suggested Socialism as a remedy—*The Jungle.* (Note, by the way, that *The Jungle,* too, was a tale of Chicago.) It is scarcely necessary to dwell upon either the strength of his presentation or the terms of his solution. They are classic. And his later novels, such as *The Millionaire,* followed their example.

Less well known, perhaps because it is very new, is *Midstream,* by Will Levingon Comfort, published this year of international disgrace, 1914. Here is a criticism not merely of the poverty-producing economic system but of all the phases of life. Society as we make it, declares Mr. Comfort, who dares to give his own real experiences as an example of what society can do, is the most perfectly inefficient thing that could be conceived by a great diabolic philosopher. The schools teach vacuity; the offices, crudeness; the army, brutality. The conception of capitalism scarce enters *Midstream,* however; and Mr. Comfort's profoundly believed solution lies in one's own development of a creative will, and in the love of good women.

But Mr. George Cram Cook, whose *The Chasm* is not so widely known as it should be, and as it certainly will be when Mr. Cook follows it with another so good a novel, joins with *The Jungle* in a perfectly definite declaration that Socialism is the solution. He does not, like Mr. Sinclair, dwell greatly on the misfortunes of the poor, except at the end of the book, where the American heroine finds herself mixed up in the Russian revolution. Rather, it is his purpose to show what is technically known as the "class-conscious worker"; the man of strong hands, not afraid of overalls, who reads wise books and speaks out his demands. *The Chasm* has been condemned as propagandist; it has been defended as significant; has been praised for the splendor of its picture of love between a girl of the classes and a real man; but no matter how it is taken, one is not likely to forget, after reading it, that there is a group of men who, right or wrong, demand social co-operation with a voice that shall be heard.

With *The Chasm* one associates Miss Susan Glaspell's second novel, *The Visioning.* Here, too, is the growth of class consciousness. The particular point of attack on the social system is in a picture of the army as a perfectly useless body of men who might—as foresters or canal-builders, say—be very useful.

And, curiously, Chicago again enters into these thoughtful romances, though most of the action in both books transpires in the Tri-Cities—Davenport, Rock Island and Moline. Both show the Midwest as a place of ferment—ferment intellectual and material. Both are in delightful contrast to the knights and artists and motorists of average fiction. For both show real life.

And does it not by now seem that practically every writer—certainly in America and to some extent in England—who is gravely seeking to present the romance of actual life as it is today, must perforce show capitalism as a thing attacked, passing—whether the writer lament or rejoice or merely complain at that passing? Few of them have any very clear idea of how the passing is to occur; as to what is to take its place. And now more than ever, with the European war shaking all the belief of the International Socialists in their might, one wonders what and how and why and when. Yet there it is, in nearly every seeing writer of today—an attack on capitalism.

Naturally, the few writers just mentioned are but a tiny proportion of the men and women doing significant work, and reacting to this matter of changing economics. Take the sharp convictions of Leroy Scott and Ernest Poole, who add, both of them, to a delightful dramatic sense a stern belief in the coming revolution (a revolution probably bloodless, they believe). Take that marvelous picture of the new class-conscious woman, *Comrade Yetta*, by Albert Edwards.

There is in *Comrade Yetta* no vague and rambling picture of a "new woman"; no yearning presentation of a woman who wants to go away from any particular Here to some magic and mythical There, to study painting or do anything else that shall keep her from housework. *Comrade Yetta* is no pleasantly illusive picture of a lady with a "temperament" written by a lady who hopes that her own divine restlessness will be recognized in the heroine. Rather, Yetta is a fighter; one who talks not at all about temperament, but a good deal about the conditions of industry, and does that talking not in scented studios, but on the hard streets during a strike. Little Yetta is a Jew of Jews, a revolutionist of revolutionists, yet a woman of women; leading her girls in the shirtwaist strike, and loving her Jewish journalist husband like a real woman.

Mr. Edwards in his picture devotes no great amount of space to a discussion of what the result of all this struggling is to be. But it is apparent that he believes some form of co-operation to be the only final solution. He presents the sweat-shop proprietor as being quite as much a victim of conditions as the girls who work for him. And, best of all, he presents both sides as real human beings. But no matter how he presents them, no matter how little he says of "capitalism," that word is the half-visible water-mark on every page of the book.

Jack London's is a name which, of course, must be thoughtfully remembered in a consideration of this sort. Though adventure is the thing for which most of his books are remembered, in such novels as *The Iron Heel* and *The Valley of the Moon*, in such short stories as "South of the Slot" one finds an unflinching opposition to large private ownership; a wonderful feeling of companionship with the man in his shirt sleeves; a grateful lack of patronage toward what even the most sympathetic writers are very often inclined to regard as "the lower classes."

In the new writers, the men of one book, the problem is not neglected. Take, for instance, Mr. Howard Vincent O'Brien, in whose *New Men for Old* is a keenly felt abhorrence for tricky business. Take still more the young English writers.

There is Hugh Walpole who, after a series of such charming novels as *Fortitude* and *The Gods and Mr. Perrin* and *The Prelude to Adventure*, novels with the magic of beauty, impregnated with a love of the sea beating on the Cornish cliffs, has at length in his latest novel, *The Duchess of Wrexe*, found his greatest task in watching the changing social condition, watching the fires they're building in the Grand Duke's woods. There is Mr. Oliver Onions—who attests to the importance of the present struggle by opposing it. In his trilogy, concluding with *The Story of Louie*, Mr. Onions devoted himself to the individual drama; but now, in *Gray Youth* he is seen turning all his attention to the forces that demand change. Socialism—feminism—eugenics—he attacks them all, with a vigor which indicates their importance. Such changes Mr. Compton Mackenzie sees in *Youth's Encounter;* such does Mr. Gilbert Cannan portray in *Old Mole*. Of all that remarkable group of young Englishmen there are scarce two who do not watch—sometimes anxiously, sometimes with bewilderment—the social drama which is so much greater than the individual drama, and find in it matter to color all their pages. (Yellow, some call the color, and some find it an inspiriting red; but there it is!)

This catalogue would, of course, be ludicrous without a consideration, direct or implied, of Bennett, Galsworthy, Conrad, Hardy, Kipling, Shaw, Chesterton, George Moore. And, except for Hardy and Moore, there is not one of these men who has not seen the matter of the power—and the possible future downfall—of capitalism as a tremendous factor in their characters' individual lives. Even Conrad, the seafaring, writes of anarchists. Even Kipling, the god of the cold bath and morning gallop and other imperialistic habits, by his very anxiety in defending the soldiers of the empire, betrays a belief that there is rather a large number of strange persons who are interested in no empire short of an international one.

As for Galsworthy, with his *Strife* and the uneasy interest of nearly every character in the changing world, and Bennett with his great gallery of plain working people, to both of them the glory of the Classes is gone; the time of the Common People has come. Marvelous is the picture of the "average man" in *Clayhanger*. And the recognition of the average man is bound to give that man a desire to try his hand at running things. And that desire, carried far enough, is likely to be disastrous to capitalism.

When, near the beginning of *Clayhanger*, Mr. Bennett suggests that Clayhanger's education has been an entirely useless and worthless training in non-existent theories, he is going very far in attacking Things as They Are.

Naturally, any one with a little time for reading and a certain amount of ingenuity can find many giant names to back up an assertion opposite to my thesis, and declare as plausibly as Chesterton that most important writers regard the passing of capitalism as a Utopian dream. Bennett himself, in a little book just published, called *The Author's Craft*, strongly advises the literary-minded to keep away from circles where the discussion of reform is the chief business of life.

But summing them all up, going from real observer to real observer, it may be contended that practically every thoughtful writer of today sees behind the individual dramas of his characters a background of coming struggle which shall threaten the very existence of this status called capitalism. Approve or disapprove—there's the struggle, mirrored in fiction.

234